MAPPING POLICY PREFERENCES II

Mapping Policy Preferences II

Estimates for Parties, Electors, and Governments in Eastern Europe, European Union, and OECD 1990–2003

HANS-DIETER KLINGEMANN, ANDREA VOLKENS,
JUDITH L. BARA, IAN BUDGE, AND
MICHAEL D. McDONALD

OXFORD
UNIVERSITY PRESS

OXFORD
UNIVERSITY PRESS

Great Clarendon Street, Oxford OX2 6DP

Oxford University Press is a department of the University of Oxford.
It furthers the University's objective of excellence in research, scholarship,
and education by publishing worldwide in

Oxford New York

Auckland Cape Town Dar es Salaam Hong Kong Karachi
Kuala Lumpur Madrid Melbourne Mexico City Nairobi
New Delhi Shanghai Taipei Toronto

With offices in

Argentina Austria Brazil Chile Czech Republic France Greece
Guatemala Hungary Italy Japan Poland Portugal Singapore
South Korea Switzerland Thailand Turkey Ukraine Vietnam

Oxford is a registered trade mark of Oxford University Press
in the UK and in certain other countries

Published in the United States
by Oxford University Press Inc., New York

British Library Cataloguing in Publication Data
Data available

Library of Congress Cataloging in Publication Data
Data available

Typeset by SPI Publisher Services, Pondicherry, India
Printed in Great Britain
on acid-free paper by
Biddles Ltd., King's Lynn, Norfolk

ISBN 0–19–929631–6   978–0–19–929631–6

1 3 5 7 9 10 8 6 4 2

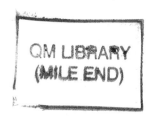

This book is dedicated to co-researchers on the Manifesto Research Project who have substantially extended its scope and depth:

Hee-Min Kim	*Richard C. Fording*
Derek J. Hearl	*Silvia M. Mendés*
Aida Paskeviciute	*Steve Lem*
Robin Best	*James Adams*

and all the coders who have worked at the coal-face, on the documents themselves.

Contents

I. PARTIES AND REPRESENTATION IN EASTERN EUROPE AND THE EUROPEAN UNION

II. METHODOLOGY AND MEASUREMENT

CD-ROM CONTENTS

List of Figures

List of Tables

How to Use the Book

This book follows on from *Mapping Policy Preferences: Estimates for Parties, Electors, and Governments 1945–1998* and its prize-winning data-set (OUP 2001). It updates the time series given in that volume for OECD countries, providing them for elections from 1990 to 2003, and incorporating voting data and other relevant information.

More importantly, it expands its geographical coverage to the countries of Central and Eastern Europe (CEE) from the first free elections in 1990 up to their consolidation in 2003, and thus provides an invaluable tool for those who study processes of democratization. By studying party election programmes, the emergent ideologies revealed in them, and the ways in which parties shaped their appeals so as to attract votes, we gain unique insights into the prime movers in the democratic process—the political parties—and how they contributed to its development over the first crucial decade of the new democracies. Analyses can now be based on the parties' own authoritative policy pronouncements and attempted dialogue with electors rather than other people's judgements about where they stood.

Following the practice of our previous volume, the numeric codings of party documents are reproduced on the CD-ROM sold with the book. They are thus ready for immediate use by readers on their own computers. The text facilitates its use by providing background to the data, full information about coding procedures, and checks on their reliability and validity. Masses of information about parties covered and party families, the documents actually coded (and those missing!), elections and voting are provided in the appendices and on the CD-ROM.

Digitalized party manifestos for the OECD countries are made available on request by the Zentralarchiv für Empirische Sozialforschung, Universität zu Köln, under certain conditions regarding their usage (the contact address is za@za.uni-koeln.de). The textual data are part of the Comparative Electronic Manifestos Project (http://research.fsw.vu.nl/DoingResearch) directed by Paul Pennings and Hans Keman, Vrije Universitat, Amsterdam, in collaboration with Ekkehard Mochmann of the ZA. This project has been financed by the Netherlands Organisation for Scientific Research (project no. 480-42-005).

The quantified data presented in the CD-ROM itself was collected as a special project of the Wissenschaftszentrum, Berlin (WZB) under the direction of Hans Dieter Klingemann and Andrea Volkens. The WZB most generously continues to finance the collection of the manifesto data. Other foundations and institutions, who have supported data collection and preparation, are the Volkswagenstiftung, Tercentenary Fund of the Bank of Sweden, the British Economic and Social

Research Council, and the Nuffield Foundation. We thank them all for their essential support.

In this book, we do not confine ourselves just to *party* policy. We also use it—with party votes—as a basis for estimating the median or middle electoral preference; thus giving an idea of what the popular majority wanted in the various elections. By identifying the (strategically important) median parliamentary party and its policy we can see how far this reflects the majority preference of voters. And by weighting the policy preferences of government parties by the proportion of legislative seats each hold, we can also form an estimate of government policy preferences. Comparing these with estimated electoral preferences provides crucial information about how well the democratic mandate performed in these countries in both its governmental and median forms (Chapter 7).

Simply mentioning these estimates for different levels of the democratic institutions of Eastern Europe gives some inkling into the immense potentiality of this data-set for answering crucial questions about the new democracies—indeed, about democracy itself, given the inclusion of OECD and other countries. The text aims at orientating users to these rich possibilities. It does this by alerting them to the methodological strengths and weaknesses of the data-set, the reliability of its estimates, wide range of uses to which it has been put, and to some of the most striking findings that have been made on its basis.

Readers who are already familiar with the previous volume and the post-war time series provided with it may well proceed directly to the new estimates provided on the CD-ROM. Even they however might wish to cast an eye over the graphs of Left-Right party movements reported for CEE countries in Chapter 1, and to assess their validity and reliability (Chapters 4–6). They should also be interested in the uses of the median and government policy estimates reported in Chapter 7.

At the other extreme there will be readers for whom a broad indication of policy trends in the new democracies will suffice. In that case Chapter 1 probably gives them all they want with regard to political parties. Estimates of what the people wanted and what governments and parties gave them are in the Policy Scales Data-Set on the CD-ROM. Country and regional specialists might wish to peruse this before going on to the data themselves.

Readers who want more information about the collection and coding of the documents, and the methodological issues involved, will find a summary in the Introduction and fuller accounts in Chapters 4–6. As data collection followed exactly the same lines as those employed previously, the major methodological discussion can be found in the original volume on *Mapping Policy Preferences* (OUP 2001). However, there have been further developments in the meantime. So, while referring back for the major checks on the reliability and validity of the data, our discussion here does include new items, for example, reliability of individual estimates and the way computerized codings of manifestos have progressively based themselves, as we have, on selective emphases in the documents (Chapter 6). This has not, of course, inhibited the development of the Left-Right (and other) policy scales, as we shall explain.

The Manifesto Research Group/Comparative Manifesto Project data (MRG/CMP data) are distinguished from more limited policy estimates such as expert judgements (Castles and Mair 1984; Laver and Hunt 1992; Huber and Inglehart 1995; Benoit and Laver 2006) by (*a*) providing information about party policy in *each* election, (*b*) thus permitting time-series analysis of party policy change while also (*c*) serving as a base for inferring the policy preferences of (median) electors, parliamentary parties, and governments. Chapters 2–7 inclusive explore the assumptions and procedures involved in this extension of the party estimates and report the substantive research into the relationships between political actors that can be done on this basis. For the first time, we are on the way to fully checking party mandate and convergence ideas and seeing how they work out in the new as well as the old democracies of Europe.

Finally, Chapter 8 provides all the information necessary, even for those embarking on this type of analysis for the first time, for putting the data on your own computer. The appeal of doing so directly rather than simply relying on published estimates, partly accounts for the success of the previous volume (reprinted in 2004) and the receipt of the APSA Comparative Politics Best Data Set Award in 2003 for the information contained in the CD-ROM.

Equally useful in approaching the data are our appendices, which contain general information, useful to country specialists as well as data users, on significant parties at each election in the various countries. The CD-ROM also provides the most recent and authoritative figures for party votes in each election 1990–2003 in both OECD and the CEE countries. These may well serve as an independent data source on their own—and are, of course, crucial in making estimates of the median voter position as well as for other measures.

The appendices provide both substantive information and technical and methodological guidance on coding procedures and documents, as well as party mean scores on various policy scales—another piece of important information immediately available from the text (see Policy Scales Data-Set on the CD-ROM). With these we hope the book provides all the orientation necessary to analyse material on the CD-ROM—together with useful information over and above that.

We cannot close without thanking all those who have collaborated on preparing the data and the text, especially Julie Snell, Claire Croft, Lizzy Suffling, John Campbell, and Eric Tanenbaum—above all our colleagues on the MRG and the coders of the CMP, whose contributions are fittingly acknowledged in the dedication. Special thanks go to those who have collaborated with us in extending the estimates in recent years—Hee-Min Kim and Richard Fording (median estimates) and James Adams, together with Michael McDonald's helpful associates Myunghee Kim, Silvia Mendés, Aida Paskeviciute, Steve Lem, and Robin Best. We also owe a considerable debt to Frances Millard and Sarah Birch for making their collections of CEE election statistics available to us and for their invaluable advice. For any remaining errors and omissions we ourselves must take responsibility. Correction is a continuing task and we appeal to readers to inform us of errors through the associated website. We also welcome information on documents we have been unable to access. Just as the data-set itself is now public property, so its expansion and correction have become a collective enterprise shared with users— who we hope will be interactive and indeed proactive in helping us improve it further.

Introducing the Manifesto Data: Background

TEXTS AS DATA

Political texts are at once the most widely available source of evidence about politics and the most neglected in terms of quantitative analysis. Practically everything that gets done politically is recorded in protocols or minutes, issued as directives or laws, or reported as proceedings of committees or legislative bodies. Political causes are advocated in recorded speeches and interviews, pamphlets, posters, and, of course, party platforms and manifestos. The latter are unique in being the only authoritative party policy statement approved by an official convention or congress. Possibly because of this they stand alone in being full 'five year plans' for the development of society.

Political historians and commentators have, of course, always used texts as their major source. But they have done so selectively—giving rise to controversy about bias and unrepresentativeness in the evidence. This extends to the reading and reporting of the texts themselves. Quantitative analyses in the form of counts of key words, sentences, or expressions can be carried out according to specified procedures over the whole range of relevant documents. This provides a superior basis for tackling problems of selection, reliability and validity, or at least specifying them clearly so they can be taken into account in evaluating results.

This book, like its predecessor, reports procedures and results for one series of political documents, the programmes parties issue for elections. All the (quasi-)[1] sentences in each document are classified into a set of policy-related categories according to an established set of rules and instructions (specified in Appendix II). Each decision is recorded on a copy of the original document so that it can be reviewed and corrected if necessary. The distribution of sentences over the categories is what distinguishes one document from another. Shifts in the distribution mark policy changes over time and highlight differences in one party's document as compared with others. Parties can be compared in this way with each other, at any one election: in terms of their 'tracks' from one election to another; and either within countries or across countries.

These dynamic estimates contrast with the other main measure commonly employed to estimate party policy positions—'expert judgements' based on survey responses of political scientists in each country to questions set by the investigators about where the national parties stand. Being essentially qualitative judgements couched in quantitative form (e.g. placement of parties on a ten-point scale) they share many of the problems of historical judgement—primarily the question of what evidence the party placements are based on, and whether this is the same as that used by the other experts involved in the survey (Budge 2000). Such judgements give a little more precision to traditional 'party family' classifications

(McDonald and Kim 2007). But being based on long-standing ideological positions they do not relate to any clearly specified time point such as a particular election, and hence lack any dynamic quality (McDonald and Mendés 1999).

Documentary estimates do possess these qualities. However, their major disadvantage is the immense amount of time and resources necessary for hand-coding large numbers of documents. The estimates reported here are based on the labours of more than fifty coders over twenty-five years, not to mention the efforts of supervisors and other members of the team, with financing from the WZB. Over the lifetime of the entire MRG/CMP programme (1979–2003 and continuing) perhaps a million and a half euros have been invested in data gathering and preparation.

This makes clear what a precious resource is being opened to readers of this and the previous Oxford University Press volume! The expense and effort involved also explain why ours is the only comparative text-based data-set of its kind and why short cuts like expert judgements are often taken. The costs are prohibitive and it is only the dedication of the original MRG and the institutional basis provided by the Wissenschaftzentrum which explain the data-set's existence.

However, for the reasons given above many such text-based data-sets are essential to the development of systematic political science. As a result efforts have increasingly been devoted to computerizing content analysis. Texts can be read in as raw data and words processed into numbers using one of several programmes now available (see Chapter 6). This may well be the way content analysis will go in the future. In Chapter 6, we consider the progress that has been made and how far computerization incorporates the basic logic of the approach we have employed in hand-coding. Before we embark on more detailed discussion, however, we should summarize the development of the manifesto data as they now stand, thus concretely illustrating the strengths and weaknesses of the estimates we present in this book.

THE MANIFESTO RESEARCH GROUP AND COMPARATIVE MANIFESTO PROJECT 1979–2004

The MRG was formed in 1979 by Ian Budge and David Robertson, both at that time in the Department of Government, University of Essex. It was constituted formally as a Research Group of the European Consortium for Political Research (ECPR) which hosted many of its early meetings and obtained funding from the Volkwagenstiftung and Tercentenary Fund of the Bank of Sweden. This supported most of its work in the 1980s.

Operationally the MRG consisted of a number of political scientists who were interested in two questions: (*a*) what political issues divided post-war political parties and (*b*) were they converging or diverging in ideological or policy terms? The last question had practical implications for interpretations of post-war politics. But it also had theoretical implications for 'rational choice' interpretations of party strategic behaviour. Downs' influential interpretation of two party competition (Downs 1957: 112–19) would lead to expectations of party convergence on the position of the median voter. The manifesto data allow us to see in practice whether this occurred.

The MRG grouped country specialists with the requisite language ability and substantive knowledge, whose interest was primarily in the politics of 'their' country, and comparativists who often had wider theoretical interests. The object was to produce a book which would analyse party divisions within separate chapters for each country—however within a common framework which permitted some comparative analysis and conclusions at the end (Budge, Robertson, and Hearl (eds.) 1987).

Robertson had already carried through a pioneering analysis of British party manifestos 1922–74 (Robertson 1976). The coding scheme based on reading these documents counted their sentences into twenty-two general policy areas. What the count of sentences over these categories recorded was the *relative emphasis* parties placed on them, not *positive* or *negative* references made to them. Political opposition was expressed by emphasizing another issue—peace, say, as opposed to military strength, freedom as opposed to planning, and so on.

It is important to emphasize two points about this coding, which formed the basis for the final MRG scheme applied to the documents covered here (Appendix II). One is that it derived from the documents themselves: relative emphases were the way in which British parties expressed themselves. Second, confrontation between the parties is there, but it takes the indirect form of emphasizing another issue rather than direct negative comment on a rival position on each issue. Budge and Farlie (1977, and especially 1983) who extended Robertson's coding to the USA (1922–76), developed a 'saliency theory' of party competition from the success of relative emphases as a coding scheme (see below and also Stokes 1966; Riker 1993; Budge et al. 2001: 78–85). However, one could use relative emphases to count words or sentences without necessarily subscribing to saliency theory.

Indeed some members of the original MRG found it hard to believe that relative emphases *were* the main way parties differentiated themselves from each other, in spite of the British and American evidence. Hence, the compromise coding scheme drawn up in 1979 created a number of pro and con categories in issue areas where direct confrontation between opposing policies seemed most likely to occur. This scheme is summarized in Table I.1 (see Appendix II for a detailed presentation).

When results from the actual coding came in about a year later it emerged that:

(*a*) national parties generally emphasized either pro or con positions but not both in any one issue area;

(*b*) the undifferentiated categories (i.e. those deriving from or developed in sympathy with the earlier relative emphases coding) performed well in differentiating parties. As a result MRG coding practices developed from then on the basis of a relative emphases approach.

Table I.1 The standard MRG/CMP coding of election manifestos 1945–98

Domain 1: External Relations
101   Foreign Special Relationships: Positive
102   Foreign Special Relationships: Negative
103   Anti-Imperialism: Negative
104   Military: Positive
105   Military: Negative
106   Peace: Positive
107   Internationalism: Positive
108   European Community: Positive
109   Internationalism: Negative
110   European Community: Negative

Domain 2: Freedom and Democracy
201   Freedom and Human Rights: Positive
202   Democracy: Positive
203   Constitutionalism: Positive
204   Constitutionalism: Negative

Domain 3: Political System
301   Decentralization: Positive
302   Centralization: Positive
303   Governmental and Administrative Efficiency: Positive
304   Political Corruption
305   Political Authority: Positive

Domain 4: Economy
401   Free Enterprise: Positive
402   Incentives: Positive
403   Market Regulation: Positive
404   Economic Planning: Positive
405   Corporatism: Positive
406   Protectionism: Positive
407   Protectionism: Negative
408   Economic Goals: Positive
409   Keynesian Demand Management: Positive
410   Productivity: Positive
411   Technology and Infrastructure: Positive
412   Controlled Economy: Positive
413   Nationalization: Positive
414   Economic Orthodoxy: Positive
415   Marxist Analysis: Positive
416   Anti-Growth Economy: Positive

Domain 5: Welfare and Quality of Life
501   Environmental Protection: Positive
502   Culture: Positive
503   Social Justice: Positive
504   Welfare State Expansion
505   Welfare State Limitation
506   Education Expansion
507   Education Limitation

Domain 6: Fabric of Society
601   National Way of Life: Positive
602   National Way of Life: Negative
603   Traditional Morality: Positive

604   Traditional Morality: Negative
605   Law and Order: Positive
606   Social Harmony: Positive
607   Multiculturalism: Positive
608   Multiculturalism: Negative

Domain 7: Social Groups
701   Labour Groups: Positive
702   Labour Groups: Negative
703   Agriculture: Positive
704   Middle Class and Professional Groups: Positive
705   Minority Groups: Positive
706   Non-Economic Demographic Groups: Positive

An unanticipated consequence of imposing these initial checks was, however, that a number of explicitly pro and con categories were built into the coding scheme. Production coding of manifestos from 1945 to 1982 had already incorporated them, and future coding had to include them to maintain comparability. The 'minority' category on each set of paired pro and con positions did not generally attract a high number of references. Hence, it was still possible to regard the coding scheme as essentially based on relative emphases. But it was not an entirely pure reflection of them.

This ambiguity carries several implications for users of the data:

(*a*) it makes the estimates more flexible, in that those who wish to devise paired confrontations from the data can do so (Table 6.1). Such confrontations include both the original pro and con codings and 'relative emphasis' categories that can be taken as opposed (e.g. 'freedom' vs. 'planning'). As we point out, it is not clear whether the different types of pairing reflect the same kind of opposition, however—a point developed below in relation to Table 6.1.

(*b*) inclusion of pro and con categories in addition to relative emphases, which might also be taken as indicating support or opposition in that specific instance, contributed to 'noise' and coding error. It was unclear whether a reference such as 'beating swords into ploughshares' should be coded simply as 'peace' or as 'military negative'. In contrasting the explicitly pro and con positions towards an issue, it is therefore unclear whether these account for all references to the topic in the manifesto or whether there has been some 'seepage' of references out to another issue area.

One reaction to these possibilities is to aggregate categories so that those which may have been somewhat confused with each other in coding are grouped on the same side of a scale thus improving overall validity and reliability. The prime example of this is the Left-Right continuum discussed below (Table 1.1).

Another consequence of early group discussions, with far-reaching consequences for coding, was the anxiety of country specialists about providing a sufficiently subtle coverage of 'their' national politics. This resulted in a multiplication of the number of categories from Robertson's original 22 (1976) to a final 56. Having more detail may be a strength. However, it turned out that many of the new categories attracted few references (between a third and a half of specific scores in the data-sets are zero). They also increased ambiguity about where to locate sentences. Less serious was the allowance made for country specialists to create subcategories under general categories of the coding scheme which could be aggregated back to the general category (Budge, Robertson, and Hearl 1987: 466–7; Budge et al. 2001: 98). Most of these, contrary to the original expectations of the researchers, were also thinly populated and so have been mostly used in aggregate form. However, they are always available for those with particular interests to pick out and use and may be of special interest to CEE specialists seeking to detail events after 1990 in specific countries (see Appendix II).

These early MRG discussions feed directly into the uses that can be made of the codings and the interpretations put upon them. New users need to be alerted to this. In Chapter 6, we take up some of these points and indicate in detail how on the one hand they permit extended applications of the data and on the other impose cautions and constraints.

With these crucial decisions made, the MRG forged ahead with production coding from 1980 to 1983, eventually covering the nineteen countries whose analysis is reported in *Ideology, Strategy and Party Change* (Budge, Robertson, and Hearl (eds.) 1987). This helped to develop many of the techniques reported above such as aggregating individual categories through factor analysis to describe the policy dimensions within which parties differentiated themselves. With regard to the two original questions which had motivated the group (*a*) the main policy dimension parties emphasized, quite against MRG expectations, was the Left-Right one (see Table 1.1 for the issues which define this), (*b*) parties did converge in Left-Right terms over the thirty-year period examined. But parties moved so much and judgements were so conditioned by the first and last years chosen for comparison that the more considered conclusion was that there was no irrevocable tendency to either convergence or divergence but simply fluctuation within a defined and consistent party policy space. (The fluctuations were probably influenced by strategic considerations (cf. Adams 2001).)

By the time the original book was published it had become clear that the MRG policy estimates were capable of adaptation and extension to many other research purposes important for democracy. From 1983, they were applied to coalition formation and policymaking (Laver and Budge (eds.) 1992), leading to the conclusion that policy proximity did not really work as an explanation of why parties joined coalitions.

By this time the MRG was winding down. Many original members left having answered their initial research questions. The data and document collections clearly had a potential for general research in and beyond political science (cf. citations in the Bibliography of Manifesto-based Research). To preserve them, the collection of original documents was partly published in microfiche (Hearl 1990) and deposited at the German Social Science Archive at Cologne. Updated and periodically extended, these collections are available for interested scholars through the archive (za@za.uni-koeln.de). The data up to 1988 was also deposited at the British Social Science Data Archive at Essex. The full data-set up to 2003 is now available at both archives.

Collection and coding of documents in most of the original countries and eventually in all OECD members was passed over to the CMP based at the WZB in 1989 and directed by Andrea Volkens, using a worldwide network of coders. At the same time a separate initiative of Hans-Dieter Klingemann and the WZB, also directed by Volkens, covered collection and coding of party programmes in all the emerging democracies of CEE, as far as the Caucasus. This is the basis for the major time series reported in this book and CD-ROM for CEE countries 1990–2003 (the corresponding OECD estimates being also reported for comparisons and checks). Needless to say the CEE project, though formally distinct, was carried through using the same procedures and coding as the OECD ones. So, they are totally comparable.

With consolidation and continuance of the time series assured, a reduced MRG carried on substantive research which supplemented the manifesto material with public policy indicators such as expenditures (Klingemann et al. 1994)—conclusion, that party emphases and expenditure change generally track each other across ten democracies, as required by mandate theory. A further investigation of the operation of the median mandate (McDonald and Budge 2005) has been published by Oxford University Press. A taster of how the manifesto median estimates enable us to investigate democratic relationships is provided in Chapter 7. Other research has focused on patterns of party interaction revealed by the estimates, within a post-Downsian perspective (Downs 1957; Budge 1994; Adams 2001). A number of further research developments, which use the manifesto estimates in different ways, can be found in Bara and Weale (2006).

The last substantive publication of the MRG itself was of course the predecessor to this volume (Budge et al. 2001). It presented the full time series for OECD countries and Israel up to 1998 on a CD-ROM available for immediate use. The text illustrated uses to which the data could be put, extended them to government and (median) electoral preferences, described coding and computational procedures, and applied tests of reliability and validity. It argued for macrolevel assessment of the estimates rather than mechanical inter-coder reliability checks, given the constantly expanding nature of the data and the different languages involved. However, a generalized measure of error for Left-Right estimates was presented (Heise 1969; Budge et al. 2001: 139). This is extended here (Chapters 4 and 5).

Previous methodological assessments are equally applicable to the data we report here, so we shall not repeat them but simply consider relevant points. Interested readers should go back to the first volume for a full account. However, some aspects of the methodology have emerged as requiring more detailed consideration and we go into them in Chapters 2–6. One topic we raise is the extent to which party election programmes (manifestos, platforms) should be considered as statements of underlying party ideology or simply of current policy. These are clearly not the same thing though they may influence each other as we argue below.

We realize, of course, that most readers will be interested primarily in what our estimates tell them about real politics, particularly in CEE over the past two decades. While methodological discussions inform us about the basis on which estimates were made they are no substitute for the estimates themselves—which we now report in Chapter 1 as 'maps' of party movement along the Left-Right dimension.

NOTE

1. A 'quasi-sentence' is defined as an argument or phrase which is the verbal expression of one idea or meaning. It is often marked off in a text by commas or (semi-)colons. Long sentences may contain more than one argument so that they need to be broken up into quasi-sentences.

Part I

Parties and Representation in Eastern Europe and the European Union

1

Uniquely! Over-Time Mapping of Party Policy Movements in Central and Eastern Europe 1990–2003

The unique strength of the manifesto data is that they measure party policy positions in each election on the basis of the specific programme the party lays down for it. That enables us to chart a party's movement over all the elections it participates in, and to estimate differences between parties at any one point in time and changes in their policy positions between one election and the next.

There are of course inevitable errors in these estimates which caution us against taking differences, especially small differences, at face value. The 'noise' surrounding estimates for a party at two consecutive elections may produce an impression of movement, whereas in fact no real change has actually taken place. Our estimates for error, already presented for Left-Right scores in our previous book (Budge et al. 2001: 139) and in Chapters 4 and 5, indicate however that it is limited to about 10 per cent of variation. While confidence intervals can be formed around each individual score on this basis the figure indicates more generally that estimates can be taken broadly at face value as indicating real change and movement in policy positions.

The graphs concentrate on movement by parties along the Left-Right continuum. This is because Left-Right differences form the central reference point in democratic discussion and analysis, confirmed by their spontaneous, near-universal emergence in our previous analyses of election programmes (Budge, Robertson, and Hearl (eds.) 1987). They are probably the single most important indicator of party policy, and a pointer to underlying ideology which meshes with membership of a generic 'family' and other distinguishing party characteristics.

This is not to say that the manifesto estimates do not cover other aspects of policy. We have also created summary indicators of support for Planning, Market Reliance, Welfare, Peace, and the EU, scores which are given along with Left-Right ones in the CD-ROM. There are also, of course, the fifty-six standard categories into which sentences were originally coded, each of which traces some aspect of party policy in detail over the post-war period.

All these indicators can be represented graphically just like Left-Right movements (Budge 1999). As it is impossible to present everything in print we concentrate on the latter here, leaving readers themselves to create comparable graphs for any series from the CD-ROM (also for governments and electorates, if they wish to focus on policy change at these levels).

The Left-Right graphs are substantively important, first of all from a descriptive point of view. They give a precise measure of where a party stands over an extended period (see Policy Scales Data-Set on the CD-ROM for mean measures of party position on the Left-Right scale). More informatively, they show how it has varied its Left-Right positions at each election. Figures 1.1–1.16 trace such movements and are well able to answer such questions as whether there is general policy convergence or divergence over time.

These questions are of particular interest in the context of Central and Eastern Europe (CEE), which the graphs in this chapter cover. A first question of course is whether Left-Right differences *are* suitable for positioning CEE parties, given that they emerged from quite a different situation, in 1990, from the one which prevailed in the West (Kitschelt 1994; Von Beyme 2001; Jasiewicz 2003). Indeed, with few exceptions, parties in CEE were largely creations or re-creations of the post-communist period and had 'not been prominent in the early stages of regime change' (Lewis 2003: 156). The suitability of the graphs, however, can be judged on such criteria as whether the parties one would expect to be on the Left (Communists and Social Democrats) usually are, at least relative to the other parties. Market Liberal and Nationalist-Conservative parties should correspondingly tend towards the Right.

One might also expect parties to sort themselves out in this way over time, and to stick generally to their own ideological area despite occasional strategic forays out of it (not unknown in the West either, as both the UK and US testify) (Budge et al. 2001: 25). This relates closely to the 'Dahrendorf hypothesis' (1990) which suggested that in the first decade following regime change, parties in CEE countries would demonstrate two major 'swings'—firstly in the direction of liberalization and subsequently towards social democracy. The first move is not simply to create distance between new parties and former regimes strongly associated with socialism, but also to create conditions for developing successful market economies. Likewise, the second move is not simply based on nostalgia for the full employment and state-sponsored welfare of the previous regime, but a reaction to the 'less palatable' aspects of capitalism. Even in established democracies parties do not always behave as one might expect in terms of reflecting left or right concerns. Indeed, their manifestos encapsulate aspects of both. Policy also changes over time. What may have been regarded as a party of the left may move rightwards on occasion—a good case in point being 'New Labour' in Britain in the 1990s. In the volatile situations at the start of regime change in CEE states it is likely that parties swing quite dramatically, irrespective of their original, self-declared locations.

The ability of the Left-Right maps to meet these criteria in a new context constitute a holistic check for the whole data-set, because the underlying scale is affected directly or indirectly by policy changes in all the areas covered by the coding frame. Holistic checks of our estimates, the first available for CEE countries, are the most appropriate ones because of the open-ended and expanding nature of the data, with new elections and countries constantly being added to it. It is a tough check because there is a real independence between the technical procedures for coding programmes and the public historical record of the post-communist period. Our conclusion is that our estimates survive the comparison to the actual historical record with enhanced credibility. But readers can judge this for themselves on the basis of the evidence below.

CREATING THE LEFT-RIGHT SCALE

First though, we must briefly describe how the scoring system was created and why it seems plausible both on theoretical and on empirical grounds. The scale is made by adding percentage references to the categories grouped as Left and Right, respectively, in Table 1.1, and subtracting the sum of the left percentages from the sum of the right percentages. This gives a score for each party-in-an-election, based on its official programme, indicating where it was in Left-Right terms.

In the figures presented in this chapter, therefore, negative scores represent left positions and positive scores represent right positions (sometimes this has been reversed in the past, as in Budge and Hofferbert 1990; Klingemann et al. 1994). At the extreme (never in practice attained) a party devoting its entire programme to left-wing issues would score −100: similarly a totally right-wing programme would score +100. In practice, parties fall in between. But one potential difference between countries is indeed the range of scores needed to accommodate party movements in the figures.

The scale generally opposes emphases on peaceful internationalism, welfare and government intervention on the Left, to emphases on strong defence, free enterprise, and traditional morality on the Right. A first question about its construction is why issues were grouped in this way? There is after all no logical or

Table 1.1. Scoring a Left-Right scale on the basis of the manifesto estimates

Right emphases: sum of %s for		Left emphases: sum of %s for
Military: Positive		Decolonization, Anti-imperialism
Freedom, Human Rights		Military: Negative
Constitutionalism: Positive		Peace
Political Authority		Internationalism: Positive
Free Enterprise		Democracy
Economic Incentives		Regulate Capitalism, Market
Protectionism: Negative	minus	Economic Planning
Economic Orthodoxy		Protectionism: Positive
Social Services Limitation		Controlled Economy
National Way of Life: Positive		Nationalization
Traditional Morality: Positive		Social Services: Expansion
Law and Order		Education: Expansion
Social Harmony		Labour Groups: Positive

inherent reason why support for peace should be associated with government interventionism though the latter might well be designed to secure greater welfare. On the other side, the three concerns of the Right could in theory vary quite independently of each other.

The fact remains however that party ideologies *do* put them together. A first guide to grouping the categories is therefore found in Marxist writings, which emphasize intervention and welfare together with the hardships of capitalist wars. Rightist ideologies are harder to pin down to a specific source, but the grouping of security, enterprise, and traditional morality is certainly familiar from the writings and speeches of theorists from Burke (1790/1955) onwards. The association of these themes in actual party documents is well attested by earlier investigations of election programmes (cf. Robertson 1976; Budge and Farlie 1977; Budge, Robertson, and Hearl (eds.) 1987).

Having grouped these categories on theoretical grounds their 'fit' with each other was investigated through factor analyses of the then existing MRG data up to broadly 1983 (Laver and Budge (eds.) 1992: ch. 2). All the categories differentiated on a priori grounds as Left-Right did indeed turn out to fit on one dimension. This dimension, scored in the percentage terms outlined above, was then input to further factor analyses to see, inductively, if further variables loaded on to it in all countries. One or two did, whose inclusion could also be justified on a priori ideological grounds. They were accordingly added into the scales.

Factor analysis introduces an element of induction (what categories actually co-vary consistently?) into the otherwise a priori, ideologically inspired creation of the Left-Right scale. But it was used to check out pre-conceived ideas rather than to suggest initial construction, for several reasons. First, factor analytic results reflect the data as they are but give no guarantee that if they change the same results will be obtained—even though in the case of our estimates actual results do not seem to vary much over time (Budge et al. 2001: 111–42). Second, because factor analysis does so well reflect tendencies over the whole of the data to which it is applied, it makes parties, which on the face of it have little to do with each other, interdependent in terms of ideological positioning. To take an extreme example, the Left-Right location of the Italian Christian Democrats in 1992 could be affected by what the Finnish communists were saying in 1948. We avoid this by using simple percentage scores without weighting, which give the same position for an individual party regardless of what the others do.

Their dependency on the data at a particular time point and interdependency of positioning seem weaknesses of other Left-Right scales based directly on factor analysis (Budge and Robertson 1987; Bartolini and Mair 1990). Gabel and Huber's attempt (2000) to construct a Left-Right scale drawing on contributions from all categories in the coding frame does have the advantage, however, of maximizing the information available from our coding.

There is a sense in which the Left-Right scale used here also draws on holistic information over all the categories. Twenty-six go directly into the measurement, with thirteen left items being added and subtracted from the sum of thirteen right items. Thus a party that makes 200 total statements with 100 (or 50 per cent) of them about left items and 40 (or 20 per cent) about right items receives a score of −30 (i.e. 20–50). This subtractive measure is consistent with saliency ideas and measurements based on relative emphases (Chapter 6). Of all the statements the party made, on balance, thirty more units were devoted to left matters than right matters. Imagine that at the next election this party's manifesto says exactly the same things it had said last time but adds 200 new statements about an issue that is not of concern to the Left-Right scale (e.g. favourable statements about protecting the environment). Now the party is making 400 total statements, and relative to that total they are making only half as many left statements (25 per cent) and half as many right statements (10 per cent) as they did for the first election. The party's Left-Right position is recorded as moving from −30 to −15. That is, the party is scored as considerably less left-leaning at the second election compared to the first. It has moved towards the centre by virtue of devoting attention to policy matters that are not within the categories relevant to the Left-Right scale.

Measuring positions in this way means that all variables, whether or not typed as explicitly Left-Right, feed into the measure. In this sense the graphs shown below summarize tendencies over the whole of the documents, not just one bit of them. This means that checks on their validity reflect on the standing of the estimates as a whole. Thus, the checks on 'predictive validity' reported in this chapter join the other holistic checks on the validity of the data-set reported below—which in combination render the manifesto estimates the most thoroughly scrutinized of any policy-indicators currently available.

Allowing the Left-Right measure to reflect tendencies in the whole document seems substantively reasonable. Election programmes, particularly those of established parties, are not made up of series of discrete statements on different areas of policy which are then stuck together without overall editing. On the contrary, it is not unusual for each document to be considered carefully by a revising committee or even by an individual—most notably the party leader: each part is checked in relation to the others and the balance of the whole finely calibrated. However, in some contexts, especially in transitional states, the process tends to be more chaotic as parties may not have established permanent bureaucracies or agreed fully on procedural rules. This is most likely to occur in the case of minor or fringe parties, even those with well-established electoral procedures. The easy way for a party to change position without offending previous supporters is to make the same sort of assertions about Left-Right issues while saying more (or less) about other matters, and either throwing them into greater relief or diverting attention elsewhere. Political rhetoric is a more subtle matter of nuances and relative emphases than is allowed by analysts who feel that parties not making blunt assertions or counter-assertions are not taking up a position at all. Part of the proof for this must, as always, be in terms of how useful and accurate are the scores that the Left-Right measure produces.

Before moving to a more detailed examination of the situations in specific CEE countries it is worth reflecting on some significant points pertaining to our data. First, our estimates are based on published programmes—if not fully fledged, dedicated election manifestos or platforms, then a surrogate document, such as a standardized newspaper summary of official policy or, on occasion, major speeches by party leaders delivered at the start of a campaign (although it has to be clear that such an alternative is an accepted surrogate for the party's election platform). Second, the estimates for each party at each election are derived directly from coding the manifesto statements into the fifty-six standard categories (and additional subcategories) (Appendix II). Sometimes, statements made in the manifestos may not form part of the debate during the election campaign, which is, of course, often framed by the mass media and reflects the concerns of interest to it. Hence, it is not unusual to find that manifesto documents prioritize policy which loomed less large in the campaign. For example, in the 2005 British General Election, Foreign Policy, mainly in terms of the Iraq war, figured prominently as an election issue in media reporting of the campaign yet was of almost no consequence in party manifestos—at least on the basis of the CMP categories. This also explains the fact that some parties may end up as Left on the basis of manifesto content, whereas the general perception of them is anything but (cf. Chapter 4).

We do not, of course, possess programmes for every party that contested elections in each country covered. This is the case for the OECD countries covered in our previous volume as well as for the CEE countries covered in this volume. Hence, we are not making final judgements about Left-Right configurations of party *systems* in terms of the whole spectrum of cases. Moreover, in the CEE cases we are dealing with material relating to periods of transition and democratization, which reflect considerable volatility in terms of the formation of party systems and the numbers of parties contesting elections. On occasion a party may not survive beyond one election, or it may disappear after one election only to re-appear after skipping one or more intervening elections. This is generally due to fractionalization or temporary amalgamation in an electoral alliance. It is not always possible to track either the origins or eventual destination of parties in all cases. Such 'flash' parties may not be recorded in our maps, even if they are a party of government. Slovakia is a good case in point.

Some parties did not produce conventional programmes which fit into our expanded coding scheme and are indeed 'more like fluid coteries of individuals than genuine collective entities' (Millard 2004: 133). These people come together to support a particular individual, as in Spain's period of transition from dictatorship to democracy, 1977–81. Such parties usually peter out or become absorbed into a larger entity. The most striking example of a party being formed to support a particular notable in CEE is probably the National Movement for Simeon II in Bulgaria. This was a political movement which grew up around the person of the last king/tsar who sought to put himself forward for election and become prime minister. Unlike many, this movement has been successful in maintaining a considerable presence in parliament without merging with any other group.

Naturally, in the first elections following a period of limited participation, large numbers of 'parties' became contenders—giving rise to significant numbers of programmes. However, these numbers diminished as the party system consolidated. Small parties found it too costly to maintain even an embryonic organization, let alone fight election campaigns. Hence, they evaporated or joined with others in order to benefit from economies of scale and increased profile (Millard 2004). This development was exacerbated in CEE countries, because some of the new systems seemed reluctant to introduce effective electoral thresholds early in the democratization process (Birch 2001; Birch et al. 2002). Electoral reforms have gradually reduced party numbers, although member parties within electoral alliances or coalitions may retain their specific identity and (for our purposes more interestingly) their own election programmes.

Apart from confronting large numbers and the tendency for parties in transitional states to both merge and fragment, we also need to be extra vigilant about name changes (which may or may not accompany these movements). Due to their high policy volatility some individual parties may indeed migrate between families and eventually settle in a different one from the one they started out in. This high degree of movement is reflected in the nature of the legenda associated with the graphical mapping of Left-Right party positions discussed below. We have often needed to adopt rather long names/acronyms for the parties, which are explained in detail in Appendix III. In especially problematic cases, notes are also provided with the graphs themselves.

In the rest of this chapter, we examine maps of Left-Right movement for CEE countries which either have joined or applied to join the EU and 'significant others' in the region such as Russia and Ukraine.

CZECH REPUBLIC, SLOVAKIA, HUNGARY, AND POLAND

We start with the former 'Visegrad' countries which all joined the EU in 2004 after long negotiations. This is because they are the most Westernized of the CEE countries, and had retained many more contacts with the rest of Europe even under Soviet domination. Both Poland and then Czechoslovakia had periods of relative liberalization and pluralism. Hungary was the scene of deliberate political and economic experimentation with a market economy in the 1980s. All also had strong popular liberation movements which staged uprisings and protests at various times in the Soviet period.

Another feature was the survival of pre-war parties such as Agrarians and Christian Democrats which had been in forced coalitions with the Communists, notably in Poland. While denied much freedom of political manoeuvre these groupings had national organizations, buildings, and funds. All of these assets gave them a solid base which was not available to other parties, when free elections came in after 1990. They rapidly distinguished themselves from the Communists. The latter themselves also carried over their material assets into the democratic set-up, and used them to advantage in staging a comeback after the first democratic governments came to be associated with economic crises and savage cost-cutting in the early 1990s.

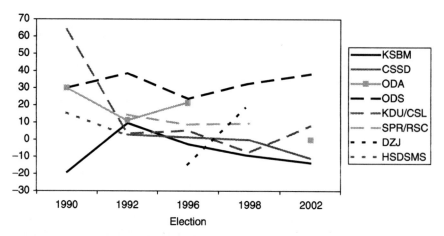

Fig. 1.1. Czech Republic 1990–2002: Left-Right movements by parties

Note: KSBM: Position for 1990 relates to 'old' Communist Party and for 1992, to the Levy Block; ODA and ODS: Position for 1990 relates to Civic Forum from which they emerged; KDU-CSL: Position for 1990–6 relates to a combination of the separate parties and for 2002 relates to position for Koalice of which they became part.

This early period was of course also an opportunity for political experimentation when new parties appeared, merged, and disappeared with extraordinary rapidity. However, Western contacts gave the Visegrad countries more familiarity with party politics than was always the case further East and more sophistication in sorting out the major from more transient contenders. In spite of a great profusion of small parties, in some cases countered by changes in electoral thresholds, the main party alternatives emerge clearly in all four countries and are characterized by quite distinctive policy stands. A good starting point is the Czech Republic (Figure 1.1) where the first election after the 1992 'velvet divorce' with Slovakia took place in 1996, but there were 'Czechoslovak' elections in 1990 and 1992.

In 1992, the Communists strategically modified their hard left line of 1990, but then have gradually returned to a more 'natural' position on the left, a trend mirrored by the Social Democrats. In 1990, Civic Forum, the former umbrella grouping of the freedom movement had started off clearly on the right. But then it split into the larger Democratic Party (ODS), which put more emphasis on its (economic) liberal position (maintained ever since, albeit with some variation) and the smaller Democratic Alliance (ODA) which took a much more social liberal approach and by 2002, clearly occupies the centre ground. The Christian Democrats (KDU CSL) emerged as the most aggressively liberalizing party in Czechoslovakia in 1990, they then clearly positioned themselves at the centre at the next election in 1992—a position they have largely maintained since—despite a short foray to the left in 1998. The three small parties, which contested more than one election, were the Autonomists (HSD SMS) the Republicans (SPR RSC), and the Pensioners (DZJ). The Republicans are a good example of a party which is perceived as being quite extreme but whose manifesto suggests that it is quite moderate. By 2002 only the Liberal ODS remained clearly on the Right. The ex-Communists, Socialists, and Christian Democrats had all moved Left. This suggests that a clear battle-line was drawn between ex-Communists and Social Democrats, on the one hand, advocating social solidarity and social provision on the Left, and the dominant free market Liberals clearly on the Right. The ex-Communists remained distinguishably to the Left of the Social Democrats in the last three elections, as party positions clarified. In general, therefore, our estimates in the figure seem to represent Czech developments quite reasonably, tracing the consolidation of the party system and the way parties got sorted out in policy terms.

Representing these same movements by party families, as we can do by sum-mating Left-Right scores of their constituent members, produces much the same patterns. Dealing with party families has the advantage of adding information about the more transient and smaller parties, especially those contesting only one election. However, the disadvantage is that it blurs the positions of the main parties which are after all the ones that survived—possibly because of the policy adjustments they are shown as making in Figure 1.1. In general therefore we shall stick with the individual parties in the other country figures, except where extreme discontinuities over time make it only realistic to rely on groupings. We shall however always check one type of figure against the other to confirm general conclusions, even where we do not mention it specifically—and, of course, readers can make their own calculations of party family positions on the basis of the estimates provided in the CD-ROM.

Slovakia was the other major component of the former Czechoslovakia, which parted company with the Czech lands in 1992.

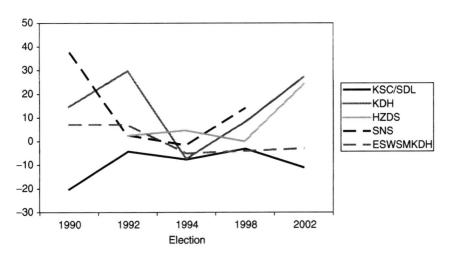

Fig. 1.2. Slovakia 1990–2002: Left-Right movements by parties

The break-up of the Czechoslovak Republic followed a campaign by Meciar's populist HZDS, which although championing Slovak interests really favoured greater autonomy for the two republics rather than the complete separation which was supported especially by the xenophobic Slovak National Party (SNS), and in the mid-1990s by the mercurial, leftist Association of Workers, not represented on the map (Williams 2003). This clearly produced party convergence in Left-Right terms during the first difficult years as a separate republic—as demonstrated by the positions of the parties at the first election after the 'velvet divorce', which took place in 1994. By the 2002 election, dominated by prospects of joining the EU, the parties for which programmes are available broadly sorted themselves out in Left-Right terms. Ex-Communists in the Democratic Left (KSC/SDL) wanted more government funding to support the interests of workers, whilst the Nationalist SNS and Christian Democratic KDH adopted clearly rightist stances. The SWS-MKDH, a party representing the interests of the Hungarian minority also campaigned for government funding to support their cultural interests, which has had the effect of positioning them near the Democratic Left on the graph. This exemplifies the way in which non-economic interests are also reflected in the scale. Slovakia's experience of regime change produced a significant number of small parties, most of which disappeared after fighting one election, their members sometimes joining larger, more successful parties.

Turning to Hungary (Figure 1.3) a close neighbour of the Czech Republic and Slovakia, a broadly similar pattern emerges. The ex-Communists, represented within the MSzP, move distinctly rightwards for both the second (which they won) and third elections, before returning Left in 2002. FiDeSz and the Free Democrats (SzDSz) are clearly distinguishable on the Right initially, though the

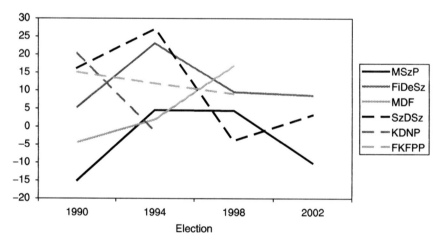

Fig. 1.3. Hungary 1990–2002: Left-Right movements by parties

Note: In 1992 and 2002, an electoral alliance was entered into by FiDeSz and the Democratic Forum.

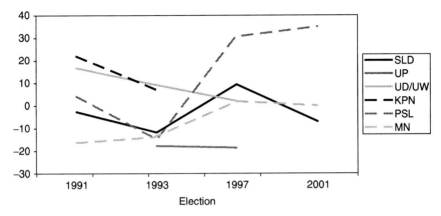

Fig. 1.4. Poland 1991–2001: Left-Right movements by parties

Note: In 2001, SLD was in alliance with UP. In 1997, UW is successor to UD.

latter spectacularly leapfrogs all parties, including their coalition partners, the Communists, in the 1998 election. In the late 1990s, it seems that all six main parties were essentially centrist in terms of ideological orientation (Tóka 2004). However, in 2002 both FiDeSz and SzDSz move to a clearer yet moderate rightist position. By the end of the period the party system thus seems to have consolidated, with these parties advocating policies consonant with overall ideological affiliations whilst the Socialist MSzP moves to a moderate left position. The aggregate party family 'mapping' based on aggregation of positions across the manifestos of the relevant family 'members' (not shown here) reflects these tendencies but shows the Liberal grouping as a whole more consistently on the Right, Christian Democrats more firmly in the centre and Agrarians, of which the FKFPP (Smallholders) are a representative, moderating their clearly right-wing tendency.

Poland is another example of a country with a huge number of flash parties which are unable to survive after a single election. However, Poland's wild card (Figure 1.4) is the sizeable Peasant Party (PSL). Close to ex-Communists (with whom it had been in forced coalition in the former regime) the PSL occupied a very leftist position for the second election. It then moved sharply rightwards in 1997 and 2001. Meanwhile the heirs of Solidarnosc faded away in party terms after they imposed extreme free market reforms producing widespread social hardship while in government from 1991 to 1993.

The ex-Communists themselves (now in the SLD Democratic Left Alliance) moved rightwards when in government (1997), only resuming a more leftward position in 2001. The Union of Labour (UP), another 'new Socialist' party, remained to the Left of the Communists (SLD) till 2001, when the two parties formed an electoral alliance. The most leftist of all until 1997—the MN—represents the interests of the German minority of Silesia and wants government help for its cultural activities. From 1997, its election platform suggests that it adopted a less extreme position. The party family mapping (not included) shows how the PSL gave way on the left to the left-populist Self-defence and the traditionally Catholic, nationalist, and Eurosceptic League of Polish Families in 2001 (Grzybowski and Mikuli 2004; Millard 2004). Other positions are much the same in aggregate. This is interesting as Poland until 1993 had so many small parties contesting elections which are too numerous and transitory to be traced in Figure 1.4. Together these affect the position of their whole family, even though this may not be reflected in the actual number of parties represented in parliament.

This most Westernized grouping of countries in the CEE seems reasonably fitted by a Left-Right representation of party movements. The parties one would expect to be on the Left, in terms of party family membership and historically based commentary, do actually appear there. By and large so do their counterparts on the Right. Few parties stick consistently to the Centre. The hard times of the 1990s in CEE perhaps made it difficult to take up a moderate position. Public policy veered between extreme liberalization of markets and trade, and demands for social protection of vulnerable groups—or indeed, may sometimes have reflected both tendencies at the same time. Looking abroad, some kind of balancing act had to be achieved between the USA and EU, without at the same time offending Russia. Creating a policy regime reasonably adapted to national conditions while adapting it to international pressure was an achievement worked out painfully over the 1990s. Given the strains this imposed it is striking that the Visegrad group have consolidated Left-Right differences so clearly.

LITHUANIA, LATVIA, AND ESTONIA

We may expect the same effects, though possibly more blurred, in the case of the three Baltic states. Relatively small, all formed part of the Russian Empire before the First World War. After independence in the inter-war period they were constituent republics of the Soviet Union from 1945 to1990. Given their historical ties with Russia and the existence of strong Russian-speaking minorities inside Latvia and Estonia, internal politics have been even more affected by foreign developments than in most other states. Even as new members of the EU they form part of Russia's 'near abroad' and have to be careful about the relationship—even though they may not always acknowledge it!

Lithuania, the most southerly and largest of the three, also has close historical and social ties with Poland. It has a Polish party, the LLS/LLRA, which like some other minority party manifesto positions we have examined emerges on the centre or centre-left (1990 and 2000) in pursuit of government support for their cultural interests (Figure 1.5). However, there is no political grouping in Lithuania like the large Polish Peasant Party.

The Lithuanian ex-Communists, the LDDP, with their somewhat ambivalent relationship with the Russians, disappeared by 2000. The LSDP–BSDK coalition of Social Democrats produced programmes which gravitated consistently towards the Left. The programmes of the Lithuanian LCJ/LCS Centre Movement have been notably Centre-Left compared with their liberalizing Visegrad counterparts.

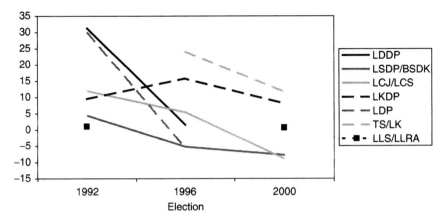

Fig. 1.5. Lithuania 1992–2000: Left-Right movements by parties

Note: In 2000, the LSDP formed a coalition with other parties, including the Russian Union and became the BSDK.

The programmes of the Christian Democrats, notably the surviving LKDP, have maintained a clear rightist stance, although they also moved significantly left-wards. The LDP on the other hand, started out from a fairly extreme rightist, economic liberal position and moved rapidly to the same position as the Social Democrats, the LSDP/BSDK, by 1996. This perhaps proved a move too far as the party then ceased to contest elections. The nationalistic Homeland Union (TS-LK) maintained its position in two elections on the Right. In 2000, the last election for which we have data, competing parties all moved leftward, although there are still considerable differences among them in Left-Right terms. It was too early to say if the LCJ/LCS's leapfrogging of the LSDP to its Left signified anything more than a strategic positioning or some more permanent shift of position. Broadly speaking the party family map showed a similar pattern. The policy positions of Lithuanian parties thus bear out assertions that they can be identified along a Left-Right axis (Duvold and Jurkynas 2004).

Latvia (Figure 1.6) is dominated by parties of the Centre. Even the national-ist Fatherland and Freedom (TB/LNNK) programmes took up moderate policy stands in 1998. 'Latvia's way's' (LC) programmes started off in a relatively rightist position but shared in the general drift leftwards of most of the other parties from 1995. The Social Democrats (LSP/LSDA) programmes, reflected an essentially left-wing position in 1995 but moved substantially towards the Centre in 1998. It should be noted that there are also many examples of flash parties contesting only one election, some of which may be moderately successful in the short term, which cannot be shown on the map (Smith-Sivertsen 2004).

The party family map for Latvia shows the same convergence between party tendencies. Latvia is both smaller in size and closer to Russia than Lithuania. The need to accommodate their giant neighbour and join the EU may account for more muted political disagreements over other matters and the consequent centrist policy convergence which shows up so clearly in the figure.

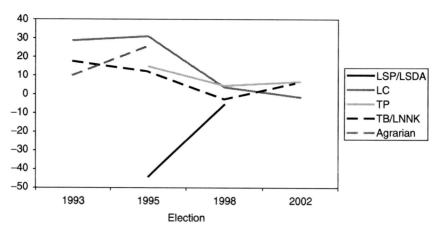

Fig. 1.6. Latvia 1993–2002: Left-Right movements by parties

Note: Social Democrats are represented by the LSP in 1995 and the LSDA in 1998.

Estonia on the other hand shows a clear and increasing differentiation between the nationalist and rurally oriented Isamaa Coalition and the other parties: Moodukad, the Liberal Reform Party (ER), and Centre (KESK). The latter three converged by 2003 but their programmatic positions were sharply distinguished from Isamaa. In territorial terms Estonia is practically a suburb of St. Petersburg, but culturally it is a detached fragment of Finland. As such it has much closer links with Scandinavia than the other Baltic states. 'Normal' internal politics may thus be easier for Estonia than Latvia. The party family mapping traces out the same tendencies as Figure 1.7.

Over the Baltic states as a whole the Left-Right representation still seems to work reasonably well in tracing out plausible policy paths for parties and

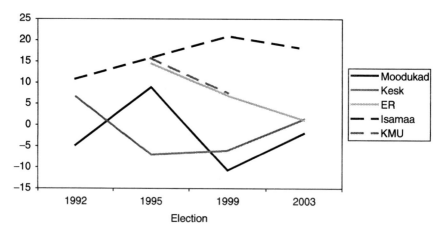

Fig. 1.7. Estonia 1992–2003: Left-Right movements by parties

differentiating them clearly. In the case of Latvia it is difficult without a longer run of cases to say if the representation is in error or conveying genuine information. We will be in a better position to make a provisional judgement about that after we have examined the whole of the CEE.

EX-YUGOSLAVIA: SLOVENIA, CROATIA, AND SERBIA

Yugoslavia set up as a Balkan state at the end of the First World War. Governed by an independent-minded Communist Party from 1945 till its break-up at the beginning of the 1990s, it split into five independent entities with two autonomous regions. We have data on all five but report mappings only for the three listed above. Though all speak Southern Slav languages (and in fact Croatia and Serbia speak substantially the same one) they all have different histories. Slovenia in the north is an old Austrian province, eastern Croatia, a Hungarian one, and western Croatia Italian and Austrian. Serbia had a long tradition of resistance to Turkish rule under Russian patronage from the 1830s. We might expect therefore to find Eastern–Western contrasts mirrored in differences between Slovenian and Croatian politics on the one hand and Serbian on the other. This is especially the case as Serbia was ruled by a highly nationalistic Communist Party, kept in office by dubious election tactics, which was only forced out by a popular rising in 1999–2000. Slovenia by contrast seceded peacefully, and Croatia's independence war with Serbia took place in the early 1990s.

   The ex-Communist parties in all three countries were associated with the maintenance of the old Yugoslav federation. So, it is not surprising in the case of Slovenia (Figure 1.8) to find the Communists (ZL/ZKS) at a rather rightist position, which perhaps accounts for their re-configuration as the United (Associated) List in 1992. Its programmes project a leftward trend from 1996 to 2000. The

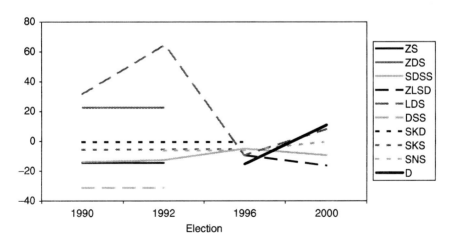

Fig. 1.8. Slovenia 1990–2000: Left-Right movements by parties

Social Democratic Party, the SDSS, starts out on the left but moves consistently rightward.

Both the Christian Democrats (SKD) and the Peoples' Party (SLS) are consistently centrist, with the latter taking the more leftward stance of the two. The Nationalist SNS also adopts a more centrist position from 1996. Indeed, all the parties represented on the map converge in Left-Right terms towards the 1996 election, but this is primarily due to the large move leftwards made by the market-oriented Liberal Democrats (LDS) after 1992. Perhaps this was due to the party having roots in the former socialist youth organization. So, this was a less dramatic move than we might imagine (Zajc and Boh 2004). However, a cautious move rightwards by the Liberal Democratic Party (LDS) in 2000 began to separate out the parties again.

This sort of behaviour is not unprecedented in Western Europe (cf. the British Conservatives and Liberals in the 1950s: Figure 1.15). It may be connected with Liberals trying to compensate strategically for the economic and social hardships brought about by marketization. However, it is extremely dramatic and one may well wonder whether ideology, as reflected by policy, was as binding for them as for comparable Western parties.

After 1996, the party system in Slovenia begins to exhibit significant change, leading to differentiation in Left-Right terms, after a period in which most parties had remained fairly static. This bears out the views of other observers (Millard 2004; Zajc and Boh 2004). But we should also be aware that the parties needed to switch policies at different elections, owing to domestic crises and international complications. These may produce uncharacteristic Left-Right emphases, such as Social Democrats expressing support for market economics or parties of the right dabbling in redistribution of wealth. Such behaviour is, of course, not unknown in the West either!

Croatia projects a contrasting pattern over time where the parties' policy positions start off from rather undifferentiated points in 1990 and differentiate themselves quite sharply over the next two elections. Croatian nationalists have generally been regarded as very much on the Right, although this is not always reflected by the policy positions mapped below. However, these positions were taken up as conflict with Serbia passed into open war, besides Croatia's involvement in a proxy war going on in Bosnia-Hercegovina.

Four parties included in the data-set—ex-Communists (SDPH), Liberal Coalition (KNS/HSLS), Peoples' Party (HNS), and especially the Democratic Union HDZ)—demonstrate rightward moves. The positions of the SDPH and the KNS/HSLS Liberal Coalition appear to stabilize by the mid-1990s. The exceptions are the traditional Peasant Party, the HSS, and the previously Radical-Nationalist-Fascist Party of Rights, HSP, which move in the opposite direction.

HSS support for policies favouring redistribution for poor peasants accounts for the party's shift to the Left from 1992 to 1995. Confusing matters from an ideological perspective is the presence of another nationalist party, the HNS (People's Party), on the Left in 1992, although by 1995 its policy positions had pushed it to the Right. Overall Croatian parties fit into patterns recognizable from the West. It

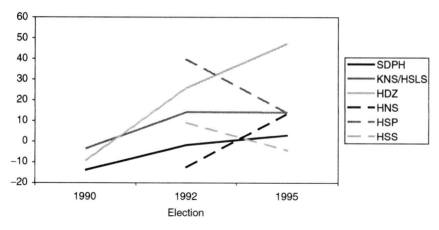

Fig. 1.9. Croatia 1990–1995: Left-Right movements by parties

will be interesting to see how these trends develop when we acquire data for later elections.

Serbia presents a different picture, as the Socialist SPS appears more right wing than left wing, certainly until 1997. SPS positions also closely mirror the policy moves of the Liberal New Democracy (ND). The SPS stance is of course explicable in terms of their dominant role as guarantors of the old order in Serbia during the 1990s. The Nationalist Radical Party (SRS) emerges further on the right and projects a further right reflection of the SPS until 1997 when it starts to show leftward tendencies. In 2000 an eighteen-party coalition, known as the Democratic Opposition of Serbia, gained a combined vote of 70 per cent and

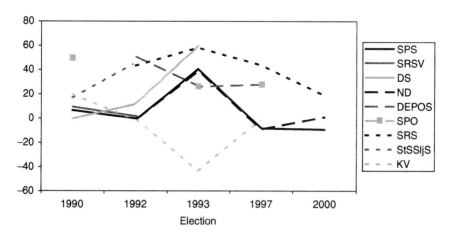

Fig. 1.10. Serbia 1990–2000: Left-Right movements by parties
Note: The SPS were in coalition with the Yugoslav Left and New Democracy in 1997.

formed a government. Among the participants were the Democratic Party (DS), New Democracy (ND), Democratic Centre, and the Alliance of Reform Forces of Vojvodina (SRSV).

An interesting feature of the Serbian map is that the minority Hungarian party, KV, is the most leftward party in the system, albeit only in terms of its 1993 programme, presumably because of favouring government support for its clients' interests. This reflects what we have found to be a general case in the CEE—one which we did not anticipate before these mappings.

BULGARIA AND ROMANIA

Bulgaria also has a minority party (DPS, representing its sizeable Turkish population) which situates itself towards the Left. The other Bulgarian parties appear to be among the most right wing in the entire CEE. The Socialist Party, the BSP, is generally to the left of the other parties but its policy positions make erratic and considerable leaps rightwards. The self-styled Union of Democratic Forces (SDS) is generally on the Right, though the BSP leapfrogged it in 1997. The Agrarian National Union (BZNS) have been more centrist in policy terms. The Business Bloc (BBB) was in 1994 well to the Right of the BSP although their policy positions leapfrogged each other quite dramatically in 1997.

While in broad terms Bulgaria maintains a general policy contrast between the parties the relationship reveals odd anomalies which seem to indicate that something more than Left-Right divisions are needed to explain its politics. The BSP are of course the former Communists and the only party to show any left of centre position (1994), although their policy positions are extremely volatile—no doubt due to pressures from continuing economic crises. In the latest election of

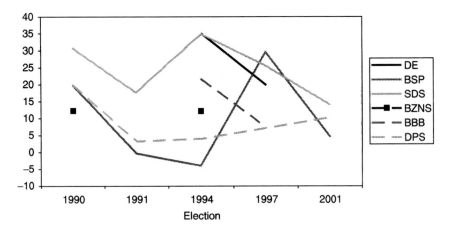

Fig. 1.11. Bulgaria 1990–2001: Left-Right movements by parties

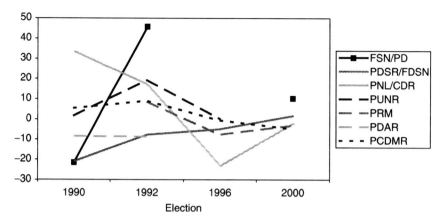

Fig. 1.12. Romania 1990–2000: Left-Right movements by parties

the series (2001) the parties appear to be taking up expected positions in Left-Right terms. But, of course, it is too early to say whether this will continue. The successful entry of the ex-King into domestic politics with a populist appeal and classic conservative claims to greater efficiency is described as being a function of 'widespread feelings of disappointment... as well as an indicator of the failure of the old parties... ' (Karasimeonov 2004: 439). But his party has not seemed to exert a stabilizing effect so far. The future shape of the Bulgarian party system is thus still unclear—as indeed its most recent election results indicate.

In Bulgaria's remaining Balkan neighbour, Romania, the preceding Ceaușescu regime was exceptionally tyrannical even by Soviet Communist standards. The brief uprising which overthrew it promoted internal divisions rather than unity, as regime stalwarts switched sides and continued to hang on to power under the guise of a new democracy. This history accounts for the ex-Communist party, the FSN/PD, taking up such an extreme right-wing position in 1992 to distance itself from its past, although it began a return towards the centre immediately afterwards.

The positions projected by the Social Democratic PDSR/FDSN, however, take up a more consistently left-wing stance within the general drift towards the Centre of all the parties including, eventually, the ex-Communists in 2001. The National-ist groupings, National Unity (PUNR), and Greater Romania (PRM) adopt more easily interpretable positions on the Centre-Right, although the latter leapfrogs the PDSR/FDSN in the last two elections (but not by much).

As representative of the interests of a sizeable, territorially concentrated minor-ity, the Hungarian Democratic Federation (PCDMR) has an important role in Romanian politics which possibly accounts for its centrist position compared to the other ethnic minorities we have examined in CEE. Its size and importance make it more than simply a promoter of government aid for its own group.

All in all the Left-Right representation fits Romanian politics surprisingly well. Convergence rather than differentiation of parties towards the end of the series can well be accounted for by pressure from the country's appalling social and economic situation, far worse than even those of its close neighbours in the Balkans and CEE.

UKRAINE AND RUSSIA

These are matched however by Romania's eastern neighbours, Ukraine and Russia—the central components of the old Soviet Union. Both of these regimes are highly presidentialized and this has stunted the development of their post-Soviet party systems (Millard 2004) In both states also the former governing party, the CPSU (Communist Party of the Soviet Union) was run by privileged cadres and wedded to the old structures of power. After independence the successor Communist parties in the two states took different paths. In Ukraine after 1994 the directly elected president used many of the party's personnel for both electoral and parliamentary purposes to consolidate his power. Paradoxically the KPU became a conservative party, dedicated to the status quo and to strong ties with Russia rather than the West.

However, one should never forget that in CEE, the old structures included an extensive state-supported health and welfare system, thus providing Communist and ex-Communist parties with an inbuilt left-wing appeal, should they care to use it. This has given them an opportunity to move from the Right when in opposition or fighting off criticisms of inefficiency and authoritarianism from other parties, as we can see in the case of the Ukraine in Figure 1.13.

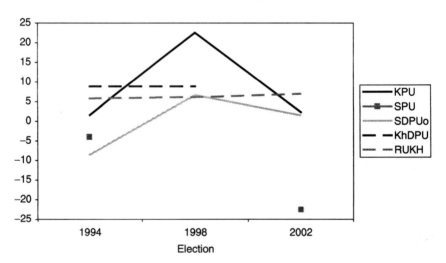

Fig. 1.13. Ukraine 1994–2002: Left-Right movements by parties

Note: Figure for Rukh, 2002 relates to Our Ukraine of which Rukh was a part.

While far and away the most right-wing party overall on the basis of its manifesto policy positions, the KPU nonetheless moved substantially leftwards in 2002 to fight off the challenge from the essentially Liberal SDPU-o (who call themselves Social Democrats). The latter have taken a perfectly comprehensible centrist position combining free market reforms with support for civil liberties and peaceful internationalism.

The most left-wing party is the SPU (Socialist Party) which has moved from being centrist in 1994 to a clear position on the left by 2002. It has increasingly supported welfare and intervention to combat the poor social conditions under which most ordinary people live. Rukh, a movement established in the late 1980s to implement glasnost, has maintained a centrist position, which is corroborated by this map. It never gained significant proportions of the vote in the 1990s (Birch 1998). However, in 2002, it was part of the 'Our Ukraine' bloc, led by Victor Yushchenko (now president), which projected a similar position in Left-Right terms. A major feature of Ukrainian politics in the post-Soviet era has been the enormous number of independent candidates standing for election. In 1994, they polled over 66 per cent of the vote!

The overall picture given by the Left-Right representation in the Ukraine is therefore comprehensible if idiosyncratic in general terms—but idiosyncratic in a interpretable way given the ambiguous position of the Communist Party.

The same could be said for Russia (Figure 1.14)—even though political positions there are even more affected by idiosyncratic developments in the 1990s. The ex-Communists, the KPRF, at that point constituted themselves as the guardians of the old Soviet legitimacy against the modernizing, directly elected presidents.

These made some attempts to organize a supportive party, Russia is our Home (NDR), which takes up an expected position on the Right in favour of order. However, the presidents have relied mostly on building up support from governments—whether their own or those of the autonomous republics inside

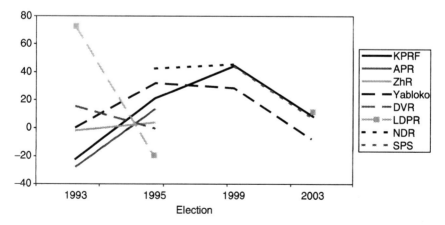

Fig. 1.14. Russia 1993–2003: Left-Right movements by parties

Russia. Thus NDR faded out after 1999. The Union of Right Forces (SPS), critical of the presidents, tracked the KPRF from 1999 as they gradually abandoned their appeal to the security and certainty of the old Soviet order in favour of a greater stress on welfare by 2003.

The so-called Liberal Democrats (LDPR) are anything but, being nationalist and contemptuous of civil rights—but are also capable of basing appeals on welfare and standing up for the 'little man', as in 1995. Hence, their policy positions over time are volatile, and it is not surprising that they mirrored KPRF and SPS positions in 2003, in opposition to the Putin presidency.

The true liberals are Yabloko standing for civil freedoms, market reforms, government efficiency, and peaceful internationalism. Stressing one of these appeals over others at different times moves them between various positions on the Centre-Right. Their classic liberal position is what we might expect in terms of party family affiliation, as indeed was the case with Democratic Choice (DVR) earlier on. The Agrarian APR, moved in parallel fashion to the Communists, with whom they were associated in 1993 and 1995.

We can thus come to a similar judgement regarding Russia as with the Ukraine. The Left-Right representation is especially idiosyncratic in these ex-Soviet republics, primarily because the Communists in light of their historical legacy have adopted a different role from elsewhere. But it is perfectly interpretable. There are also some signs of other parties, such as the Liberals, adopting 'normal' policy positions which parallel those of their counterparts in other countries.

OVERVIEW

Perhaps the most prudent conclusion to draw from the various applications of the Left-Right framework to CEE countries is that it is not obviously wrong. In a majority of countries it orders the parties as we expect and maps their movements plausibly. Even where the representation is not a 'normal' one, as judged from a Western perspective, it is plausible for the country concerned. The crucial question is whether after democratization the Communists or their successors took on their traditional role of defending workers' interests against the ravages of the free market: or whether they continued (usually in government) to defend the Soviet-era regime.

As expected we find the former situation more prevalent, and a conventional party system tending to function along established Left-Right lines, in the countries of Central Europe as opposed to Eastern Europe. Indeed, many of the 'maps' reflect our experience in working with OECD countries. The exceptions become more numerous, and country-based explanations more necessary, the further East we go. The contrast has an obvious explanation: Central Europe and the Baltic inherited more established pre-Second World War social and political institutions and cultural norms than the East. So, the Left-Right distinctions already associated with these and embedded in pre-existing party ideology were available to organize party competition (an exception seems to be Latvia). In the East, with less of the pre-Soviet political culture surviving, politics were less clear and often overwhelmed by war and unrest and a much deeper social and economic collapse.

Under these circumstances we have refrained from mapping other countries for which we have data such as Belorus and the Caucasian republics where democracy has only been tenuously established and is continuously threatened. Their inclusion would only have strengthened the contrast between Central Europe and Eastern Europe.

If Left-Right works better where institutions and processes are better established may we expect it to take more hold, to produce clearer and more consistent party distinctions, as time goes on and democratic structures are consolidated? There is some evidence for this in our maps. In some cases parties had become more differentiated by the time of the last election. In others, however, a considerable degree of policy convergence seems to be taking place. A prudent conclusion is, therefore, that the time series of elections is too short to discern trends with any certainty.

The same reasoning applies to many countries where the overall positioning of the parties looks good in Left-Right terms but there are one or two dramatic and anomalous moves by major players, that is, a party either crosses quite deeply into opposed ideological terrain (e.g. Hungarian and Polish ex-Communists in the mid-1990s) or leapfrogs on to the other wing (Slovenian Liberals) or both. Is this substantive information—for strategic or other reasons a party changed policy positions quite dramatically for a particular election? Or does the anomaly invalidate the whole Left-Right representation?

Some light can be cast on this question by considering Figures 1.15a and 1.15b, which map parties in the long-established democracy of Britain. The figures allow us to contrast a short- and long-time perspective and the inferences one might be tempted to make from them. If we consider elections from 1945 up to and including 1959 this shows the normally rightist conservatives moving from Right of Centre in 1945 to well within the Left in 1955. The Liberals also change position though Labour maintains substantially the same left-wing position throughout. This period, covering five elections in the aftermath of the War and great internal changes, provides an equivalent picture for Britain to those we have been examining for the CEE countries. We have only the four or five elections of the period in which 'normal' party competition re-established itself after the War. But it was not altogether normal. The parties fall into their 'correct' Left-Right positions (e.g. Conservatives and Liberals are consistently to the Right of Labour). On the other hand the Conservatives make a totally uncharacteristic foray to the Left, particularly in 1955. Is this an anomaly or substantive information conveyed by the Left-Right mapping? Inspection of the overall map (1945–2005) covering a much longer time period reassures us about the validity of the representation. Nineteen fifty-five was simply a particular strategic adjustment by Conservatives who edged back in the 1960s to a right-wing position they have held more or less ever since. The move Left in the 1950s has been interpreted by historians as the 'Social Democratic Consensus' in which Conservatives sought to convince electors

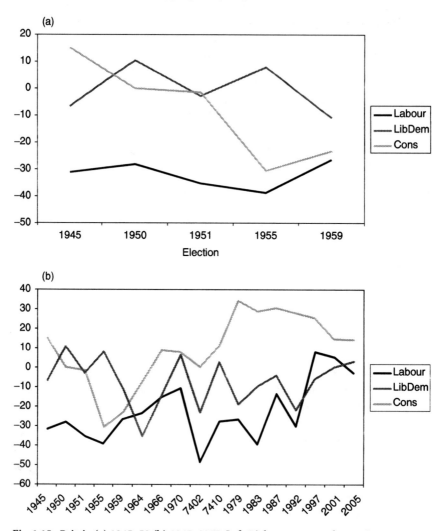

Fig. 1.15. Britain (a) 1945–59 (b) 1945–2005: Left-Right movements by parties

that they could safely be entrusted with the administration of the new Welfare State and a mixed economy.

We are not yet able to put our information about the CEE countries into such an extended time perspective. But the British example shows how seemingly anomalous moves can actually represent quite real party policy changes. We should be wary about interpreting them as diminishing from the credibility of the representation when actually they enhance it.

Figure 1.16 illustrates party development in the Western European case most analagous to the CEE, Portugal. Portugal emerged from a forty-year dictatorship

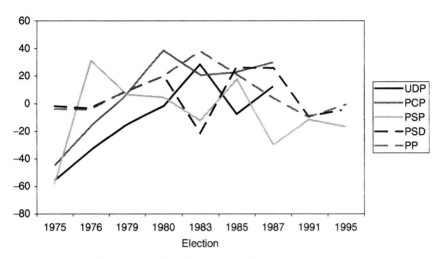

Fig. 1.16. Portugal 1975–95: Left-Right movements by parties

in 1974, as the result of an army coup. The early years of restored democracy were quite chaotic and confused, with Socialists (PSP) leapfrogging positions of the Centre (Christian) Social Democrats (PSD). Only later, in the 1980s and 1990s, did the Socialists pursue a more distinct and left-wing line. We may expect the same developments to take place across CEE: they have already almost crystallized in Central Europe and the Baltic.

CONCLUSIONS

If we adopt the hypothesis-testing approach to a Left-Right representation that our previous book advocated (Budge et al. 2001: 62) then we can certainly say that the analyses of this chapter do not refute the idea that voting and party competition occur primarily in a one-dimensional Left-Right space. We have argued previously that this concept has so many theoretical and analytical advantages that we should stick with it until conclusive evidence emerges against. None has in this chapter. On the contrary the majority of country representations present patterns which are plausible and fit with Left-Right ideas. Where they do not there are historical reasons for them not doing so and the Left-Right representation still makes a good starting point for exploring the national political situation.

We shall, of course, also explore these points in greater detail below. Mapping the CEE countries makes a good starting point for further discussion however, as it has shown our spatial representation to work *in extremis*, and certainly under circumstances which were never envisaged when it was first proposed.

2

Beyond the Left-Right Dimension: Policy
Profiles and Programmatic Coherence of
Party Groupings in the European Parliament

EP PARTY GROUPINGS AND DISCRIMINANT ANALYSIS

This chapter is concerned, like Chapter 1, to see how far our manifesto-based policy estimates fit the new democracies—and new political developments—in Europe. However, it extends the inquiry from the Left-Right divisions we have been examining so far to all the issues covered by the coding frame. One of the most direct ways to see if these are relevant to contemporary politics is to use them to explain the evolution of party groupings in the European Parliament (EP). These have often been said to rest on strategic or pragmatic considerations (the arguments are reviewed in Volkens 2006). Our own feeling is that the groups—which in their present forms were formally constituted only recently (2004), after the enlargement of the EU to take in eight new CEE members—have a strong basis in the old party families and hence are grounded in their policies and ideologies rather than in situational and strategic influences. This implies that policy similarities between parties extend across the divide between 'Old' and 'New' Europe, a point we also examine.

We can check these ideas by using party policy statements as laid out in the manifestos to assign probabilities to national parties of being members of particular EP groupings. The policy-based probabilities can then be compared with actual membership of the groupings to see if they correspond. In the following analyses we take the parties in each parliamentary grouping in turn and assign probabilities, on the basis of their programmatic statements, of their belonging to the group in question, or to one of the others.

The data-analytic technique we use to do this is multiple discriminant analysis. The aim of this type of analysis is to maximize differences between selected groupings of cases. It essentially answers the question: Given the information we have about tendencies over a whole set of party documents, how far can we use this for unequivocal typing of individual party programmes as belonging to the grouping? Like regression, discriminant analysis averages prediction variables in the best linear combination to predict (or more properly to 'postdict') the cases into the original target variable categories (i.e. the parliamentary groups).

We thus take groupings of parties, and try to put a particular manifesto into a particular party grouping. If we can do this—if, say, a large number of manifestos written by Green parties across several countries are accurately typed as being in the Green Grouping of the EP—we have shown that our coding schemes pick out the essence of party ideologies in a way that transcends both the cultural and the national context. Also we have answered our substantive question about whether the groupings are ideology—and policy—driven.

We are actually able to do more. The linear combinations of predicting variables, like a factor analytic solution but unlike a regression equation, can be interpreted as measures of an underlying continuum. Thus we can make informed guesses as to what particular policies make parties alike. We can sketch what makes Greens resemble other Greens, and different from Liberals or other Centrists, and so on.

This in fact is what we start off doing in the next section before coming to the actual results of the discriminant analysis itself. We can anticipate its predictive success here by reporting that, out of the total 133 parties included in the analysis, 68 per cent were classified in the correct EP grouping. An additional 15 per cent were put into groups ideologically 'next door' to the one under examination. Only 17 per cent were misclassified into groupings further away, and hence ideologically alien to the grouping in question. We can therefore regard programmes and policies, as classified into our coding scheme, as providing a great deal of information about parties' ideological groupings and 'families'. Which particular aspect of these is most informative is examined in the next section before proceeding to the classification exercise itself.

POLICY DIFFERENCES BETWEEN GROUPINGS

In order to do a high-level discriminant analysis, of course, one has to have information to analyse. This is contained in the manifesto (quasi-)sentences as classified into our coding scheme and counted as percentages of the total. In order to maximize the information available, particularly for CEE, the scheme we use here is organized differently from the original (Table I.1) although it relates closely to it. In coding CEE countries, many subdivisions were made within the original coding categories to accommodate the special conditions there, particularly during the transition in the early 1990s. Thus 'government authority' (305 in our coding scheme) often involved questions about keeping former Communists in the bureaucracy. The coding for CEE created a separate subcategory (3053) into which such references could be coded and distinguished. Such subcategorizations—which have always been used to deal with conditions in particular countries—do not affect the generality or integrity of the overall MRG coding scheme because they can always be aggregated 'up' to the original categories.

However, to maximize discrimination between policies, particularly for the ex-Communist members of the EU, some of these subcategories were transferred

Table 2.1. Coding scheme adapted for discriminant analysis and used to classify policy positions of political parties as expressed in their election programmes

Code	Policy areas
State Policy	
POL1	Freedom and Human Rights
POL2	Democracy
POL3	Constitution
POL4	Centralization
POL5	Decentralization
POL6	Modes of Government
POL07	Communists, pro
POL08	Communists, con
Economic Policy	
ECO1	Market Economy
ECO2	Planned or Mixed Economy
ECO3	Economic Infrastructure
ECO4	Environmental Protection
ECO5	Agriculture
ECO6	General Economic Orientation
Social Policy	
SOC1	Traditional Morality, Law and Order
SOC2	Cultural Libertarianism
SOC3	Welfare State, Limitation
SOC4	Welfare State, Expansion
SOC5	Social Group Politics
Foreign Policy	
FOR1	Military Strength
FOR2	Peace and Détente
FOR3	Nationalism
FOR4	International Cooperation
FOR5	Special Relationships

across the boundaries of the original categories to form part of new policy bundles. Experimental analyses indicated that they yielded more information for discrimination in this way. The re-ordered scheme is illustrated in Table 2.1. It is clearly close to the original one. Categories have however been amalgamated and their contents modified to a limited extent by transferring subcategories. The details are given in the chapter appendix. Here, we need only note that it is the categories in Table 2.1 which have been input to the analysis reported later and which appear as explicit categories in Tables 2.2–2.5 following.

We now use them to take a broad look at policy differences between old and new EU states and between the party groupings, before going on to more technical procedures. Although our analysis is primarily concerned with differences between party groupings, Table 2.2 as a matter of interest looks at differences in the policy

Table 2.2. The political agenda in the old and new member states
of the European Union as reflected in party election programmes

Policy area	*Old* Mean (91)	*New* Mean (42)	*Total* Mean (133)	Sig.*
State Policy				
Freedom and Human Rights	2.35	1.47	2.07	.067
Democracy	2.93	2.04	2.65	.053
Constitution	0.48	1.23	0.72	*.003*
Centralization	0.10	0.16	0.12	.526
Decentralization	3.57	3.79	3.64	.761
Modes of Government	**8.50**	**11.38**	**9.41**	.024
Communist, pro		0.30*		
Communist, con		0.26**		
Economic Policy				
Market Economy	**7.69**	**7.72**	**7.70**	.974
Planned or Mixed Economy	1.68	2.36	1.89	.136
Economic Infrastructure	**7.01**	**6.43**	**6.82**	.504
Environmental Protection	**6.65**	3.29	**5.59**	*.002*
Agriculture	2.19	**5.57**	3.26	*.000*
General Economic Orientation	2.16	3.06	2.45	.047
Social Policy				
Traditional Morality, Law and Order	**7.55**	**6.98**	**7.37**	.627
Cultural Libertarianism	0.21	0.15	0.19	.466
Welfare State, Limitation	0.40	1.78	0.83	*.000*
Welfare State, Expansion	**24.69**	**22.57**	**24.02**	.000
Social Group Politics	**6.64**	4.43	**5.94**	*.000*
Foreign Policy				
Military Strength	0.77	1.99	1.15	*.000*
Peace and Détente	1.06	0.29	0.82	*.000*
Nationalism	4.02	**5.28**	4.42	.322
International Cooperation	**6.06**	4.23	**5.48**	0.14
Special Relationships	0.37	1.34	0.68	*.001*

Notes: Bold face: average of 5.00 and above; bold face italics: difference of means test
significant at the .005 level.
*Analysis of variance, between group differences, *F* test.
**Categories used for CEE countries only.

agenda between old and new states as such. The general conclusion must be that it
is very similar. With a few exceptions the same topics get emphasized to very much
the same extent between East and West. The most emphasized topics are shown
in bold type. Five out of nine of these receive a lot of attention on both sides of
the divide, and of the remaining four it is only on environmental protection and
agriculture that there could be said to be a considerable difference.

What does differentiate the regions is usually some little-emphasized area which
does however get more attention on one side than the other. Thus for obvious
reasons the new members are more concerned with constitutional questions than

the old, even if they are not a topic of burning interest. Parties do talk about welfare limitation in CEE, even if the emphasis is minimal compared to support for welfare expansion. In the West parties hardly talk about limitation at all, so this constitutes a policy difference between them. There are also differences of emphasis on foreign policy: the new states, highly conscious of their proximity to Russia, are more concerned than the old with military strength and special relations with other states (Russia again).

In terms of heavy emphasis and differences between the Western and Eastern blocks, it is however the opposition of environment to agriculture that most differentiates them—again understandable in terms of their economic situation, where older states can pay off farmers with the Common Agricultural Policy and thus afford the luxury of worrying about the environment, while CEE feels (up to now) it cannot.

As neither East nor West can be said to have uniform social and economic conditions across countries, we would expect to find this division, like the others, less directly reflected in differences between states than in divisions between party groupings and the relative distribution of their member parties in the new EU states as compared to the old. We can check *their* policy agendas in Table 2.3.

Table 2.3 orders the party groupings from Left to Right in terms of their overall ideological tendency. Their positioning is indicated both by our general scales and by expert opinion (e.g. as expressed in party family classifications). The Union for a Europe of Nations (UEN) consists of traditional State Nationalist parties, not necessarily Eurosceptics but highly concerned with their own national interest, interventionist, but as much for law and order as welfare. 'Independence and Democracy', on the other hand, is distinguished by Euroscepticism on the one hand and suspicion of all state intervention on the other. Both groupings are understandably placed on the Right. The name adopted by the non-affiliated group might suggest that they wish to transcend Left-Right divisions. In practice however they consist of parties like the National Front in France which would conventionally be regarded as extreme Right. Not unsupportive of state handouts on welfare, they strongly oppose immigration and want cultural integration round traditional national values.

Table 2.3 bold types are the issues on which groupings put most relative emphasis compared to other groupings. As one can see from looking up and down the columns these are not always the topic it most emphasizes over all its programmes—the three most important are ranked internally (1, 2, or 3 in brackets). Take the case of the European Greens/European Free Alliance (EG/EFA), in the second column. As expected they distinguish themselves most from other parties by their emphasis on environmental protection (bold type, 15.23 per cent). However, this is not the topic they emphasize most compared to the others in their programme. Environment is actually second to welfare expansion (23.83 per cent). However, most party groupings in the table support welfare expansion very strongly. So this is not a distinctively Green issue in the way the environment is.

Overwhelming support for more welfare is however what picks out the United Left/Nordic Green Left (EUL-NGL) (32.74) from other groupings, and is also by far their biggest issue. They also distinguish themselves from others on social groups (trade union and the working class), democracy, economic intervention, peace, and cultural libertarianism. These are classic Leftist policy stances. Their relatively strong endorsement here shows the coherence of EUL-NGL in policy terms.

Generally, we would expect ideology to become less of a binding force as we went from Left to Right. However, most groupings distinguish themselves from others by their relative emphasis on at least one very characteristic issue. The Socialists (PES) are almost as keen on welfare as the EUL-NGL. Relatively speaking, however, they cohere round the need for building the infrastructure—a solid 'non-political' issue for a moderate group influenced by 'New Labour' and a 'Third Way'. The Alliance of Liberals and Democrats for Europe (ALDE) are fittingly characterized by decentralization internally and international cooperation including the EU. While again supporting welfare expansion in line with traditional Christian social doctrine, the more secular wing of the European People's Party (EPP) puts its most characteristic gloss on policy by emphasizing market economy coupled with welfare limitation.

Besides giving an interesting insight into what the policies of the EP groupings are, Table 2.3 also reveals that there are enough differences between them to support the idea that their boundaries are primarily ideological, and provide a good basis for the analysis which is going to discriminate systematically between them. It is noticeable that the categories which might be said to do most work in the table are, in effect, the original categories of the MRG Coding Scheme (Table I.1) (like the Welfare one).

Comparisons of policy emphases can only take us so far. For a more intensive examination of the policy profiles we look at the discriminant functions. In order to make predictions of what parties belong to what groupings we have to average the input variables (in our case, the percentage mentions of a set of policy topics) into one or more linear combinations which best separate the groups; each such combination, a discriminant function, being uncorrelated with the others. While theoretically there are $N-1$ such combinations (where N = the number of classification groups), they are extracted in decreasing importance as separators. In the present case seven significant functions, the maximum for eight groups, are derived, and all are statistically significant. They are chosen so that each makes the maximum contribution to differentiating between a particular pair of categories, regardless of the others. Thus if there is some combination of original variables that distinguishes between, say, Communism and Liberalism, with no particular relevance to the difference between Socialists and Conservatives, this will be derived. One thus has a truly multi-dimensional portrayal, with no preconceptions that what distinguishes between the far Left and far Right should also distinguish the centre-left and centre-right. The results are empirical, not theoretically constrained, and are all the more useful as a result.

In addition to doing the actual work of classification (Table 2.6 in the next section), we can use the correlations between the original coding categories for policy areas, and each function, to fill in what the function is telling us about

Table 2.3. Similarities and differences in the political agenda of the eight party groupings of the European Parliament

Policy area	European United Left–Nordic Green Left (EUL-NGL) (16)	European Greens–European Free Alliance (EG-EFA) (14)	Party of European Socialists (PES) (25)	Alliance of Liberals and Democrats for Europe (ALDE) (25)	Europe People's Party–European Democrats (EPP-ED) (37)	Union for a Europe of Nations (UEN) (6)	Independence and Democracy (IND-DEM) (4)	Non-affiliated (NA) (6)
State Policy								
Freedom and Human Rights	1.98	2.40	1.61	2.83	1.71	0.58	*5.88*	1.73
Democracy	*4.98*	4.67	2.14	2.05	2.14	0.30	1.25	2.70
Constitution	0.61	0.90*	0.57	0.90	0.67	0.59	*1.07**	0.54
Centralization	0.11	0.04	0.20	0.03	0.09	0.35	*0.66*	0.00
Decentralization	2.29	5.40	3.17	5.58	3.10	2.63	1.44	2.88
Modes of Government	5.77	7.74(3)	9.36(2)	8.95(3)	10.96(2)	9.42(3)	10.30(3)	*14.93(2)*
Economic Policy								
Market Economy	5.53	4.16	6.56	9.51(2)	*9.89(3)*	5.49	6.87	8.14
Planned or Mixed Economy	*3.41*	1.57	2.75	1.08	1.32	2.40	1.00	2.09
Economic Infrastructure	4.51	4.75	4.39	7.02	7.21	8.54	7.72	4.29
Environmental Protection	6.34(3)	*15.23(2)*	8.75(3)	5.10	3.55	2.67	3.54	5.01
Agriculture	2.65	2.15	2.36*	2.39*	3.47	*9.03*	6.26*	5.80
General Economic Orientation	2.17	*1.34**	2.91	2.45	2.60	2.33	*3.99*	2.02

Social Policy

Traditional Morality, Law and Order	2.40	3.92	6.09	7.06	10.13	10.87	*12.22(2)*	11.53(3)
Cultural Libertarianism	*0.58*	0.25	0.17	0.19	0.09	0.00	0.00	0.00
Welfare State, Limitation	0.15	0.03	0.57	1.24	*1.45*	0.28	0.49	0.96
Welfare State, Expansion	*32.74(1)*	23.82(1)	29.38(1)	21.34(1)	22.21(1)	16.18(1)	8.21	19.64(1)
Social Group Politics	*7.24(2)*	7.16	5.98	5.87	5.43	5.74	3.11	5.06
Foreign Policy								
Military Strength	0.26	0.25	0.87	1.08*	2.03	0.97	0.10	*2.63*
Peace and Détente	*2.42*	1.94	0.61	0.45	0.27	0.53	0.22	0.32
Nationalism	5.03	2.34	2.92	3.56	3.50	10.49(2)	*21.50(1)*	5.67
International Cooperation	4.81	7.01	6.02	7.66	4.92	1.82	1.29	2.35
Special Relationships	*1.27**	*0.28**	0.49	0.65	0.73	*1.33*	0.16	0.37

Note: *Difference between party election programmes of the old and new member states significant (F test, .005 level). Highest average in bold italics.

Numbers in parentheses ranking of importance of policy area to grouping (1–3).

the policy dimensions which divide groupings. As noted above, the functions can be interpreted as measures of underlying policy continua, yielding a condensed picture of what unites and divides parties. Examining which policy categories load positively and negatively tells us what the nature of these dimensions is.

Function 1 clearly picks up traditional Left-Right differences, opposing all the habitual concerns of the Left (Peace, Welfare, and Democracy) to the traditional order. This is the most important function: the numbers 1–7 put functions in decreasing order of importance from the point of view of distinguishing groups. The fact that it is so clearly Left-Right provides further proof (if proof were needed) of the pre-eminence of such divisions in party politics. Function 2 opposes State Nationalism to support for international cooperation, including the EU. Here we have the European dimension so often talked about in politics, for or against further expansion of EU powers. Function 3 is environmental. Function 4 expresses concerns with internal (government) and external strength. Function 5 could be interpreted as economic managerialism. Function 6 groups hostility to individualism and libertarianism with some support for welfare (expressed as opposition to its limitation). These seem like attitudes normally associated with the extreme Right. Function 7 with its positive stress on decentralization, mixed economy, and agriculture, and opposition to centralization and economic development seems to reflect agrarian and rural suspicions of urban expansion, while not despising (planned) agricultural subsidies.

The policy concerns summarized in these dimensions of European politics reflect both old and new political divisions. Of the cleavages outlined by Lipset and Rokkan (1967)—class, religion, centre–periphery, and urban–rural—function 1 (Left-Right) has absorbed the first two, class and religion. At the other end, the least important function (7) seems to absorb both centre–periphery and urban–rural.

In between, functions reflect new issues like the shape of Europe itself (2), the environmental crisis (3), national strength against increasing threats to the traditional nation state (4), and opposition to its dilution (6). In face of and exposure to increasing globalization managerialism (5) forms a response which, for example, the European Socialists (PES) seem to be taking up.

In all, therefore, the seven discriminant functions provide a good summary of the policy cleavages shaping the new European politics. We should expect them therefore, if ideology and policy indeed are the determining influences behind the formation of the parliamentary groups, to do a relatively efficient job of classifying member parties into them. We report this in the next section.

CLASSIFYING NATIONAL PARTIES INTO EP GROUPINGS ON THE BASIS OF THEIR ELECTION PROGRAMMES

Each discriminant function is a linear combination of predictor variables (coding categories), which gives a probability that a particular national party will be a member of a grouping, given its particular pattern of emphases on the categories. The seven probabilities produced by the functions can be combined to yield joint probabilities for the party belonging to a particular EP grouping. Usually but not always one probability predominates so much that we can assign a party confidently and fairly uniquely to one of the groupings.

These probability distributions are illustrated for the European People's Party–European Democrats (EPP-ED) in Table 2.5. The EPP-ED is currently the largest single party grouping in the EP with more than one-third of the seats (36.6 per cent). It is based on a fusion of Christian Democrat with Conservative parties, so cutting across one of the old family divisions and to some extent blurring their traditional ideologies. The broad ideological appeal of this combination consequently caused many of the CEE parties to join because they felt themselves to be broadly centrist and neither socialist nor extreme right. The combined effect of crossing party family lines and attracting new parties from the new democracies is to make classification on ideological and policy criteria more difficult.

In this sense Table 2.5 constitutes a worst-possible case for our analysis with almost equal numbers of parties correctly and incorrectly classified (though a third of the latter are placed in the ideologically contiguous Liberal grouping). Actually the analysis does quite well, postdictively, in Western Europe (70 per cent of cases correctly classified). It is among the new parties in new EU members that extensive misclassification occurs. This is understandable in policy terms: new parties have not had time to sort themselves out programmatically and have less of a past record to root them in one ideological place.

Table 2.5 shows how the discriminant analysis works. The member parties of each party grouping in turn are given probability values of belonging to the groupings on the basis of the sum of the emphases they have given to each policy area (cf. Table 2.4 rows) weighted by the values they assume on each discriminant function (cf. Table 2.4 columns). This calculation gives the probabilities of belonging to each grouping, which constitute the cell entries in the table and together add up to 1.00 along the rows. Sometimes parties are assigned to their own grouping, the EPP-ED, with such a high probability that there is clearly no question about where they belong (e.g. the Finnish National Coalition at .913). Sometimes they are classified with almost equally high values in the EPP-ED and a neighbouring group. Take the first entry in the table, the Swedish Christian Democrats: in this case, the correct grouping just wins out (.437 to .425). By convention, we take the highest probability and count this as a successful classification. This is balanced by cases where the 'wrong' group just leads and is counted as a misclassification (the Spanish Popular Party). In other cases, a very high probability is given for belonging elsewhere (the Swedish Moderate coalition party).

While there is an element of arbitrariness in just regarding probabilities as evidence of 'success' or 'failure', the arguable cases balance out to a considerable extent, leading to the conclusion for this particular grouping that the analysis works out poorly. Of course, it is possible that the probabilities are actually telling us more than simple 'success' or failure. They may also indicate which parties are likely defectors and which grouping they may move to in the future. This is a point

Table 2.4. Relationships between policy areas and discriminant functions used to classify EP groupings

Policy areas	Func1 Left-Right	Func2 pro/anti EU	Func3 environment	Func4 strength	Func5 economic managerialism	Func6 anti-pluralism	Func7 agrarian
State Policy							
Freedom and Human Rights	-.030	.092	.160	-.224	.336	**-.388**	.071
Democracy	**.374**	.093	.112	.186	.263	-.153	-.146
Constitution	-.008	.014	.084	-.058	.003	-.124	-.022
Centralization	-.076	.185	-.111	-.210	.082	.160	**-.319**
Decentralization	.024	-.138	.274	-.111	-.215	-.143	**.386**
Modes of Government	-.167	-.054	.022	**.201**	.140	.188	.152
Economic Policy							
Market Economy	-.204	-.251	-.031	.141	.068	**-.519**	-.164
Planned or Mixed Economy	.152	.070	-.241	-.033	.042	.315	**.342**
Economic Infrastructure	-.144	-.112	-.117	-.261	-.119	.273	**-.316**
Environmental Protection	.304	.142	**.521**	.023	-.056	.296	-.205
Agriculture	-.174	.281	-.104	.164	-.260	.118	**.324**
General Economic Orientation	-.089	-.016	-.117	-.142	**.161**	-.013	-.148
Social Policy							
Traditional Morality, Law and Order	**-.356**	.020	-.018	.240	.018	.014	-.239
Cultural Libertarianism	.243	.028	-.088	-.058	.047	**-.310**	.089
Welfare State, Limitation	-.127	-.161	-.003	.103	.027	-.256	-.171
Welfare State, Expansion	**.378**	-.234	-.300	-.046	.135	.310	-.021
Social Group Politics	.157	-.017	.016	.011	-.157	.023	.054
Foreign Policy							
Military Strength	-.215	-.205	-.052	**.463**	.051	-.009	-.069
Peace and Détente	**.550**	.307	.027	.021	-.035	-.144	-.012
Nationalism	-.176	**.476**	-.088	-.200	.217	-.226	.108
International Cooperation	.121	-.315	.219	-.258	-.118	-.172	.064
Special Relationships	.035	.033	-.141	.056	-.193	-.205	.014
Canonical Correlation	.822	.710	.696	.569	.435	.382	.200
% of Cases Correctly Classified	67.7						

Note: Cell entries are pooled within-groups correlations between discriminating variables and canonical discriminant functions. Bold type for most important correlations for each policy areas.

we may check four years on but on which we have no independent information at the moment.

Table 2.6 summarizes results for eight tables all set up like Table 2.5 for each grouping in turn, starting with the United Left and going through the EPP-ED to non-affiliated. It thus puts the somewhat disappointing results from Table 2.5 in their place, showing that the overall success rate for all groupings, at 68 per cent is higher than that for the EPP-ED at a mere 51 per cent. In all cases 'near-misses' in terms of placing parties with a contiguous group are listed separately: these are 15 per cent (one-seventh) of all cases and cannot be regarded as being as much of a failure as classifying a party further away from its actual grouping.

The only other large grouping which approaches the EPP-ED in terms of being badly classified is the ALDE—another centrist coalition. Traditionally, the Left is distinguished more than other party *tendences* by having a tightly defined and coherent ideology. Initially, therefore, we expected the classification to be more successful on the Left and success rates to go down progressively as we moved from Left to Right. Success rates are clearly high for the EUL-NGL and Greens and respectable even for the sizeable PES (second largest grouping in the EP). However, success rates are also higher on the extreme right, excepting Independence and Democracy.

Success rates for old and new member states are also shown in italics under the overall rate for each EP grouping. From these it is clear that there is no overall contrast between Western Europe and CEE. Classification problems are concentrated particularly on new parties from new member states within the centre groupings—ALDE and EP-ED. It is likely that many of these—not really clear about how they defined themselves ideologically—were attracted by the broad centrist groupings which were themselves less clearly defined than those on Right and Left. In terms of what we said about misclassifications indicating future deviants and defectors, it is likely (*a*) that centre groupings will be the least stable in terms of membership when they reconstitute themselves at the next parliament and (*b*) that this will be most true for parties from the new member states.

CONCLUSIONS

This analysis prompts two sets of conclusions: one substantive and the other methodological. Following through on the substantive considerations, we can say that the success of our classifications demonstrates the programmatic coherence of the European groupings and the fact that they are primarily based on policy agreements between their member parties. This is true also for members in the new states, even though those in the centre groupings are likely to shift and sort themselves out more in the future.

These findings are important in a broader perspective because the EU, if it is going to be a democracy at all, will have to be a party democracy. Parties are the essence of modern representative democracy. They are the link between electorates

Table 2.5. Applying discriminant analysis based on coded national party manifestos to classify the members of the European People's Party–European Democrats (EPP-ED)

CMP-ID	Party name	EUL-NGL	EG-EFA	PES	ALDE	EPP-ED	UEN	IND-DEM	NA
11520	Christian Democratic Community, 1 (Sweden)	.000	.019	.056	.425	**.437**	.000	.000	.061
11620	Moderate Coalition Party, 4 (Sweden)	.000	.000	.005	**.945**	.049	.000	.000	.000
13620	Conservative People's Party, 1 (Denmark)	.000	.000	.014	.212	**.762**	.005	.000	.004
14620	National Coalition, 4 (Finland)	.000	.000	.012	.072	**.913**	.000	.000	.002
21521	Flemish Christian Democrats–New Flemish Alliance, 4 (Belgium)	.000	.005	**.352**	.250	.269	.000	.000	.121
21522	Walloon Christian Democrats, 1 (Belgium)	.000	.000	.432	.030	**.453**	.000	.000	.082
22521	Christian Democratic Appeal, 7 (the Netherlands)	.000	.001	.138	**.483**	.363	.007	.000	.005
23520	Christian Social People's Party, 3 (Luxembourg)	.000	.000	.296	.226	**.448**	.002	.000	.25
316626	Union for a Popular Movement, 17 (France)	.001	.003	.187	.056	**.439**	.006	.000	.305
32522	Christian Democratic and Centre Union, 5 (Italy)	.000	.000	.057	.093	**.448**	.307	.041	.050
32610	Go Italy, 16 (Italy)	.000	.000	.057	.093	**.448**	.307	.041	.050
33610	Popular Party, 24 (Spain)	.000	.001	.064	**.468**	.407	.000	.000	.058
34511	New Democracy, 11 (Greece)	.000	.002	.111	.130	**.654**	.001	.000	.098
35313	Social Democratic Party, 7 (Portugal)	.000	.000	.198	.111	**.633**	.000	.000	.055
35520	Popular Party, 2 (Portugal)	.000	.000	.230	.043	**.491**	.000	.000	.234
41521	Christian Democratic Union/Christian Social Union 49 (Germany)	.000	.000	.026	.120	**.820**	.002	.000	.029
42520	People's Party, 6 (Austria)	.001	.001	.140	.087	**.683**	.001	.000	.084
51620	Conservative Party, 27 (United Kingdom)	.002	.016	.078	.211	**.334**	.061	.000	.295
51621	Ulster Unionist Party, 1 (United Kingdom)	**.615**	.277	.005	.007	.070	.007	.000	.015
53520	Fine Gael, 5 (Ireland)	.019	.000	**.631**	.123	.202	.017	.000	.005
54620	Nationalist Party, 2 (Malta)	.003	.000	**.832**	.033	.127	.000	.000	.002
55711	Democratic Coalition, 2 (Cyprus)	.000	.008	.073	**.566**	.325	.000	.000	.023
82413	Civic Democratic Party, 9 (Czech Republic)	.000	.000	.000	.000	.037	.000	.000	**.961**
82523	Christian Democratic Union–Czech People's Party, 2 (Czech Republic)	**.340**	.003	.219	.115	.306	.007	.000	.007
83710	Pro Patria, 1 (Estonia)	.000	.000	.006	.084	**.611**	.001	.000	.294
86421	Alliance of Young Democrats–Hungarian Citizens' Party, 12 (Hungary)	.000	.001	.019	.015	.410	.005	.000	**.545**

ID	Party								
86521	Hungarian Democratic Forum (Hungary)	.000	.000	.009	.220	.000	.753	.000	.016
87423	New Era, 2 (Latvia)	.000	.000	**.469**	.056	.009	.423	.000	.345
87610	People's Party, 1 (Latvia)	.000	.000	.091	.052	.002	**.508**	.000	.345
88620	Homeland Union, 2 (Lithuania)	.000	.000	.059	.057	.002	**.745**	.000	.135
92435	Citizen Platform, 15 (Poland)	.000	.000	.030	.019	.001	.383	.000	**.565**
92811	Peasant Alliance, 4 (Poland)	.000	.000	.054	**.347**	.184	.254	.000	.156
96521	Christian Democratic Movement, 3 (Slovakia)	.000	.000	.000	.005	.000	.153	.000	**.841**
996523	Democratic and Christian Union, 3 (Slovakia)	.000	.000	.004	.074	.000	**.721**	.000	.200
96952	Hungarian Coalition, 2 (Slovenia)	.000	.000	.070	**.858**	.000	.069	.000	.000
97320	Social Democratic Party, 2 (Slovakia)	.001	.000	**.849**	.100	.000	.045	.000	.001
97522	New Christian People's Party, 2 (Slovenia)	.021	.000	**.743**	.131	.000	.099	.000	.003
	Classification results	2	0	6	6	0	19	0	4
	Old Member States (20)	1		2	4		14	0	—
	New Member States (17)	1		4	2		5		4

Note: Figure after each party is number of members it has in EP.

Table 2.6. Success of discriminant analyses based on adapted Manifesto Coding Scheme in classifying national parties into the correct EP grouping

	European United Left–Nordic Green Left (EUL-NGL)		European Greens–European Free Alliance (EG-EFA)		Party of European Socialists (PES)		Alliance of Liberals and Dems for Europe (ALDE)		European People's Party–European Democrats (EPP-ED)		Union for a Europe of Nations (UEN)		Independence and Democracy (IND-DEM)		Non-affiliated		Total	
	N	%	N	%	N	%	N	%	N	%	N	%	N	%	N	%	N	%
Total correctly placed	14	88	12	86	19	76	15	60	19	51	4	67	2	50	5	83	90	68
Old members	*13*	*87*	*11*	*80*	*13*	*76*	*12*	*70*	*14*	*70*	*2*	*66*	*1*	*33*	*3*	*75*	*69*	*75*
New members	*1*	*100*	*1*	*100*	*6*	*75*	*3*	*37*	*5*	*30*	*2*	*66*	*1*	*100*	*2*	*100*	*21*	*48*
Placed in nearest grouping(s)	0	0	1	7	3	12	9	36	6	16	1	16	0	0	0	0	20	15
Incorrectly placed	2	13	1	7	3	12	1	4	12	32	1	16	2	50	1	16	23	17
Total to be classified	16	100	14	100	25	100	25	100	37	100	6	100	4	100	6	100	133	100

and governments. They organize the voting choice for electors, by presenting them with programmatic alternatives to choose between and endorse. And they seek to carry these through in government, thus creating the necessary democratic link between popular preferences and public policy.

Given its size and heterogeneity, these considerations are even more true for the EU than for the traditional states of Europe. The EU needs parties to provide uniform voting choices across the Union and to link these with parliamentary decisions and with governance. It is true that no one party grouping is ever likely to get a parliamentary majority, with the consequence that no one programme will automatically become the parliamentary guideline. However, as we point out below (Chapter 7) following McDonald and Budge (2005), the strong Left-Right line-up in the EP means that the median grouping (currently the Liberals) will have a strong strategic position in pushing their policies through. Compromises between the Socialists and EPP-ED will typically settle somewhere near the Liberals.

However, for this process of representation of the middle voter by the middle parliamentary party to work out, it is essential that the parties act in a programmatically coherent and disciplined way, both electorally and in parliament. The organization of the parliament round the party groupings aids this. The EU has often been accused of a 'democratic deficit' however in that even in the European elections, the parliamentary groupings are weak and in most cases it is the *national* political parties who decide on and run candidates. The question then arises, in choosing one or other national party alternative in the European elections, are voters really allowed to register their preferences about which way the increasingly powerful EP should go?

It seems from our analysis that they are because there is such a strong congruence (in some groupings, identity) of national parties' ideology and policy with that of the EP grouping they belong to. This remains to be tightened up in the ALDE and EPP-ED. But we can see the process taking place. It has already happened in Western and Northern Europe and may be expected to occur in the CEE over the next few years. A 'programmatic supply' (Thomassen (ed.) 2005) of homogeneous policy alternatives across the Union will then ensure that the European voter is able to express clear political preferences which get fed in by parties to European decision processes, thus rendering the EU more of a united democratic entity than it has been in the past.

The methodological import of our discriminant analysis is twofold. On the one hand it shows that our general coding scheme, modified slightly for CEE conditions, is well able to distinguish between the European party groupings. This is a severe test of the manifesto data's continued relevance to new political developments and of their ability to reflect the complexities of countries other than the ones they were originally generated from. But they pass it.

Indeed, the high success rate achieved with the modified coding even suggests that we were overcautious in modifying it in the first place. It is our original categories which load the highest on the most important discriminant functions (Table 2.3). This suggests that with our original coding scheme (Table II.1:

Appendix II), we might have had a similar success in distinguishing party groupings.

Pressures of time leave this for the future, but what we can say here is that the modified scheme makes a very useful contribution to distinguishing EP groupings in policy terms and demonstrating their programmatic coherence. In turn this suggests that European elections will become even more relevant to voters, thus helping to overcome the EU's democratic deficit.

APPENDIX: MODIFYING THE MRG-CMP CATEGORIES TO ADAPT BETTER TO PARTIES IN CEE

As explained in the chapter, the original coding scheme (Table II.1: Appendix II) had numerous subcategories added to cope with the very particular political conditions in CEE, particularly under the transition to democracy. Many subcategories were created within the original categories as detailed in Appendix II. This was in line with previous practice by national investigators who were anxious to record particular features of a country's politics. The practice does not affect the integrity of the original coding scheme as subcategories can always be regrouped to reflect the original categorization.

Amalgamating the original categories does not affect their integrity either and may indeed increase their discriminating power and eliminate 'noise' (Laver and Budge (eds.) 1992: 24). Indeed, the amalgamations detailed below bear a considerable resemblance to those just referenced, and these in turn to the Robertson–Budge categories round which the original MRG coding was built (Chapter 6).

Where the modified scheme does more fundamentally alter the original is where certain subcategories under one of the original categories have been transferred out of it and amalgamated with another category. An example from the detailed description given below is where 'withdraw the Russian army' (1031) has been grouped with peace (106). This cuts across categories in the original MRG-CMP scheme. Of course, it is open to anyone using the data to do this for their own purposes, provided that they explain clearly what they are doing. The purpose of this appendix is to unambiguously specify the modifications introduced for the analysis of Chapter 2.

A first point to note is that the modified coding scheme involves much more straightforward amalgamation of the original categories than transfers between them. Such transfers are in fact few and involve thinly populated subcategories. Thus we can regard the modified coding scheme as a near twin of the original, and likely to generate results very similar to those the latter would have produced if it had been applied. The similarities can be seen from the very detailed set of instructions which follow:

The modified classification scheme: An overview
State policy

POL1	Freedom and Human Rights
POL2	Democracy
POL3	Constitution
POL4	Centralization
POL5	Decentralization
POL6	Modes of Government
POLO7	Communists, pro
POLO8	Communists, con

Economic policy

ECO1	Market Economy
ECO2	Planned or Mixed Economy
ECO3	Economic Infrastructure
ECO4	Environmental Protection
ECO5	Agriculture
ECO6	General Economic Orientation

Social policy

SOC1	Traditional Morality, Law and Order
SOC2	Cultural Libertarianism
SOC3	Welfare State, Limitation
SOC4	Welfare State, Expansion
SOC5	Social Group Politics

Foreign policy

FOR1	Military Strength
FOR2	Peace and Détente
FOR3	Nationalism
FOR4	International Cooperation
FOR5	Special Relationships

THE MODIFIED CLASSIFICATION SCHEME: DEFINITION OF CATEGORIES

State Policy (POL)

Freedom and Human Rights (POL1)

Favourable mentions of importance of personal freedoms and human rights, such as freedom from coercion in the political and economic sphere; freedom of speech, freedom from bureaucratic control; individualism (201). Freedom of nations to decide freely (1033).

Democracy (POL2)

Favourable mentions of democracy as a method or goal in national and other organizations; involvement of all citizens in decision-making, as well as generalized support for a country's democracy (202). General references to the transition process of one-party states to pluralist democracy (2021).

Constitution (POL3)

Preferences for specific constitutions; use of constitutionalism as a policy argument (203, 204). Preferences for a Republic (2032), a Monarchy (2041), or a Presidential regime (2031). Reference to citizenship and election laws (2022, 2023). Support for checks and balances and separation of powers (2033).

Centralization (POL4)

Opposition to political decision-making at lower political levels; support for more centralization in political and administrative procedures (302).

Decentralization (POL5)

Support for federalism or devolution; more regional autonomy for policy or economy; support for keeping up local and regional customs and symbols; favourable mentions of special consideration for local areas; deference to local expertise (301). Support for a strengthening of republican powers (3011). Negative references to exerting strong influence (political, military, and commercial) over other states; negative references to controlling other countries as if they were part of an empire; favourable mentions of decolonization; favourable references to greater self-government and independence of colonies; negative references to imperial behaviour of countries (103). Cultural diversity, communalism, cultural plurality, and polarization; preservation of autonomy of religious, linguistic heritages within the country, including special educational provisions (607). Favourable mentions of cultural autonomy in general (6071).

Modes of Government (POL6)

Favourable mentions of strong government, including government stability; party's competence to govern and/or other parties' lack of such competence (305). Need for efficiency and economy in government and administration; cutting down civil service; improving governmental procedures; appeal to make the process of government and administration cheaper and more effective (303). Need to eliminate corruption, and associated abuse in political and public life (304).

Communists, Positive (POL07)

Cooperation with former authorities and communists in the period of transition; pro communist involvement in the transition process; 'let sleeping dogs lie' in dealing with the nomenklatura (3052). 'Hunting the witches': negative references to the situation in public life, after the elections to the Supreme Council (3051). References to the need of a broader political coalition, need for cooperation at the political level, and necessity of collaboration of all political forces, including the communists in the current crises situation (3055). Rebuilding the USSR (6012). Negative references to physical restitution of property to previous owners (4131).

Communists, Negative (POLO8)

Against communist involvement in democratic government; weeding out the guilty and the collaborators from government service (3053). References to civic rehabilitation of politically persecuted people in the communist era; references to juridical compensation concerning communist expropriations; moral compensation (3054). Favourable references to physical restitution of property to previous owners (4013).

Economic Policy (ECO)

Market Economy (ECO1)

Favourable mentions of free enterprise, capitalism; superiority of individual enterprise over state and control systems; favourable mentions of private property rights, personal enterprise and initiative; need for unhampered individual enterprises (401). Favourable references to privatization (4011) and of privatization by vouchers (4014). Negative references for general need for direct government control of the economy (4012). Support for the concept of free trade (407). Need for reduction of budget deficits; retrenchment in crisis, thrift and savings; support for traditional economic institutions such as the stock market and banking system; support for strong currency (414). Need for wage and tax policies to induce enterprise; encouragement to start enterprises; need for financial and other incentives (402). Need for regulations to make private enterprises work better; actions against monopolies and trusts; and in defense of consumer and small business; encouraging economic competition (403).

Planned or Mixed Economy (ECO2)

Government ownership, partial or complete, including government ownership of land (413). General need for direct government control of the economy; control over prices, wages, rents, etc. Favourable references to creation or preservation of cooperative or non-state social ownership within a market economy (4121). Favourable references to mixed ownership within a market economy (4122). Favourable mentions to publicly owned industry (4123). Position references to socialist property and negative references to privatization (4124); Positive use of Marxist-Leninist concepts for an analysis of the economic situation (415). Demand-oriented economic policy, economic policy devoted to the reduction of depressions and/or to increase private demand through increasing public demand and/or through increasing social expenditures (409). Favourable mentions of extension or maintenance of tariffs to protect internal markets; other domestic economic protectionism such as quota restrictions (406). Favourable mentions of the need for the collaboration of employers and trade union organizations in overall economic planning and direction through the medium of tripartite bodies of government, employers, and trade unions (405). Favourable mentions of long-standing economic planning of a consultative or indicative nature, need for government to create such a plan (404). Negative references to privatization (4132).

Economic Infrastructure (ECO3)

Importance of modernization of industry and methods of transport and communication; importance of science and technological development in industry; need for training and research (411). Need to encourage or facilitate greater economic production; need to take measures to aid this; appeal for greater production and importance of productivity to the economy; the paradigm of growth (410).

Environmental Protection (ECO4)

Preservation of countryside, forests, etc.; general preservation of natural resources against selfish interests; proper use of national parks, soil banks, etc.; environmental improvement (501). Favourable mentions of anti-growth politics and steady-state economy; ecological orientation as a way of life; Green politics (416).

Agriculture (ECO5)

Support for agriculture and farmers; any policy aimed specifically at benefiting agriculture and farmers (703).

General Economic Orientation (ECO6)

Overall General Interest of Parties in Economics (408).

Social Policy (SOC)

Traditional Morality, Law and Order (SOC1)

Favourable mentions of traditional moral values; prohibition, censorship, and suppression of immorality and unseemly behaviour; maintenance and stability of family and religion

(603). Enforcement or encouragement of cultural integration (608). Better law enforcement; actions against crime; support of and more resources for the police; tougher court action (605). General sense of crisis and alienation (6061). Negative mentions of cultural autonomy of Roma (6081).

Cultural Libertarianism (SOC2)

Opposition to traditional moral values; support for divorce, abortion, etc. (604). Multiculturalism, pro Roma (6072).

Welfare State, Limitation (SOC3)

Limiting expenditure on social services or social security (505). Necessity of private welfare provisions because of economic constraints; desirability of competition in welfare service provisions; private funding in addition to public activity (5031, 5041). Limiting expenditure on education (507). Necessity of private education because of economic constraints; desirability of competition in education (5061). Necessity of restrictive provisions because of economic constraints; private funding in addition to public activity (5021). Abuse of power of trade unions (702).

Welfare State, Expansion (SOC4)

Favourable mentions of need to introduce, maintain, or expand any social service or social security scheme; support for social services such as health service or social housing (504). Need to expand and/or improve educational provision at all levels (506). Need to provide cultural and leisure facilities including arts and sport; need to spend money on museums, art galleries, etc.; need to encourage worthwhile leisure activities and cultural mass media (502). Favourable references to labour groups, working class, unemployed; support for trade unions; good treatment of manual and other employees (701). Concept of equality; need for fair treatment of all people; special protection for underprivileged; need for fair distribution of resources; removal of class barriers; end of discrimination such as racial, sexual, etc. (503).

Social Group Politics (SOC5)

Favourable references to middle class, professional groups, such as physicians or lawyers; old and new middle class (704). Favourable references to underprivileged minorities who are defined neither in economic nor in demographic terms, for example, the handicapped, homosexuals, immigrants (705). References to ethnic minorities in foreign countries (7051). References to ethnic minorities living in the country such as Latvians living in Estonia, and so on (7052). Favourable mentions of, or need for, assistance to women, old people, young people (706), war participants (7061), refugees (7062), linguistic, and all other special interest groups (706).

Foreign Policy (FOR)

Military Strength (FOR1)

Need to maintain or increase military expenditure; modernizing armed forces and improvement in military strength; rearmament and self-defence; need to keep military treaty obligations; need to secure adequate manpower in the military (104).

Peace and Détente (FOR2)

Peace as a general goal; declarations of belief in peace and peaceful means of solving crises; desirability of countries joining in negotiations with hostile countries (106). Favourable mentions of decreasing military expenditures; disarmament; 'evils of war'; promises to reduce conscription (105). Need to withdraw the Russian army (1031).

Nationalism (FOR3)

Appeal for national effort and solidarity; need for society to see itself as united; appeal for public spiritedness; decrying anti-social attitudes in times of crisis; support for public interest (606). Favourable mentions of national independence and sovereignty as opposed to internationalism (109, 1032). Support for, or need to maintain national security in all spheres of societal life: politics, economy, science, etc. Policy devoted to this goal (6013). Hostile mentions of the EU; opposition to specific European policies which are preferred by European authorities (110). Appeals to patriotism and/or nationalism; suspension of some freedoms in order to protect the state against subversion; support for established national ideas (601). Against cooperation in the Nordic Council or in a Yugoslav Federation (1025, 1026).

International Cooperation (FOR4)

Need for international cooperation; need for world planning of resources; need for international courts; support for any international goal or world state; support for UN (107). Favourable mentions of EU in general; desirability of expanding the EU and/or increasing its competence; desirability of joining or remaining a member (108). Position references to cooperation in the Nordic Council (1015). Against patriotism and/or nationalism (602).

Special Relationships (FOR5)

Mentions of particular countries with which the country has a special relationship. For example, in the British case: former colonies; in the German case: East Germany; in the Swedish case: other Scandinavian countries (101, 102). In the East European countries special relationships refer to positive mentions of countries formerly belonging to the USSR and the rest of the former CMEA bloc (1011, 1021). In addition they refer to positive or negative mentions of Germany and other Western states (1012, 1022), Eastern European countries (1013, 1023), Baltic countries (1014, 1024), and in a positive way to the former Yugoslavian countries (1016). Included in this category are also mentions of the Karabakh and Cyprus issues (6011, 6014).

A Modified Left-Right Scale Based on This Classification Scheme

A logical further development of this coding scheme is to produce a modified Left-Right scale—again closely related to the MRG original and based on similar theoretical concerns, but more sensitive (in foresight anyway) to CCE politics. This is used in Chapter 3 and defined as follows:

The modified Left-Right scale used in Chapter 3

'Right' is defined as the sum of percentages of quasi-sentences in the following categories:

POL1   Freedom and Human Rights
ECO1   Market Economy
SOC1   Traditional Morality, Law and Order
SOC3   Welfare State, Limitation
FOR1   Military Strength

   'Left' is defined as the sum of percentages of quasi-sentences in the following categories:
POL2   Democracy
ECO2   Planned or Mixed Economy
SOC2   Cultural Liberalism
SOC4   Welfare State, Expansion
FOR2   Peace and Détente

The Left-Right score is calculated as follows:
   Left-Right = RIGHT − LEFT

3

A Common Space for Electoral Communication? Comparing Party and Voter Placements on a Left-Right Continuum in Western Europe and CEE

Parties are the major vehicle for the communication of electoral preferences to parliament and government within present-day representative democracies. We have seen from the two previous chapters that they distinguish themselves in policy-terms sufficiently to provide a clear basis for policy choice by voters particularly between Left, Centre, and Right. In this chapter, we ask whether electors are conscious of this party differentiation and act upon it—in the new as well as in the old democracies of Europe.

In doing so, we base ourselves on a previous study which asked the same question about how parties and voters line up (Klingemann 1995). Here, we use Eurobarometer self-placements to locate party family supporters and manifesto data to locate party families themselves—all in Left-Right terms. The previous analysis was inevitably confined to Western Europe. Moreover, it used country-specific Left-Right scales to locate parties, although they certainly overlapped in content—with each other and with the general Left-Right scale used here.

In this chapter, we use the same Left-Right scales for all countries. These are the self-placements for voters, who are generally asked to place themselves on a 'scale' or 'ladder' of ten intervals between Left and Right. This has been transformed linearly into the +100 to −100 Left-Right metric normally used for the party documents, as the object is to make comparisons between these electoral positions and the party families' programmatic location as measured on the basis of the manifesto data.

The scale we use for this is however the modified version of the general MRG Left-Right scale described in the Appendix to Chapter 2. The reason for modifying the measure is that the original coding categories were regrouped for the discriminant analysis reported in Chapter 2, so as to be more sensitive for use in CEE. In particular, they made use of the new subcategories which had been developed for coding manifestos there, when it made sense to aggregate them across the boundaries of the old categories. However, the correlation between the standard Left-Right scale used in Chapter 1, and the modified one used here, is $r = .83$, indicating a comprehensive overlap between the two.

The nature of the modification is explained in the Appendix to Chapter 2, on the basis of the new coding categories. Scale construction is detailed there so that the new summary measure can be explicitly related to the associated coding classification scheme. As the scale can also be presumed to be more sensitive to politics in CEE, particularly in the transitional period of the early 1990s, it is the one used here. However, we should stress that party family locations hardly differ between the general MRG-scale of Chapter 1 and the alternative scale, so the conclusions we reach below would be broadly the same whichever manifesto-based Left-Right scale we applied.

The main finding from Klingemann's study (1995) was the good overall match between voters and 'their' party's position, particularly at the individual country level. However, supporters of the right tended to take up more extreme positions than the average one held by their party family. We can see whether this recurs, and particularly how relationships work out within the CEE, by comparing the earlier voter–party positions with those presented below.

PARTY FAMILIES AND THEIR SUPPORTERS IN CENTRAL AND EASTERN EUROPE

Figure 3.1 shows the positions of party families from 1990 to 2003 on the top side of the line running across the page, which represents the Left-Right continuum, and self-placements of the family supporters along the bottom side of the line.

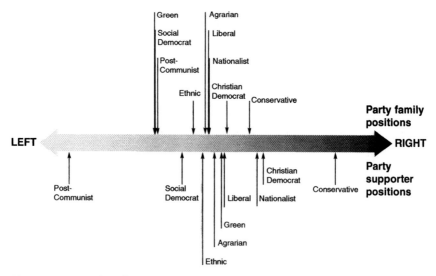

Fig. 3.1. Mean Left-Right positions of party families and their supporters in ten CEE countries (1990–2003) using Eurobarometer self-placements by supporters

Three major impressions arise immediately from these distributions. First, the parties' own policy positions are much closer to each other than those of their supporters. The party families' mean positions lie within a range of −15 to +11— Centre Left to Centre Right. Supporters' positions run from the Communists at −41 to Conservatives at +34. However, if we discount the two outliers we have a range from −14 to +19, practically matching the party one.

The second striking fact about the figure is that the ordering of parties from Left to Right is substantially the same on both sides, if we discount overlapping by the Greens and Social Democrats, and Nationalists and Liberals, on the party family side; with Communists being very much more towards the Left, on the supporter side.

The third finding relates to the closeness of party supporters to their own party family. In general it has to be said, family supporters are generally closer to another family's mean policy position than they are to their own, and in the case of Communist and Conservative supporters at any rate, they are substantially removed from the latter. However, within the middle area more thickly populated with party families and supporters, both are so squashed up that (*a*) minor discrepancies might not be very noticeable when choosing a party to support and (*b*) in some cases are likely due to measurement error.

In terms of Klingemann's earlier findings about Western Europe there *is* a tendency for right-wing supporters to be rightwards of their parties (Klingemann 1995). More noticeably we find supporters at both extremes of the ideological spectrum going very far out beyond the positions of their party families.

As families rather than individual parties are involved in these comparisons it is difficult to draw exact conclusions about party–voter relationships from them. Parties within the same family may take up very different policy positions at any one time, and thus more finely tune their policy distance to their national supporters. On this the correlations between party and supporters' views within each country are much more illuminating than Figure 3.1. We discuss these in relation to Table 3.1.

PARTY-SUPPORTER AGREEMENT ACROSS EUROPE

Table 3.1 presents the correlations we are immediately interested in—between the Left-Right positions of the individual parties and their supporters within each CEE country over the national elections between 1990 and 2003. Individual party and supporter positions on each side are measured as for Figure 3.1, but the difference is that we are dealing here with the individual parties rather than aggregated party families. The general impression from column two is that the distances between CEE party and supporter positions in the figure are somewhat reduced. The average correlation between them is 0.46—not remarkable but still indicating a fair degree of convergence between party and party–voter positions.

Table 3.1. Relationship of Left-Right party policy position and Left-Right self-placement of party supporters by country

Western Europe	Time period	Pearson's r	N	Central and Eastern Europe	Time period	Pearson's r	N
Spain	1982–9	.92	9				
Sweden 1	1968–88	.86	28				
France	1973–88	.85	117				
Denmark 1	1973–88	.85	35				
Germany 2	1976, 1983–98	.85	26				
Norway 1	1973–89	.83	20				
Denmark 2	1979, 1984, 1990–8	.83	45				
				Czech Republic	1990–2002	.78	23
Sweden 2	1968, 1973–98	.76	58				
Netherlands 1	1972–89	.71	18				
				Lithuania	1992–2000	.70	13
Norway 2	1973–97	.69	47				
Luxembourg	1969–89	.66	20				
Netherlands 2	1971–98	.66	47				
United Kingdom 2	1964–74; 1983–2001	.66	33				
				Bulgaria	1990–2001	.62	20
				Hungary	1990–2002	.61	17
United Kingdom 1	1970–87	.58	15				
				Latvia	1993–2002	.57	20
Belgium W	1971–87	.54	19				
				Slovakia	1990–2002	.49	18
Germany 1	1972–87	.45	15				
Belgium F	1971–87	.44	21				
Italy	1972–87	.40	15				
				Estonia	1992–2003	.37	20
				Poland	1991–2001	.34	26
Ireland	1973–89	.26	23				
				Romania	1990–2000	.12	23
				Slovenia	1990–2000	−.02	26
Western Europe pre-1990		.64	255	Central and Eastern Europe post-1990		.46	206
Western Europe post-1990		.74	256				

Like many averages, however, this one masks considerable variation between countries. There is clearly substantial convergence between parties and their voters in the Czech Republic and Lithuania, and to a lesser extent in Bulgaria, Hungary, and Latvia. In Romania and Slovenia on the other hand there is very little. Poland produces a surprisingly low correlation of 0.34. But this may be explained by the enormous number of shifting parties and electoral coalitions which appeared in the first election of the 1990s, when no less than twenty-nine parties and groups were represented in parliament—the majority of them abruptly disappearing after the next two elections.

On the whole there is not the sharp contrast between Centre and East within CEE which might have been expected due to the consolidation of policy voting in the former compared with the latter. There are slightly more Central European countries at the top of the column and slightly more Eastern European at the bottom, but Lithuania, for example, is ranked second top and Poland third last. CEE countries mix in the middle.

We can get a better take on the new democracies by comparing them with the longer established ones of Western Europe before and after 1990. The average correlation between individual parties' Left-Right position and that of their voters is 0.64 before 1990 and 0.74 afterwards. This is quite a difference and could be taken as indicating an improvement in the efficiency of party representation over time. The difference between the CEE average of 0.46 and that of Western European countries before 1990 (0.64) is not insurmountable. In light of the increased correlation after 1990 in Western Europe one might well anticipate a greater convergence of views between electors and their party representatives in CEE as the party system consolidates there.

This expectation is particularly upheld by the fact that the Western European country where party positions best reflect supporters' Left-Right preferences is Spain—itself a new democracy consolidated only at the beginning of the 1980s. The low position of Ireland at 0.26, however, serves as a warning that convergence is not simply a reflection of a general process of consolidation but also of the party alternatives on offer and the voting rules. In the 1970s and 1980s, Ireland had an unusual number of electoral and government coalitions. Under its Single Transferable Vote system there was a premium on supporters of the larger party in the coalition voting for the smaller one, which in itself creates some discrepancy of views between parties and their voters. Strategic voting also probably accounts for the relatively low correlations shown for the UK.

Some Western European countries appear twice in the first column of the table (usually labelled '1' and '2'). This is because the opportunity has been taken to use other available survey series which had Left-Right self-placements, often over a slightly different time period. As a result it is difficult to say whether the varying correlations they produce are the result of formatting or question differences, or time differences. In the absence of clear criteria for privileging one estimate over another they have been averaged together to produce the mean figures at the bottom of the column. Flemish and Walloon Belgium have been treated as separate cases because of their different parties and party systems.

Whatever artefactual differences are created by the differing survey evidence, it is clear that there is almost as much variation between Western European countries as between those in CEE in terms of party representativeness. Six countries—almost half the total—rank above even the Czech Republic, the highest ranking Central European country. At the lower end of the column there is however a lot of overlap between East and West. Neither group of countries is clearly marked off from the other, which is cheering news for these who maintain that democracy is on the rise in all parts of Europe.

PARTY FAMILIES AND THEIR SUPPORTERS IN WESTERN EUROPE COMPARED WITH CEE

As we have stressed, Table 3.1 gives more information than a general party family comparison does on the exact degree of convergence between party positions and voters' views. However, it is still interesting to check general family relationships to see what the variation is among the traditional ideological groupings—whether, for example, some are closer to their supporters' views than others. From Figure 3.1, we saw this was more apparent in the case of parties on the Centre-Left. Does the same occur in Western Europe? We can check this from the corresponding graphical representation in Figure 3.2, for six matching Western European countries.

In this case both the parties and their supporters spread out along the spectrum, Left-Socialists almost going off the page at over −50 towards the Left. Conservative

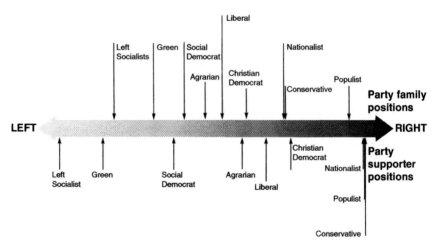

Fig. 3.2. Mean Left-Right positions of party families and their supporters in six Western European countries (1990–2003) using Eurobarometer self-placements by supporters

and Populist party family supporters are almost equally far towards the Right (over 40).

The absence of any major concentration in the middle, on the part either of families or their supporters, means that the two are generally further apart in Figure 3.2 than they were in Figure 3.1. Supporters of leftist families are further towards the Left and the same is true in reverse for Centre-Right and Right. Even populist parties (in this context mainly Scandinavian ones like the Danish Progress Party) are distinctly more moderate than their supporters.

This contrast between the two parts of Europe is unexpected. Were the figures unlabelled we would tend to associate the centripetal tendencies of Figure 3.1 with the West and the centrifugal tendencies of Figure 3.2 with the East, instead of this being reversed! It is possible that the 'averaged' moderation shown in CEE in Figure 3.1 is in fact due to some of the major moves in a contrary ideological direction shown for parties of the Left in the graphs of Chapter 1— particularly when they were in government after the second round of elections and had to defend their record. However as we also saw, parties in the West are prone to take such leaps from time to time, so we cannot simply regard this as evidence for greater party instability in the East. Whatever the detail, we can conclude broadly that the party families of the East show no signs of greater extremism in the Left-Right stands they take—quite the contrary. While parties may moderate their supporters' views to some extent most families' supporters there are moderate too. So, there is no indication that they represent popular views less faithfully than Western parties. The balance in fact is all on the other side.

Taking a broader view, we can say that party families order themselves in roughly the same way in East and West, with a few changes of position between contiguous parties (Liberals and Agrarians, for example). In both areas supporters order themselves from Left to Right in much the same way as families do—only they are consistently more extreme in the West than they are in the East.

FAMILY PREFERENCES AND PARTY VOTERS: AN OVERVIEW

In our discussion above we have largely commented on the efficiency with which parties and party families represent the Left-Right preferences of their supporters in Western Europe and the CEE. This is a substantive concern, with major implications for the EU and European democracy in general, which we can now address with better evidence than we have had before.

Our comparisons yield fairly definite answers. There seems little difference in communicative and representational potential between East and West, or between the old and new members of the EU. Parties seem to have much the same relationships among themselves and with their supporters in both groupings (as do supporters with parties and each other). It seems confirmed that Left-Right differences form a major if not the major framework for political discourse and political communication, within which parties and preferences are ordered as a basis for choice.

This conclusion confirms much other evidence about the primacy of the Left-Right space for party and above all electoral politics (e.g. Pierce 1999). However, the figures presented in this chapter also raise some questions, particularly in terms of the distance between party family and supporter positions and in some cases the greater proximity of one party family to supporters of another family. We devote the rest of the section to this question as it has considerable bearings on our estimation of voter positions in Chapter 7.

Of course, the anomalies we identify occur more in relation to party families than to individual parties, and individual parties are what individual electors vote for. From the correlations presented in Table 3.1 these parties are close to their voters in many countries. Nevertheless, there are some in which policy representation is looser. Where does this leave our later estimates of voter opinion based on a median calculation which assumes proximity voting?

One qualification on the previous analyses is that inevitably, given the limits of the data, supporters are defined in terms of votes at the last election. Depending on how recent that was, this may be a reasonable operational definition or a bad one. Particularly given the state of flux and emergence of new parties in the 1990s— not only in the CEE (cf. Chapter 4), many former voters may well be thinking of voting for a new party alternative closer to their policy position next time. This seems particularly to explain the low correlations in Poland (Table 3.1) where sharp fluctuations in the party alternatives devalue past votes as an indicator of current support, even if it is the best basis available.

A more fundamental explanation of the anomalies may, however, come from the limited comparability of the metrics involved on the party and family side of the comparison, on the one hand and on the electors' side on the other. The rank-orderings of party families from Left to Right may be comparable between levels but the exact distances may not.

The reason for saying this goes back to the fact that, in nearly all countries, the median (middle) voter positions identified by mass surveys are quite similar (Powell 2000: 162, 180–5). For example, the median citizen in Norway is recorded by surveys to be at the same Left-Right position as the median citizen in Australia, and even as the median citizen in the USA (Powell 2000: 162). This is implausible when one thinks of the general differences between these countries' politics. Norway by almost any account is well to the left of Australia or the USA. One consequence is that, but for three countries that stand three or four standard deviations to the Left of all the others in these surveys (namely, France, Italy, and Spain), the cross-national correlation between median citizen positions identified by surveys in the 1980s with those in the 1990s is almost non-existent and, worse, negative— that is, $r = -0.14$. It appears, therefore, that voters in surveys report they are on the Left, in the Centre, or on the Right within the context of their own country's political space, rendering their exact self-placements suspect for any comparative analysis and, more damning for present purposes, for matching to the party-position data that do contain valid cross-national differences along the Left-Right dimension. The Kim–Fording (1998) measure used in Chapter 7 and reported in the CD-ROM (see Policy Scales Data-Set on the CD-ROM) uses leverage gained from the party system cross-national difference and has been validated in part by tests that pay attention to national political differences (Kim and Fording 1998). And, we can note, the overtime $r = +0.44$ for the Kim–Fording measure applied to the same elections in the same fifteen nations for which Powell's survey data correlation is -0.14.

The party and family metrics, based on their election programmes, *are* designed to have meaningful cross-national variation—that is, if Norwegian parties locate themselves on average to the Left of Australian parties of the same family (e.g. Social Democrats and Conservatives) this can be taken as indicating that the Norwegian Left-Right locations are Left of Left-Right locations in Australia. This feature holds for the manifesto data as well as for 'expert' survey data (Mair and Castles 1997: 150–7). Mass survey data on respondents' Left-Right positions, on the contrary, are much more country specific.

This implies that we should regard party family supporters' aggregated and averaged positions in Figures 3.1 and 3.2 with some reserve. It is informative on the rank-orders of supporters from Left to Right, and these can be matched with the rank-orderings on the party and family side to give a general idea of the representativeness and responsiveness of the party system to their supporters. But the specific metrics on both sides are not closely comparable.

The same applies to the correlations in Table 3.1 for individual parties and supporters, which should be taken as indicating rough correspondences which in some cases emerge as very low, partly because of measurement incompatibility. It is the rank-ordering of countries in terms of representational efficiency rather than the exact value of the correlations that we should concentrate on here.

Within these limits the comparisons carried out in this chapter have very interesting implications. They enable us to relate two levels of the political system to each other, complementing some of the dynamic analyses that have appeared linking movements on the two sides. For example, Evans and his associates demonstrated a direct link in Britain (1970–97) between class-based voting in elections, measured from election surveys, and party polarization on the standard Left-Right scale (Evans, Heath, and Payne 1999: 94–100). In a comparative analysis of eight countries Adams and associates (2004) linked electoral shifts of opinion measured on the Eurobarometer surveys to party movements on the standard Left-Right scale. Parties were found to respond systematically to negative movements of opinion against them by adjusting their own position in the same direction. This forms a powerful indication that a voter–party dialogue is going on and that it is conducted in Left-Right terms.

Interestingly, in light of the points made above, Adams (2005) has also argued that although survey-based electoral and manifesto-based party positions are not directly comparable, movements between them are, at least in terms of direction. This gives further scope to analysts who want to put the two kinds of data together. In Part II, we will additionally show how vote shares can be combined with party Left-Right positioning to produce other estimates of electoral opinion in the shape of the median voter's preference. These estimates work out quite convincingly for CEE, as well as Western Europe, providing confirmatory evidence on the comparability of party and electoral politics across all these regions.

Part II

Methodology and Measurement

4

Evaluating Validity with the Standard Left-Right Scale: Matching Measurements to Conceptual Intentions

The mappings based on the standard MRG Left-Right scale distinguish between parties reasonably well and in plausible ways, grouping them to Left and Right as we would broadly expect and identifying changes which we can link to known historical events. This is true not only for the ex-Communist countries studied in Part I but also for the range of established post-war democracies examined in our previous volume (Budge et al. 2001: 24–50). Thus far, therefore, our representations pass the test of face validity.

Here we want to push the issue further and move beyond our own interpretations of the valid confirmations we think we see in the data. One is entitled to ask, for instance, whether the rich cross-temporal variation we see in Left-Right scores is really informative or, instead, reflects errors in recording essentially stable and ideologically fixed policy positions of the parties (Pelizzo 2003). This is particularly pertinent as the major alternative measures of party positions, expert judgements, do give relatively stable and fixed estimates (Budge et al. 2001: 128–30). One is also entitled to ask whether this rich cross-national variation really allows us to use Left-Right scores to validly analyse cross-national comparisons of policy choices by voters, parliaments, and governments.

VALIDITY: WHAT IS INTENDED FOR LEFT-RIGHT MEASUREMENTS?

To address the question of measurement validity, one asks how well the scores assigned to parties match what one intends to measure. Chapter 1 described the thinking and procedures that gave rise to the content of the MRG/CMP Left-Right scale. There we also remarked that our intention has been to produce a Left-Right score for each party-in-an-election based on its official programme. With valid election-specific information of this sort one can inquire about party competition in an electorate (Budge and Farlie 1977; Budge, Robertson, and Hearl 1987), policy-based coalition formation (Laver and Budge 1992), parties in the policymaking process (Budge and Hofferbert 1992; Klingemann et al. 1994), and parties in the democratic process generally (McDonald and Budge 2005). Both the input intention, in relation to scale construction, and output intention, in regard to scale application, are equally important considerations. Together they reveal all the major elements necessary for evaluating the validity of our Left-Right scores: we want comparable cross-national and cross-temporal Left-Right scores that signal parties' policy commitments to the electors they are promising to represent.

A major alternative to the CMP Left-Right scores are the Left-Right scores produced by expert surveys. They have been produced with the same intentions. Peter Mair and Frank Castles report that their expert survey was motivated by two concerns: (*a*) 'left-right differences between parties had a major relevance for public policy outcomes' and (*b*) 'left right differences between parties were ... relevant to policy-based coalition[s]' and 'crucial to the functioning of party systems more generally' (Mair and Castles 1997: 151). And eschewing reliance on personal impressions or party family distinctions, they felt that 'what was needed ... was a more systematic data base, in which variations across a common cross-national scale could be compared, and in which real differences between parties could be measured' (Mair and Castles 1997: 151).

Both approaches are in the best tradition of a scientific research programme. They start with impressions, translate the impressions into hypotheses, and recognize that personal impressions are not necessarily interpersonally comparable— what looks leftist to us may look mainstream centrist to you. They also refuse to take the easy road by relying on easy-to-access extra-personal categories, such as party families. Family affiliation is a good rough indicator of party positions within a nation, but relying on family affiliations across nations requires us to ignore differences within family groupings. That would make all cross-national differences entirely dependent on which families are present in a party system, and it would require acceptance of static positioning across time. The question at hand is how far do the two approaches carry the scientific programme towards a valid conclusion, to a valid set of measurements.

We undertake four analyses. The first involves the preliminary step of showing that the CMP Left-Right party positions are a good match to three expert surveys—Castles and Mair (1984), Laver and Hunt (1992), and Huber and Inglehart (1995). With that as the backdrop, our second analysis proceeds to ask whether there are dynamics in the Left-Right party positions that are worth recording and taking into account. Our third analysis considers cross-national comparisons by asking how far expert surveys and the CMP carry the measurements beyond the impoverished designations based on party–family affiliations. Our fourth and final analysis looks into the reportedly anomalous cases of radical-right parties where, despite their historical extremism, the CMP does not always designate these parties as the most extreme-right parties in a nation.

The results allow us to draw a rather sharp distinction between what the expert surveys and CMP are measuring. On the expert survey side we see a record of party positions based on long-run reputation. Party reputations are mostly stable, so the expert surveys lack a dynamic quality. Reputations are also so strongly associated with a party's family affiliation that the survey results lack some degree of cross-national comparability. Third, extreme-right parties have reputations based principally on select policy issues, and expert surveys appear to add extra weight to those issues when assigning Left-Right positions to such parties.

On the CMP side of the line we see a record of policy promises. There are identifiable dynamics in party position taking; at least one-third of parties take systematically different positions across time. There are within-family cross-national differences that matter for making valid cross-national comparisons. And, while radical-right parties are characterized as extremists for their authoritarian and exclusionary policies on social integration and immigration, their positions across the whole set of issues that comprise a Left-Right dimension are not so extreme after all.

LEFT-RIGHT PARTY POSITIONS IN THE CMP AND EXPERT SURVEYS

Left-Right is the core currency of political exchange in Western—and indeed new—democracies (cf. Chapter 3). It is ever present in our thinking about politics even though it cannot be said to tell us everything we want to know. Here we want to know how similar the tale is when recorded by expert survey and CMP data. The three expert surveys and the CMP cover in common seventy-nine parties in seventeen Western nations.[1] The Castles–Mair and Huber–Inglehart surveys were expressly designed to locate parties in the Left-Right space. Laver–Hunt asked experts to place parties along a pro–con continuum in each of eight policy categories.

Figure 4.1 records the commonality in Left-Right party scores for the two Left-Right expert surveys and the CMP, as located in a factor space defined by those three scores and the eight policy categories scores from Laver–Hunt. Five of the eight Laver–Hunt issue categories are highly correlated with Left-Right, though party alignments on the environment, urban interests, and decentralization leave room to manoeuvre. After extracting two dimensions (varimax rotation, with dimension extraction for eigenvalues ≥ 1.0), we rotated the axes so that the first factor would indicate Left-Right as marked by Castles–Mair while having no relationship to the second factor. This makes factor one something close to a Left-Right factor and nothing else. With that, each squared loading (communality, h^2) on factor one can be interpreted as a statement of the validity of each measure as an indicator of party Left-Right positions.

Castles–Mair and Huber–Inglehart are, by the factor analytic standard applied here, the two most valid measures. Each has a communality, h^2, in the vicinity of 0.9. The CMP is a valid indicator, again by the standards of validity founded on this factor analysis, but about a sixth of its variance is distinctly different from that of the expert surveys, i.e. $h^2 = .87^2 = .76$, and 1 $(.76/.90) = .16$.

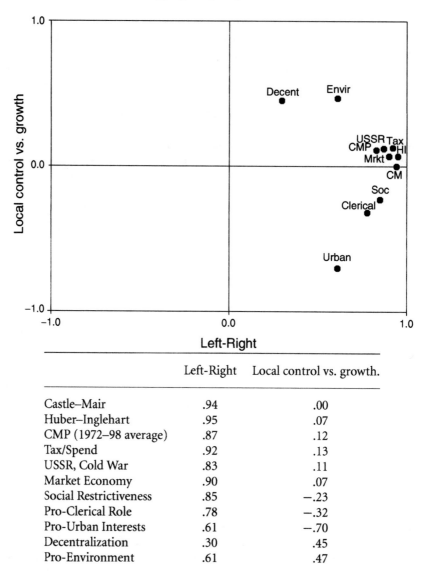

Fig. 4.1. Factor analysis of Left-Right scorings in two expert surveys and the MRG/CMP scale, together with expert placements of parties on eight specific policy scales

	Left-Right	Local control vs. growth.
Castle–Mair	.94	.00
Huber–Inglehart	.95	.07
CMP (1972–98 average)	.87	.12
Tax/Spend	.92	.13
USSR, Cold War	.83	.11
Market Economy	.90	.07
Social Restrictiveness	.85	−.23
Pro-Clerical Role	.78	−.32
Pro-Urban Interests	.61	−.70
Decentralization	.30	.45
Pro-Environment	.61	.47

What contributes to CMP distinctiveness? One possibility is that the CMP contains one-sixth more noise than the expert measures. Another possibility, which our analyses support, is that the so-called specific variance in CMP scores (where total variance is composed of commonly shared plus indicator-specific plus error variances) is informative cross-temporal and cross-national variation that goes unrecorded by the expert scores.

PARTY POSITION DYNAMICS

Elsewhere McDonald and Mendés have shown that three sets of expert survey scores from the early 1980s through early 1990s are highly reliable but have very little dynamic variation (McDonald and Mendés 2001: 100). Ninety-eight to 99 per cent of the reliably estimated cross-time variation is stable. A re-analysis that extends the analysis to 2002–3 is very much in line with these stability estimates.[2] This is troubling because it presents us with the possibility that the expert scores are akin to locating parties in the Left-Right space according to their party–family affiliation. Measurements based on family affiliations would be highly reliable from one decade to the next, but we would be hard-pressed to find dynamic variation.

Are the expert scores missing any important dynamic variation? We investigate that possibility for party Left-Right locations of eighty-one parties in seventeen Western nations.[3] Except for two Danish parties and with allowance for the special circumstances of Belgium, France, Italy, and the Netherlands, the eighty-one parties include those for which we have data on coded manifestos in consecutive elections totalling more than half of a nation's elections from the late 1940s through 1998.[4] The Belgian parties split along the lines of language during the period 1968–77, and we treat the pre- and post-splits as separate party systems. Parties under France's Fifth Republic, but not the Fourth Republic, are included. The analysis of Italian parties stops in 1992 after which many of the Italian parties reconfigured. Finally, the three separate Christian parties in the Netherlands combined at the time of the 1977 Dutch election to form the CDA; the three parties and the CDA are treated as four separate parties.

Our approach to uncovering evidence of systematic change, in this chapter, is based on estimating an autoregressive equation on each party's series of positions—in Chapter 5, we return to this question and consider alternative approaches to uncovering the dynamics. Party positions that shift over the long run, such as those forming a trend, will result in an autoregressive equation that indicates whether a party's long-run expected value (a sort of dynamic mean) is different from its mean as reported in Figure 4.2.[5] A party that changes by drifting away from its mean position for a sustained period but later coming back to it—a characteristic of cyclical movements—will result in an autoregressive equation with patterned change that leaves the long-run expected value and the mean close to one another. Finally, results from an autoregressive equation that indicates that the mean is a reasonable description regardless of a party's position at the previous election, are situations where parties are moving as if randomly around their respective mean positions, neither trending nor drifting.

To describe in more detail how the autoregressive equation can be used to identify what we label as *changers*, *drifters*, and *homeostatic wanderers*, we start with the equation as applied to any one party's Left-Right position. It takes this form:

$$\text{LR}_t = a + \beta\,\text{LR}_{t-1} + \varepsilon_t$$

where LR$_t$ is a party's Left-Right position for the current election; LR$_{t-1}$ party's Left-Right position at the previous election; α the intercept; β the slope; and ε_t a set of (assumed to be) well-behaved (homoscedastic and non-autocorrelated) errors in party positions at the current elections. When the estimated value of β is not distinguishable from zero, it indicates that the movements around the party Left-Right mean are, so far as we can tell, random deviations from its typical (mean) position, to which a party can be expected to return at the next election. When β is distinguishable from zero and in the interval -1 to $+1$ (all our estimates are in that interval), party movements show signs of sustained changes through time. For example, a statistically significant slope of .75 indicates that a deviation from a party's long-run typical Left-Right position is expected to move towards (but not to) that position at the next election. The speed at which it approaches that long-run typical position is $(1 - \beta)$. In the case of the example $(1 - \beta)$ is $1 - .75$, or .25; therefore, that party is expected to move one-quarter of the way from where it was at the last election towards where it is expected to be in the long run.

The difference between where we can expect a party to be in the long run and where it is on average is one way to describe how and by how much a party has changed. To estimate where a party's Left-Right position will be in the long run, we divide the intercept by 1 minus the slope, i.e. $[\alpha/(1 - \beta)]$ (see Spafford 1971; Price and Sanders 1993).

As we see, there are parties for which the slope is distinguishable from zero, and the difference between the mean and the party's long-run expected position is large. We call these parties *changers*. There are also instances of parties with slopes distinguishable from zero but with small differences between mean versus long-run expected value. These are parties that drifted one way, then the other— going through cycles of reliably predictable and moderately sustained movements. We call these parties *drifters*. Finally, there are parties that diverge from and converge towards their mean values in an essentially unpredictable manner. For these parties, movements away from their mean positions are expected to be short lived, with an expectation of each one returning to its mean position at the next election. We call these parties *homeostatic wanderers*.

For a party with patterns of change that show a shift to a new position, as would be true for a party whose positions create a trend, we have said there is a large difference between its mean Left-Right position and its long-run expected Left-Right position. Figure 4.2 is a histogram that displays these differences for each of the eighty-one parties. Not many parties show much difference. Only 10 of the 81 parties (12.3 per cent) have expected long-run positions that differ from their respective mean positions by more than ±4 points. Two of those 10 parties— the Dutch CDA and Italy's PSI—show changes larger than ±4, but their changes are based on estimated slopes that we deem to be unreliable.[6] That leaves eight parties that changed their Left-Right positions through time in a reliably estimated manner. They are the eight, so-called, *changers*.

The eight *changers* are listed in Table 4.1. There, too, we provide a description of the pattern of change along with each party's mean value over the period, its so-called target position (which is where, based on our analysis, we expect the

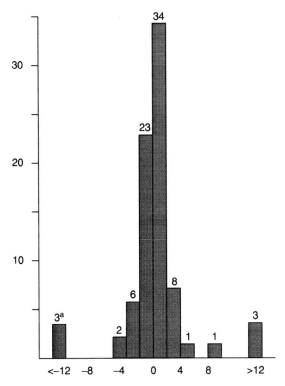

Fig. 4.2. Histogram of the difference between a party's mean and long-run expected Left-Right position over eighty one parties 1945–98

Source: Compiled by authors from CMP data (Budge et al. 2001).

[a] One large leftward changer (−34, Dutch ARP) is not fully depicted in this representation; it is one of the three cases in the category labelled < −12

party Left-Right position to settle over the long run), and its Left-Right position by decade. The first thing to notice is that of the eight *changers*, four no longer existed in the same organizational form in the mid- to late 1990s. Two Italian parties, the PSDI and PRI, each of which had been moving to the right, were themselves transformed when the party system as a whole changed after the 1992 election. In addition, two other *changers* are Dutch Christian parties—ARP and CHU—that combined, also with the Catholic KVP, to form the Christian Democratic Appeal (CDA), in the 1970s. The movements of both Dutch (Protestant) Christian parties show a trend leftward, and after they merged into the CDA, they held a centre-left position. That leaves four parties that have different Left-Right positions in the 1990s compared to where they stood in, say, 1960.

Patterns of change for these four still-in-existence *changers* are consistent with what informed observers of these parties tell us was happening throughout the period. The Austrian FPÖ is reported to have placed itself to the left during the

Table 4.1. Identification and description of movements by *changers*[a]

| Country | Party | CMPid | L-R | | Pattern of change |
			Mean	Target	Numerical value of L-R mean by decade
Austria	FPÖ	42420	2.5	14.2	Started centre, moved left, then steadily back to centre and continued on past centre to right 50s = +4.5 60s = −26.8 70s = −13.8 80s = +4.6 90s = +39.5
Ireland	FG	53520	11.1	6.5	Started right, moved steadily to centre-left until 80s, then moved to centre-right 50s = +46.6 60s = −2.0 70s = −17.6 80s = +2.8 90s = +9.3
Italy	PSDI	32330	−12.2	−4.5	Started left and moved rather steadily towards and to centre 50s = −28.5 60s = −24.1 70s = −5.3 80s = +3.5 90s = +2.3
Italy	PRI	32410	−0.7	15.3	Started left-centre and moved, in step-like manner rather steadily to right 50s = −17.0 60s = −10.0 70s = −1.0 80s = +22.8 90s = +36.7
Netherlands	ARP	22523	5.0	−29.6	Steady movement from centre-right to centre-left when it ended in early 70s 50s = +16.1 60s = +1.6 70s = −16.1 80s = ∿∿ 90s = ∿
Netherlands	CHU	22525	8.9	−3.1	Started right, moved to centre in the 60s and ended in centre-left in the early 70s 50s = +21.5 60s = +4.0 70s = −17.7 80s = ∿∿ 90s = ∿
Norway	SP	12810	−5.3	−17.3	Started right-centre, moved steadily and quickly left, reaching left-centre by mid-60s and stayed there 50s = +18.8 60s = −12.7 70s = −16.6 80s = −15.7 90s = −15.6
USA	DEM	61320	−12.8	−1.9	Started left-centre into the 1980s, then moved steadily to and through centre to centre-right 50s = −19.1 60s = −15.6 70s = −20.4 80s = −14.1 90s = +10.5

[a] A changing party takes Left-Right positions in a manner that changes predictably from one election to the next and produce an estimated long-run Left-Right position removed from its mean Left-Right position over the post-war period (beyond ±4 points).

Source: Estimations and compilations by authors based on CMP data (Budge et al. 2001).

1960s in order to gain favour with the SPÖ for government coalition bargaining purposes, but then gave up that strategy and moved strongly to the right (Müller 2000: 87). Mair (1986) reports that Fine Gael took noticeable steps to the left during the 1960s and 1970s and stood clearly to the left of Fianna Fáil during that time. Hanne Marthe Narud and Kaare Strøm have said of the leftward drift of Norway's SP that 'the party's opposition to European integration has gradually generalised into a greater scepticism towards market economies' (Narud and Strøm 2000: 164). Finally, US Democrats, most especially under the leadership of President Clinton but presaged by smaller movements towards the centre during the 1980s, are generally understood to have moved there over time (see, e.g. Erikson, MacKuen, and Stimson 2001).

Nineteen parties are classified as *drifters*, more than twice the number of *changers*. The *drifters* are listed in Table 4.2. Recall that our classification criterion for *drifters* versus *changers* is that, while a *drifter*'s position undergoes predictable and sustained changes, in the long run its Left-Right position is not much different from its mean position over the entire period. This is reflected in the column in the middle of the table, where the mean and (long-run) target values are reported. One general pattern of drift covers the Anglo-American parties. In Australia, New Zealand, the UK, and the USA, the *drifters* each moved towards the right—a movement that also describes the US Democrats in Table 4.1. The reason many of these appear to be *drifters* rather than *changers* is that along the way their movements were erratic enough not to provide a firm basis for describing them as trends. Among the *drifters* in Belgium (if we were to add in the combined liberals of the 1950s and 1960s), the Netherlands, Norway, and Sweden, the movements follow a pattern where the 1960s and 1970s show a leftward shift followed by rightward shifts during the 1980s and 1990s. Four other parties did not head towards the right side of the spectrum during the 1980s and 1990s—the Irish FF, Danish CD and KrF, and the Swiss CVP. Fianna Fáil moved rightward in the 1960s and 1970s only to move leftward towards the centre in the 1980s and 1990s. The two Danish parties, CD and KrF, started on the right, both having won seats for the first time in the traumatic 1973 Danish election, and tended to move slightly leftward towards a centre-right position. The Swiss CVP appears to have moved erratically but decidedly to the left over the entire period.

The modal outcome is that of the *homeostatic wanderers*. There are 54 of them, 66.7 per cent of all the parties analysed—too many to be reported in a table. These are parties that, as the wandering portion of their label suggests, have moved around without developing patterns of sustained change across time. We say of them, then, that, so far as we can tell from the autoregressive estimations, their movements are as if random. Of course, the 'homeostatic' qualifier in the label indicates that a party's wandering is anchored in a meaningful position, presumably meaningful for their leaders as well to voters.

It is proper to enquire further whether the wandering is untethered or homeostatic. A set of completely random numbers will have a mean; hence, having a mean can hardly be a justification for inferring that these parties have an identifiable ideological home. The inference of homeostasis therefore rests on how widely these parties wander away from their respective mean positions. The standard deviations around the mean positions of *homeostatic wanderers* are actually slightly smaller on average than the standard deviations around the regression lines of the *changers* and the *drifters*. Among the 54 *homeostatic wanderers*, the average standard deviation is 12.4; for the *changers* and *drifters*, the average standard deviation around their regression lines is 13.1 (average s_e values). In that

Table 4.2. Identification and description of movements by *drifters*[a]

| Country | Party | CMPid | L-R | | Pattern of drift |
			Mean	Target	Numerical value of L-R mean by decade
Australia	LAB	63320	−11.1	−7.3	Started left, stayed left through the 70s, drifted to varied positions at and around the centre 50s = −22.5 60s = −14.2 70s = −22.1 80s = +3.2 90s = +5.6
Belgium	CVP	21521	−1.9	1.5	Started centre-left in late 60s, moved steadily to centre-right in 80s, and moved to centre 50s = ~~~ 60s = −12.8 70s = −8.2 80s = +7.7 90s = +1.7
Belgium	VU	21913	−2.9	−3.4	Started centre, veered to centre-left in late 60s, climbed back centre-right and moved to centre 50s = ~~~ 60s = −5.8 70s = −8.4 80s = +4.7 90s = −2.9
Canada	PC	62620	4.2	6.2	Centre until mid-70s and drifted to right-centre thereafter 50s = −2.4 60s = −0.6 70s = +2.3 80s = +14.9 90s = +17.6
Denmark	CD	13330	21.9	21.3	Started right (70s), stayed right in 80s and moved to centre in 90s 50s = ~~~ 60s = ~~~ 70s = +26.7 80s = +25.1 90s = +6.0
Denmark	KrF	13520	20.3	18.6	Started right (70s), moved to centre-right in 80s, and stayed 50s = ~~~ 60s = ~~~ 70s = +30.0 80s = +12.2 90s = +12.3
Ireland	FF	53620	6.4	8.3	Started centre, moved right in 60s and 70s, jumped back to centre in late 70s and stayed centre 50s = +8.0 60s = +22.4 70s = +26.5 80s = −10.2 90s = +0.7
Netherlands	PvdA	22320	−25.0	−25.5	Started left (60s), moved steadily left in 60s and 70s, and back towards and to centre-left in 80s and 90s 50s = −21.3 60s = −27.6 70s = −43.3 80s = −22.5 90s = −8.9
Netherlands	D'66	22330	−18.3	−18.3	Started left (60s), moved further left in 70s, and to centre-left in 80s and 90s 50s = ~~~ 60s = −18.3 70s = −30.8 80s = −11.7 90s = −13.0
NZ	LAB	64320	−24.4	−24.5	Started left, moved steadily towards centre in 60s and 70s, drifted unsteadily back to left in mid-80s and 90s 50s = −34.6 60s = −29.4 70s = −16.4 80s = −11.2 90s = −22.2

Table 4.2. (*Continued*)

Country	Party	CMPid	L-R Mean	L-R Target	Pattern of drift numerical value of L-R mean by decade
Norway	KF	12520	0.1	−2.4	Started centre-right, drifted steadily to centre-left til 90s, and jumped back to centre 50s = +15.7 60s = −4.5 70s = −5.2 80s = −13.8 90s = +2.0
Norway	Høyre	12620	4.2	3.2	Started centre-right, drifted steadily towards centre-left from 60 till mid-70s, and moved back to centre-right 50s =+16.4 60s = 0.0 70s = −14.2 80s = −2.3 90s = +14.4
Sweden	SDP	11320	−23.2	−20.6	Started left, moving a little further left in 60s, jumped to centre-left in early 70s, drifted back left, only to move to centre in 90s 50s = −32.7 60s = −46.0 70s = −18.9 80s = −21.2 90s = +4.7
Sweden	FP	11420	−4.2	−6.4	Started centre-right, jumped to left in 60s, and gradually drifted back to centre-right 50s = +10.8 60s = −33.4 70s = −15.6 80s = +3.3 90s = +12.5
Sweden	MSP	11620	36.9	34.9	Started right, moved to centre-right in 70s, moved back to right 50s = +51.8 60s = +40.3 70s = +14.0 80s = +40.5 90s = +40.5
Sweden	CP	11810	−3.3	−0.7	Started centre drifting right, swung centre-left in 60s and stayed until early 80s, drifted to centre-right 50s = +2.5 60s = −6.5 70s = −16.2 80s = −6.8 90s = +12.9
Switzerland	CVP	43520	10.1	6.6	Started right, jumped to centre in mid-60s and stays centre 50s = +25.1 60s = +19.9 70s = +1.2 80s = +0.6 90s = −6.8
UK	CON	51620	7.9	10.5	Started variably though slightly left, drifted towards centre-right through 60s and 70s and to right in 80s and 90s 50s = −8.0 60s = +0.8 70s = +11.0 80s = +29.7 90s = +26.8
USA	REP	61620	13.9	15.9	Started erratically around centre, more reliably centre in late 60s and 70s, and moved right in 80s and 90s 50s = +7.0 60s = +4.3 70s = +3.7 80s = +28.5 90s = +27.3

[a] A drifting party takes Left-Right positions in a manner that changes predictably from one election to the next but has an estimated long-run Left-Right position close to its mean Left-Right position over the post-war period (within ±4 points).

Source: Estimations and compilations by authors based on CMP data (Budge et al. 2001).

sense, the unpredictable variation of the *homeostatic wanderers* based on their means is slightly less than the unpredictable variation based on the otherwise predictable movements of the *changers* and *drifters*. In short, a mean position of a *homeostatic wanderer* generally characterizes its positions and a regression equation a position of a *changer* or *drifter*.

Our evidence indicates that one-third of the eighty-one parties changed their Left-Right positions in detectable, systematic ways. Given the systematic change, it is really necessary to try to capture the dynamic aspects of party positioning. On the other hand, only four ongoing parties have changed their long-run positions to a substantial degree. This limited number of *changers* makes it understandable that long-run perceptions of party positions, what we think is recorded by expert surveys, would record high degrees of stability.

In anticipation of what we will have to say in Chapter 5, a word of caution is in order. The dynamic variation beyond that which we have here labelled systematic should not be thrown on the junk pile, as if it amounts to nothing more than noise. Much of it has been explained as systematic policy adjustments to the circumstances of each election (Budge 1994; Adams 2001; Adams et al. 2004). Statistical models of cross-temporal attributions of stability, change, and noise require one to have in mind a model of 'true behavioural change' in order to be able to separate noise in the measurements from change in the behaviour (Heise 1969)— an issue we take up directly in Chapter 5. Here we have employed a commonly used model of 'true' behaviour change in the form of a Markovian process. In effect, the assumption we are making here says that when behaviour truly changes it does so by way of particular forms of systematic Markovian process movements, depending on a party's current position, but not on its previous positions nor on how long it has taken its current position. It then adds by implication that to the extent behaviour is not following a Markovian process, the remaining portion of the measured signal is noise.

A close examination of systematic change by parties would reveal widely accepted real changes that do not show themselves as such in our results. One clear example is Britain's Labour Party. Surely it has moved from left to right under the leadership of Tony Blair and the CMP records that movement. But, because it showed up so late in the CMP series, this is effectively left as noise because, by 1998, it was still too early to say whether the movement was systematic in the statistical sense (cf. our similar point in Chapter 1 about the British Conservatives' move to Left in the 1950s if we cut the series off at 1959 (Figure 1.15a)).

CROSS-NATIONAL VARIATION

An important purpose of party position indicators is to provide valid indications of party differences across nations. Party–family affiliations are not up to the task of drawing consistent distinctions between parties across nations, even though family affiliations are surely useful for rank orderings within nations (see, e.g. the within-nation rank orders from different studies in Mair 2001: 21–2).

Under the assumption that family affiliation does not travel especially well across countries, one has to expect that some part of the variation within families comes from national influences on individual parties. Norway's political space, for example, while containing variance that is largely associated with parties from different families, makes its own contribution to the location of Norwegian parties. In other words, we expect that Norway's political parties are generally to the left of parties of the same family in, say, Australia and the USA. This is because Norway's Labour Party (DNA), an affiliate of the social democratic family, is to the left of social democratic Australian Labour and American Democrats, and the Norwegian Høyre (conservative family) is to the left of Australian Liberals and American Republicans (also belonging to the conservative family).

This analysis focuses on seventy-nine parties belonging to one of eight families in seventeen nations, the same nations used in the factor analysis above (see Note 1). We include parties from eight families: Communists, Greens, Social Democrats, Liberals, Christians, Agrarians, Conservatives, and Nationalists. To create a Left-Right score from the Laver–Hunt data, we follow the recommendation in McDonald and Mendés (2001: 99) and calculate a weighted sum of the Laver–Hunt scores on their *public ownership*, *tax/spend*, and *social permissiveness* policy dimensions. The CMP scores are based on average Left-Right scores over the period 1978–96 (except for Italy for which we calculate a CMP mean through the 1992 elections). For convenience, we linearly transformed all four sets of scores so that each one's metric ranges from a minimum of zero (0 = extreme left) to a maximum of ten (10 = extreme right). In the case of the CMP data, for which possible maximum left and right values are far removed from the observed maximum values, the re-scaling set $-50 = 0$, $0 = 5$, and $+50 = 10$, i.e. the rescaled CMP scores equal $[(CMP + 50)/10]$.

Variation Across Families

We begin by asking how the four sets of Left-Right scores line up by party family. The family averages are shown in Table 4.3. As one would expect, on average, Communists are far left; Greens and Social Democrats are on the left; Liberals, Agrarians, and Christians are centre to centre-right; Conservatives are on the right; and Nationalists are far right. On this general ordering, all four data-sets agree.

With respect to variability across and within families, however, the CMP data stand distinct. Perhaps most noteworthy is that there is more cross-family variation and less within-family variation in the expert survey sets compared to the CMP. The experts record more homogeneity within families and more distinctiveness between and among families compared to the latter. The R^2 values at

Table 4.3. Average party Left-Right positions by party family

Party family	N	Mean (std. dev.)			
		Manifesto project	Castles and Mair	Laver and Hunt	Huber and Inglehart
Communist	8	1.83	1.70	1.77	1.86
		(.99)	(.48)	(.35)	(.43)
Social Democrat	22	3.75	3.54	3.80	3.74
		(1.18)	(.98)	(1.08)	(.82)
Green	4	3.62	3.83	3.45	2.85
		(1.29)	(.83)	(.70)	(.71)
Liberal	13	5.35	5.84	6.10	6.01
		(1.52)	(1.17)	(1.33)	(1.30)
Agrarian	5	5.16	6.10	6.19	6.39
		(1.60)	(.99)	(.66)	(1.35)
Christian Democrat	11	5.67	6.31	6.79	6.27
		(1.08)	(.70)	(.49)	(.99)
Conservative	14	6.13	7.18	7.12	6.95
		(1.63)	(.73)	(.87)	(.77)
Nationalist	2	7.89	9.45	8.55	9.63
		(1.06)	(.50)	(.95)	(.53)
All parties	79	4.70	5.09	5.23	5.12
		(1.91)	(2.08)	(2.05)	(2.06)
Summary statistics					
R^2		.553	.832	.844	.812
R^{-2}		.509	.815	.829	.793
s_e		1.336	.892	.850	.936

Notes: Table entries are for party families mean Left-Right locations based on 0–10 metrics for all four data-sets. Summary statistics come from regressing the party positions onto dummy variables for each of seven families, withholding one family to serve as the baseline category.

the bottom of the table indicate that sizeable proportions of the Left-Right variation for the expert data are associated with family affiliation; all three exceed .8. Given that error variance (simple noise) almost surely constitutes between 5 and 10 per cent of the total variance of each set of expert scores, these R^2s are probably too high. At a minimum, this is contrary to the stated purpose of moving beyond family to more finely graded Left-Right scores. Therefore, at first reading, the expert survey data do not appear to tell us much about Left-Right party positions beyond what party–family affiliations, standing alone, could have told us. The CMP data are not so strongly associated with party family. Compared to the expert survey data, the CMP data have a smaller standard deviation for the seventy-nine parties considered overall ($s = 1.91$ vs. about 2.06). Also, within each and every party family the CMP standard deviation is larger than the corresponding standard deviation in the expert data. It follows, then, that the R^2 value when predicting CMP scores from party family is more modest.

Only 55 per cent of the variation in CMP Left-Right scores is associated with family affiliation.

Variation Aross Countries

One way to estimate where in Left-Right space each nation's party system operates relative to the space of other nations' party systems is to calculate the distance between each party's Left-Right position and its family mean, and then average those distances by nation.[7] For nations whose parties stand uniformly to the left of their respective family means, the average distance will be negative; for nations whose parties stand uniformly to the right of their respective family means, the average distance will be positive.

Table 4.4 reports the national averages. For the CMP data, a statistically significant 38 per cent of the variation in these party differences is associated with the nations. Among the expert survey sets of scores, the constructed Left-Right score for Laver–Hunt has the highest percentage of variance associated with nations: 32 per cent, but with such a large number of dummy variables, it falls short of statistical significance ($F = 1.780$, $p = .055$). For the Castles–Mair as well as the Huber–Inglehart scores, the variance associated with the nation dummy variables is clearly not greater than chance.

The findings suggest that party locations identified by expert surveys, especially Castles–Mair and Huber–Inglehart, correspond so closely to party–family affiliation that information about nations does not tell us very much about party positions. This conclusion is troubling but should not be overdrawn. It is conditional on a statistical analysis that considers all nations jointly. When attention is switched to specific nations, one can see common tendencies that have to be taken to mean that not all the expert results, for each and every country, are just noise. All four data-sets, for example, have parties in Canada placed to the left of their family counterparts. On the other side as well, the CMP and expert surveys place parties in Australia to the right of their respective families, on average. Given such commonalities, it has to be said that there is some degree of cross-national validity, or at least reliability, in all four studies.

The question is whether the selected common tendencies are generalizable? We can look at the generalizability by correlating the four sets of national positions reported in Table 4.4. The six correlations are ($N = 17$):

CMP and C-M = .575 (p = .008)

CMP and L-H = .703 (p = .001)

CMP and H-I = .329 (not significant, p = .099)

C-M and L-H = .427 (p = .049)

C-M and H-I = .036 (not significant, p = .445)

L-H and H-I = .742 (p < .001)

Table 4.4. Average distance, by nation, between party Left-Right positions and party family means

Country	N	Average distance (standard deviation)			
		Manifesto project	Castles and Mair	Laver and Hunt	Huber and Inglehart
Canada	3	−.64	−.52	−1.20	−1.01
		(1.07)	(.17)	(.51)	(.92)
Norway	6	−1.38	−.48	−.57	−.31
		(.65)	(.77)	(.52)	(.78)
UK	3	−.42	−.56	−.39	−.25
		(1.80)	(1.02)	(1.49)	(.96)
Ireland	4	−.90	−.06	−.34	−.37
		(.83)	(.58)	(.34)	(.88)
Spain	5	−.61	.59	−.58	−.56
		(.43)	(.82)	(.93)	(.61)
Finland	7	−.46	−.20	−.06	.58
		(1.35)	(.45)	(.47)	(.96)
Germany	5	.02	−.01	−.13	−.34
		(.85)	(1.04)	(.69)	(.64)
France	6	−.51	−.13	−.08	.11
		(.90)	(.70)	(.54)	(.67)
Sweden	4	.51	−.21	.05	−.03
		(1.49)	(.52)	(.45)	(.89)
Italy	7	.84	−.13	.17	.12
		(1.15)	(.97)	(.74)	(.76)
Belgium	7	.18	.13	.14	−.23
		(.82)	(.97)	(.87)	(.64)
Netherlands	4	−.29	.22	.23	.20
		(1.01)	(1.19)	(.81)	(.59)
New Zealand	2	−.53	−.46	.67	.82
		(.25)	(1.02)	(1.31)	(1.09)
Austria	3	1.05	−.03	.51	.82
		(.58)	(.86)	(.72)	(1.50)
Australia	4	1.33	.83	.42	.18
		(1.08)	(1.08)	(.56)	(1.43)
Denmark	7	.91	.35	.68	.41
		(1.88)	(.98)	(1.01)	(1.07)
USA	2	1.25	.44	.72	−.35
		(.59)	(1.16)	(.38)	(.15)
Summary Statistics					
R^2		.376	.182	.315	.233
R^{-2}		.216	−.029	.138	.035
s_e		1.129	.863	.753	.877

Notes: Entries are average within-nation differences between a party's location and its respective family mean. Negative/positive values mean that parties within a given nation are on average to the left (negative) or right (positive) of their party family mean. Summary statistics come from regressing the differences onto sixteen nation-specific dummy variables, with one nation serving as the baseline. Standard deviations are reported in parentheses. Reporting the standard deviations supplies the greatest flexibility for readers to test hypotheses about individual nations. The homoscedastic standard errors for nation i are equal to $s_e/\sqrt{n_i}$, where s_e is the standard error of estimate from the regression (reported under summary statistics at the bottom of the table). The standard errors corrected for heteroscedasticity through weighted least squares equal $(s/\sqrt{n_i})$, where s is the standard deviation reported in the table. For testing paired comparisons without assuming homoscedasticity, the standard error for any pair of nations, a and b, is $\sqrt{(s_a/n_a + s_b/n_b)}$, where s_a is the standard deviation for nation a and s_b nation b. Nations are ordered top to bottom according to the average Left-Right national position across all four data-sets, with left-most nations at the top.

The evidence of generalizable commonalities across the four studies is mixed. The Castles–Mair national spaces share essentially no variance with Huber–Inglehart (r = .036; therefore, r^2 = .001). The CMP and Laver–Hunt country locations share something in the vicinity of 50 per cent of variance. In between, the CMP and Castles–Mair share about a third of their variation and Castles–Mair and Laver–Hunt one-sixth.

Close inspection of the country-specific numbers in Table 4.4 reveals that the mixed generalizability comes in large part from five nations being located in very different positions in one or another of the data-sets. Castles–Mair places Spanish parties substantially to the right in relation to their party families, while the other three studies have Spanish parties substantially to the left relative to their party families. Also, Castles–Mair locates the Austrian system near the centre while the other three place it considerably to the right. Huber–Inglehart locates Finland's parties on the right; the other three have Finland on the left. Even more surprising, Huber–Inglehart places the US Democrats and Republicans to the left of their family counterparts; the other three studies arrive at the more commonly held view that American parties are substantially to the right of family affiliates. Finally, the four studies render a rather dramatically split decision on New Zealand's party system. Castles–Mair and the CMP put New Zealand's party system on the left, relatively speaking, while Laver–Hunt and Huber–Inglehart report that New Zealand's party system is on the right.

Re-calculating the correlations of national spaces across data-sets after excluding the five anomalous nations shows the following (N = 12).

CMP and C-M = .706 (p = .005)

CMP and L-H = .753 (p = .003)

CMP and H-I = .597 (p = .021)

C-M and L-H = .794 (p = .001)

C-M and H-I = .635 (p = .013)

L-H and H-I = .926 (p < .001)

Within the restricted set of twelve countries, all the correlations are statistically significant.

The evidence on cross-national comparability shows that party Left-Right locations identified in expert surveys are much more strongly conditioned by party–family affiliation than is the case for the CMP, which says meaningful cross-national variation in expert survey scores is muted relative to what we see in the CMP scores. On this aspect of measuring what is intended to be measured, the CMP has a substantial edge. The evaluation should not be read as an all-or-nothing judgement, of course; some of the reasons for the missing variation in expert surveys can be identified, and, to the extent it is, it can be remedied.

RADICAL-RIGHT PARTIES

Our final inquiry into the validity of the CMP's Left-Right scale takes its motivation from commentators who have told us there must be something wrong with the scale because it misrepresents the positions of some radical-right parties (Gabel and Huber 2000: Special Issue of *Electoral Studies* (ed.) 2007 passim). A prominent case in point is Italy (Pelizzo 2003). The neo-fascist *Alleanza Nazionale* (MSI from 1948 to 1972 and MSI-DN from 1972 to 1994) has been and is by all accounts a party on the extreme right. On average, however, the CMP scores AN as a centre-right party. Two particular features of the CMP Left-Right construction account for the AN centrism in the CMP data. The first is, again, related to reputation; the second has to do with how the CMP calculates Left-Right scores. Both are core matters of validity—what do we intend to measure?

The AN gains much of its radical-right reputation from its fascist heritage, fierce anti-communist rhetoric, and monarchist sympathies. At times, however, it takes positions that accord with policies associated with the left, as in the mid-1980s when it supported the PCI (communist) referendum measure to raise the ceiling on the wage indexation system. The AN like some other radical-right parties is not always hostile to welfare state provisions, and supports a strong state with many forms of intervention into the economy—necessary in their eyes to safeguard national integrity.

Data from a recent expert survey acknowledge as much (Benoit and Laver 2006). They asked country experts to place parties along a Left-Right dimension and along several specific policy dimensions, one of which is a pro-welfare versus anti-welfare state indicator of raising taxes to increase public services versus cutting public services in order to cut taxes. The AN, along with its dissident members who formed the MS-FT and the anti-immigrant LN, are by the experts' rendering the three most extreme-right parties in Italy as of 2003. All three are also judged to be the most socially conservative and anti-immigrant of the Italian parties. On the welfare state indicator, however, the AN is judged to be moderate, and its MS-FT offshoot is left-leaning. How does a party with a moderate or leftist position on the welfare state end up being a party located at the extreme right end of the political spectrum? The very real possibility is that its reputation precedes it. Given that 'everyone knows' that the AN, MS-FT, and LN—by the very labels they are given, viz. radical- and extreme-right parties—are very far to the right, the reputation associated with the label is the score assigned.

The reputational issue is not one just associated with Italian parties. Figure 4.3 shows the relationship between the Benoit–Laver Left-Right and pro-tax versus anti-tax and spend positions in five countries, including Italy, each with one or more radical-right parties (the designation of which parties are among the radical right comes from Norris 2005: Table 3.1). In all five countries, radical-right parties are the parties standing farthest to the right in the system in the experts' judgements. Nevertheless, with the single exception of the *Fremkridtspartiet* (FrP, Progress Party) in Denmark, the radical-right parties are not the ones judged to stand farthest right on taxing and spending within the context of their respective

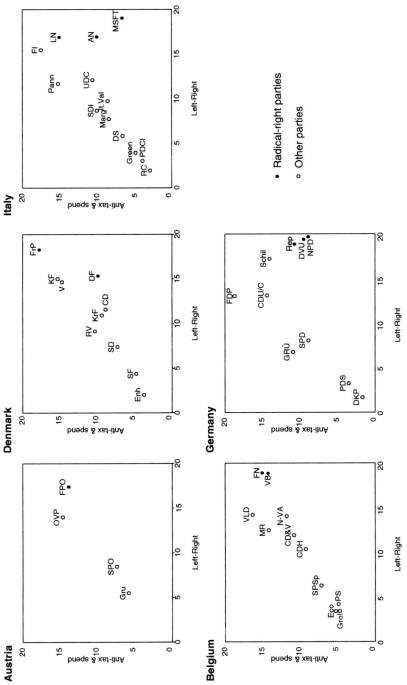

Fig. 4.3. Relationship between expert judgements of party Left-Right placement and tax and spend positions in five countries in 2003

party systems. In several cases, including the AN in Italy, as we have said, the radical-right party positions on taxing and spending are judged to be downright centrist.

Given the policy mix of the radical-right party issue positions, where do they belong along the Left-Right spectrum? As with all questions related to measurement validity, the answer depends on one's intention. If the intention were to ensure that the measurement comports with the descriptive labels or to ensure a match with the experts' perceptions, the CMP has a validity problem (which, as we will see below, could be solved). But, since the intention is to record the policy promises to electors and to be able to check whether the policies they pursue while in parliament and government square with those promises, placement of a party such as the AN by the CMP is not necessarily out of line. In sum, the difference between the CMP and expert survey placements is principally a function of experts scoring party reputations more than specific party promises and policy commitments.

A second reason the AN score in the CMP appears to be out of line with expert perception is a consequence of how the CMP calculates Left-Right scores. It takes Left-Right to be indicated by the difference between summations of thirteen right and thirteen left policy categories. Parties that do not say much about these twenty-six policy categories receive scores around zero, near the centre on the Left-Right dimension. The AN is a party that typically has little to say about issues in the CMP's twenty-six Left-Right categories. With little to say about issues that identify where it stands in the Left-Right space, it looks rather centrist.

To identify this scoring decision as a part of the source of a seemingly anomalous AN Left-Right placement is a long way from justifying the decision, certainly. The diagnosis does not so much answer the criticism as raise a different question: Is the difference in summations the valid form for calculating a Left-Right score? An alternative scoring procedure could be applied. Hee-Min Kim and Richard Fording introduced a ratio-calculation alternative to the CMP's difference scoring (Kim and Fording 1998; see also Laver and Garry 2000). They subtract the scores in thirteen left categories from scores in the thirteen right categories, *but* they then divide the difference by the sum total of all Left-Right scores, i.e. $[(\text{Right} - \text{Left})/(\text{Right} + \text{Left})]*100$. This has the effect of consciously wiping out how salient Left-Right issues are to a party and, instead, scores a party for its Right versus Left emphasis among only the Left-Right issues it values enough to include in its manifesto.

One congenial result produced by the ratio measure is to score the AN, on average, as among the most right-leaning parties in the data-set. Of the 135 parties in Western democracies for which we have five or more manifestos, the MSI average Left-Right ratio score ranks as the nineteenth most right-leaning.

That is the good news, seemingly. The bad news is that its re-scored position imposes a validity problem or, more accurately said, creates an invalidity problem. While the ratio scoring now puts the AN in line with the Left-Right location one would think a radical-right party would have, it glosses over the fact that often the AN is not telling voters much about where it stands over the full range of

Left-Right issues. The ratio scoring has the effect of handing the relative weight given to specific issues over to the party (a good thing in and of itself) not on the sole basis of how much it values a particular issue but on the additional basis of how much it does not value issues associated with Left-Right policies. A near obsession with government support for agriculture and a statement or two about education expansion in rural areas does not make a party an extreme-left party; as well, a near obsession with government support for agriculture plus a passing statement or two favouring protectionist policies does not make a party an extreme-right party.

Parties face people and circumstances involving a broad swathe of issues. A party may choose to put its emphasis on one or a small set of issue domains or even subcategories within a domain. Such a focused interest forms an important concern to the CMP data collection, relying as it does on saliency. But when a party chooses not to make Left-Right issues much of a concern they are not staking out an extreme position on the Left or Right. That is what the CMP Left-Right scoring records, validly given the intention of the scale.

✦ SUMMARY AND CONCLUSION

The validity of the CMP Left-Right scale stands up rather well to the empirical scrutiny brought to bear on it in this chapter. Parties' average positions match the positions along the Left-Right dimension that experts see. *And* the CMP's measurements move beyond the collective judgements of experts by recording positional dynamics and cross-national differences. Identifying typical positions, observing dynamics, and facilitating comparisons across nations are goals that prompted the creation of the MRG. The project continues to respond to critics and other commentators who want the data to be accurate in all its particulars. Attention to specific objections helps to focus attention in useful ways. Sometimes there are actual problems. But more often, as with Left-Right locations of radical-right parties, the commentary assists in clarifying the very concept the CMP intends to measure. What might at first look like a validity problem is sometimes more a matter of the commentator wanting to measure something different.

We have leaned heavily on expert scoring as the major alternative to the CMP and found it wanting in three respects—largely because it depends too much on parties' long-term reputations. Long-term reputational scoring washes out most dynamic variation, mutes the variance associated with party systems of different nations, and gives extra weight to particular issue categories. The CMP-expert comparisons in this chapter have not been intended as criticisms; rather, they have been used to spotlight three key elements that have to be considered as part of a validity evaluation. The expert survey scores are what they are. Given what they are—records of various parties' reputations—they are reliable. But they lack important variation that would make them more valid, given the intentions of the survey administrators and of the CMP.

There is, of course, safety in numbers and comfort in the consistency that gives rise to the experts' reliability. But this is not all that is important, and it is not what is centrally important to validity. The downside to safety in numbers, when the numbers involve appeals to experts, is the risk of committing the combined fallacies of ad populum appeals to authority. In the spirit of a scientific programme, of which the CMP and expert surveys form parts, it is the evidence that matters most, not anyone's or, for that matter, everyone's impression. The findings presented in this chapter indicate that the evidence compiled and used by the CMP to construct its Left-Right scale is valid.

NOTES

1. The nations are Australia, Austria, Belgium, Canada, Denmark, Finland, France, Germany, Ireland, Italy, the Netherlands, New Zealand, Norway, Spain, Sweden, the UK, and the USA. Unfortunately, the CEE countries are not covered in all the surveys, so we have to omit them from the analysis. We also take the CMP data only up to 1998 to facilitate comparison with the expert surveys conducted in the 1980s and 1990s. We could have added data from Kenneth Benoit's and Michael Laver's 2002-3 expert survey, which we do use in an analysis later in this chapter, but that would have forced us to drop France, because they did not solicit Left-Right information on French parties, and Italy, because the Italian party system was transformed after 1992 (Benoit and Laver 2006).
2. We re-estimated the stability based on the Castle–Mair (early 1980s), Huber–Inglehart (early 1990s), and Benoit–Laver (early 2000s) surveys (see Note 1). Because we lose parties from France and Italy (Benoit–Laver does not record left-right scores for France, and the Italian party system has been remade) and a few other parties, the common pool of parties (conditioned by a party having had to appear in the Laver–Hunt survey of the late 1980s), numbers 56. Estimated stability for the early 1980s to 1990s under the truncated set of parties and using the Castles–Mair, Laver–Hunt, and Huber–Inglehart data is .947. Using the Castles–Mair, Huber–Inglehart, and Benoit–Laver data, the estimated stability is a similar .942. Both estimates are lower than the previously reported .982, but that apparently is due to the different set of parties included in the analysis rather than having arrived at something different. That is, if we were arriving at something different, the re-estimate from the three previously used data-sets would be in the vicinity of .982, and not of .942.
3. These are not exactly the same seventeen nations used in the factor analysis. Here we exclude Spain, because the number of elections since democratization is too small and we include Luxembourg, which was not present in the factor analysis because its parties had not been scored by Castles and Mair.
4. A few of the manifesto data points are estimated from the party's manifesto at an earlier election. Such carryover data present problems for our analyses on two counts. They artificially reduce variation and create autocorrelation. Therefore, we exclude carryover manifestos. The exclusion is usually for one election at the beginning or end of a party's series. The single election exclusions are the Belgian PVV in 1995, the Belgian FDF in 1965, the Belgian VU in 1958, the Canadian SC in 1972 and 1974, all Danish parties in 1998, all Norwegian parties in 1997, and the Swiss SVP in 1947. Dropping the 1998 Danish data caused observations on the Danish CD and KF to go from 11 of 22 (half)

to 10 of 21 (less than half). Still, we decided to keep both Danish parties in the analyses. In the case of the French Conservatives, the entire series had to be excluded because several of its manifestos are recorded as estimates. Finally, the single manifesto score of the United Socialists in Italy for the 1968 election is the 1968 score that we assign individually and separately to the PSI and PSDI.

5. As we explain immediately below, the dynamic mean is distinguishable from the mean conceived as the average of all cases. The dynamic mean is the end-state towards which changes tend. It can be calculated by estimating an autoregressive equation and seeing whether the slope is zero. If the slope is zero, then the mean value of Y at any given time is estimated to be equal to the autoregressive intercept. If the slope is different from zero, then the mean, which is estimated to vary, is estimated by the intercept divided by one minus the slope. For informative discussions about autoregressive equations, with substantive applications to politics, see Spafford (1971) and Sanders and Price (1991).

6. We take what could be considered a liberal approach to a decision rule for reliably estimated relationships, but what we have done in fact is to take account of the effect of measurement error. Errors in an X variable reduce the magnitude of an estimated slope, and errors in both the X and Y variables are likely to increase the slope's standard error. Given that a t-ratio is (b/s_b), the effect of measurement errors makes tests of statistical significance at conventional levels (e.g. $p < .05$) prone to Type II errors. Therefore, we loosen the conventional standard of, say, $p < .05$, so that reliably predicted behaviour is deemed to exist when a slope's t-value has a magnitude such that $t < -1.5$ or $t > 1.5$. Twenty-one parties show a statistically significant relationship at conventional levels, compared to 27 using our looser 1.5 t-value. Note that the liberal decision rule has no effect on our subsequent analyses and evaluations, except to cause us to provide detailed descriptions of change for twenty-seven instead of twenty-one parties in Tables 4.1 and 4.2.

   Tests of statistical significance could also be affected by autocorrelated errors. We have checked for autocorrelation for each of the eighty-one party series. When a lagged value of Y is on the right hand side, the test (e.g. Durbin's h) is a large sample test and is not especially powerful. With our small samples of between six and twenty one elections for any one party, about half of the tests are not calculable. However, we have calculated values of *rho* for all parties. We find an estimated *rho* between $\pm.25$ for 72 of the 81 parties. Therefore, in no more than a few cases could it be said that a concern about autocorrelation is warranted.

7. Analysing difference-score variables can create inferential complications. They assume that the coefficient on X, in a $(Y–X)$ calculation is 1.0. If it is not, then analysing the reasons for the differences reflects in part the reasons for the differences themselves and in part the reasons why the coefficient is not 1.0. We have checked to ensure that such complications do not confound our analyses of cross-national differences. In addition to asking how the difference scores relate to nation dummy variables, we created a variable from the party family means and moved it to the right-hand side of the equation. Thereafter, we regressed the respective party scores onto the mean party family values (i.e. Y-hat from the party family regression) plus the nation dummy variables. That allows us to check whether the coefficient on that variable equals 1.0. It very nearly equals 1.0 for all four sets of party Left-Right scores—CMP, Y-hat slope, = 1.003; Castles and Mair = 1.010; Laver and Hunt = 1.009; and Huber and Inglehart = .994.

5

Information or Error?
Reliability of Policy Time Series

The preceding chapter examined variation on our standard Left-Right scale and showed that it is a valid measure, in the main. The measurements provide the kinds of distinctions between parties which are useful for making comparisons across time and across nations.

Stated in a concise way, the measured Left-Right positions have this form.

$Position_{it} = Ideological\ Home_{it} + Dynamic\ Movement_{it} + Specific\ Forces_{it} + Noise_{it}.$

The position of party i at time t reflects its ideological home position, which will be signalled in large part (but not entirely, depending on the remaining terms) by something like its family affiliation (Communist, Social Democrat, ..., Conservative, and Nationalist). For various reasons—electoral strategy, changes in party leadership, etc.—parties move around their home area from one election to the next. Positions are also influenced by specific forces, such as the nation-specific circumstances of an open or closed economy and varying degrees of cross-cutting or reinforcing cleavages, among many others. These are the measurements' main elements. The details matter too. In this chapter, we want to focus on the details with our attention concentrated on the last element in the measurements, noise.

Anything more than a cursory glace at the comparative over-time mapping of policy movements in established democracies (Budge et al. 2001: 19–50; McDonald and Budge 2005: 68–70) reveals that nearly all parties are anchored in their home location, seldom leapfrogging other parties in the system. But almost all of them show substantially more variation across time than most observers would have anticipated—certainly much more than is evident in expert surveys. Some part of that within-party variation reflects erratic party behaviour, but another part reflects measurement error. Here, we provide as thorough an evaluation as we can of how much measurement error exists in the CMP Left-Right scores.

RELIABILITY: GENERAL

Overall Considerations

How much can one rely on the Left-Right scores to tell us about 'real' party differences and movements? That is one way to put the issue of measurement reliability;

measurements need to be accurate. No one has definite information on what the real and accurate positions of parties are. Hence, the empirical observation of reliable Left-Right measurements partitions variation of the measured qualities into parts that are reproducible by independent observations versus ones that are not reproducible. If a measured observation of a phenomenon can be reproduced time and again, we can rely on it. If, however, we cannot reproduce it, we cannot really rely on the score we recorded because it depends on how we measured what we observed rather than on what we observed.

In technical terms, reliability can be stated in a formula. We start with the simple fact that

$$Measured\ Score_{it} = True\ Score_{it} + Error_{it}$$

The measured score of party i at time t is a result of what we truly want to measure plus random errors of measurement. We do not have a record of the true score and that shortcoming forces us to evaluate reliability as a relative matter based on the variances of scores. In theory,

$$Reliability = var_{\text{true}}/var_{\text{measured}}$$

and in fact

$$Reliability = var_{\text{reproducible}}/var_{\text{measured}}$$

where *var* refers to the variation in scores.

This fact has two important implications. First, it means that reliability estimates depend on the degree of variance in what has been observed. If all parties have, hypothetically, five units of error and we are looking at the entire range of parties, from die-hard Communists to staunch Conservatives, the estimated reliability is much higher than if we restrict our view to parties in a single family. That is, estimating reliability on the basis of all parties generally, within and across families with a wide coverage of nations, contains a good deal of between-family and cross-national variation. Five units of error per party, hypothetically speaking, would pale in comparison to the total variation found among all kinds of parties in many nations. On the other hand, five units of error might be a substantial portion of error for any one party that is wandering around the vicinity of its Left-Right home space. In the first case, the proverbial glass looks nearly filled with reproducible variation given all of the observed variation, but, on the other, only half full with respect to variation of a single party. Scrutiny of the scores of a single party makes a critic say there is too much error for confidence. But application of the scores involving many parties bolsters one's confidence a great deal. In sum, reliability coefficients are relative statements, depending very much on the total variation being observed.

The other important implication of the reliability formula as estimated in practice, in contradistinction to theory, is that reliability estimation concentrates on reproducible variation. The label 'measurement error' tends to make one think first of a faulty instrument. But, as we have said, two sources of noise arise when measuring party positions. One comes from the erratic behaviour of the parties themselves and the other comes from measurement error. Commentary on erratic party behaviour has a long tradition. A party 'cannot be defined in terms of its principles' (Schumpeter 1962: 283). Parties are 'ever hungry for new members' (Michels 1949: 374). Parties are motivated by a specific goal of maximizing votes (Downs 1957: 30). Parties engage in a political strategy that 'appears to center on finding out what the public wants to hear and marketing the product accordingly' (Farrell and Webb 2000: 122).

Thus, unpredictable party positions are not necessarily a product solely of the measuring instrument. In what is surely the best-known investigation of measurement error in political science, Philip Converse's thesis of *non-attitudes* among the American public arose from his estimation of measurement error in mass attitudes. Finding a lot of it, Converse indicted the public's inconsistent self-reported attitudes as its source (Converse 1964, 1970), a verdict he stands by thirty-six years later despite attempts by others to indict the measurement instrument (Converse 2000). In short, reliability evaluations depend on the quality of the models we have for predicting (reproducing) what has been measured.

Approaches

Reliability of the CMP Left-Right scores could be estimated through four general approaches: (*a*) multiple coders, (*b*) alternative forms of measuring Left-Right, (*c*) split halves, and (*d*) retest. Each of these has played some role in previous attempts to evaluate how reliable the CMP data are.

Having multiple coders of the same document is instructive and has been employed in several, limited instances. Just after the coding frame was created (1978–9), members of the MRG were understandably anxious about the instructions being intelligible and uniformly applied. Many therefore carried out check-codes on their national data-set with satisfactory results—conventionally at that time over 90 per cent coincidence between individual coding decisions (Budge, Robertson, and Hearl (eds.) 1987: 23–4, 48, 78, 119, 140, 183, 237, 276, 332, 355, 375). The German data 'at the lower scale of tolerance' (301–2) were recoded in the early 1990s. However desirable, employing multiple coders has practical limitations. Five experts recoding each of 3,000 documents and devoting 1–5 hours per document would consume between 15,000 and 75,000 work hours for the coding, to say nothing of the time to train coders and collate the results.

The alternative-form approach to reliability can be operationalized in various ways. For instance, in addition to coding election manifestos, one could code speeches, commercials, and statements sponsored by parties during election campaigns and see how far they produced the same assessments (e.g. of the importance of issues). This, too, has practical limitations in terms of time, organization, and expanse. Another alternative-form approach was undertaken in the previous chapter (and elsewhere) when the CMP data were matched to expert survey results (see Figure 4.1). The limitation here was that the terms of the comparison were defined by the expert surveys and therefore related mostly to the long-term Left-Right reputations of the parties.

The split-halves approach takes the total set of categories that go into a Left-Right score and divides them into two subcomponent scores, each of which is supposed to be an indicator of the same observable concept. These are related to each other, corrected for the reduction in variation due to the subdivision, and result in a reliability estimate. We undertake this form of analysis below.

The retest method assessing how much variation is explained by a plausible model, and how much is not, has been employed in varying ways on several occasions—with the CMP Left-Right scale (Budge et al. 2001: 115–24, 138–40, 243; McDonald 2006; McDonald, Mendés, and Kim 2007). Reported reliabilities have varied between .79 and .94, depending on nations covered, parties included, time periods surveyed, and measurement models employed. The difficulty in retest estimations, as applied to the CMP data, is more theoretical than practical. 'Real' change in party behaviour, including seemingly erratic change, has to be separated from unreliability. We repeat the retest analysis below, with particular attention to alternative assumptions about how parties 'really' change positions.

The reliability assessments here proceed through six steps. In sequence, we (*a*) create a series of split-halves tests, (*b*) estimate a full-scale retest reliability, (*c*) hone the full-scale test by using the Heise (1969) model of retest reliability, (*d*) investigate the credibility of the assumptions about change that undergird the Heise model, (*e*) use estimations from Budge's model (1994) of change to look specifically at the apparent errors in measured positions nation-by-nation and party-by-party, and (*f*) close the circle from validity to reliability and back to validity by showing how well the measurements perform when predicting actions by governments.

RELIABILITY: SPLIT HALVES

Left-Right is measured on the basis of twenty-six policy categories. These have been recombined into five sets of mutually exclusive split-halves measured by random assignment of six or seven left and right categories, after which each left sub-summation was subtracted from its respective right sub-summation. For example, the first set of split-halves randomly assigned seven left items to create one sub-form—i.e., Left1a = per104 + per305 + per401 + per402 + per407 + per603 + per605. The remaining six categories formed a second sub-form—i.e., Left1b = per201 + per203 + per414 + per505 + per601 + per606. Similarly, seven categories were randomly selected for the first Right half—i.e., Right1a = per103 + per105 + per106 + per406 + per413 + per504 + per701—and the remainder formed its second sub-form— i.e., Right1b = per107 + per202 + per403 + per404 + per412 + per506. Subtracting the respective sub-forms creates two split-halve Left-Right measures—i.e., Left-Right1a = Right1a − Left1a, and Left-Right1b = Right1b − Left1b.[1]

Table 5.1. Factor analysis of ten split-halves measure-ments of the MRG/CMP Left-Right scale

	Split-halve	Loading	Communality
1a	Left-Right a1	.831	.690
2a	Left-Right a2	.778	.605
1b	Left-Right b1	.792	.628
2b	Left-Right b2	.869	.755
3a	Left-Right c1	.767	.589
3b	Left-Right c2	.833	.694
4a	Left-Right d1	.794	.631
4b	Left-Right d2	.786	.617
5a	Left-Right e1	.759	.576
5b	Left-Right e2	.850	.723

The final result is ten split-halves measurements of Left-Right. The results of a principal component analysis of these ten half forms, using all established Western democracies in the CMP data-set,[2] are shown in Table 5.1. To generalize, the estimated reliability of the Left-Right measurements is about .78. Each component loading is, itself, about .8, and therefore each has a communality of about .64. Once we correct those communalities for the fact that split-halves have less variance than the overall, twenty-six category measurement, the reliability in each instance is about .78.[3]

RELIABILITY: RETEST

The CMP scores parties at each election. That makes it possible to estimate reliability through the retest method, where each party's measured position at one election is 'retested' in relationship to its measurement at one or more subsequent elections. This has been done several times in several different ways (Budge et al. 2001: 243; Hearl 2001; McDonald and Mendés 2001; McDonald 2006; McDonald, Mendés, and Kim 2007). The major complication in retest analysis is being able to separate actual changes in party positions from differences due to errors of measurement. Here, we re-perform retest analyses and give special attention to (*a*) how estimated reliability varies depending on assumptions used to separate actual and measurement error changes and (*b*) how the measurement error estimates vary across nations and parties.

A Preliminary Model

A full-scale and easy application to retest analysis uses data on all parties with long-term series, late 1940s through early 2000s ($N = 975$),[4] and relates each one's current position to its immediately preceding position. The result is

$$Position_{it} = -1.7 + .675\, Position_{it-1}, \text{ with } R^2 = .467.$$

$$(.55)\ \ (.023)$$

where *Position* is party *i*'s position at the current (*t*) and preceding election (*t* − 1). The .675 slope tells us that if party positions are perfectly stable so that all differences are due to measurement errors, then nearly one-third of the variation (.325, from 1 − .675) is due to error. Stated the other way around, .675 of the variation is reliable, since assuming a true slope of 1.0, perfect stability, the less than 1.0 value estimated would have been discounted only due to errors of measurement (i.e. reliability = true slope/estimated slope). If, however, the measurements are perfectly reliable, then 32.5 per cent of the variation in positions is due to actual change in party positions. Surely, the truth lies somewhere in-between—either perfect stability or perfect reliability. Possibly, therefore, we could be looking at 10 per cent of the variation due to real change, and thus we could be looking at a reliability of .75 (.675/.9). If actual change accounts for 20 per cent of the variation, then reliability is .84 (.675/.8). And, if as much as 30 per cent of the variation is actual change, then the measured positions are almost totally reliable (.675/.7 = .96). In the end, the reliability has to be above .67 and, if the dynamic analysis from Chapter 4 is accepted as giving an accurate view of actual change, which amounts to about 20 per cent of the total, then the reliability is around .84.

Heise Model

David Heise created a retest measurement model expressly designed to separate reliability and stability estimates (Heise 1969). He accomplished this by working in a causal modelling framework, requiring three successive measurements, and assuming (*a*) constant reliability at all three time points,[5] (*b*) a Markovian change process, which holds that a party's current position is what matters to where it might move at the next election, (*c*) whatever external forces cause parties to move between times one and two are unrelated to whatever causes them to move between times two and three, and (*d*) measurement errors are uncorrelated across time with either themselves or with the 'true' scores.

The wealth of CMP data, across nearly sixty years, allows the Heise estimations to be performed in a large number of ways. Originally (McDonald and Mendés 2001: 139) applied it to a three-wave panel of elections closest to 1984, 1989, and 1993, getting an estimate of .94. A three-wave panel of elections closest to 1975, 1985, and 1995 in 19 nations (76 parties in all) produced a reliability of .83, a result consistent with the split-halve analysis above. We next applied it to a three-wave panel of elections closest to 1955, 1965, and 1975 among the same seventy-six parties. The result is a reliability of .75, a little lower than alternative estimations but similar. The two other possibilities for equally spaced three-wave estimates among the set of five panel waves—1965–1975–1985 and 1955–1975–1995—signal cause for alarm. The 1965–1975–1985 reliability is an unacceptably low .54 and the 1955–1975–1995 is an unacceptable .52.

What might account for the mixed results? One possibility is that the measurements in the more recent period, 1975–95, are more reliable. But that does not explain the good reliability in the 1955–75 timeframe. A more likely possibility is that something changed fundamentally between 1965 and 1985. A check on the assumptions shows that the residuals from the 1965 scores predicted from the 1955 scores are statistically significantly and negatively correlated with the residuals from the 1985 scores predicted from the 1975 scores, in violation of the assumptions of the Heise model. That raises the strong possibility that there was some form of fundamental change in party Left-Right positioning that runs contrary to a change process describable as Markovian. It is as if some common force entered the world of these parties—e.g., the oil shocks and associated stagflation—that caused the parties to change in unpredictable ways.

Whatever the particular cause, the mixed results raise the very real possibility that the Heise model does not ever and always allow the correct approach to separate stability and reliability—or, otherwise stated, separate actual party change from measurement error. When its assumptions are met, we have reliability estimates from .80 to .94. When the assumptions are violated, the reliability estimate seems itself unreliable.

Errors: The Flip Side

Observed reliability estimates, as we remarked earlier, are calculated as variance ratios. There is thus a temptation to take a reliability coefficient to mean that each score of each party in each nation is, say, 90 per cent on the mark but has ±10 per cent error. But this has to be resisted. The variance ratios are not saying that. Indeed, reliability, taken alone, does not tell us much about errors in measurement for national party systems or individual parties. Communist parties might be mostly consistent, whereas mass parties might be taking quite varied positions in their search, as some theories suggest, for the median voter. Ten per cent of 10 units of variation gives errors of ±1 units, but 10 per cent of 80 units of variation means errors of ±8 units.[6]

With the proper model of change, we could identify the amount of error for nations and parties and that is what we attempt below. We say attempt because, to repeat, error identification is conditional upon having the proper model of change.

We know from Budge's analysis (1994) of parties in twenty nations that the predominant process of change in the CMP data has parties staying in their own ideological neighbourhood but frequently zigzagging from one election to the next. Budge calls this an Alternation Model of party movement, where parties alter policy priorities in different directions between elections. A leftward shift in the current election is followed by a rightward shift at the next. This is consistent with the negative residual correlation we found in the 1965–85 period when checking on the assumptions of the Heise model. It is also consistent with a re-check of the full-scale model that estimated the relationship between current and immediately past positions for 1975 cases. There, too, the residuals at one election and the next are statistically significantly negatively correlated ($r = -.19$, $t = 5.8$). And it is also consistent with the fact which an equation which includes a lag position across two and three elections shows that a party's current position is related not just to the preceding elections but to the additional lag positions as well, though the effect attenuates over time.

$$Position_{it} = -.84 + .39\,Position_{it-1} + .27\,Position_{it-2} + .16\,Position_{it-3}, \quad R^2 = .541.$$

$$(.52)\ (.03)\ (.03)\ \ (.03)$$

The zigzag pattern with its negatively correlated residuals and the lag-two and lag-three effects are contrary to a Markovian change process, because a current position near the centre but more centrist than at the preceding election suggests the party is expected to move back towards its preceding, less centrist position. Or, in other words, how a party moves depends on where it is currently *and* where it was at the preceding election and the one before that. Given these tendencies, one has to believe the dynamics uncovered in Chapter 4 understate the full dynamics because the alternations make it more difficult to uncover trends in the data. Some substantial part of a party's variation—at least of some parties' variation—involves back and forth fluctuations.

Here, we adopt a variation of the Alternation Model and estimate change as a consequence of a party's position at the preceding election plus a time-trend term. That is,

$$Position_{it} = a + \beta Position_{it-1} + \lambda Time_{it} + \varepsilon_{it}.$$

The model is applied to each party series separately rather than estimating an alternation or trend for all parties generally, as an alternation or trend for one party may be moving in a direction opposite that of another.

Assuming the Alternation Model captures all that is important and systematic about party position changes, the residuals record remaining errors. These have been aggregated by nation, Table 5.2, and by individual parties, Table 5.3.

Errors in two nations stand out most especially, Finland and Iceland. Typically, the standard deviation or errors after estimating party positions from the Alternation Model is about 13 units. The average in Finland is 20.8, and in Iceland it is 18.3. There are several possible reasons for this. One is that these party systems are more fickle than others in Left-Right terms. Another possibility is that because these two nations have the lowest average number of quasi-sentences in their manifestos, it is more difficult to score the parties accurately. There may also be nation-specific issues that cross-cut parties of the Left and Right in a manner different from how those issues operate elsewhere. Two candidates in this regard are political authority (category 305) and social harmony (category 606). All parties in Iceland give at least twice as much emphasis to political authority compared to the average party. In Finland, all but the SSDP give more than average emphasis to political authority. The SSDP is quite varied in the emphasis it gives to social harmony; throughout the post-war period it averages five times more emphasis in its manifestos than the average party. Two other nations that stand out on the high side are Ireland and Australia. Their parties, too, score high on emphasis to political authority and social harmony.

Table 5.2. Variation of within party errors, by country [a]

Country	Std. Dev. of Errors	N
Sweden	13.3	85
Norway	8.0	81
Denmark	11.7	104
Finland	20.8	66
Iceland	18.3	52
Belgium	9.9	54
Netherlands	10.3	56
Luxembourg	11.4	43
France	12.5	36
Italy	11.8	71
Germany	12.1	42
Austria	15.7	46
Switzerland	12.4	55
Great Britain	12.0	42
Ireland	16.6	48
USA	9.1	26
Canada	8.8	51
Australia	16.0	64
New Zealand	12.0	38
Total	13.1	1,060

[a]Estimation of predictable variation based on Alternation Model as estimated for each party separately, where the Alternation Model is specified as

$$Position_{it} = \alpha + \beta Position_{it-1}, + \lambda Time_{it} + \varepsilon_{it}.$$

A reanalysis of Left-Right reliability, where Left-Right is calculated without the addition of political authority and social harmony and assuming that 20 per cent variation in party positions records true movements, produces a reliability coefficient of .91. But we are not prepared to declare that the two categories do not belong to the Left-Right calculation. Rather the point has been to present in great detail the amount of error that might exist in the CMP Left-Right scores, *given a particular model of change and thereby assuming that movements not covered by the model leave only measurement errors.*

What can one make of the individual party estimates of error? To make any use of them, one has to start with some model of change. The simplest model would be to assume that all movement is error. That is the naive model (null hypothesis model) that stands behind the investigation of dynamics in Chapter 4 and the Alternation Model used in this chapter. If one finds a series of elections runs consistently above or below the party mean at a level beyond two times the quantity of the errors divided by the square root of number of observations on the party (both *s* and *N* are reported in Table 5.3) there is evidence of a persistent shift. Persistent shifts by this definition appear in the USA Republican series before and after Ronald Reagan and in Britain's Conservative Party series before and after Margaret Thatcher. On the other side, Democrats and Labour, shifts by this

Table 5.3. Variation of within party errors, by party [a]

Party	Std. Dev. of Errors	N
SWE: Vp Left Party	4.3	17
SWE: SdaP Social Democratic Labour Party	14.4	17
SWE: FP Liberal Peoples Party	19.8	17
SWE: MSP Moderate Conservative Party	15.2	17
SWE: CP Centre Party	8.9	17
NOR: SV Socialist Left Party	8.7	14
NOR: DNA Labour Party	6.3	14
NOR: V Liberal Party	10.0	14
NOR: KrF Christian Peoples Party	8.7	14
NOR: H Conservative Party	9.9	14
NOR: SP Centre Party	6.2	14
DEN: DKP Communist Party	12.4	19
DEN: SD Social Democratic Party	11.5	22
DEN: RV Radical Party	9.2	22
DEN: V Liberals	11.8	22
DEN: KF Conservative Peoples Party	14.9	22
FIN: SKDL Peoples Democratic Union	18.7	16
FIN: SSDP Social Democrats	23.6	14
FIN: KK National Coalition	24.6	12
FIN: SK Finnish Centre	19.4	14
FIN: RKP SFP Swedish Peoples Party	19.4	14
ICE: Ab Peoples Alliance	15.4	9
ICE: A Social Democratic Party	13.0	15
ICE: Sj Independence Party	17.7	16
ICE: F Progressive Party	27.1	12
BEL: SP Flemish Socialist Party	10.7	17
BEL: PS Francophone Socialist Party	10.8	17
BEL: VLD Flemish Liberals and Democrats	12.2	17
BEL: PRL Francophone Liberals	11.4	17
BEL: CVP Christian Peoples Party	6.3	17
BEL: PSC Christian Social Party	7.9	17
NET: PvdA Labour Party	10.3	17
NET: VVD Peoples Party for Freedom and Democracy	8.8	17
NET: KVP Catholic Peoples Party	14.5	17
NET: ARP Anti-Revolutionary Party	8.0	17
NET: CHU Christian Historical Union	13.9	17
LUX: PCL KPL Communist Party	14.6	9
LUX: POSL LSAP Socialist Workers Party	12.0	12
LUX: PD DP Democratic Group	9.5	10
LUX: PCS CSV Chr Social Peoples Party	11.3	12
FRA: PCF Communist Party	13.8	14
FRA: PS Socialist Party	11.3	14
FRA: Gaullists	13.3	11
ITA: PCI-PDS Democratic Party of the Left	12.1	11
ITA: PSI Socialist Party	12.9	10
ITA: PSDI Democratic Socialist Party	5.9	9

Table 5.3. (*Continued*)

Party	Std. Dev. of Errors	N
ITA: PRI Republican Party	12.8	9
ITA: PLI Liberal Party	16.6	11
ITA: DC-PPI Italian Popular Party	5.5	11
ITA: AN National Alliance	15.4	10
GER: SPD Social Democratic Party	9.0	14
GER: FDP Free Democratic Party	10.1	14
GER: CDU-CSU Christian Democrats	16.7	14
AUT: SPO Social Democratic Party	13.6	16
AUT: FPO Freedom Movement	18.2	14
AUT: OVP Peoples Party	16.4	16
SWI: SPS PSS Social Democratic Party	10.4	14
SWI: FDP PRD Radical Democratic Party	12.0	14
SWI: CVP PDC Christian Dem Peoples Party	14.0	14
SWI: SVP UDC Peoples Party	14.3	13
UK: Labour Party	13.4	15
UK: Liberal Party	13.7	15
UK: Conservative Party	10.2	15
IRE: LP Labour Party	9.5	16
IRE: Fine Gael	20.6	16
IRE: Fianna Fail	18.8	16
USA: Democratic Party	7.6	13
USA: Republican Party	10.7	13
CAN: NDP New Democratic Party	8.8	17
CAN: LP Liberal Party	9.0	17
CAN: PCP Progressive Conservative Party	9.0	17
AUL: ALP Labour Party	12.4	22
AUL: LPA Liberal Party	16.1	22
AUL: NPA National Party	19.8	20
NEW: LP Labour	8.7	19
NEW: NP National Party	14.8	19
Total	12.9	1,153

[a] Estimation of predictable variation based on Alternation Model as estimated for each party separately, where the Alternation Model is specified as

$$Position_{it} = \alpha + \beta Position_{it-1}, + \lambda Time_{it} + \varepsilon_{it}.$$

yardstick occur before and after Jimmy Carter (beginning in 1984 and 1988, not just with Bill Clinton, who appears to have completed rather than started the shift) and before and after Tony Blair, though presaged by Neil Kinnock's reform tendencies in 1987. A similar judgement could be reached about the German CDU's shift to the right while out of power in the 1970s. And the list could go on. The point is that with a baseline idea of, in these examples, no change, the error estimates provide a basis for placing a confidence interval of mean values on the individual party series to ask whether two-three-four- ... election shifts lie persistently outside the bounds of error.

Alternatively, one could look at the possibility of alternation, zigzagging, in a similar way. Assume as a baseline idea that there has been no change and then check on whether the individual party series fluctuates above and then below its average position in a manner beyond two times the standard error of the mean.

It helps tremendously to have a baseline model and an actual model of change in mind; otherwise investigating change versus error can too easily cross the line between analysis and data mining. But, then, what is one to do about assessing one-off abrupt movements? The types of error-versus-change analyses just described assumed one is looking for shifts that persist for two, three, four, or more elections, using a confidence interval around a mean value.

To look at one-off abrupt shifts, a confidence interval around the individual data point is what is needed. For that, one needs to use a value of two times the errors reported in Table 5.3. Those errors are, so far as we can tell, the standard deviations around individual scores. Where there is a greater than two standard deviation shift, there is a strong indication that one is looking at a shift beyond what could normally be attributed to error. The Goldwater shift in the USA 1964 election is a case in point. Schroder's centrist tendency as leader of Germany's SPD in 1998 is another. Michael Foot's Labour Party lurch to the Left in 1983 is a good candidate, and the lurch is recorded in the CMP data. But it would not pass this two-times-error test. While we are not prepared to write-off Labour's position in 1983 as 'just so much error', in a structured analysis with a black-or-white decision rule, one could make a case for no real change (beyond what might be reasonably attributed to error).

The useful news is that the error estimates can be used in a variety of ways to look at error versus change in individual estimates, short series, and long series. How one should approach the data, it probably could go without saying, is influenced a great deal by the model of change one carries into the analysis and the depth of information one has about the party or parties under investigation.

FINAL CONSIDERATIONS

In the final analysis, the issue of good measurement, reliability and, before that, validity, comes down to whether the measurements can be used profitably to analyse politics and policy. Unreliable measurements attenuate estimated relationships; thus to the extent unreliability gets in the way, analyses using poor measurements inform analyses in weak ways. Invalid measurements measure concepts other than those intended and except by accident have little to tell us about theoretically important relationships. In this final analysis, we exploit what we know happens with poor measurements by reviewing and previewing analyses of policy choices by governments. The first looks at a series of policy positions taken by US presidents, the second looks at a series of cross-sectional analyses of government spending.

US Presidential Policy Positions

James Stimson and his colleagues have constructed models of dynamic representation and, more generally, of the macro-polity in the USA (Stimson, MacKuen, and Erikson 1995; Erikson, MacKuen, and Stimson 2001). One of their indicators is presidential position taking on legislation before the US Congress. This serves well as a policy indicator predictable from US party manifestos (aka party platforms in the USA), because it has a faster-paced dynamic than actual policy (McDonald, Budge, and Hofferbert 1999). That last analysis demonstrated that presidential policy position taking is predictable from a dummy variable indicating which party controls the presidency *and* the party position taken by the controlling party in the preceding election. Now we want to predict the presidential policy position from three different measurements of policy positions without the party dummy.

The three measurements are the CMP election-by-election Left-Right scores, the smoothed estimate of party positions developed by Stimson (see Stimson, ND), and the smoothed positions estimated above on the basis of the Budge Alternation Model. Figure 5.1 shows how each measurement tracks the party positions from 1956 through 2000. Taken at face value, the CMP scores appear more reasonable than the others (to us, at least). The shift to the right in 1964, when the conservative wing of the Republican party won control and nominated Goldwater, is reflected in the CMP data but all but missed by the smoothed measurements based on the Stimson and Budge models. Furthermore, the abrupt shift to the right by Republicans in 1980, under the leadership of Ronald Reagan, is apparent in the CMP data but muted in the smoothed measurements. And, finally, the strong shift towards the right—to the right-centre—by Democrats when they nominated Bill Clinton in 1992 and again in 1996 shows up in the CMP data but, again, is muted in the Stimson–Budge measures.

Face-value assessments and apparently accurate measurements are interesting, but how well does each work as an actual predictor of policy? The results of three separate analyses, Table 5.4, show all three measurements have predictive power. Perhaps surprisingly, however, the smoothed measurements based on the Budge Alternation Model provide a better fit than the CMP scores and the Stimson smoothed measurements. For any final determination of which is the 'better' indicator, we would need a firmer theoretical basis for accepting one over the others.

Table 5.4. Estimating US presidential policy positions from three different measurements of party Left-Right positions

	CMP	Stimson	Budge
Intercept	40.8	39.3	43.0
(Std. Error)	(.98)	(1.4)	(.98)
Slope	−.67	−1.01	−.96
(Std. Error)	(.08)	(.10)	(.06)
R^2	.67	.74	.88
s_e	9.6	8.4	5.7

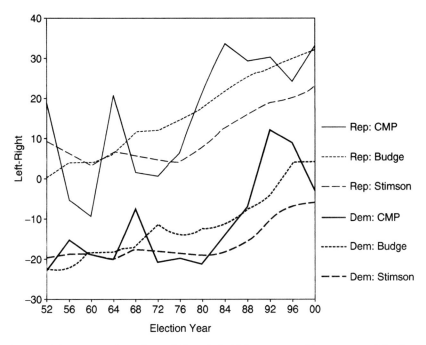

Fig. 5.1. US Democratic and Republican Left-Right party position measured by three methods, 1952–2000

Note: *CMP* = original CMP Left-Right score

Stimson = party position estimation created by Stimson (ND) based on the following formula

$$Position_{it} = .2\,CMP_{it} + .8\,Position_{it-1}$$

where the 1952 position is calculated from .2 times the 1952 CMP recorded position and .8 times the 1948 CMP recorded position.

Budge = the Budge (1994) Alternation Model estimated earlier in this chapter using the formula

$$E\,(Position_{it}) = \alpha + \beta Position_{it-1}, + \lambda Time_{it}$$

As a strictly empirical matter, however, smoothing out some part of the rough edges of the CMP measurements, even though they appear the most credible, can have its advantages.

Cross-national Comparisons of Government Size

Analysis of the role of politics in the choice of public policies has had a chequered history. Reported findings have often found no role for politics, raising the two questions of 'do politics matter' and 'do parties matter?' Difficulties arise in two ways. The first comes from how party positions are measured. The second comes from the slow pace of policy change in contrast to the rapid pace of political change.

Often the colour of government, meaning its Left-Right leaning, is pre-categorized as the percentage of left-party controlled seats in parliaments or governments (e.g. Cameron 1978; Blais, Blake, and Dion 1993). Alternatively, expert party scores are used to create a weighted average of parliamentary or government policy preferences (e.g. Rueda and Pontusson 2000). Either approach to measuring party positions leaves out the dynamics associated with parties changing their positions between elections. And as we have just seen in regard to US presidential policy advocacy, changing positions of parties are important. The slow pace of policy change is an obstacle to uncovering political effects because a change of government from Left control to Right control, or vice versa, cannot reasonably be expected to show itself immediately. Policy choices have a momentum all their own, which is seldom overturned in a year or two—or three or four (McDonald and Budge 2005: 171–97).

These two difficulties have resulted in trace elements for party effects being found in large-scale analyses with data pooled across nations and across time. In more detailed year-by-year or cross-national analysis, however, the role of politics has often been unobservable. A study of government spending by Andre Blais and his colleagues is often cited in this regard (Blais, Blake, and Dion 1993). They show that in a series of twenty-eight cross-sectional analyses, one per year from 1960 through 1987, Left-Right partisanship of governments has virtually no predictive power for government spending. However, after analysing the data aggregated in a pooled cross-national time series, a small partisan effect appears: 'governments of the left spend a little more than those of the right. Parties do make a difference, but a small one. The difference, ... , is confined to majority governments and takes time to set in' (Blais, Blake, and Dion 1993: 57).

We undertake the same form of analysis here. To address the measurement issue we use the CMP data to measure the Left-Right position of the median party in parliament (MPP) and to address the slow pace of policy change we use a twenty-year moving average of the MPP position.[7] The spending data and the centralization control variable cover 1972 through 1995 and come from various reports by the IMF (see McDonald and Budge 2005: 167).

The pooled analysis results are stronger than those reported by Blais et al., but in a similar vein do show a partisan effect.

$$G\$_t = 5.92 + .81G\$_{t-1} + 2.54C - .056MPP\ LR_{MA20}$$

$$\quad\ (.85) \qquad (.03) \qquad\ \ (.39) \qquad\quad (.016)$$

where $G\$_t$ and $G\$_{t-1}$ are variables indicating central government spending as a percentage of GDP in the current and preceding years, C_t is a three-category variable indicating government revenue centralization (-1 = low; 0 = medium; 1 = high), and $MPP\ LR_{MA20}$ is the twenty-year moving average of the MPP Left-Right position. All three independent variables are significantly related to government spending. The slow pace of change is indicated by the .81 coefficient on spending in the previous year. The political effect of a shifting centre of gravity in parliament of, say, ten points on the CMP Left-Right scale (something like from a typical social democratic party's standing to a typical liberal party's standing) is estimated to result in just over a half a percentage point shift (.056 × 10 = .56) in the short-run. In the long-run, however, the effect will be to shift spending by almost three-percentage points—i.e., (.056 / (1 − .81) = .29) and (.29 × 10 = 2.9).

The important payoff from use of the CMP measures comes from year-by-year analyses of cross-sections. The results for the political partisan effect are shown in Table 5.5. Blais and his colleagues found statistically significant effects of governments, at the p < .1 level, in six of twenty-eight years. Worse, in twelve years the estimated effects of the colour of governments ran in the direction opposite to that hypothesized. In Table 5.5, we see all estimated effects are in the proper

Table 5.5. Slope estimates using twenty-year moving average Left-Right positions of median parties in parliament to predict total spending by central governments, controlling for revenue centralization, in successive cross-sections, 1972–95

Year	Slope	t-value
1972	−.17 **	−2.25
1973	−.14	−1.60
1974	−.10	−0.90
1975	−.04	−0.34
1976	−.08	−0.72
1977	−.15	−1.46
1978	−.20 **	−1.85
1979	−.23 **	−1.91
1980	−.23 **	−1.82
1981	−.27**	−1.90
1982	−.28 *	−1.73
1983	−.30 **	−1.87
1984	−.28 *	−1.74
1985	−.29 *	−1.73
1986	−.34 **	−2.37
1987	−.38 ***	−3.05
1988	−.42 ***	−3.63
1989	−.42 ***	−3.22
1990	−.37 **	−2.59
1991	−.34 **	−2.07
1992	−.32 *	−1.67
1993	−.37 *	−1.74
1994	−.31 *	−1.60
1995	−.29 *	−1.42

*p < .1, **p < .05, * * *p < .01.

Sixteen nations: Australia, Austria, Belgium, Canada, Denmark, France, Germany, Ireland, Italy, the Netherlands, New Zealand, Norway, Sweden, Switzerland, the United Kingdom, and the USA.

Missing values on central government spending: Italy 1972 and 1995, New Zealand 1989, and Switzerland 1985–90.

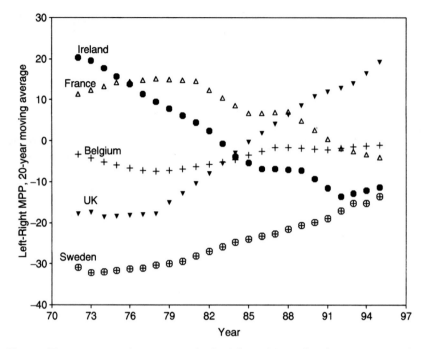

Fig. 5.2. Twenty-year moving averages of Left-Right positions of median parties in parliaments of five nations, 1972–95

direction; in nineteen of twenty-four years the effect is statistically significant, at least at the $p < .1$ level and more often beyond that; and the coefficients themselves are reasonably stable except during the period surrounding the first oil shock of the 1970s. There is not a small and conditional effect of politics on policy but a robust one, in this analysis premised on the CMP Left-Right measurements.

Could all this predictability be the result of washing out dynamic variation in the within-nation political series by using the twenty-year moving average? Not at all. Figure 5.2 serves as a visual check. There we have selected five nations to illustrate how the long-term Left-Right position of MPPs tracks through time. As probably all observers would anticipate, the parliamentary centres in Ireland and France moved from right to left from the early 1970s through the mid-1990s. The parliamentary centre in Britain, as everyone knows, moved from left to right. The parliamentary centre in Sweden underwent a bit of a power shift as the right-of-centre MUP gained ground, while the SDA had its grip on parliament and governments loosened and, itself, moved rightward after 1975. Only in Belgium, among these five nations, is there little movement to report. The CMP Left-Right scores capture the movements and, with that, predict the policy effects.

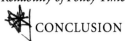CONCLUSION

Few measurements in political science have been subjected to as many checks on their reliability as the CMP Left-Right scale. The repeated evaluations usually show reliability estimates in the range of .8 to .9. These can be taken to mark the low and high points. Reliability of the CMP's Left-Right score is certainly no worse than .8 and possibly a bit better than .9. The sternest and most important test of all, combining concerns for validity with those for reliability, shows the information contained in the CMP Left-Right can profitably be used to understand the politics of the policy process in a single nation through time and across a set of politically diverse nations. Repeated attempts to pursue important theoretical questions of politics and policy where knowledge of the policy positions of parties is crucial will be the ultimate arbiter of both the reach and limitations of the CMP data.

As we have said repeatedly in this chapter, reliability is a relative matter, depending on how much total observable variation there is in a set of scores. That total, in turn, depends on which countries and parties are analysed. As is true for most inferential analyses, the more variation the better—that is, the stronger one's confidence will be in the inferences drawn. With that in mind, we have taken the additional step of looking at the flip side of reliability, the amount of error, and reported these 'errors' by country and by individual party. For any one party there is more error than we would like, but just as surely there is real dynamic variation for at least one-third of the parties. How exactly one chooses to separate errors from actual party movements depends on the model of change one has in mind together with one's knowledge about the party systems under investigation. Making such judgements is helped by the reliability and error checks reported here.

NOTES

1. The four other split-halves are constructed from additional random assignments.
   Left2a = per104 + per203 + per402 + per414 + per601 + per606.
   Left2b = per201 + per305 + per401 + per407 + per505 + per603 + per605.
   Right2a = per105 + per202 + per404 + per406 + per413 + per504.
   Right2b = per103 + per106 + per107 + per403 + per412 + per506 + per701.

   Left3a = per201 + per203 + per305 + per402 + per407 + per601 + per606.
   Left3b = per104 + per401 + per414 + per505 + per603 + per605.
   Right3a = per106 + per202 +per404 + per406 + per413 + per504 + per506.
   Right3b = per103 + per105 + per107 + per403 + per412 + per701.

   Left4a = per201 + per203 + per305 + per402 + per407 + per601.
   Left4b = per104 + per401 + per414 + per505 + per603 + per605 + per606.
   Right4a = per103 + per105 + per106 + per403 + per413 + per701.
   Right4b = per107 + per202 + per404 + per406 + per412 + per504 + per506.

   Left5a = per201 + per203 + per402 + per505 + per601 + per603 + per606.
   Left5b = per104 + per305 + per401 + per407 + per414 + per605.
   Right5a = per103 + per106 + per107 + per403 + per412 + per413 + per504.
   Right5b = per105 + per202 + per404 + per406 + per506 + per701.

2. The nations are Australia, Austria, Belgium, Canadá, Denmark, Finland, France, Germany, Iceland, Ireland, Italy, Luxembourg, the Netherlands, New Zealand, Norway, Portugal, Spain, Sweden, Switzerland, the UK, and the USA.

3. The loadings are the estimated correlation between the measure and the underlying concept—Left-Right. The communalities are the shared variance between the alternative measurements, which, as such, are the reliability estimations. However, splitting the categories into halves reduces the variance of a full-scale left-right measurement and therefore has to be corrected via the Spearman–Brown formula—reliability of full-scale = (2 × reliability of split-half) / (1 + reliability of split-half), or .78 = 1.28 / 1.64.

   No extra leverage is gained by analysing all ten split-halves simultaneously, as opposed to analysing each pair of halves on their own. Either way, the analysis results in communalities around .64.

4. In order to have series of party positions that extend back into the 1950s for application of the Heise model (below) we have dropped Portugal and Spain from the retest analyses (see Note 2). We also treat each of the Belgian Social Democratic, Christian, and Liberal parties that split into language groups as six continuous parties, with each post-split party given the score of its pre-split party. We do something similar for each of the three Dutch parties as three continuous series, with each one receiving the score of the CDA after they combined. Finally, because we later apply two and three election lags to the analysis, for comparability reasons we have here excluded cases that we would lose later when we add the third lag.

5. This assumption could be modified by the Wiley-Wiley three-wave panel model, which assumes the amount of measurement error, not the reliability, is constant across the three waves (Wiley-Wiley 1970). The alternative assumption adds a good deal of complexity to the calculation but usually little difference in results, as the Wiley-Wiley time-two reliability is the same as the constant Heise reliability.

6. If we *were* pressed to give a general estimate of error in individual Left-Right scores it would be ± 4 units on the standard Left-Right scale. This relates to what we have identified as a significant difference between estimated long-term equilibrium and mean values in the previous chapter, and to unpublished research on relationships with other variables showing that cut-off points under this value have only a limited effect on these relationships. Both results imply that moves of ± 4 units on the Left-Right scale, if maintained, are associated with important long-term changes in the party. Any individual move of this magnitude thus has the potential to contribute to real change, as opposed to moves under this magnitude which can be attributed to measurement error masking underlying stability.

7. The choice of twenty-years comes from a .81 estimated per annum stability in total government spending as a percentage of GDP (see below). At that level of stability, it takes about 20 years for 99 per cent of an effect to be incorporated—i.e., $.81^{20} = .01$.

6

Quantifying Policy Emphases in Texts Using the CMP Approach: Comparisons with Alternative Aproaches

INTRODUCTION

Chapter 5 worked down from macro-level assessments of the quality of our main policy indicator to agreement estimates for sub-sets of scores. These are useful for comparing two scores (say for different parties in 1992 or the same party between 1942 and 1997), and deciding whether they are really different or whether their basic identity is masked by error. As the figures show, our measurements are generally reliable, so most differences can be taken as telling us something about real-life politics.

We have however always argued that the major guarantes of our data are to be found in macro-level procedures and controls. This is because the data themselves are always changing, as new elections produce new documents to be coded and integrated into the set, and new countries like CEE democracies are added in. The data in this volume are very different from those in the last, and the basic data-set from which they are drawn has already expanded in 2004 and 2005.

Conventional measures of reliability and validity generally apply to closed, finite sets, like a typical survey collected over a limited time period and over a predetermined set of cases. Once checks and tests are done, they definitively designate the state of the data. Contrast this with the manifesto data where any test-statistic is necessarily provisional and needs to be extrapolated to the data as they are now, not yesterday or ten years ago.

This caution applies even to the statistics presented in Chapter 5, which are as up to date as we can make them and apply across as much of the data as they prudently can. Surveys of experts asked to locate their national parties on a scale can be examined to see what the variability in national judgements has been, and these can be summarized as error estimates for individual figures (leaving aside the broader question of how they compare cross-nationally). But this is because the judgements constitute only a snapshot at one point in time and can be regarded as definitive only because they tell us nothing about dynamics and movement.

It is precisely because of these dynamics and the unique capacity of our data to expand over time that we have put our emphasis on the stability and transparency of procedures for collecting and coding them rather than on any finite statistical checks. A continuous process of gathering and coding needs sound and detailed procedures to guarantee comparability and quality. It is in these rather than on quickly dated, extrapolated tests of inter-coder agreement that confidence in the data is founded. That was the reason why in our previous volume we put so much emphasis on our centrally controlled and carefully worked out coding procedures (Budge et al. 2001: 93–110). Checks for the reliability and validity of the data should match their scope and deal with numbers of countries and parties across decades rather than years (Budge et al. 2001: 111–42).

As procedures and coding have so much importance, we deal with them in the first section of this chapter before going on to related questions of what exactly the data tell us, how they should be organized, and whether they could be collected by other means—computers, for example.

QUANTIFYING ELECTION PROGRAMMES: CODING PROCEDURES AND CONTROLS

In this section we simply summarize Volkens' authoritative account in Chapter 4 of *Mapping Policy Preferences* (Budge et al. 2001). Any reader encountering the data for the first time, or who wants necessary detail should go back to that discussion. With this said we cover the main points about coding and procedures here:

(a) It is clear from the history of the MRG/CMP project outlined earlier that the data collection as a whole falls into two stages—the estimates from 1945 to 1983 coded by members of the MRG and/or assistants working under their supervision[1] and those produced under the CMP from 1983 on. In *Mapping Policy Preferences*, Chapter 5, Hearl in fact takes advantage of this to confirm that analytic results do not differ between the 'MRG data-set' and the full set up to 1996, thus testing the reliability of the estimates holistically.

The data in this volume, from 1990 onwards, have been exclusively produced by the CMP. So, it is CMP procedures we are concerned with here. As we have stressed, exactly the same procedures and direction were employed for the OECD countries and CEE, so formally there is no difference in the status of the two sets of estimates.

(b) The CMP hires coders, usually political scientists from the countries concerned, who are native speakers of the language, to collect the relevant programmes and content analyse them according to the standard scheme described in Appendix II and on the CD-ROM (see also Budge et al. 2001: Appendices II, III, and CD-ROM). Before quantifying the documents, coders are required to study procedures outlined in a printed handbook, which includes actual applications of the scheme to an English language manifesto. After doing so they have to code another English language manifesto blind and send the document to the supervisor in Berlin with the coding decision on each (quasi-)sentence of the document clearly marked. This is compared with the standard coding of a document retained there, and the results are reported back to coders. Those who do well on the test then proceed to production coding. Those who perform poorly are retrained and kept under close supervision from Berlin when they do pass on to production. E-mail allows for regular contact with all coders, discussion of difficult decisions and even decisions being made by the supervisor on sentences translated into English. Copies of the original documents are sent in with every coding decision recorded on them, so they can be subjected to later review and revision if required.

(c) It is impossible to emphasize too strongly that the inter-coder reliability test described above is one taken by trainee coders in the course of their training. It is not a final figure relating to the reliability of the MRG/CMP data as a whole—quite apart from the fact that the test relates only to a single document of the early 1980s (now altered to one of the mid-1960s). Unfortunately, the overall 0.72 correlation between trainee results, and their variation in performance, has on occasions been misquoted as figures for agreement between trained coders (e.g. in Laver, Benoit, and Garry 2003: 317). This is clearly misleading since the reliability of the final codings, due to the procedures followed, is much higher particularly in the cases of those who performed more poorly on the test. Correlations for coders who undertook another contract and redid the test document average 0.88.

Neither of these figures apply to actual production coding of course. It is in any case misleading to regard inter-coder reliability as a direct measure of the reliability of the indicators themselves. Inter-coder agreement at best can only be regarded as an indirect check on the actual estimates. It belongs more properly to the actual procedures of coding as feedback on the quality of what is being done. Reliability and validity of indicators themselves are better assessed on the basis of their actual performance within the data-set.

Conventional content analyses can produce final figures for inter-coder agreement because they usually deal with a finite set of documents in the same language. Such tests were performed for individual countries by the original MRG investigators with satisfactory results (Budge, Robertson, and Hearl (eds.) 1987: 23–4 and passim). Clearly, however, what we would most like to know is whether, for example, Portuguese documents from the 1970s are being coded in the same way as Lithuanian ones from the 1990s—and so on for all the country/language documents covered.

Constraints of time and resources, space, and compatibility of linguistic knowledge clearly render this comparative check impossible—as it also does for 'expert' surveys of party stands, of course. So far as reliability is concerned our main trust has to be put in standardized procedures and close communication between coder and supervisor. This does not of course eliminate error altogether—particularly between smaller and more ambiguous coding categories. We shall be outlining procedures for dealing with this below. As we saw in Chapter 5, general reliability estimates can be associated with individual figures in our data-set. But it is always a wise precaution to discount small differences or changes over time, which is what a mechanical reliability estimate would lead one to do anyway.

However, one feature of our data also helps in sorting out genuine changes and differences from others. This is its over-time and comparative nature. If overall patterns can be discerned from a broad spread of data, showing that small differences fit into an overall tendency, then they can certainly be given more credence. This is in fact what various researchers have done. A good example is Adams (2001), whose theory of party competition leads to a prediction of Left-Right movements by each party alternating at each election. The prediction can be checked against overall tendencies in the data which do in fact take on this form.

Seen in this broad context, reliability figures for each individual estimate seem of limited importance. Given the over-time and comparative nature of the data-set, it is difficult to conceive of uses being made of it which depend crucially on a single estimate rather than general tendencies and patterns. Most analyses are in fact examinations of multivariate relationships which generate their own error statistics. We ourselves would certainly advise readers to build on these particular strengths in addressing reliability questions—while discounting small individual differences just as a more formal measure would do.

Building on these considerations *Mapping Policy Preferences*, Chapters 5 and 6 carried through holistic reliability and validity checks on broad patterns in the data. Derek Hearl repeated the factor analyses reported in Budge, Robertson, and Hearl (eds.) (1987) with the full data-set up to 1996, and confirmed that results were essentially the same, testifying to the stability of estimates through the transfer from the MRG to CMP. McDonald and Mendés (Table 6.1) reported results for the Heise (1969) measurement model applied to various Left-Right scales produced from MRG data and confirm that the main ones are reliable, while allowing for meaningful movement. Chapter 5 extended this treatment to reliability statistics which can be applied to each individual estimate. From these it also appears that the data-set taken as a whole is reliable, and passes tests which estimates subject to more conventional assessments have yet to undergo.

WHAT DO THE MANIFESTO ESTIMATES TELL US?

As indicated by the title of the earliest MRG publication, *Ideology, Strategy & Party Change* (Budge, Robertson, and Hearl (eds.) 1987), party programmes and the derived numeric estimates have been regarded within this project as indicating how party 'identity and programmatic themes are mixed to capture electoral consent' (Pelizzo 2003: 87). In other words, they reflect *both* strategic considerations of how to shape policy positions in the current election so as to consolidate or attract votes, and the constraints imposed by long-standing ideology. Ideology imposes limits from which parties only rarely break out, because of leadership commitments and core electoral attachments. These assumptions have formed a framework for studies of strategic movement by parties (Budge 1994: Adams 2001; Adams et al. 2004).

Perhaps because of the influence of Downs (1957) and our consequent concern to map party policy manoeuvres, the idea that specific party programmes should wholly and faithfully reflect party ideology never occurred to us until the issue was raised by Pelizzo (2003). The expectation that programmes must stably reflect underlying ideology may however explain why some analysts such as Kitschelt (1994: 139) rejected the manifesto estimates as invalid, because they put the French Socialists left of the Communists in 1962 and 1973. This is in contrast to 'party family' classifications or expert judgements which locate Communists invariantly to the left of Socialists.

From the point of view of most analysts, however, this is precisely the strength of the MRG/CMP data. They do reveal party movement and change over time, as well as variation in the extent to which individual members of the same party family may formulate policy on the basis of their ideology (Chapter 4). Instead of invalidating the estimates, this variation provides unique substantive information on individual party positions and over-time movements—which expert judgements, rooted in a panoramic view of the party system based on Left-Right ideology, are incapable of providing.

Pelizzo's argument proceeds by identifying anomalies in first Italian and then in other national parties' specific placements on the MRG Left-Right scale[2]— anomalies that is, in terms of the parties' general and ascribed ideology. After resolving questions about the validity of the estimates, he then however reasons through to the conclusion quoted above—that in fact programmes are not a pure reflection of ideology but are instead prompted by a mixture of strategic and ideological considerations. This is indeed the perspective we started from and have continued with. We are glad to have it confirmed by detailed analysis.

This exchange highlights two additional points which have come up in other analyses:

(a) Convergent validation of the manifesto data with the main alternative measure of party position—expert judgements—have found a tendency for extreme parties of the Left or Right to be placed at surprisingly moderate policy positions on the basis of their programmes (e.g. the Italian MSI-AN, Danish Progress, French FN, Communists, and so on) (cf. Gabel and Huber 2000). On reflection, these placements again tell us less about the validity of the data than provide substantive information. Extreme parties competing in elections will naturally present a more moderate image to attract votes. To establish a claim to run government they also have to venture outside their specialized issues and comment on the whole nexus of domestic and international problems—on many of which of course they do not necessarily have extreme positions. They also support extensive government intervention to strengthen the nation. All of these pressures on programme writing raise an expectation that their declared policy positions will be more moderate than their general image, and may indicate that in the long run the parties become more moderate in themselves. Some established parties like the Swedish Conservatives for similar strategic reasons may take up more extreme positions than those indicated by their general image. Some such variation may surely be expected and constitutes reliable information once the general validity of the estimates is established.

(b) Related to the points made about extremist parties is the tendency of new parties (not necessarily extremist ones) to change positions a lot on policies beyond their immediate concerns. This will register as strongly alternating movement in their first 2–3 elections. Eventually, however, they establish a settled stance on a wide range of issues and take up more stable positions. This is clearly evident for some of the CEE parties examined in Chapter 1—though perhaps the more surprising finding is that some parties took up fairly stable policy stances from the first election on.

    Stability of course is a relative concept. As Pelizzo concluded, programmes will always show some movement owing to specific and strategic pressures. We would however be disconcerted if the Italian Communists' average positions over time were not to the left, the DC in the centre, and the ANs to the right. It is to their mean or median values over time on the Left-Right and other scales that we should look for the underlying ideological tendencies in parties. We have already reported these figures for the OECD countries (Budge et al. 2001, Figure 2.1: 54–6) and for the CEE (see Policy Scales Data-Set on the CD-ROM). High correlations have always been shown between MRG mean positions and expert judgements of party location (Budge et al. 2001: 136–7) because of course the mean figures pick up the ideological leanings which form the basis of the experts' judgements. The two sets of estimates are very closely correlated. This finding should serve to counter criticisms that the MRG estimates fly in the face of ideological positioning. They do not. But they have the additional merit of tracing policy variation around these ideological positions over time. Analysts should always be careful to distinguish between a party's policy position in any one election and its underlying ideological tendency (mean, median, or range of scores on the Left-Right scale).

    It follows from the variation in policy options offered at specific elections that parties stress different items from their ideological repertoire at different times. As noted, when we discussed the basis and composition of the Left-Right scale (Table 1.1), a pure leftist position groups together emphases on peaceful internationalism, government social and economic intervention, and welfare in general. The rightist end groups together emphases on a strong military posture internationally, with emphases on order and tradition and freedom and rights domestically.

    It is of course perfectly possible for parties to elevate one of these themes over the others in any particular election. If electors are more concerned about international than economic themes or vice versa, parties might well be concerned for strategic reasons to emphasize one over the other at a particular election or even for a series of elections. So long as they are not actively repudiating the themes they do not stress, they can probably get away with the new emphases without alienating too many activists and supporters. They also have flexibility in that other issues, not traditional Left-Right ones, can be brought into the current policy package thus diluting Left-Right content overall.

If the Left-Right scale were a posteriori and inductive and based on factor-analyses of our data-set at a given time, these different stresses and emphases might lead to concerns about the representation being dated and new dimensions entering politics. It was however precisely to avoid this possibility that the Left-Right groupings were made on an a priori basis in line with ideological writings (Marx and his successors; Burke, Green, and others). The conceptual basis of our Left-Right representation remains stable in face of varying party emphases over time, because it has a theoretical justification rather than an empirically derived and contingent one.

There is of course an empirically relevant question attached to its use rather than to its construction—that is, does a Left-Right representation still catch the main divisions in politics and produce useful mappings of the parties—as well as relate to other aspects of their behaviour? Much of this and our previous volume have checked these questions out. Their results are pretty conclusive: so far at any rate our Left-Right placements fully match expert and other representations (cf. Gabel and Huber 2000) and produce illuminating mappings of parties. They also perform well in theory testing (McDonald, Budge, and Pennings 2004; McDonald and Budge 2005). As the representation has passed all the checks that other scales have and then some, we can take its empirical relevance to date as established. Of course, its relevance is always subject to other tests such as the mappings of CEE countries reported above (Chapter 1).

We should note that the question of whether overall Left-Right confrontations have become outdated is a very different one from the question of whether they are equally relevant at all stages of the political cycle. There seems a variety of evidence—quoted in Chapter 3—that election debate takes on an essentially unidimensional Left-Right form and that this simplifies and organizes choices for voters. McDonald and Budge (2005) have however pointed out that inter-election parliamentary debate tends to separate out Left-Right into specific dimensions, as well as reintroducing other unrelated issues passed over in the election debate. This is because parliamentary debate is structured by the division of administrative responsibilities into ministries; legislative and administrative enactments within each area are considered on their own, often without reference to any wider context. When a new election looms they are again drawn together within a Left-Right framework, of course, but this may not hold for the legislative arena.

This multi-dimensional deconstruction of legislative policy space complicates both political relationships and political analysis. To take one example, if the overall Left-Right median party in parliament is the mechanism by which the median voters' preference gets injected into the policy process (Chapter 7), it has also to be at the median on the specific policy dimensions if it is to get its way on these. McDonald and Budge (2005) were able to investigate this possibility quite extensively by relating our Left-Right scale to the specific scales also constructed from the manifesto coding categories and described in Appendix I.

Such specific policy scales are of course equally available for readers' use: median voter and government position estimates are also provided, as for the EU scale. There is of course nothing to prevent other scales being constructed from the basic manifesto coding categories to meet other analytic needs (e.g. the environment). The next section discusses some of these.

ORGANIZING THE MANIFESTO DATA IN CONFRONTATIONAL FORM

As our historical sketch in the Introduction indicated the main MRG/CMP codings were developed on a relative emphases basis, inductively, from pilot codings of British manifestos and US platforms (Robertson 1976; Budge and Farlie 1977: 410–48). Each party defined its policy position by selecting and emphasizing its own pet themes rather than expressing direct opposition to other party positions within identical policy areas. This tendency also appeared in other systems such as the multi-party, continental ones. Since emphases differ sharply between parties we can use these to distinguish them quite clearly, and in fact can build scales expressing party opposition out of such emphases—like the Left-Right scale and specific policy scales discussed above. Relative emphases are at the heart of the new computerized approaches to coding texts (see below).

As noted above, there has always been a certain amount of scepticism about a relative emphases approach. Commentators have found it hard to believe that the major mode of party confrontation was not direct opposition on the same issues (cf. Laver (ed.) 2001: 67–73). As a result of early doubts on this, pro and con positions were distinguished by the MRG on the issues considered most likely to provoke direct opposition. In spite of one or other of the opposed categories usually collecting limited references, and the success of the remaining 'emphasis' categories in distinguishing between parties, the pro and con categories were embedded into the coding scheme and have remained part of it ever since.

This gives those who wish to do so the opportunity of setting up the manifesto data in a confrontational manner. Some unipositional, relative emphases categories can also be contrasted in this way. We should emphasize again that this would not be our own preferred way of treating the coding categories as we think party competition normally proceeds in a more indirect fashion. But we have no right to legislate for readers who have other views and wish to use the data differently. In setting up categories in a directly oppositional way, certain precautions do need to be observed however—in particular against the possibility there may be ambiguity and 'coding seepage' between the con position on one issue and another 'relative emphasis' category which also expresses opposition to the 'pro' position, though indirectly. One of the clearest examples is per105 'military negative' and per106 'peace'. 'Beating swords into ploughshares', quite a common expression in political rhetoric, could be coded under either. We therefore feel it is useful to report in Table 6.1, in which other categories might be included on each side of the oppositions. Such (bracketed) categories might or might not be combined with the pro or con one depending on analysts' own purposes and experiments with the data. Hopefully, the table provides a starting point for such experiments.

To take the first case in the table, a positive evaluation of special relationships with other countries is contrasted with a negative one. Such relationships are often a relic of colonial days (the British Commonwealth, French Union), so opposition to the old Empire often merges into a negative view of special relationships. This possibility is noted by bracketing per103 anti-imperialism under foreign special relationships: negative to show a possible overlap. On the other hand, support for special relationships (US–Britain, US–Israel, Russia and the 'near abroad') often merges into support for military alliances, so there is a potential general overlap between stances on foreign special relationships and military preparations.

Such overlaps should not be regarded purely as error. The related categories are ones into which pro or con references would have gone had a pure relative emphases coding been applied. They do express opposition to the 'other side' reported in Table 6.1, but in a more indirect way than envisaged in a directly confrontational pro–con coding.

Of course our procedures and coders try with some success to guarantee that references are being coded consistently and clearly into appropriate categories, compensating for the ambiguity inherent in imposing pro and con codings on what is basically a relative emphases scheme. The most important point to note is that not all references to an issue area will be necessarily comprehended in the explicitly 'pro' and 'con' categories.[3] This is illustrated in the case of the public services (welfare and education), where references to saving money are often expressed as enhancements to government efficiency (per303) rather than opposition to the service itself.

One or two of the relative emphases categories themselves can be set up as pro–con contrasts as is done at the bottom of Table 6.1. Again the oppositions cannot be taken as entirely straightforward. 'Regulation of Capitalism', for example, is often proposed as defending free enterprise by eliminating monopolies and cartels. So, it is not the same thing as a controlled economy, although related. Most of the relative emphases categories in the coding frame however do not lend themselves to a pro–con treatment as parties nowhere oppose, e.g. social justice or productivity or peace as such.

Emphasizing other issues in a positive light seems to be the major way in which parties express opposition to each others' policies. However on occasion some parties do take up a more directly confrontational stance. Disaggregating our data by country and party reveals that new, small or extreme parties often

Table 6.1. Setting up the MRG categories to express 'pro' and 'con' positions in the same issue areas

Pro and con positions directly coded as such (with related categories bracketed)

Pro		Contra	
External Relations			
PER101	Foreign Special Relationships: Positive (Per104 Military: Positive)	PER102	Foreign Relationships: Negative (Per103 Anti-Imperialism)
PER104	Military: Positive	PER105	Military: Negative (Per106: Peace: Per107 Internationalism: Positive)
PER 107	Internationalism: Positive	PER 109	Internationalism: Negative
PER 108	European Community: Positive	PER 110	European Community: Negative
Freedom and Democracy			
PER203	Constitutionalism: Positive	PER204	Constitutionalism: Negative
PER302	Centralization (Per303: Governmental & Administrative Efficiency) (Per305: Government Authority)	PER301	Decentralization
Economy			
PER 406	Protectionism: Positive	PER407	Protectionism: Negative
Welfare and Quality of Life			
PER504	Welfare State Expansion (Per503 Social Justice)	PER505	Welfare State Limitation (Per303 Government Efficiency)
PER506	Education Expansion	PER507	Education Limitation (Per303 Government Efficiency)
Fabric of Society			
PER601	National Way of Life: Positive (Per606 Social Harmony)	PER602	National Way of Life: Negative
PER603	Traditional Morality: Positive (Per 605 Law & Order: Per606 Social Harmony)	PER604	Traditional Morality: Negative
PER607	Multiculturalism: Positive (Per705 Underprivileged minority groups: Per706 Non-Econ. Demographic groups)	PER608	Multiculturalism: Negative
Social Groups			
PER701	Labour Groups: Positive	PER702	Labour Groups: Negative (Per704 Middle class)

Possible pro and con positions not directly coded as such (with related categories bracketed)
Economy

PER401	Free Enterprise	PER412	Controlled Economy (Per403 Regulation of Capitalism) (Per413 Nationalization)
PER414	Economic Orthodoxy	PER409	Keynesian Demand Management (Per404 Economic Planning)

define their position in direct contrast to mainstream party policy. This may tie in with the general development noted above whereby new parties emerge with a particular cause to promote in opposition to the mainstream (ecology, environment, regional independence, etc.). This gets them a niche electoral following. To move beyond this however they have to widen their appeal. There is also pressure to bolster their governmental credibility by dealing with all major societal problems in their programme. In expanding their programme they muffle their original confrontational stances and introduce more relative emphases—ending up like other mainstream parties if they are successful in doing so, or remaining marginalized like most Western Communist parties if they do not. However this may be, the pro–con categories may prove particularly useful for readers who want to look at green, minority nationalist, agrarian, or small communist parties, particularly at early stages in their development.

Our own preferred strategy for dealing with possible overlaps and ambiguities between pro and con and relative emphases categories and with thinly populated or ambiguous categories in general, is to combine them into broader scales. Examples of these are the overall Left-Right continuum (Table 1.1) or the policy scales reported in Table 6.2, and the Policy Scales Data-Set on the CD-ROM. As these combine closely related categories, the coding errors created by ambiguity between these are eliminated. The overall measures are thus more stable and reliable than any one of their components. All the strategies which parties use to differentiate their policies are reflected by them so that a variety of clearly distinguishable positions are available for parties to take. However, the scales themselves (apart from EU support) are not set up in a directly confrontational manner though it would be possible to do so with 'planned eonomy' and 'market economy', for example. The reason why we do not regard these as necessarily constituting two ends of the same continuum is because of the ambiguous nature of 'regulation of capitalism'—this is not clearly for or against a market economy as we noted. However, readers could always set them up confrontationally if they wished.

Table 6.2. Five policy scales combining manifesto coding categories

1	2	3	4	5
Planned economy	Market economy	Welfare	International peace	European Union*
403 Regulation of capitalism	401 Enterprise	503 Social justice	102 Special foreign relations: negative	108 European community: positive
404 Economic planning	414 Economic orthodoxy	504 Social services: positive	105 Military: negative	110 European community: negative
412 Controlled economy			106 Peace	

*Unlike scales 1–4 where category percentages are additively combined, the EU scale subtracts negative references in per110 from positive ones in per108.

RELATIVE EMPHASES, MRG/CMP CODINGS, AND COMPUTERIZED WORD COUNTS

Whatever the *additional* information obtained from the pro and con oppositions in our data, the *main* information is obtained from the relative emphases parties give to the different messages they wish to transmit to electors. Operationally this is measured by the space given to each of the coding categories in the party election programme. It is the percentage distribution of quasi-sentences coded into these categories which constitute our data.

It is important to emphasize two points in relation to our coding and counting procedures:

(a) By and large they emerged inductively from our reading of the election programmes themselves—initially from British and American programmes, later from those of other Anglo-Saxon and Continental party systems. It is mainstream parties themselves which most of the time seem to distinguish themselves, in their own documents, by stressing different issues and policy areas from their rivals. Across countries, parties of the same 'family' also stress similar issues and policy areas, as one would expect given their common ideological base.

(b) This relative emphases approach is, as we have stressed, inductive and data-driven. It can be used as a measurement technique without any theoretical underpinnings. Some of the computer-based word counts discussed below have in fact used it in this way. Nevertheless, it is natural to ask *why* parties try to give prominence to some issue areas and downplay others rather than arguing directly with each other on the same issues.

We have suggested (Budge et al. 2001: 81–9) that a plausible interpretation of parties' selective emphasis of different areas is to be found in the saliency theory of party competition. This regards most party strategists as reacting to what they see as a majority electoral position on most issues—not advocating tax rises for example because this would be hugely unpopular. They also see electors as identifying particular parties with their favoured course of action in particular areas. This gives these parties 'ownership' of certain issues, in the sense that the centrality of a certain issue in an election will increase its vote. To compete effectively therefore a party will emphasize its 'own' issues in an election—for example, socialists will oppose the idea of cutting taxes with that of increasing services. This constitutes indirect opposition, giving rise to differential emphases on the two areas because the two courses of action do not entirely preclude each other (governments can borrow, for example, in order to finance services).

Saliency ideas provided the theoretical context within which the MRG/CMP developed and applied their relative emphases approach to coding. They certainly provide plausible reasons why parties should write their programmes in this way—indeed, as far as we are aware, saliency is the only theoretical explanation that has been advanced to explain why they do so. (Stokes' 'valence issues' (1966) and Riker's 'dominance' principle (1993) are closely related variants on the same ideas.)

Nevertheless, saliency does add some additional theoretical assumptions to a relative emphases approach which readers who might be happy to adopt the approach itself might not accept. They certainly need not, though they may then face a challenge to provide some alternative theoretical justifications for what they are doing.

A measurement approach and a theory are however clearly not the same thing though they may be related. The rest of this section discusses the former without involving the latter. In this light we consider how far computerized coding procedures adopt the same relative emphases approach as the MRG/CMP. This discussion is important for two reasons:

(a) To the extent that wholly automated procedures reproduce the MRG/CMP ones, we can look forward to them eventually taking over the processing of texts with enormous savings of time and money for coding, and an extension of content analyses from programmes to actual policy outputs (e.g. laws).

(b) Such procedures however need to be validated before they can be applied to the mass production of estimates, particularly in regard to their over-time mapping of policy movements. The unique independent source for over-time mappings is the MRG/CMP. The check becomes more direct and more interpretable if both the hand-coding and computerized procedures rest on the same assumptions.

An obvious difference between the hand and computer procedures is in the unit coded—in the first case, the sentence and in the second, the word. It is clearly easier for the computer to operate with the most basic unit, the word, and for human coders to deal with sentences. However, both the word and the sentence measure relative emphases. Measurement bias associated with the units might certainly produce differences between estimates. But that is contingent and certainly not inherent in their nature.

Indeed Kleinijenhuis and Pennings (2001: 164–8) apply a word count to the task of automatically scoring election programmes on all fifty-six of the MRG/CMP categories. Their procedure was as follows:

(i) The original codes (101–706) in a set of party programmes formed the 'calibrating set'. Each quasi-sentence in each programme had already been assigned by a human coder to one MRG/CMP category, giving an overall percentage distribution and a score for each category.

(ii) A set of fifty-six probabilities was then assigned to each word occurring in the calibrating set: one probability for each of the fifty-six categories of MRG scheme. The extent to which a given word is an indicator of a given MRG category depends on the empirical probability of it occurring in each of the fifty-six MRG categories in the calibrating set.

(iii) Words that occurred less than five times were removed from the dictionary. Words that occurred extremely often but did not discriminate between the categories were removed also, for example, function words like 'the'.

(iv) The probabilistic dictionary derived in this way was applied to the 'application set' of party programmes to be coded. For a complete party programme, the 'frequency' of a specific MRG category in that party programme can be computed as the sum of the frequencies of the word from the calibrating set in the application set, weighted by their respective probabilities of pointing towards the MRG category under review.

The calibrating set in this analysis consisted of three of the five Dutch party programmes of 1998 (PvdA, VVD, CDA). The application set was all other Dutch party programmes in the period 1946–98. The estimated percentages were then aggregated for each programme in the 'application set' (1946–98 inclusive) to form scores on a Left-Right scale (not the standard MRG one in Table 1.1 but formed along the same lines). An overall 'map' of Dutch party movement was formed from the estimated scores and compared with the map based on original scores (like Figure 1.1). The two maps were broadly similar, locating parties in basically the same positions in regard to each other over time. However, some party locations, and party moves from one point in time to another, did not correspond exactly.

The technique is very promising, particularly as it could be applied to word counts in any language, even ones unknown to the analyst. There have of course to be initial scorings of categories for the calibrating set. For fifty-one countries, however, these are already supplied in this and the previous volume.

The results of the check may not have been as good as they could have been, however, as 1998 does not seem obvious as the choice for the base year. The application was to the whole of the post-war period. Possibly the mean percentages for all party programmes 1946–98 might have been used. Word probabilities could then have derived from these and been applied to the individual programmes.

Laver, Benoit, and Garry (2003) have developed the Klennijenhuis/Pennings procedure into a computer programme (Wordscores), which they have published electronically. Their approach differs in that it starts from an overall policy scale on which the different party programmes have already been scored for a given time point. The probabilities or weights assigned to each word thus refer to its relative frequency over all the party programmes in the 'calibrating' or 'reference set' in the given year. These provide weights which can be applied to the word distributions in the 'virgin texts' to be scored, giving rise to an estimated position for each manifesto on the policy scale which can be compared with the original party position (e.g. original scores for 1992 can be compared with estimated ones for 1997). A figure for the uncertainty of the new estimate can be interpreted as a reliability measure, and movement between the two years judged to be genuine or the result of measurement error.

It is useful to have a reliability measure for single estimates. However, the measure is limited in the sense that it says nothing about the more important question of the reliability (or validity) of the extraneous policy scale on which the manifestos in the reference set are located in the first place—only that, given these locations, we can say that there has been a significant shift between the known one and the estimated one over the two time points involved.

A second question of 'macro-reliability' is whether movement estimated to have occurred from 1992 to 1997 would be the same as movement estimated from 1997 to 1992? There is no a priori reason for using one as the reference rather than the other, so really both the 1992–7 and the 1997–1992 estimates have to concur if we are to make firm judgements about party change. Even if they concur in this particular case we would have to have some guarantee that they will generally concur. If this question is left unresolved then firm estimates of party movement become purely contingent.[4]

Laver et al. used expert locations of parties on economic and social scales both to provide the initial party policy locations and external indications of what movement actually occurred on the scales. (For the UK and Ireland the authors had expert judgements of where the parties were for both 1992 and 1997.) The Wordscores procedures placed parties in plausible positions relative to each other, as Kleinijenhuis and Pennings succeeded in doing with the Dutch parties. It also did so with German parties using manifesto texts in German. Estimates of party shifts on social and economic policy for the years in question broadly concurred with evidence from expert judgements in three out of four cases.

The Wordscores procedure therefore is clearly promising—also for analysing other texts such as reports of legislative debates. Validation, however, in contrast to Kleinijenhuis and Pennings (2000) was confined to only two time points (although a wider range of countries). The procedure also raises broader questions about reliability (discussed above). An independent check (Budge and Pennings 2007*a*, *b*) confronted both these questions, using mean MRG Left-Right scores and aggregated word frequencies of British manifestos (1979–97) as the calibrating (reference) set, and the individual party manifestos to be analysed as 'virgin' texts, to give estimated locations for the three British parties in the elections of 1979, 1983, 1987, 1992, and 1997. The advantage of proceeding in this way are that mean and aggregated data for the whole time period give an authoritative base for estimate without possible discrepancies between a 'backward' and 'forward' look at movement. Moreover, the MRG data provide an independent time series against which results can be evaluated rather than just a two-point comparison. Unfortunately, results were disappointing in that Wordscores like earlier computerized analyses (Bara 2001*b*) proved unable to detect important changes in party positions. Other computerized coding schemes have, however, produced positive results. These focus essentially on saliency and thus avoid problems related to establishing pro and con positions (Bara 2006).

It seems that the word frequency approach, though promising, needs further development before it can substitute for the MRG/CMP as the major mode of analysis for political texts. This may simply be a matter of time. An important question therefore is to what extent these computerized analyses take over the basic assumptions of our project—in particular, the relative emphases approach to analysing texts? To the extent they do, this will guarantee a smooth transition between the body of data reported in this and the preceding volume and the estimates they will start to generate in the future.

With regard to Kleinijenhuis and Pennings (2001) comparability is guaranteed. After all their whole procedure is geared to estimating the MRG categories—largely, as we have seen, relative emphasis categories. To the extent they succeed, estimates would simply carry on from MRG ones in an unbroken time series.

With the Wordscores procedure the comparison is not quite so simple. Word probabilities have been adapted here to estimate positions on an extraneously given scale, on which parties have already (again extraneously) been located at a given point in time. Of course, as we have seen, the extraneous scale can be the MRG Left-Right scale—and potentially any policy scale based on the MRG/CMP data.

Mechanically, therefore, an improved Wordscores can be applied to the MRG scales and in this sense generate continuations of the time series—once validated against pre-existing estimates of course. A relevant question however is how far the underlying logics of our hand-scoring and these computerized procedures resemble each other, as this strengthens confidence in the underlying unity of the time series produced by both approaches.

One obvious resemblance in light of the controversies over confrontational versus relative emphases approaches is that the later computerized approaches base themselves entirely on the relative word frequencies in establishing estimates of party locations. As noted by Laver et al. (2003: 329–30):

> this almost certainly has to do with the way words are used in practice in the advocacy of particular policy positions. With regard to our own technique, take the individual word used in our earlier example—'choice'. Of course the word choice has several meanings, while each meaning can also be qualified with a negative or even a double negative. Someone coming to computational text analysis for the first time might reasonably feel for these reasons that the relative frequency of the word choice in a given text does not convey substantive information ... our approach works because particular words do, empirically, tend to have policy-laden content. Thus, in post-Thatcher Britain, those using the word choice in relation to education or health policy, for example, tended to be advocating greater choice of schools or health providers and correspondingly less central control. Those opposing such policies tended, as a matter of empirical observation, not to argue for 'no choice' or 'less choice' but rather to talk about the benefits of central planning and coordination.

We could not put this better ourselves! In our opinion this constitutes one of the more powerful statements justifying a relative emphases approach. Paradoxically these very authors have only recently been converted to using emphases rather than directly contrasting pro and con positions (Laver and Garry 2000).

Of course one *could* argue that the scale locations of parties used as input to Wordscores provide contrasting and potentially confrontational positions at the start—placing them at opposing Left-Right positions, for example. In that case however there is no difference from MRG/CMP procedures, which similarly locate

Table 6.3. Similarity of the scoring procedures used in CMP and computerized word probability approaches to scoring manifestos

Stages	CMP Procedures	Wordscores
1. Extraneously given scale	Theoretically driven groupings of coding categories to form the scale (cf. Table 1.1)	Selection of a priori scale which assigns numeric score to each party in calibrating/reference set
2. Weighting procedure	Each coding unit (category) in scale weighted equally in absence of extraneous theoretical advice on how to weight	Each coding unit (word) weighted in accordance with its frequency over the calibrating/reference set manifestos
3. Scoring of new (virgin) manifestos	Party scores calculated by adding for each manifesto the percentaged frequencies of quasi-sentences in each category in, e.g. Left and Right and subtracting Left sum from Right sum	Party scores are calculated by adding weighted word scores for each manifesto in the application (virgin) set

Sources: Mapping Policy Preferences, 21–2, Kleinnijenhuis and Pennings, 2001; Laver, Benoit, and Garry (2003: 314–19).

parties in contrasting Left-Right and other policy scale positions (cf. Tables 6.2 and 6.3, Policy Scales Data-Set on CD-ROM).

An explicit illustration of the underlying identity of Wordscores and CMP procedures is given in Table 6.3. This divides the procedures into three stages:

1. Selection of a scale which is 'given' in the sense of existing before the procedures are applied. In the CMP case, this is given from pre-existing ideological writing, which stresses certain themes as important to one or other ideological point of view, left or right. The full set of opposing themes then form the two ends of the scale. The Wordscores procedure simply takes a pre-existing set of scale scores which could be produced either by experts or by the MRG or by other means.

2. The coding unit to be used in the estimation is weighted. The weighting is a priori in the case of the CMP; mostly ideological discussions do not indicate how each theme or issue is to be weighted in relation to others, so by default they are given equal weights. Obviously, if a relevant theory did attribute a greater weight to some categories they could be weighted differentially. The computerized procedure estimates weightings for each word empirically, on the basis of its frequency in each of the calibrating set of manifestos applied to the scale score of the corresponding party.

3. The weighted frequencies of the coding unit in the application set (the 'virgin' documents) are added to form an estimated scale score for each party. In the case of Wordscores this can be compared with the original scale position to see how far the party has changed policy. The MRG scores can of course be calculated independently for each party manifesto and compared (Figures 1.1–1.16).

Procedures therefore differ in detail between the two techniques but share the same underlying logic in proceeding from extraneously given scale to weightings to calculation of final scores. Wordscores is sensitive to differences between the original and new types of texts, so the authors advise against estimating positions on widely varying documents (e.g. manifesto and legislative texts). Hopefully, such sensitivity will be overcome in future developments as this constitutes a severe constraint on our ability to see how far party intentions have been incorporated into public policy—a crucial question in political science. The MRG scales have already been applied to government as well as party documents (Budge et al. 2001: Appendix VI).

The basic point to take away from the methodological comparison of Table 6.3 is however that the CMP estimates come from procedures conceptually similar to those involved in generating computerized word probability estimates. This makes them ideal—even essential—for checking out and validating the latter. It also means that the latter—once they are refined and developed—can take over seamlessly from hand-coding procedures, in producing time series for the central policy scores. Until such refinement and development take place, the CMP estimates remain essential however.

SUMMARY AND OVERVIEW

This chapter has reviewed some of the main methodological issues which have come up since the publication of our previous volume. In particular it has summarized coding procedures and controls, particularly as these have evolved over the lifetime of the CMP, clarified what the manifesto policy estimates actually tell us—the current position of the party, shaped by situational and strategic concerns as well as its underlying ideology; and shown how some manifesto coding categories can be organized as pro and con alternatives, even though the main thrust of the coding scheme is towards capturing the relative emphases laid by manifestos on various areas. Finally, we have reviewed the new computerized word probability approaches to coding party documents and shown how these rely on selective emphases to score political parties just like the CMP.

For more detailed discussion of methodological issues, the interested reader should turn back to the previous volume. We hope here to have summarized the most relevant points and also to have extended them—particularly how computerized approaches have perforce adopted the relative emphases approach to coding which has always characterized the MRG/CMP. We realize of course that most readers will be interested primarily in what the estimates tell them about substantive politics, particularly in CEE over the past two decades! While methodological discussions inform us about the basis on which estimates were made they are no substitute for the estimates themselves.

Chapter 7 shows how these can be applied to some interesting research questions which go to the heart of representative processes, and which could equally be raised about the new, as they already have about the old, democracies.

NOTES

1. Even in this case there was central control and coordination through the research officer of the MRG, Derek Hearl, who coded either by himself or with assistance the programmes for Belgium, Luxembourg, Austria, Australia, New Zealand, and the USA.
2. Pelizzo does not explicitly cite his source for the manifesto data he processes. He misinterprets Austrian Left-Right placements which in MPP Figure 1.13 (p. 37) show the Freedom Party under Heidar moving sharply rightwards (we think correctly). The Dutch PvdA's move rightwards in 1994 signalled a precedent-breaking coalition with the right-wing Liberals, thus we would regard it as informative rather than wrong (Pelizzo 2003: 76, 78).
3. Nor under a pure relative emphases scheme would all 'con' references necessarily remain in that issue area, as they would in that case have been assigned to the alternative issue the party was trying to promote in indirect opposition to the pro position.
4. Of course, a substantive research design might point to either a forward-looking or backward-looking perspective as more relevant, thus resolving the problem for a particular analysis. But it remains in general.

7

Exploiting Manifesto-Based Estimates of the Median for Multi-Level Analysis: Relating Electoral, Legislative, and Government Policy Preferences

This chapter complements the various methodological assessments made in Part II by giving a practical example of how the strengths of the manifesto data can be exploited to tackle a major research question. The question relates to how representative processes work out in practice in Western democracies and how they are affected by voting rules. In theory, the latter should make 'a necessary connection' (May 1978; Saward 1998: 51) between popular preferences and public policy. To what extent do they do this? And which set of rules is best for ensuring the connection?

To investigate these points we obviously need measures of popular preference and government intentions for a reasonably extended range of democracies over the whole post-war period. This book and its predecessor supply all of these. This chapter focuses particularly on the measures of median voter and government preferences which can be derived from our data, so it forms a good introduction to the estimates presented in the CD-ROM.

ESTIMATING GOVERNMENT POLICY POSITIONS

Building on measures pioneered by Kim and Fording (1998, 2001*a*) our previous volume (or rather its accompanying CD-ROM) provided estimates of the median voters' Left-Right position in twenty-five democracies 1945–98. It also (Kim and Fording 2001*b*: 166–72) presented a way of measuring government policy preferences by adding the weighted Left-Right scores of the parties making it up. The weights are the proportion of legislative seats each party contributes to the total government share. (In turn, this relates closely to the proportion of cabinet position it holds.) More specifically, the measure is

$$\Sigma \{\text{Left-Right party position*(no seats/total seats}\}$$

where Σ is the summation sign.

Using a *weighted* average to indicate the government's overall Left-Right position is based on the reasonable assumption that parties in government influence policy in proportion to the seats they contribute to it and the cabinet posts they occupy (which are closely related—Browne and Franklin 1972). When there is just one party in government that party's Left-Right position is the government's position; the party holds 100 per cent of the weight of parties in government. When there are two parties in government, one with seventy-five seats and the other with twenty-five, then the position of the first has three times as much weight in the calculation.

A comparison of policy scores obtained in this way with others based on a similar calculation but using expert scores shows a correlation of r = 0.82, for 32 governments of the early 1980s and 1990s (Powell 2000: 180–5). However, the manifesto-based measure can also, of course, be calculated for every post-war government and vary over time.

Estimates of government preferences calculated along these lines should not be confused with the estimates for actual government policy declarations which were reported on the previous CD-ROM (Budge et al. 2001). These were based on a coding of separate documents—the government's publicly stated programme at its investiture debate—and covered only ten countries over a thirty-year period. To avoid confusion, estimates based on Kim and Fording's formula were not reported earlier. In this volume, however, they are reported for all countries from 1990 to 2003. This gives readers an opportunity to replicate or extend the analyses of representation summarized below using our estimates for government and party preferences, median parliamentary preferences and median elector preference. Unfortunately, the analyses which have been done only extend to Western democracies since data for CEE has not been available up to now. Our examples show, however, how a similar analysis of representation could easily be extended to Eastern Europe.

MEASURING ELECTORAL POLICY PREFERENCES—THE MEDIAN VOTER

Our measurement of a median voter's position also relies on a procedure developed by Kim and Fording (1998, 2001a). It differs from a survey-based measure in three respects. First, surveys asking respondents to locate themselves on a Left-Right scale often do not permit the identification of the party for whom a respondent had voted in an earlier election. That requires the survey-based measure to refer to a median citizen rather than a median voter. Second, and more importantly, surveys that ask a Left-Right self-placement question are infrequently available, so they are not up to the task of providing a good match to the party-position data. The latter data are designed to have meaningful cross-national variation—that is, if Norwegian parties locate themselves on average to the left of Australian parties of the same family (e.g. Social Democrats and Conservatives), this can be taken as indicating that the Norwegian Left-Right space is left of the Left-Right space in Australia. This feature holds for the CMP data as well as for some 'expert' survey data (Mair and Castles 1997). Mass survey data on respondents' Left-Right positions, on the contrary, appear to have no such cross-national variation (see Chapter 3).

In nearly all countries the median voter positions identified by mass surveys are quite similar (Powell 2000: 162, 180–5). For example, the median citizen in Norway is recorded by surveys to be at the same Left-Right position as the median citizen in Australia or the USA. This is implausible when one thinks of the general differences between these countries' politics. One consequence is that (but for three countries that stand three to four standard deviations to the left of all the others (namely, France, Italy, and Spain)), the cross-national correlation between median citizen positions identified by surveys in the 1980s with those in the 1990s is almost non-existent and, worse, negative—i.e. r = −0.14. It appears, therefore, that survey respondents report they are on the left, in the centre or on the right within the context of their own country's political space, rendering their self-placements suspect for any comparative analysis and, more damning for present purposes, for matching to the party-position data that do contain valid cross-national differences along the Left-Right dimension. The Kim–Fording measure uses leverage gained from party system cross-national differences and has been validated in part by tests that pay attention to national political differences. And, we can note, the overtime r = +0.44 for the Kim–Fording measure applied to the same elections in the same fifteen nations for which Powell's survey data correlation (2000) is −0.14. The formula used by Kim and Fording is:

$$M = L + [\{(50 - C)/F\} \times W]$$

Here:

M = median voter position, Left-Right.

L = lower end on the Left-Right dimension of the interval containing the median.

C = the cumulative vote percentage frequency up to but not including the interval containing the median.

F = the vote percentage of the party in the interval containing the median.

W = the width of the interval containing the median.

In a three-party system, with parties P, Q, and R at Left-Right positions of −12, +2, and +8 and vote percentages of 47, 12, and 41, the median voter position is:

$$M = (-5) + [\{(50 - 47)/12)\} \times 10]$$
$$M = -2.5$$

Basing a measure of popular policy preference in part on the policy positions taken by the parties is justified on two grounds. First, to register any public choice at all, voters must decide between the alternative programmes offered by the parties. In modern representative elections there simply is no other choice available and demonstration of support for a public alternative represents a more considered choice than preferences privately expressed in a survey.

Second, Chapter 3 has shown that electors and parties do see the choices in Left-Right terms which they line up in broadly the same way. This justifies us in attributing a Left-Right ordering both to governments and to voters and to parties in parliament (which in conjunction with the distribution of seats there enables us to determine the party with the median legislator, an important element in the investigation reported in a later section).

MEDIAN VOTER AND POPULAR MAJORITY

Being able to estimate the median voter position is important because it is the best indicator we can have of what the popular majority wants. This proposition has been proved mathematically (Black 1958) and can also be seen intuitively—most readily in the case of a single-dimensional policy continuum like the Left-Right one.

To see why, consider Figure 7.1, where voters prefer any policy closer to their own preference on a Left-Right continuum. This puts C, at the median, in the most powerful position. Voters both to left and right need C to form a majority. They can only attract C by putting their collective preference close to hers—otherwise the alternative grouping will be more attractive and become the majority. Compared to the policy positions of voters on the other wing, C's position will be preferred, whichever coalition she joins. Thus C's position will constitute the point towards which majority-backed policy always tends in practice. That is why it is such a good indicator of what a majority would want if it formed. It also has a certain normative appeal, being the policy position which gives all voters the maximum satisfaction they can expect with equal suffrages under the existing distribution of preferences.

The same argument also applies, with necessary modifications, to the situation of the Median Parliamentary Party (MPP). To the extent that parliamentary divisions focus around Left-Right differences, the median party should be able to bring the final outcome close to its own position by swinging its vote between the two sides.

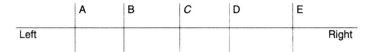

Fig. 7.1. The dominant position of the median actor, C, in a one-dimensional policy space

INVESTIGATING REPRESENTATION

The main object of this chapter is to summarize investigations which have used these median measures and concepts to investigate political representation in the modern world. Most studies of modern representation have focused on the extent to which the legislative seat shares given to parties reflect the vote shares they gained in the election. This relationship is in large part determined by the rules under which elections are held—the election system. The two main alternatives are proportional representation (PR), aimed at ensuring that seat shares match vote shares as closely as possible: and a single member district plurality system (SMD) more concerned with ensuring a decisive result by awarding seats to whichever party gets the largest number of votes.

The concern of most of the literature with party seats rests on the implicit assumption that parties are the carriers of different policies so that the distribution of seats will affect the outcomes of public policy. This is true of course. Parties *are* the carriers of policy and can be seen as hewing to a reasonably consistent policy line over time at least in Left-Right terms (Castles (ed.) 1982). Nevertheless, they do vary their policies between election and election—and as far as individual elections are concerned, sometimes quite considerably (consider the variation in ex-Communist policy positions mapped in Chapter 1). Such changes not only affect the choices offered to electors, and what they can be seen as voting for. It also alters the policies parties promote once in office.

Fortunately the manifesto data offer a direct source of evidence on party policy change. These enable us to take direct cognizance of what the parties themselves say about their election policy in their only authoritative pronouncement—the platform or manifesto—and to map it in terms of party Left-Right movement as in Figures 1.1–1.16 in Chapter 1. Similar maps could be presented for all our countries and form the basis for the Tables 7.1 and 7.2.

Having individual election positions for parties allow us to see what electors are actually voting for and permits a more refined investigation of the effects of election rules over electoral preference formation and public policy in different countries. We can now answer questions such as whether rules are more important than cultural differences (Anglo-Saxon vs. Continental, European vs. American) or types of party system in shaping policy representation.

REPRESENTING PUBLIC PREFERENCES

With measures both of popular policy preferences and of government intentions we are in a position to measure the correspondence between the two. This is a first step towards examining the effects of voting rules on representation, by seeing how the correspondence varies between countries with different types of election system.

Table 7.1. Representational distortion, bias, and responsiveness between Left-Right positions of governments, weighted by party size, and Left-Right position of median voters, twenty-one democracies from 1950s to 1995

System	Country	Short-term distortion[a] Mean (Std. Dev.)	Long-term bias[b] Mean (Std. Dev.)	Responsiveness[c] Intercept (s_a)	Slope (s_b)	R^2	s_e	N
SMD	Australia	18.2 (9.1)	7.1 (19.4)	7.7 (3.9)	.64 (.35)	.12	19.4	25
	Canada	6.1 (7.8)	3.6 (9.3)	3.1 (2.7)	.85* (.39)	.23	9.6	17
	France	18.6 (8.2)	11.3 (18.6)	7.0 (4.4)	.53 (.45)	.05	18.4	27
	New Zealand	12.4 (7.0)	1.2 (12.4)	−2.6 (4.7)	.56 (.40)	.08	14.4	22
	United Kingdom	14.6 (11.1)	4.1 (18.2)	10.3 (5.5)	1.55** (.32)	.59	17.3	18
	USA	15.4 (7.4)	−0.3 (17.7)	−4.2 (6.1)	2.46* (1.29)	.25	17.5	13
SMD Summary		14.7 (9.4)	5.3 (16.7)	5.0** (1.6)	.93** (.15)	.24	16.8	122
PR	Austria	6.6 (4.4)	−1.6 (8.0)	−1.5 (2.0)	.89** (.15)	.75	8.2	18
	Belgium	5.5 (4.8)	0.4 (7.4)	−.9 (1.5)	.88** (.17)	.46	7.2	27
	Denmark	16.1 (11.6)	1.4 (20.0)	1.1 (4.5)	.83** (.44)	.15	20.4	27
	Finland	13.6 (14.9)	6.6 (19.2)	3.8 (5.1)	.92** (.25)	.23	18.8	32
	Germany	9.4 (9.0)	2.3 (13.0)	1.7 (2.5)	1.45** (.26)	.58	12.5	21
	Iceland	7.5 (8.4)	4.2 (10.5)	4.5 (3.2)	1.04** (.25)	.52	10.6	18
	Ireland	8.5 (8.8)	0.6 (8.5)	1.7 (2.7)	.70** (.17)	.51	11.7	19
	Italy	1.8 (1.8)	0.9 (2.4)	1.6 (0.6)	1.07** (.06)	.87	2.8	42
	Luxembourg	4.3 (3.4)	−0.6 (5.6)	2.4 (3.0)	1.17** (.17)	.79	5.7	14
	Netherlands	7.3 (4.0)	1.4 (8.5)	−.1 (2.1)	.79** (.14)	.67	7.3	14
	Norway	10.3 (7.3)	2.7 (12.4)	−.7 (11.4)	.86* (.45)	.16	12.7	21
	Portugal	4.7 (2.8)	2.9 (4.7)	3.7 (2.1)	1.12** (.22)	.77	4.9	10
	Spain	3.6 (2.3)	1.1 (4.3)	3.7 (2.9)	1.24** (.23)	.86	4.3	7
	Sweden	8.8 (7.7)	−3.1 (11.4)	1.5 (3.8)	1.25** (.17)	.75	11.0	21
	Switzerland	4.5 (3.2)	0.6 (5.5)	.6 (1.0)	1.00** (.10)	.68	5.6	45

Table 7.1. (*Continued*)

System	Country	Short-term distortion[a]	Long-term bias[b]	Responsiveness[c]					
		Mean (Std. Dev.)	Mean (Std. Dev.)	Intercept (s_a)	Slope (s_b)	R^2	s_e	N	
PR Summary		7.6 (8.5)	1.4 (11.3)	1.1 (0.7)	.95 (.05)	.55	11.3	336	

*p < .05; **p < .01; two-tail critical values for intercepts and one-tail critical values for slopes.

[a]Distortion is the absolute value of the difference between the weighted-mean Left-Right position of governments (with weights proportional to the number of seats held by each party in government) and the Left-Right position of median voters. N is the number of governments. Totally congruent systems have a mean equal to zero.

[b]Bias is the average arithmetic difference between the weighted-mean Left-Right position of governments (with weights as above) and the Left-Right position of median voters. N is the number of elections. A zero mean indicates accurate (i.e. unbiased) long-term representativeness.

[c]Responsiveness is evaluated by the linear relationship between the weighted-mean Left-Right position of government (Y) and the Left-Right position of the median voter (X) on the basis of a regression equation covering all post-war elections in the country. Left positions are negative, centre equals zero, and right positions are positive.

There are three aspects of policy correspondence which we can examine. The first is the most obvious—the average absolute difference between median voter position and government position on the Left-Right scale after each election. However, we can also bring in time by seeing how this works out over the long run, since negative and positive deviations from the popular position at each election could, over the long term, average out close to the long-term popular preference. Finally, we can see how well changes in the popular position from election to election get reflected in changes in government position—a simple regression equation is all that is needed to relate the two. The last two measures have not been used before because they build on the ability of the manifesto data to reflect changes over time, which have been lacking in most previous investigations of representative relationships based on surveys or expert judgements (e.g. Powell 2000). Yet they are essential to get a rounded view of how popular–representative relationships work out over a given period—surely essential to a full evaluation of the *lasting* impact of election systems.

Table 7.1 provides figures for Western democracies (but we hope later to extend our investigation eastward) which enable us to make these three kinds of comparison, each casting light on some aspect of policy representation. The first (column 1 of Table 7.1) simply averages the absolute differences after each election between the Left-Right preference of the median voter[1] and the (weighted) Left-Right preferences of the subsequent government (we label this 'distortion'). The second measure, of long-term bias, averages these differences arithmetically, taking account of positive and negative values. It is designed to show how far individual election distortions might balance each other out in the long run. The third measure, responsiveness, shows how far a change in the position of the median voter produces a corresponding change in the government position after each election.

Applying these measures to the individual countries in the table we can see, for example, that Australia commonly produces governments with quite a large incongruence between the median voter (majority) preference and the government-policy position. This is reduced, however, when we average these distortions arithmetically over time because positive ones balance out negative ones. There is still quite a substantial discrepancy of 7.1 but it is much reduced from the 18.2 post-electoral incongruence. The figure for responsiveness (slope) at .64 does not differ significantly from 1.00, a one-to-one relationship, showing considerable sensitivity of government policy to shifts in popular opinion. In the case of the UK and USA, this might be considered over-sensitivity as small swings in public support produce disproportionate changes in government positions—as in Germany, to cite a PR system which also produces disproportionate change.

In all countries, long-term bias is less than short-term distortion—a reassuring finding for the representative democrat! The reduction is particularly marked for Denmark and the USA, which approach almost perfect correspondence in the long run after showing a lot of short-term distortion. The much criticized electoral and party systems of Italy produce a good correspondence on all indicators, provoking the heretical reflection that possibly the median Italian voter got what she wanted out of the old political system (at least as far as government policy intentions were concerned). Italy contrasts with France which performs badly on all representation measures.

ELECTION SYSTEM AND POLICY REPRESENTATION

A major interest is, of course, less in individual country differences than those between election systems. The table shows that SMD systems (largely as a result of electoral pluralities being transformed into parliamentary majorities) produce considerably more incongruence between popular and government preferences than PR systems—an average of 14.7 compared to 7.6. However, over time, these tend to cancel out, as a leftward incongruence is succeeded by a rightward incongruence—average bias is 5.3 (SMD) compared to 1.4 (PR). Thus long-term policy representation under SMD compares much more favourably than short-term representation with that of PR systems, although the comparison still favours the latter.

Responsiveness is often considered the great strength of SMD compared to PR—shifts in electoral opinion being immediately transformed into changes of governments and their policies, while legislative bargaining over coalition formation impedes this. However, we can see from the third column of Table 7.1 that this sweeping generalization is not upheld. In fact, most PR systems show a quite impressive level of responsiveness to changes in popular preferences while the lowest responsiveness appears in New Zealand and France.

The French case contrasts with that of Britain, which shows ultra-high responsiveness to shifts in electoral opinion. The USA is even more responsive but also more erratic in registering a response as indicated by the (bracketed) standard error of the slope. In terms of individual election distortions France and Britain both show high levels—resulting both from pluralities being represented as parliamentary majorities and possibly also from having a limited number of party alternatives to choose from, given that effective choice in France is between Left and Right. In spite of having even more limited party alternatives, majoritarian voting in the USA as associated with a better—indeed almost perfect—match between individual election preferences and government policy over the long run (-0.3).

When it comes to long-term bias we have seen that alternation between Left and Right substantially reduces the electoral-government gap in Britain, bringing it closer to the USA in this regard. However, the French system still reveals itself the least sensitive system so far as reflecting popular preferences is concerned—not only in regard to Britain and the USA but also to all the other countries in the table. The majoritarian run-off system, and possibly the interventions of an autonomous presidency in government negotiations, undermine policy representation by governments.

Over-responsive to change at one level, and insensitive to current popular preferences at the other, Britain hardly appears as a model of representation either. The majoritarian system of the USA created by party competition for the presidency appears somewhat more capable of reflecting and responding to popular demands. Of course by considering only presidential intentions, we are not taking into account the effect of the separation of powers and hostile Congressional majorities. These probably impede the actual implementation of policy intentions—a complication which is however beyond the scope of discussion here.

Examining differences among SMD systems themselves—interesting and neglected as they often are—should not be allowed to obscure the major differences in representational efficiency which emerge between the PR and non-PR systems in the table. The main lesson is that proportional representation does the job it was designed for in policy terms as well as in the reflection of vote shares in seats—and probably *because* it equates seat with the vote shares, giving parliamentary influence to parties in proportion to the popular support they get (McDonald, Mendés, and Budge 2004). On all the indicators in Table 7.1, PR systems perform better or equally well as SMD systems on average—and indeed also compare well at the individual country level, with the intriguing exception of Canada.

This finding echoes the conclusions of previous studies such as Powell's (2000). Perhaps an even more important finding once the extra dimension of time is introduced is that long-term bias is reduced in SMD systems by alternation between governments with different policy positions. Individually, these may be out of tune with their electorate. Abrupt alternations of policy direction seem in the end, however, to add up to an average position which is not too far removed from the average over-time preference of electors. Alternation and confrontation may not be the best way to get a correspondence (Anderson and Guillory 1997;

Lijphart 1999). But it is reassuring from the democratic point of view that the major alternative form of voting to PR does achieve it in the end.

PARTY SYSTEMS AND POLICY REPRESENTATION

One way in which electoral systems might exert an effect is through the kind of party system they promote. Since Duverger (1951) it has been recognized that PR tends to encourage more parties and SMD less. More parties might offer more nuanced policy alternatives through which the median preference might more sensitively be reflected by the government. (Though of course Downs [1957: 142–50] has cautioned that multiparty coalition governments form without much regard to popular votes, which makes rational choice of party by electors difficult.)

Table 7.1 however shows few differences that could be associated with party numbers as such. Austria, with $2^1/_2$ parties like Britain, scores better than the UK on all measures. Italy and Denmark, both with highly fragmented party systems, turn in different performances, as does France. There seems clear evidence, therefore, that election systems exert some direct effects on representation, not ones wholly mediated by the party system.

We can check this conclusion directly by tracing distortion and bias to their roots in elections and parties. The party system can distort the representation of median voter preferences by offering party policy packages that are all quite distant from those preferences, even in terms of the closest alternative which attracts her support. By measuring the distances in Left-Right terms between the median voter and the closest party at each election and taking the absolute sum and mean of these, we get an estimate of how much distortion each party system with its range of offerings introduces into policy representation. By adding these distances arithmetically and allowing for their positive and negative signs, we can estimate the bias of the party system.

For its part the election system is supposed to make the party policy chosen by the median voter the median one in parliament. The measure of how far it departs from this is the Left-Right distance between the policy position of the party chosen by the median voter and that of the parliamentary median. Distortion and bias can both be estimated from this as previously.

As misrepresentation can last a longer or a shorter time, the estimates here, unlike those in Table 7.1, are weighted by the time between elections to get a truer picture of how far representation is generally exact or off the mark. (However, unweighted estimates produce much the same results). There are other sources of distortion and bias in the representative process—distance between the policy position of the parliamentary median party and that of the government for example, which are not noted in the table. However, it does provide a basis for judging the extent to which party systems or election systems contribute most to representational gaps.

Of course, these factors in turn are not wholly independent of each other. PR may sustain more parties than SMD and the number of parties then affects both election results and the parliamentary situation. A first step in examining interrelationships is surely however to look at the direct effects on representation which each produces and this is what Table 7.2 does.

Answers are mixed. In SMD systems, the source of distortion varies very much between individual countries, from New Zealand where the party system contributes much more to distortion than the election system to Britain where the reverse is very strongly true. Under SMD, election and party systems seem to contribute equally to distortion. Distortion is less in general under PR, but the party system makes almost three times the contribution to it that the election system does.

Switching our attention to long-term bias—which allows distortions in different directions to compensate each other over time—shows that contrasts between the types of electoral and party system diminish sharply. The result is, of course, achieved by different routes. Under PR constant negotiation and compromises produce the generally satisfactory matches between government policy intentions and those of the popular majority (measured as the median voter) (Lijphart 1999). Under SMD the route is by alternation between governments with different policy inclinations which in the long run cancel each other out to land up near the median voters' policy preference (McDonald and Budge 2005: 101–33). Whether this is as satisfactory to the general public as having a government at all times closer to them is a moot point (Anderson and Guillory 1997).

What we have shown here is that by considering time—which the manifesto policy estimates unlike any others allow us to do—the contrasts between SMD and PR in terms of representational efficiency are sharply reduced. Responsiveness, however, (Table 7.1) seems just as great under PR as under SMD. Both findings are enough to set the debate about the relative merits of different representational systems on a new footing.

SUMMARY AND CONCLUSIONS

This chapter has explored some uses to which manifesto-based estimates of government intentions, party policy, and electoral preferences can be put. Linking the three main actors in democratic policymaking, they offer an unparalleled basis for exploring the process of representation as it operates in modern democracy. For the first time we can more or less exactly measure bias and responsiveness and attribute it either to election rules or the workings of the party system. The measurements have so far been made only for Western countries but the data provided in the CD-ROM and illustrated in Chapter 1 allow them to be applied also to CEE. We hope they soon will be, either by authors or readers.

One methodological point needs to be tackled before we pass on to the wider implications of this research. The fact that both the median voter measure and

Table 7.2. Electoral system and party system effects on representational distortion and bias over twenty-one democracies from 1950s to 1995

System	Country	Distortion		Bias	
		Electoral system	Party system	Electoral system	Party system
SMD	Australia	9.1*	15.6**	0.8	4.6
		(3.9)	(1.7)	(4.5)	(4.0)
	Canada	4.1	4.3**	2.6	0.5
		(2.6)	(1.1)	(2.7)	(1.6)
	France	12.4**	8.1**	6.8	2.4
		(3.5)	(1.7)	(4.9)	(3.1)
	New Zealand	3.4	10.1**	3.4	0.9
		(1.6)	(1.6)	(1.6)	(3.1)
	United Kingdom	19.4**	6.6**	12.7	−2.7
		(4.2)	(1.2)	(6.0)	(2.1)
	SMD Summary	9.3*	9.4**	4.8*	1.3
		(1.6)	(0.7)	(1.9)	(1.4)
PR	Austria	3.6	6.7**	0.5	2.6
		(2.3)	(1.1)	(2.5)	(2.1)
	Belgium	0.5	2.3*	0.5	1.8
		(0.3)	(0.9)	(0.3)	(1.0)
	Denmark	0.7	4.7**	0.7	−3.7**
		(0.6)	(1.0)	(0.6)	(1.2)
	Finland	1.0	2.3**	0.7	−0.1
		(0.9)	(0.6)	(1.0)	(0.9)
	Germany	0.0	5.0**	0.0	0.4
		(—)	(0.8)	(—)	(0.4)
	Iceland	0.5	2.7**	0.5	−1.6
		(0.4)	(0.5)	(0.4)	(0.8)
	Ireland	5.6	7.9**	5.6	−5.2
		(3.6)	(1.9)	(3.6)	(2.5)
	Italy	0.2	1.5**	0.2	1.4**
		(0.2)	(0.4)	(0.2)	(0.4)
	Luxembourg	1.6	4.5**	−1.0	4.4**
		(1.7)	(0.7)	(1.8)	(0.7)
	Netherlands	0.0	3.2**	0.0	1.6
		(—)	(0.6)	(—)	(1.0)
	Norway	1.3	3.6**	0.2	−1.4
		(0.8)	(0.8)	(0.9)	(1.3)
	Portugal	0.2	3.8**	0.2	1.0
		(0.4)	(0.8)	(0.4)	(1.6)
	Spain	2.4	1.7	2.4	1.6
		(1.7)	(0.7)	(1.7)	(0.7)
	Sweden	5.7	7.2**	0.6	−2.3
		(3.3)	(1.9)	(3.6)	(2.6)
	Switzerland	0.0	1.8**	0.0	0.6
		(—)	(0.5)	(—)	(0.7)
	PR Summary	1.6**	4.1**	0.8	−0.3
		(0.4)	(0.3)	(0.5)	(0.4)

*p < .05; **p < .01.

Note: We have not reported figures for the USA here because in this period the major party supported by the median voter always won, so distortion and bias are zero—it thus seems better to confine comparisons to parliamentary democracies.

Distortion: Cell entries are means and their standard errors (bracketed) from early 1950s to 1995. Calculations are weighted by the time between elections. Distortions are defined as follows:

Electoral system: the absolute value of the difference between the party Left-Right position closest to the median voter and the median parliamentary party Left-Right position.

Party system: the absolute value of the difference between the median voter Left-Right position and the Left-Right position of the party closest to the median voter.

Bias: cell entries are means and their standard errors from early 1950s to 1995. Calculations are weighted by the time between elections. Biases are defined as follows:

Electoral system: the arithmetic difference between the party Left-Right position closest to the median voter and the median parliamentary party left right position.

Party system: the arithmetic difference between the median voter Left-Right position and the Left-Right position of the party closest to the median voter.

government policy position are calculated from party policy positions may raise some doubts about a potential tautology in evaluating results. When we consider the details of the calculations in each case it can be seen however that they are quite capable of varying independently of each other—as the tables in fact demonstrate. We have already shown that substituting another measure would produce similar results in the case of government policy (r = 0.82 with Powell's expert estimates (2000: 173–4)). So other measures would produce similar results, although they could be applied only to distortion rather than to long-term bias and responsiveness, lacking the time dimension of the manifesto data. From a wider theoretical perspective, it can be said that any tautology is inbuilt to the structure of modern representative government, which forces voters to express their public preferences by voting for party programmes and then commissions the same parties with their declared programmes to make up government. We investigate the links between these. But representative government itself creates the situation in which they become substantively important.

What we are investigating by comparing median voter preferences with median parliamentary ones, and both with government intentions, are therefore rule-based rather than strictly causal relationships. Modern representative theory says that parliaments and governments ought to reflect popular preferences, and we investigate the extent to which it can be said that they do. Because of limits on space we have not discussed here the mechanisms by which such congruence might come about, whether by parties converging on the median voter (Downs 1957: 114–18) or through them offering fairly clearly differentiated and stable alternatives to electors (Downs 1957: 122–7).

It is clear from our mapping of party positions whether in the West (Budge et al. 2001: 19–50) or in CEE (Chapter 1) that parties generally stick within the same ideological range which differentiates them from each other in terms of current policy. This supports a mandate rather than a convergence approach to representation. We have raised elsewhere (McDonald, Mendés, and Budge 2004) the question of what kind of mandate operates. The difficulty with the idea that elections select and empower a government with a majority mandate to carry through its party programme is that elections so rarely do so (only in 12 per cent of all cases according to our calculations). An alternative can be found in the idea of a median mandate, where election rules ensure that the party the median voter supports becomes the median and hence the pivotal party in parliament.

A full specification of these ideas with an investigation following out the fulfilment of majority preferences, not only in relationship to government policy *intentions* but to the actual policy they make, can be found in a volume just published by Oxford University Press (McDonald and Budge, *Elections, Parties, Democracy: Conferring the Median Mandate*). This brings together the manifesto-based estimates described in this chapter together with expenditure data from the 1960s to 1990s to check out the extent to which modern Western democracies conform to median mandate prescriptions. The same research can now be applied to CEE with the data now made available in this book and CD-ROM, to which we turn in the next chapter.

NOTE

1. The study we report made two modifications to the calculation. First, in the case of Iceland and Portugal the category 'effective authority' was omitted from the Left-Right calculation, as inspection indicated this was not an indicator of right-leaning attitudes in these two countries. Second, when the furthest left or furthest right party in a system is involved in the formula, it is assumed that the voters on its 'outer side' occupy an interval symmetrical with that on its 'inner side' rather than stretching out to +100 or −100, which would render them unrealistically extreme. The correlation between estimates made on these assumptions and the original Kim–Fording ones are still of the order of $r = .95$ however.

8

Using the Data

This chapter moves on to a discussion of the material contained in the CD-ROM and of the ways in which this may be utilized and extended. The CD-ROM contains the data described in the earlier chapters, organized so as to facilitate the further analyses suggested there or in other appropriate investigations. We begin by describing data organization, and continue with suggestions about how this could be utilized to answer questions about party policy positions within and among the countries discussed in the text. We conclude with procedures for coding other party manifestos or related documents for MRG-type analyses.

THE FILES

The CD-ROM holds four types of files. *Documentation* files describe the procedures used to create the policy indicators from the original party platforms and manifestos. These are in *Adobe pdf* format which can be accessed with the *Acrobat 7* reader supplied on the CD-ROM. *Data* files hold the policy preference indicators. These appear in three formats: (*a*) Comma-delimited text, (*b*) Excel spreadsheets, and (*c*) SPSS[1] portable files. *Text* files include samples of the original material used by the MRG to produce the substantive policy codes underlying the analyses reported earlier in this book. *Utility* files include two programs designed to facilitate use of the documentation and data files by readers who do not have computer programs that can access these files. Each set of files will be described in turn.

DATA FILES

The data files contained in the CD-ROM cover four topics related to the broad theme of policy preferences: (*a*) Party Policy Positions, (*b*) Party Mean Scores on Six Policy Scales, (*c*) Median Voter Preference, and (*d*) Government Policy Positions.

Three data formats are used for each topic area to enhance the material's accessibility by different computer programs. Files with an '.xls' extension are designed for the *Microsoft Excel* spreadsheet programs and are compatible

The CD-ROM included with the book is compatible with both
MAC OS and Windows 95 (and above) computer systems.

Instructions for using the CD-ROM appear on the CD-ROM label.

WINDOWS

The CD-ROM will start automatically when inserted in a PC
operating under Windows. To enter the CD-ROM's contents, click
on Start.

MAC OS

A CD-ROM icon will appear when the CD-ROM is inserted. Click
on the icon.

OTHER

The files described in Chapter 8 are stored in subdirectories
on the CD-ROM. Subdirectory names are described
in the section entitled 'The Files'. Individual file names are intuitively
meaningful; it will be clear what each topic designates.

Fig. 8.1. Using the CD-ROM: System requirements

with releases 5 onwards of that program.[2] As the Excel format is becoming a
de facto data transfer standard, users of other analysis programs will likely find
that their programs will easily convert this file format. Files with a '.por' extension
are designed for the SPSS analysis system, popular with many social scientists.
Indeed, it is so commonly available, that files formatted for SPSS are often directly
usable by other statistical analysis programs. Finally, files with a '.csv' extension
are stored as text files in which each unit of information is set off (or delimited)
by a comma. Files in this format should be accessible to any programs used to
manipulate structured data.

The information is presented in a further two ways. Information for all the
countries can be accessed simultaneously or the data for individual countries can
be accessed separately. Individual country data are presented in straight character
(ASCII) format with the separate fields delimited by commas. These files are
provided for readers who cannot use the .xls or .por files. Because these readers
may have difficulty in categorizing the observations by countries, separate country
files were created.

PARTY POLICY POSITIONS

As Table 8.1 shows, this file contains the major country-by-country across-party
over-time manifesto policy codes. These form the basis of all the analyses reported
in the earlier chapters and lend themselves to further analyses.

Table 8.1. Party policy positions

Name	Meaning
COUNTRY	Country Code
COUNTRY NAME	Name of Country
EDATE	Day-Month-Year of Election
PARTY	Party Identification Number; These Are Structured to Identify Party Type. See Appendix II on the CD-ROM
PARTY NAME	Full Party Name
VOTEEST	Original or Estimated Figure for Votes: (0) Original and (1) estimated
PRESVOTE	Percentage of Votes in Presidential Elections
ABSSEAT	Absolute Number of Seats
TOTSEATS	Total Number of Seats in Parliament
PROGTYPE	Type of Program Data
DOMAIN 1	EXTERNAL RELATONS
PER101	Foreign Special Relationships: Positive
PER102	Foreign Special Relationships: Negative
PER103	Anti-Imperialism
PER104	Military: Positive
PER105	Military: Negative
PER106	Peace
PER107	Internationalism: Positive
PER108	European Community: Positive
PER109	Internationalism: Negative
PER110	European Community: Negative
DOMAIN 2	FREEDOM AND DEMOCRACY
PER201	Freedom and Human Rights
PER202	Democracy
PER203	Constitutionalism: Positive
PER204	Constitutionalism: Negative
DOMAIN 3	POLITICAL SYSTEM
PER301	Decentralization
PER302	Centralization
PER303	Government and Administrative Efficiency
PER304	Political Corruption
PER305	Political Authority
DOMAIN 4	ECONOMY
PER401	Free Enterprise
PER402	Incentives
PER403	Market Regulation
PER404	Economic Planning
PER405	Corporatism
PER406	Protectionism: Positive
PER407	Protectionism: Negative
PER408	Economic Goals
PER409	Keynesian Demand Management
PER410	Productivity
PER411	Technology and Infrastructure
PER412	Controlled Economy
PER413	Nationalization

Table 8.1. (*Continued*)

Name	Meaning
PER414	Economic Orthodoxy
PER415	Marxist Analysis
PER416	Anti-Growth Economy
DOMAIN 5	WELFARE AND QUALITY OF LIFE
PER501	Environmental Protection
PER502	Culture
PER503	Social Justice
PER504	Welfare State Expansion
PER505	Welfare State Limitation
PER506	Education Expansion
PER507	Education Limitation
DOMAIN 6	FABRIC OF SOCIETY
PER601	National Way of Life: Positive
PER602	National Way of Life: Negative
PER603	Traditional Morality: Positive
PER604	Traditional Morality: Negative
PER605	Law and Order
PER606	Social Harmony
PER607	Multiculturalism: Positive
PER608	Multiculturalism: Negative
DOMAIN 7	SOCIAL GROUPS
PER701	Labour Groups: Positive
PER702	Labour Groups: Negative
PER703	Agriculture and Farmers
PER704	Middle Class and Professional Groups
PER705	Underprivileged Minority Groups
ADDITIONAL SUBCATEGORIES USED FOR CEE COUNTRIES	
	For Comparisons Between OECD and CEE Countries, Subcategories Can Be Aggregated into one of the fifty-six Standard Categories Used in all Countries
PER1011	Russia/USSR/CIS: Positive (Subcategory of PER101)
PER1012	Western States: Positive (Subcategory of PER101)
PER1013	Eastern European Countries: Positive (Subcategory of PER101)
PER1014	Baltic States: Positive (Subcategory of PER101)
PER1015	Nordic Council: Positive (Subcategory of PER101)
PER1016	SFR Yugoslavia: Positive (Subcategory of PER101)
PER1021	Russia/USSR/CIS: Negative (Subcategory of PER102)
PER1022	Western States: Negative (Subcategory of PER102)
PER1023	Eastern European Countries: Negative (Subcategory of PER102)
PER1024	Baltic States: Negative (Subcategory of PER102)
PER1025	Nordic Council: Negative (Subcategory of PER102)
PER1026	SFR Yugoslavia: Negative (Subcategory of PER102)
PER1031	Russian Army: Negative (Subcategory of PER103)
PER1032	Independence: Positive (Subcategory of PER103)
PER1033	Rights of Nations: Positive (Subcategory of PER103)

Table 8.1. (*Continued*)

Name	Meaning
PER2021	Transition to Democracy (Subcategory of PER202)
PER2022	Restrictive Citizenship: Positive (Subcategory of PER202)
PER2023	Lax Citizenship: Positive (Subcategory of PER202)
PER2031	Presidential Regime: Positive (Subcategory of PER203)
PER2032	Republic: Positive (Subcategory of PER203)
PER2033	Checks and Balances: Positive (Subcategory of PER203)
PER2041	Monarchy: Positive (Subcategory of PER204)
PER3011	Republican Powers: Positive (Subcategory of PER301)
PER3051	Public Situation: Negative (Subcategory of PER305)
PER3052	Communist: Positive (Subcategory of PER305)
PER3053	Communist: Negative (Subcategory of PER305)
PER3054	Rehabilitation and Compensation (Subcategory of PER305)
PER3055	Political Coalitions: Positive (Subcategory of PER305)
PER4011	Privatisation: Positive (Subcategory of PER401)
PER4012	Control of Economy: Negative (Subcategory of PER401)
PER4013	Property Restitution: Positive (Subcategory of PER401)
PER4014	Privatization Vouchers: Positive (Subcategory of PER401)
PER4121	Social Ownership: Positive (Subcategory of PER412)
PER4122	Mixed Economy: Positive (Subcategory of PER412)
PER4123	Publicly Owned Industry: Positive (Subcategory of PER412)
PER4124	Socialist Property: Positive (Subcategory of PER412)
PER4131	Property Restitution: Negative (Subcategory of PER413)
PER4132	Privatization: Negative (Subcategory of PER412)
PER5021	Private–Public Mix in Culture: Positive (Subcategory of PER502)
PER5031	Private–Public Mix in Social Justice: Positive (Subcategory of PER503)
PER5041	Private–Public Mix in Welfare: Positive (Subcategory of PER504)
PER5061	Private–Public Mix in Education: Positive (Subcategory of PER506)
PER6011	The Karabakh Issue: Positive (Subcategory of PER601)
PER6012	Rebuilding the USSR: Positive (Subcategory of PER601)
PER6013	National Security: Positive (Subcategory of PER601)
PER6061	General Crisis (Subcategory of PER606)
PER6071	Cultural Autonomy: Positive (Subcategory of PER607)
PER6072	Multiculturalism Pro-Roma (Subcategory of PER607)
PER6081	Multiculturalism Against Roma (Subcategory of PER608)
PER7051	Minorities Inland: Positive (Subcategory of PER705)
PER7052	Minorities Abroad: Positive (Subcategory of PER705)
PER7061	War Participants: Positive (Subcategory of PER706)
PER7062	Refugees: Positive (Subcategory of PER706)
ADDITIONAL STATISTICS	INFORMATION ABOUT CODING UNITS
PERUNCOD	Uncoded Quasi-Sentences
TOTAL	Absolute Number of Quasi-Sentences

Table 8.1. (*Continued*)

Name	Meaning
SUMMARY POLICY INDICATORS	SUMMARY PARTY POLICY STANDS
RIGHTLEFT	Left-Right Index
PLANECO	Planned Economy
MARKECO	Market Economy
WELFARE	Welfare References
INTPEACE	International Peace
EUROP	European Integration Index

Note: Extended field definitions are provided in Appendix I, 164.

Table 8.1 shows the layout of the material in the file. There are three distinct groups of estimates covered in the CD-ROM, all of which pertain to elections between 1990 and 2003. First, those for the twenty-four OECD countries and Israel, the countries which formed the subject matter of *Mapping Policy Preferences*, 2001. Second, estimates for CEE countries which have recently experienced a transition to democracy. (Eight of these countries are recent EU accession states.) Third, other countries which are EU accession states, notably Malta and Cyprus. (Particular elections in different countries for which no estimates are included are noted in Appendix I.) The file has the percentage of quasi-sentences[3] for each specific policy area in each party's manifesto for elections occurring between 1990 and 2003. Besides these specific policy preferences, individual party scores are given on the six general policy scales (market economy, planned economy, welfare provision, international peace, and European integration as well as the party's general Left-Right stance). This information is combined with details of each party's electoral success as indicated by the percentage of votes and seats gained in the election.

MEDIAN VOTER

These files contain estimates of median voter positions inferred from party positions and votes. The approach is fully described in the previous chapter which exemplifies how the basic policy estimates can be extended to new areas. Table 8.2 describes the file contents.

Two other aspects of this work can be mentioned under the broad heading of extensions. First, Table 8.2 shows how policy estimates can be combined to create new composite indicators. Second, median positions can be calculated for countries not presently in the data-set when new information becomes available. Government policy positions are structured in exactly the same manner with appropriate changes in terminology. These latter estimates use the same government identification system as that set out in Woldendorp, Keman, and Budge (2000) and are explained in Table 8.3.

Table 8.2. Median voter position file structure

Field name	Meaning
COUNTRY	Country Numeric Code
COUNTRY NAME	Country Name
ELECYR	Election Year
EDATE	Year-Month of Election
PEACEMED	Voter Position on Peace (Calculation: per102+per105+per106)
WELFMED	Voter Position on Welfare (Calculation: per503+per504)
PLANMED	Voter Position on Planned Economy (Calculation: per403+per404+per412)
MARKECOMED	Voter Position on Market Economy (Calculation: per401+per414)
RIGHTLEFT	Voter Position on Left-Right Spectrum (Code: left(−100) <- - -> right(+100)
EUROPMED	Voter Position on European Integration (per108 − per110)

Table 8.3. Government policy position

Field name	Meaning
COUNTRY	Country Number
COUNTRY NAME	
GOVID	Government ID after Woldendorp, Keman, and Budge (2000)
INAUGDAT	Day-Month of Government's Inauguaration
GOV POSITIONS	Estimated Government Policy Positions

TEXT FILES

The data files described above are based on substantive codes assigned to party manifestos by members of the CMP working to a common coding scheme. Inter-coder consistency was achieved by asking new coders to work on a sample manifesto with known substantive content. The new coder's work could then be compared to this standard. Sample manifesto text files are included on the CD-ROM to allow the reader to replicate this training, either because he or she wants reassurance about the procedure or, to code additional manifestos similarly.

The files contain, inter alia, extracts from two manifestos: (*a*) Great Britain's Liberal/SDP Alliance Party 1983 document 'Working Together for Britain' and (*b*) New Zealand's National Party 1972 document 'A Guide to What the Next National Government Will Do for New Zealand.' *Original Documents* holds the text as it originally appeared. *Quasi-Sentences* breaks this material into coding units, in preparation for the reader's own application of the coding rules. Appendix II: (Manifesto Coding Instructions) on this CD-ROM provides details of this. *Coded Sentences* contains the codes assigned by the CMP which can be used to verify the reader's codes.

DOCUMENTATION FILES

Documentation files contain supporting material for the analyses reported here and elsewhere. Moreover, they provide essential background for the further use of the Data files on the CD-ROM. The files and their contents are:

Appendix I: Description of manifesto data-set
    lists the contents of Policy Positions with more extensive detail about each indicator than is provided in Table 8.1.

Appendix II: Manifesto coding instructions[4]
    describes the MRG's coding procedure. It begins by describing how it developed over-time and then shows how it can be applied to a sample manifesto (contained on the CD-ROM in original documents). The file contains extensive definitions of the separate coding categories.

Appendix III: Political parties included in the data-set
    shows how the numeric party identifiers signify the party–family basis for classifying parties within each country and lists every party included in the data-set, both in English and in the original language—transliterating where necessary. The elections for which estimates are available for the parties are also provided.

Appendix IV: Missing party documents
    lists the active parties in the period 1990–2003 for which no party platforms are available. Consequently, these parties are excluded from the summary data-sets on the CD-ROM.

Appendix V: Party programmes, titles, and sources
    lists the programmatic documents on which each set of party policy estimates is based, together with the actual sources from which they were obtained.

UTILITY FILES

Program files will install utilities that allow browsing of the .xls data files, SPSS files, and the .pdf documentation files:

Adobe Reader 7.0
    To install 'Acrobat 7.0' click on Acrobat. Then follow the instructions that appear on the screen.

Excel 97 Viewer (not for MAC OS)
    To install the 'Microsoft Excel 97 Viewer' under the Windows 95/98/ME operating system, click on MS Excel Viewer. Then follow the instructions that appear on the screen.[5]

SPSS Set-up for Data-Sets.

SUGGESTIONS FOR FURTHER RESEARCH

Several topics were explicitly suggested in the earlier chapters but many more will have occurred to the reader. Indeed, the motive for including our latest data in this text is to stimulate a continuation of the work begun by the original MRG in 1979.

The text itself synthesizes the work done to date by the original MRG and its successor, the CMP. This provides a launch pad for other analyses to advance our understanding of the policy process by replication and extension. The CD-ROM can fuel further exploratory trips through the data, further types of extension. Several possible analyses are described below. Readers however may also wish to add more party systems and/or new time periods to those covered here. Since they would need to start by coding new party manifestos, we also describe how the researcher can extend the material provided on the CD-ROM.

FURTHER ANALYSES

The data in the Party Policy Position file can be the basis for many further investigations. Examples are:

- Excel users can use the *correl* function to assess the extent to which particular policy stances move together within parties. For example, positive correlations among *per607: Multiculturalism-Positive* and *per705: Minority Groups* and *per606: Social Harmony* may reveal attitude structures underlying policy makers' assessment of this area. The inter-relationship between policy indicators can be visualized by using several of the multi-indicator charts provided by Excel. Indeed the different policy stands and indices included in Appendix VI are calculated in this way. Here, the emphasis is on the policy areas themselves—the parties are simple vehicles for these policy characteristics. However, within-country and/or over-time evaluation of the relationship among policy areas, showing the differences that time and place can make, are also feasible with these data, as the next example suggests.

- Showing time and place differences in relationships requires the judicious sorting of the individual observations (or parties) into either country groups or time periods or into within-time and country groups together. Multiple rearrangements of data are a particular strength of spreadsheet programs like Excel. The analyses can then be conducted on the data contained within these groupings.

- The impact of policy stances on electoral success can be gauged by regressing either the proportion of votes earned or the number of seats won onto one or more policy estimates. This can be done with Excel's *Regression analysis tool* (part of the analysis toolpack) or with Quattro Pro's *@Regression* function.

- Researchers interested in party strategy can also use these data and their program's regression functions, in conjunction with these programs' data transformation routines, to evaluate the success of different vote attraction strategies. For example, an analyst interested in the impact of a changing emphasis on minorities could score each party on how its emphasis on per705: Minority Groups changed between elections. Similarly, their changed success, say as measured by a new variable created by scoring inter-election changes on abseats ÷ totseats could be regressed on the 'change in per705' indicator.

- Profiles of any country's policy agenda for a particular year can be established by calculating the within-year policy scores. This will provide a description of the policy marketplace available to that country's electorate in a particular election—not every party has to offer Protectionism (per406: Protectionism Positive–per407: Protectionism Negative), but the elector interested in it should have at least one party purveying it in return for her vote. Changed emphases across time can then be plotted using one of the charting functions.

- Additional policy scales can be constructed which might be of particular interest for specific countries, groups of countries, or parties. For example, we could compare positive 'special foreign relations' between the fifteen West European members of the EU and the eight new CEE members by creating an index which subtracts per102 Foreign Relations Negative from per101 Foreign Relations Positive, which would also include the extensions constructed to catch the special interests of CEE countries.

ADDING OBSERVATIONS

The data in the Party Policy Position file also provide the basis for contextual analyses. Several authors, in works cited in this text's bibliographies, began with the MRG's policy estimates to establish similar ratings for parties operating in other countries and/or in other time periods. Indeed, several of the substantive contributions to this volume exemplify how the estimates can be extended by adding new types of data. This can be taken further, for example they could be pooled with survey and public opinion data (see, e.g. Adams et al. 2004), or new categories based on survey materials can be established (see, e.g. Bara 2006). Adding new party systems to the data-set requires a different approach, for the appropriate party documents have to be transformed to an MRG compatible form before they can be analysed. In other words, each new party document must be coded by applying the MRG coding frame *in the same way* that a member of the MRG would. Deviation in procedures would introduce incompatibilities which render subsequent comparisons invalid.

Adding new parties is a two-stage process. First, the researcher must become operationally conversant with MRG procedures. Second, these procedures must be applied. Each stage will be discussed in turn.

LEARNING TO CODE

File 'Appendix II Manifesto Coding Instructions' on the CD-ROM is the best starting point for the training process. This material, in conjunction with Chapter 4 of *Mapping Policy Preferences*, 2001,[6] establishes the MRG's guiding ethos.

Having read the material, we suggest that the sample manifesto material, extracts from the 1983 British Liberal-Social Democratic Alliance and the 1972 New Zealand National Party programmes, be coded using the MRG procedures. This will require, first, that the text be edited into quasi-sentences, the basic MRG coding unit. The MRG coding framework, presented in file 'Appendix II: Manifesto Coding Instructions', can then be applied. Finally, the results of the reader's own coding can be compared to the MRG-applied codes. Any deviations can be reasoned through by looking at the MRG procedures for further guidance.

Three files on the CD-ROM support this training exercise. As mentioned earlier, *Original Documents* holds the extracts in their published formats, *Quasi-Sentences* shows what the document looks like after the MRG rules have been applied to produce the coding units, and *Coded Sentences* shows the grouping of sentences into the MRG topic codes.

The structure of these three files lead to our recommendation about how the second stage of the addition of new parties should be organized. Budge, Tanenbaum, and Bara (1999) found that the spreadsheet format eased the coding of new party documents, reduced clerical errors, and facilitated the analysis of the coded material. It also facilitated comparisons between manual and computerized coding, such as that discussed in Chapter 6.

Using this approach clearly requires that the party documents be in computer-readable format. While this may entail scanning printed documents, our experience is that recent party documents are available on the World Wide Web sites maintained by many parties or at the Zentralarchiv Cologne (za@za.uni-koeln.de). Consequently they can be downloaded as electronic files.[7]

They may, however, have embedded formatting instructions. These will be immediately recognizable when the document file is opened with a word processor and can therefore be easily removed with the word processor's 'find and replace' function. The word processor can also be used to transform the original document into the quasi-sentences demanded by the MRG's coding procedure. Essentially, this just means inserting a physical line break by doing a 'carriage return'[8] at the appropriate point in the text. If the resulting file is saved as a text file, it will be straightforward to input it to a spreadsheet programme.

SUMMARY

When the MRG began its work in the 1970s, it did not imagine that the work would launch such an extensive, open-ended investigation into the democratic policy making process. This book is evidence that it has. This chapter has shown how investigations might be extended even further. Its discussion of the CD-ROM included as an intrinsic part of the book suggests how the data can be analysed and developed, by independent researchers in totally new directions, which will enrich and enhance the collection in future years.

NOTES

1. Statistical package for the social sciences (also now known as statistical product and service solutions).
2. These files can also be viewed, but not manipulated, with the XLViewer programs supplied on the disk.
3. Extended field definitions are given in Appendix III.
4. The MRG's coding procedures are described in Andrea Volkens 'Quantifying the Election Programmes: Coding Procedures and Controls,' in Budge et al. (2001) *Mapping Policy Preferences: Estimates for Parties, Electors and Governments, 1945–98.*
5. Although comments are directed to Microsoft Excel users, the functions that are described are generic and will have equivalent implementations in *any* spreadsheet programs. The suggestions have been tested with Quattro Pro 9 and Lotus 1-2-3.
6. Volkens (2001) ibid.
7. As stated in the introductory chapter, it is also the case that digitalized party manifestos for the OECD countries are made available on request by the Zentralarchiv für Empirische Sozialforschung, Univesität zu Köln, under certain conditions regarding their usage (the contact address is za@za.uni-koeln.de). The textual data are part of the Comparative Electronic Manifestos Project (http://research.fsw.vu.nl/DoingResearch) directed by Paul Pennings and Hans Keman, Vrije Universitat, Amsterdam, in collaboration with Ekkehard Mochmann of the ZA.
8. On some keyboards, this key is labelled *Enter*; on others it is called *Return*.

Description of Manifesto Data-Set

Units	Parliamentary parties at national elections
Data Sources	Content analysed election programmes or their nearest equivalents (see Appendix II for details) and publicly available election statistics
Number of countries	51; including 24 OECD countries; 24 CEE countries, among which are 4 OECD members; 3 other countries, of which 2 are EU members
Number of parties	651
Number of elections	185
Time period covered	1990–2003; except all semi-free elections of 1990 in CEE countries and of 2000 in Belorussia; except Moldova 1998 and 2001. One extra election is also included for Britain (2005) and the USA (2004).
Number of cases	1,314; including 108 cases of estimated programmatic data for missing programmes (Progtype = 3), among them all cases for the following elections:

Albania 2001,
Belgium 2003,
Bosnia 2002,
Croatia 2000 + 2003,
Iceland 2003,
Japan 2003,
Macedonia 2002,
Montenegro 2002,
Portugal 2002, and
Turkey 2002; including 140 cases of parties without seats in parliament (Absseat = 0). These 140 cases comprise programmes of single parties that have been assigned to party blocs or joint programmes that have been assigned to single parties (see variable progtype) and some parties that are not represented in parliament at all.

Number of variables	9	identification variables
	3	data quality variables
	5	electoral data variables
	113	programmatic data variables
	5	programmatic dimensions

Identification Variables:
I. OECD countries

Country	Two digit code:

11	Sweden
12	Norway
13	Denmark
14	Finland

15   Iceland
21   Belgium
22   Netherlands
23   Luxembourg
31   France
32   Italy
33   Spain
34   Greece
35   Portugal
41   Germany
42   Austria
43   Switzerland
51   Great Britain
53   Ireland
61   USA
62   Canada
63   Australia
64   New Zealand
71   Japan
74   Turkey

II. CEE countries
75   Albania
76   Armenia
77   Azerbaijan
78   Belarus
79   Bosnia-Herzegovina
80   Bulgaria
81   Croatia
82   Czech Republic
83   Estonia
84   Georgia
85   German Democratic Republic
86   Hungary
87   Latvia
88   Lithuania
89   Macedonia
90   Moldova
91   Montenegro
92   Poland
93   Romania
94   Russia
95   Serbia
96   Slovakia
97   Slovenia
98   Ukraine

III. Other Countries
54   Malta
55   Cyprus
72   Israel

Countryname	Name of country in English (string variable)
OECD	0 not OECD member
	10 OECD member countries as of 2004
EU	0 not EU member
	10 25 EU members as of 2004
	20 EU applicants as of 2004
Edate	Day, month, and year of national election (DD.MM.YY)
Date	Year and month of national election
Party	The party identification code consists of five digits. The first two digits repeat the country code. The third, fourth, and fifth digit are running numbers.
Partyname	Abbreviations of names of parties in original language and names of parties in English (string variable)
Parfam	Tentative grouping of political parties and alliances into the following party families (party family origin):

10	ECO	Ecology parties
20	COM	Communist parties
30	SOC	Social democratic parties
40	LIB	Liberal parties
50	CHR	Christian democratic parties
60	CON	Conservative parties
70	NAT	Nationalist parties
80	AGR	Agrarian parties
90	ETH	Ethnic and regional parties
95	SIP	Special issue parties
98	DIV	Electoral alliances of diverse origin without dominant party
99	MI	Missing information

Data Quality Variables:

CoderID	Identification number of coder, three digit code:
	First digit: 1 MRG/CMP group member
	2 hired coder
	8 specifically trained coder
Coderyear	Year during which coding took place
Reltest	Result of reliability test as given in coding handbook: test of accuracy in comparison to the master copy;
	999 no handbook during first phase of coding/test not done by MRG member or specifically trained coder

Electoral Data Variables:

Pervote	Percentage of votes gained by each party; in CEE countries also percentage of votes gained by party blocs; for mixed electoral systems with both a proportional and a majoritarian components, votes for proportional component only;
	99.99 no votes available (for Belarus 1995 and Montenegro 1990)
Voteest	**0 Original figure from data source**
	As a rule, election statistics present votes and seats for each party in parliament. However, in CEE countries electoral coalitions are quite frequent and votes and seats are only available for blocs of parties.

1   Estimated
In OECD countries, blocs of parties are less frequent and seats are given for each single party in the electoral coalition. Here, votes for parties in electoral coalitions often have been estimated on the basis of the distribution of seats between them.

Presvote   Percentage of votes in presidential elections; for USA only; 99.99 for all countries besides the USA.

Absseat   Absolute number of seats held by each party or party bloc.

Totseats   Total number of seats in parliament.

Programmatic Data Variables:

Progtype   **1   Programme of a single party**
As a rule, each party issues one programme for each election.

2   Programme of two or more parties
In a number of countries, parties compete as programmatic coalitions by issuing joint programmes. In these cases, the joint programmes were assigned to each of the parties of the programmatic coalitions.

3   Estimate
For calculating median voter or median party figures, missing election programmes have been estimated on the basis of available programmes whenever a party obtained seats in parliament. Estimates were derived either by computing averages between two adjacent programmes or by duplicating programmatic data (see Appendix V on CD-Rom for details).

4   Programme taken from main party of electoral coalition
In CEE countries especially, parties often compete as electoral coalitions which means that blocs of parties receive joint votes and seats, but the single parties in the blocs still issue separate programmes. When the electoral coalition is dominated by one strong party, the programme of the main coalition party was used to measure positions of the 'electoral coalition' as a whole.

5   Average of all members of an electoral coalition
When the electoral coalition consists of equally strong parties, the average of platforms from all coalition parties was used to measure positions of the electoral coalition as a whole.

6   General programme
Some parties did not issue separate election programmes but contested elections with their general programmes.

8   Party bloc programme
Some party blocs issue joint programmes. Rather than providing electoral statistics for the single parties making up the bloc as is the case for type 2 programmes, electoral statistics are given for the party bloc as a whole.

9   Other type of programme
Other types of programmes not specified by types 1 to 8 (see Appendix V on CD-Rom for details).

Data entries   Percentages of quasi-sentences in each of fifty-six categories grouped
per101–per706   into seven major policy areas. Because of differences in the length

of the documents, the number of (quasi-)sentences in each category is standardized taking the total number of (quasi-)sentences in the respective documents as a basis. In the data-set each of these categories is a variable represented by the percentage.

Domain 1: External Relations

per101   *Foreign Special Relationships: Positive*

Favourable mention of particular countries with which the manifesto country has a special relationship. For example, in the British case: former colonies; in the Swedish case: the rest of Scandinavia; the need for cooperation with and/or aid to such countries.

per102   *Foreign Special Relationships: Negative*

Negative mention of particular countries with which the manifesto country has a special relationship; otherwise as 101, but negative.

per103   *Anti-Imperialism: Anti-Colonialism*

Negative reference to exerting strong influence (political, military, or commercial) over other states; negative reference to controlling other countries as if they were part of an empire; favourable mention of decolonization; favourable reference to greater self-government and independence for colonies; negative reference to the imperial behaviour of the manifesto and/or other countries.

per104   *Military: Positive*

Need to maintain or increase military expenditure; modernizing armed forces and improvement in military strength; rearmament and self-defence; need to keep military treaty obligations; need to secure adequate manpower in the military.

per105   *Military: Negative*

Favourable mention of decreasing military expenditures; disarmament; 'evils of war'; promises to reduce conscription, otherwise as 104, but negative.

per106   *Peace: Positive*

Peace as a general goal; declarations of belief in peace and peaceful means of solving crises; desirability of countries joining in negotiations with hostile countries.

per107   *Internationalism: Positive*

Need for international cooperation; cooperation with specific countries other than those coded in 101; need for aid to developing countries; need for world planning of resources; need for international courts; support for any international goal or world state; support for UN.

per108   *European Integration: Positive*

Favourable mention of European integration in general; desirability of expanding the European Union and/or of increasing its competence; desirability of the manifesto country joining (or remaining a member).

per109   *Internationalism: Negative*

Favourable mention of national independence and sovereignty as opposed to internationalism; otherwise as 107, but negative.

per110   *European Integration: Negative*

Hostile mention of the European Union; opposition to specific European policies which are preferred by European authorities; otherwise as 108, but negative.

Domain 2: Freedom and Democracy

per201   *Freedom and Human Rights: Positive*

Favourable mention of importance of personal freedom and civil rights; freedom from bureaucratic control; freedom of speech; freedom from coercion in the political and economic spheres; individualism in the manifesto country and in other countries.

per202   *Democracy: Positive*

Favourable mention of democracy as a method or goal in national and other organizations; involvement of all citizens in decision-making, as well as generalized support for the manifesto country's democracy.

per203   *Constitutionalism: Positive*

Support for specific aspects of the constitution; use of constitutionalism as an argument for policy as well as general approval of the constitutional way of doing things.

per204   *Constitutionalism: Negative*

Opposition to the constitution in general or to specific aspects; otherwise as 203, but negative.

Domain 3: Political System

per301   *Decentralization: Positive*

Support for federalism or devolution; more regional autonomy for policy or economy; support for keeping up local and regional customs and symbols; favourable mention of special consideration for local areas; deference to local expertise.

per302   *Centralization: Positive*

Opposition to political decision-making at lower political levels; support for more centralization in political and administrative procedures; otherwise as 301, but negative.

per303   *Governmental and Administrative Efficiency: Positive*

Need for efficiency and economy in government and administration; cutting down civil service; improving governmental procedures; general appeal to make the process of government and administration cheaper and more effective.

per304   *Political Corruption: Negative*

Need to eliminate corruption, and associated abuse, in political and public life.

156 *Mapping Policy Preferences II*

per305   ***Political Authority: Positive***

Favourable mention of strong government, including government stability; manifesto party's competence to govern and/or other party's lack of such competence.

Domain 4: Economy

per401   *Free Enterprise: Positive*

Favourable mention of free enterprise capitalism; superiority of individual enterprise over state and control systems; favourable mention of private property rights, personal enterprise and initiative; need for unhampered individual enterprises.

per402   *Incentives: Positive*

Need for wage and tax policies to induce enterprise; encouragement to start enterprises; need for financial and other incentives such as subsidies.

per403   *Market Regulation: Positive*

Need for regulations designed to make private enterprises work better; actions against monopolies and trusts, and in defence of consumer and small business; encouraging economic competition; social market economy.

per404   *Economic Planning: Positive*

Favourable mention of long-standing economic planning of a consultative or indicative nature, need for government to create such a plan.

per405   *Corporatism: Positive*

Favourable mention of the need for the collaboration of employers and trade union organizations in overall economic planning and direction through the medium of tripartite bodies of government, employers, and trade unions. (This category was not used for Austria up to 1979, for New Zealand up to 1981, and for Sweden up to 1988.)

per406   *Protectionism: Positive*

Favourable mention of extension or maintenance of tariffs to protect internal markets; other domestic economic protectionism such as quota restrictions.

per407   *Protectionism: Negative*

Support for the concept of free trade; otherwise as 406, but negative.

per408   *Economic Goals*

Statements of intent to pursue any economic goals not covered by other categories in Domain 4. This category is created to catch an overall interest of parties in economics and, therefore, covers a variety of economic goals.

per409   *Keynesian Demand Management: Positive*

Demand-oriented economic policy; economic policy devoted to avoiding depression, mitigating effects of depression, and/or to increasing private demand through boosting public demand and/or through increasing social expenditures.

per410　　　*Productivity: Positive*

Need to encourage or facilitate greater production; need to take measures to aid this; appeal for greater production and importance of productivity to the economy; increasing foreign trade; the paradigm of growth.

per411　　　*Technology and Infrastructure: Positive*

Importance of modernization of industry and methods of transport and communication; importance of science and technological developments in industry; need for training and research. This does not imply education in general (see category 506).

per412　　　*Controlled Economy: Positive*

General need for direct government control of economy; control over prices, wages, rents, etc.; state intervention into the economic system.

per413　　　*Nationalization: Positive*

Favourable mention of government ownership, partial or complete, including government ownership of land.

per414　　　*Economic Orthodoxy: Positive*

Need for traditional economic orthodoxy, e.g. reduction of budget deficits, retrenchment in crisis, thrift, and savings; support for traditional economic institutions such as stock market and banking system; support for strong currency.

per415　　　*Marxist Analysis: Positive*

Positive reference (typically but not necessary by Communist parties) to the specific use of Marxist-Leninist terminology and analysis of situations which are otherwise uncodable. This category was not used for Austria 1945–79, for Australia, Japan, and the USA up to 1980; for Belgium, Ireland, the Netherlands, and New Zealand up to 1981; for Italy and Britain up to 1983; for Denmark, Luxembourg, and Israel up to 1984; for Canada, France, and Sweden up to 1988.

per416　　　*Anti-Growth Economy: Positive*

Favourable mention of anti-growth politics and steady-state economy; ecologism/'Green politics' especially as applied to economic policy; sustainable development. This category was not used for Austria 1945–79, for Australia, Japan, and the USA up to 1980; for Belgium, Ireland, the Netherlands, and New Zealand up to 1981; for Italy and Britain up to 1983; for Denmark, Luxembourg, and Israel up to 1984; for Canada, France, and Sweden up to 1988; and for Norway up to 1989. Test codings, however, have shown that parties before the beginning of the 1990s hardly ever advocated anti-growth policies.

Domain 5: Welfare and Quality of Life

per501　　　*Environmental Protection: Positive*

Preservation of countryside, forests, etc.; general preservation of natural resources against selfish interests; proper use of national parks; soil banks, etc.; environmental improvement. 'Ecologism'/'Green' politics as applied to environmental policy.

per502   *Culture: Positive*

Need to provide cultural and leisure facilities including arts and sport; need to spend money on museums, art galleries, etc.; need to encourage worthwhile leisure activities and cultural mass media.

per503   *Social Justice: Positive*

Concept of equality; need for fair treatment of all people; special protection for underprivileged; need for fair distribution of resources; removal of class barriers; end to discrimination on the grounds of race, sex, gender, disability, age, sexual orientation, etc.

per504   *Welfare State Expansion: Positive*

Favourable mention of need to introduce, maintain, or expand any social service or social security scheme; support for social services such as health service or social housing. This category excludes education.

per505   *Welfare State Limitation: Positive*

Limiting expenditure on social services or social security; otherwise as 504, but negative.

per506   *Education Expansion: Positive*

Need to expand and/or improve educational provision at all levels. This excludes technical training which is coded under 411.

per507   *Education Limitation: Positive*

Limiting expenditure on education; otherwise as 506, but negative.

Domain 6: Fabric of Society

per601   *National Way of Life: Positive*

Appeals to patriotism and/or nationalism; suspension of some freedoms in order to protect the state against subversion; support for established national ideas.

per602   *National Way of Life: Negative*

Opposition to patriotism and/or nationalism; opposition to the existing national state; otherwise as 601, but negative.

per603   *Traditional Morality: Positive*

Favourable mention of traditional moral values; prohibition, censorship, and suppression of immorality and unseemly behaviour; maintenance and stability of family; religion.

per604   *Traditional Morality: Negative*

Opposition to traditional moral values; support for divorce, abortion, etc.; otherwise as 603, but negative.

per605   *Law and Order: Positive*

Enforcement of all laws; actions against crime; support for enhancing resources for police, etc.; tougher attitudes in courts.

per606   *Social Harmony: Positive*

Appeal for national effort and solidarity; need for society to see itself as united; appeal for public spiritedness; decrying anti-social attitudes in times of crisis; support for the public interest.

| per607 | *Multiculturalism: Positive* |

Favourable mention of cultural diversity, communalism, cultural plurality and pillarization; preservation of autonomy of religious, linguistic heritages within the country including special educational provisions.

per608   *Multiculturalism: Negative*

Enforcement or encouragement of cultural integration; otherwise as 607, but negative.

Domain 7: Social Groups

per701   *Labour Groups: Positive*

Favourable reference to labour groups, working class, unemployed; support for trade unions; good treatment of employees.

per702   *Labour Groups: Negative*

Abuse of power by trade unions; otherwise as 701, but negative.

per703   *Farmers: Positive*

Support for agriculture and farmers; any policy aimed specifically at benefiting these.

per704   *Middle Class and Professional Groups: Positive*

Favourable reference to middle class, professional groups, such as physicians or lawyers; old and new middle class.

per705   *Underprivileged Minority Groups: Positive*

Favourable reference to underprivileged minorities who are defined neither in economic nor in demographic terms, e.g. the handicapped, homosexuals, immigrants, etc.

per706   *Non-economic Demographic Groups: Positive*

Favourable mention of, or need for, assistance to women, the elderly, young people, linguistic groups, etc.; special interest groups of all kinds.

Data Entries per1011–per7062   Subcategories used for CEE countries. For comparisons between OECD and CEE countries, subcategories can be aggregated into one of the fifty-six standard categories used in all countries.

per1011   *Russia/USSR/CIS: Positive*

Favourable mention of Russia, the USSR, the CMEA bloc, or the Community of Independent States.

per1012   *Western States: Positive*

Favourable mention of Western states, including the USA and Germany.

per1013   *Eastern European Countries: Positive*

Favourable mention of Eastern European countries in general.

per1014   *Baltic States: Positive*

Favourable mention of the Baltic states, including other states bordering the Baltic Sea.

per1015   *Nordic Council: Positive*

Favourable mention of the Nordic Council.

per1016   *SFR Yugoslavia: Positive*

Favourable mention of countries formerly belonging to SFR Yugoslavia including special relationships with Montenegro, Macedonia, Slovenia, Croatia, and Bosnia-Hercegovina.

per1021   *Russia/USSR/CIS: Negative*

Negative mention of Russia, the USSR, or the Community of Independent States.

per1022   *Western States: Negative*

Negative mention of Western states, including the USA and Germany.

per1023   *East European Countries: Negative*

Negative mention of Eastern European countries in general.

per1024   *Baltic States: Negative*

Negative reference to the Baltic states.

per1025   *Nordic Council: Negative*

Negative reference to the Nordic Council.

per1026   *SFR Yugoslavia: Negative*

Negative mention of countries formerly belonging to SFR Yugoslavia including negative reference to Montenegro, Macedonia, Slovenia, Croatia, and Bosnia-Hercegovina.

per1031   *Russian Army: Negative*

Need to withdraw the Russian army from the territory of the manifesto country; need to receive reparations for damage caused by the Russian army or other Soviet institutions.

per1032   *Independence: Positive*

Favourable mention of the independence and sovereignty of the manifesto country.

per1033   *Rights of Nations: Positive*

Favourable mention of freedom, rights, and interests of nations.

per2021   *Transition to Democracy*

General reference to the transition process of one-party states to pluralist democracy.

per2022   *Restrictive Citizenship: Positive*

Favourable mention of restrictions in citizenship; restrictions in enfranchisement with respect to (ethnic) groups.

per2023   *Lax Citizenship: Positive*

Favourable mention of lax citizenship and election laws; no or few restrictions in enfranchisement.

per2031   *Presidential Regime: Positive*

Support for current presidential regime; statements in favour of a powerful presidency.

per2032	*Republic: Positive*
	Support for republican forms of government as opposed to monarchy.
per2033	*Checks and Balances: Positive*
	Support for checks and balances and separation of powers, and specifically for limiting the powers of the presidency by increasing legislative/judicial powers, or transferring some executive powers to the legislature or judiciary.
per2041	*Monarchy: Positive*
	Support for a monarchy, including conceptions of constitutional monarchy.
per3011	*Republican Powers: Positive*
	Favourable mention of stronger republican powers.
per3051	*Public Situation: Negative*
	Negative reference to the situation in public life after the founding elections.
per3052	*Communist: Positive*
	Cooperation with former authorities/Communists in the transition period; pro-Communist involvement in the transition process; and 'let sleeping dogs lie' in dealing with the nomenclature.
per3053	*Communist: Negative*
	Against Communist involvement in democratic government; weeding out the collaborators from governmental service; need for political coalition except Communist parties.
per3054	*Rehabilitation and Compensation: Positive*
	Reference to civic rehabilitation of politically persecuted people in the Communist era; reference to juridical compensation concerning Communist expropriations; moral compensation.
per3055	*Political Coalitions: Positive*
	Positive reference to the need of broader political coalition; need for cooperation at the political level; necessity of collaboration among all political forces.
per4011	*Privatization: Positive*
	Favourable reference to privatization.
per4012	*Control of Economy: Negative*
	Negative reference to the general need for direct governmental control of the economy.
per4013	*Property-Restitution: Positive*
	Favourable reference to the physical restitution of property to previous owners.
per4014	*Privatization Vouchers: Positive*
	Favourable reference to privatization vouchers.

per4121   *Social Ownership: Positive*

Favourable reference to the creation or preservation of cooperative or non-state social ownership within a market economy.

per4122   *Mixed Economy: Positive*

Favourable reference to mixed ownership within a market economy.

per4123   *Publicly Owned Industry: Positive*

Positive reference to the concept of publicly owned industries.

per4124   *Socialist Property: Positive*

Positive reference to socialist property, including public and cooperative property; negative reference to privatization.

per4131   *Property-Restitution: Negative*

Negative reference to the physical restitution of property to previous owners.

per4132   *Privatization: Negative*

Negative reference to the privatization system; need to change the privatization system.

per5021   *Private–Public Mix in Culture: Positive*

Necessity for private provision due to economic constraints; support for private funding in addition to public activity.

per5031   *Private–Public Mix in Social Justice: Positive*

Necessity for private initiatives due to economic constraints.

per5041   *Private–Public Mix in Welfare: Positive*

Necessity for private welfare provisions due to economic constraints; desirability of competition in welfare service provisions; private funding in addition to public activity.

per5061   *Private–Public Mix in Education: Positive*

Necessity for private education due to economic constraints; desirability of competition in education.

per6011   *The Karabakh Issue: Positive*

Positive reference to the unity of Karabakh and Armenia or the recognition for an independent Republic of Karabakh; rendering assistance to Karabakh.

per6012   *Rebuilding the USSR: Positive*

Favourable mention of the reunification of all republics and nations living on the former territory of the USSR into a new common (democratic) state or into a common economic space whereby the new union would be the guarantor of the manifesto country's sovereignty; negative reference to the dissolution of the USSR and the respective treaties.

per6013   *National Security: Positive*

Support for or need to maintain national security in all spheres of social life; policies devoted to this goal.

per6061	*General Crisis*
	Identification of a general crisis in the country.
per6071	*Cultural Autonomy: Positive*
	Favourable mention of cultural autonomy.
per6072	*Multiculturalism pro Roma: Positive*
	Favourable mention of cultural autonomy of Roma.
per6081	*Multiculturalism pro Roma: Negative*
	Negative mention of cultural autonomy of Roma.
per7051	*Minorities Inland: Positive*
	Reference to manifesto country minorities in foreign countries; positive reference to manifesto country minorities.
per7052	*Minorities Abroad: Positive*
	Reference to ethnic minorities living in the manifesto country such as Latvians living in Estonia.
per7061	*War Participants: Positive*
	Favourable mention of, or need for, assistance to people taking part in the war on the territory of the former Yugoslavia.
per7062	*Refugees: Positive*
	Favourable mention of, or need for, assistance to people who left their homes because of the war (e.g. on the territory of the former Yugoslavia) or were forcibly displaced.
Peruncod	Percentage of uncoded (quasi-)sentences
Total	Total number of quasi-sentences
	Programmatic dimensions:
Rile	Right-Left position of party as given in Michael Laver/Ian Budge (eds.): Party Policy and Government Coalitions, Houndmills, Basingstoke, Hampshire: MacMillan Press 1992:
	(per104 + per201 + per203 + per305 + per401 + per402 + per407 + per414 + per505 + per601 + per603 + per605 + per606) − (per103 + per105 + per106 + per107 + per403 + per404 + per406 + per412 + per413 + per504 + per506 + per701 + per202).
Planeco	per403 + per404 + per412.
Markeco	per401 + per414.
Welfare	per503 + per504.
Europ	per108 − per110.

Manifesto Coding Instructions

1. Introduction

The object of content analysing election programmes as pursued by the MRG/CMP is to measure policy positions of parties across countries within a common framework. Election programmes are taken as indicators of party policy emphases and policy positions at a certain point in time. Therefore, election programmes are subjected to quantitative content analysis. A classification scheme was designed to allow for the coding of all the content of election programmes for the post-Second World War period in a variety of countries.

A first version of the classification scheme was developed by Robertson (1976: 73–5) for analysing modes of party competition in Britain. In 1979, the 'Manifesto Research Group' (MRG) was constituted as a research group of the European Consortium for Political Research (ECPR) by scholars interested in a comparative content-analytic approach to policy positions of parties. During the period 1979–89, the classification scheme was extended and revised to fit additional countries.

Since 1989 the Social Science Research Centre Berlin (WZB) has provided resources for updating and expanding the MRG data-set. This appendix forms an introduction to the application of the coding scheme for coders who may not have the background knowledge of the MRG-members. Moreover, it provides investigators in countries not covered by the MRG/CMP with all the relevant information, definitions, and sources to apply the coding scheme to their respective countries.

2. Selection of Programmes

Programmatic statements are central features of parties. In party programmes, the political ideas and goals of parties are put on record. Although only few voters actually read party programmes, they are disseminated widely through the mass media.

Among the different kinds of programmes which are issued in many countries, *election programmes* are used as the basis of our research. The advantages of taking election programmes as a source for identifying political goals of parties are manifold:

1. Election programmes cover a wide range of political positions and themes and, therefore, can be seen as a 'set of key central statements of party positions' (Budge, Robertson, and Hearl 1987:18).

2. Election programmes are authoritative statements of party policies because the programmes are usually ratified in party conventions.

3. Election programmes are representative statements for the whole party, not just statements of one faction or group within the party or of individual party members.

4. Election programmes are published before every election. Thus, changes of policy positions of parties over time can be studied.

According to the special significance of election programmes, the documents to be collected are the platforms of parties which are published for the election of representatives in the national assembly of a respective country. The sources for gathering the programmes may be the parties themselves, associated research and training institutes or publications in newspapers, magazines, or books.

⇥In some countries parties do not always distribute election programmes. In this case, the above given description of election programmes serves as an 'ideal type' of a document which is to be searched for. The only documents available may be newspaper summaries of the parties' election pledges or reports of party spokesmen about policy positions and goals for the upcoming legislature. In any case the ideal type of a document which summarises authoritative statements of the party's policy positions for electioneering should be used as far as possible.

3. Selection of Parties

Collections should cover all significant parties which are represented in the national assembly. The 'significance' of parties is defined as the coalition (governmental) or blackmail potential of a party in a given party system (Sartori 1976: 121–5). Coalition potential is defined as (1) actual or former membership in a government or (2) the possibility (feasibility) of becoming a government party. Blackmail potential is defined as the party's impact on 'the tactics of party competition particularly when it alters the direction of the competition—by determining a switch from centripetal to centrifugal competition either leftward, rightward, or in both directions—of the governing-oriented parties' (Sartori 1976: 123). These criteria for selection need to be considered in situations where small parties, especially new ones like Green parties, may affect party competition despite their size.

4. The Coding Procedure

The election programmes are analysed by means of content analysis which is 'a research technique for the objective, systematic, and quantitative description of the manifest content of communication' (Berelson 1971: 18). This method can be applied to a wide range of different materials and research questions. The purpose of this section is to describe the specific form of content analysis to be undertaken in manifesto research.

This kind of internal, quantitative analysis relates particularly to ideas, policies, issues, and concerns that parties stress in their platforms. The methods of coding are also designed to be comparable over a wide range of countries irrespective of cultural and socio-economic differences. Therefore, a classification scheme with fixed general categories is used to cover the total content of election programmes by identifying the statements of preference expressed in the programmes. This classification scheme contains fifty-six different categories grouped into seven major policy domains: Each of the fifty-six categories summates related issues in such a way that changes over time can be measured both across parties and across cultures. Thus, the coding procedure comprises a quantification (*how many* statements do parties make?) and a classification (*what kind* of statements do parties make?) of election programmes.

4.1. Quantification: The Coding Unit

The coding unit in a given programme is the '*quasi-sentence*', defined as an argument—that is, the verbal expression of one political idea or issue. In its simplest form, a sentence is the basic unit of meaning. Therefore, punctuation can be used as a guideline for identifying arguments. The starting point of coding is the sentence, but what we are aiming for is an argument. In its shortest form, a sentence contains a subject, a verb, and an attribute or an adjective.

> Examples: 'We will cut taxes.'
> 'We will reduce our military forces.'

Obviously, these two sentences contain two different arguments which are easy to identify and to distinguish. But unfortunately, language is more complex, and different forms or styles may be used to express the same political ideas.

> Example: 'We will cut taxes and reduce our military forces.'

In this case, the two statements are combined in one sentence, but for our purposes are still treated as two different arguments. Long sentences are broken down into 'quasi-sentences' if the sense changes within the sentence. In most cases, one sentence which covers two (or more) arguments can be easily transformed into two (or more) quasi-sentences by repeating substantives and/or verbs. Thus, a quasi-sentence is a set of words containing, one and only one, political idea. It stops either at the end of an argument or at a full stop (period).

In many cases, arguments are combined and related into one sentence.

> Example: 'Because we want freedom, we need strong military forces.'

These are *two* quasi-sentences, because there are two political goals, that is, freedom and strength of military forces, which can be transformed into two quasi-sentences:

> Examples: 'We want freedom.'
> 'We need strong military forces.'

Thus, long sentences may combine two or more arguments which are often contained by commas, semicolons, or colons. A list of arguments, sometimes marked with hyphens or bullet points, is treated as if separated with full stops.

> Example: 'In international policy we shall take new initiatives.
>
> We will:
>
> – promote peace;
> – ban chemical weapons;
> – refuse to deploy cruise missiles;
> – begin discussions for the removal of nuclear bases;
> – increase aid to developing countries;
> – take action to protect the status of refugees.'

This text contains seven quasi-sentences. Three of the arguments—(1) ban chemical weapons, (2) refuse to deploy cruise missiles, and (3) begin discussions for the removal of nuclear bases—express the same general idea, that is, disarmament, but refer to different issues in this policy field. Because distinct policies are mentioned for disarmament, three different quasi-sentences are identified. This list of policies may be given in the following way for which the same number of quasi-sentences is coded as for the list given above:

'In international policy we shall take new initiatives. We will promote peace, ban chemical weapons, refuse to deploy cruise missiles, begin discussions for the removal of nuclear bases, increase aid to developing countries, and take action to protect the status of refugees.'

Thus, if different issues—however short—are dealt with in the same sentence they constitute different quasi-sentences even if they apply to the same policy field. Conversely, the same argument may be very long and may occupy a lot of space, but still be only one quasi-sentence.

Step No. 1: Identifying Quasi-Sentences

(1) *Photocopy the respective party programme. Then, (2) start with reading the first paragraph, (3) look at each sentence of the first paragraph, (4) identify the number of arguments by transforming them into quasi-sentences, and (5) mark all quasi-sentences in the first paragraph as shown in sample texts in section 5.*

Some parts of the platform, like statistics, tables of content, and section headings are not considered as text to be coded and, therefore, do not count as quasi-sentences. Introductory remarks by party leaders are equally ignored since the ideal-type of a platform is defined as authoritative statements by parties. All the other parts of a platform constitute the basis of analysis. The total number of units of analysis equals the total number of quasi-sentences identified for the relevant text of a given platform.

4.2. Classification: The Standard Coding Frame

The CMP uses three types of comparison: (*a*) comparison of changes in policy positions or in emphases over time within specific parties; (*b*) comparison of differences in policy positions or in emphases across parties, and, (*c*) comparison of differences across countries. The basic data sought to support such comparisons are the proportions of election programmes devoted to each category in a set of standardized issue areas. Comparison requires standardization. The manifesto project, after much experimentation and discussion, developed a coding system, whereby each quasi-sentence of every election programme is coded into one, and only one, of the following fifty-six standard categories. The fifty-six standard categories are grouped into seven major policy areas or domains (Table II.1). The coding categories are designed, as far as possible, to be comparable between parties and countries, and over time.

After identifying the quasi-sentences in the first paragraph, the next stage of the coding procedure is to decide which of the fifty-six categories of the Standard Coding Frame a respective quasi-sentence expresses. Each category of the Standard Coding Frame is specified by a set of typical issues and political ideas which are given in Section 7 of this appendix. Before starting the coding procedure, the coder should read through the Standard Coding Frame and its defining ideas and issues several times. With only fifty-six categories the Standard Coding Frame is reasonably compact so that titles of categories and their defining characteristics can be memorized easily. The more effectively the coder can memorize the categories and their specifications, the easier and faster the coding procedure will be.

For the example given above, the category numbers (105) 'Military: Negative', (106) Peace, (107) 'Internationalism: Positive', and (201) 'Freedom and Human Rights' are noted down at the margin of the copied election programme:

107 In international policy we shall take new initiatives. We will:
106 - promote peace;

Table II.1. The standard coding frame: fifty-six categories in seven domains

Domain 1: External Relations
101	Foreign Special Relationships: Positive
102	Foreign Special Relationships: Negative
103	Anti-Imperialism: Anti-Colonialism
104	Military: Positive
105	Military: Negative
106	Peace: Positive
107	Internationalism: Positive
108	European Integration: Positive
109	Internationalism: Negative
110	European Integration: Negative

Domain 2: Freedom and Democracy
201	Freedom and Human Rights: Positive
202	Democracy: Positive
203	Constitutionalism: Positive
204	Constitutionalism: Negative

Domain 3: Political System
301	Decentralization: Positive
302	Centralization: Positive
303	Governmental and Administrative Efficiency: Positive
304	Political Corruption: Negative
305	Political Authority: Positive

Domain 4: Economy
401	Free Enterprise: Positive
402	Incentives: Positive
403	Market Regulation: Positive
404	Economic Planning: Positive
405	Corporatism: Positive
406	Protectionism: Positive
407	Protectionism: Negative
408	Economic Goals
409	Keynesian Demand Management: Positive
410	Productivity: Positive
411	Technology and Infrastructure: Positive
412	Controlled Economy: Positive
413	Nationalization: Positive
414	Economic Orthodoxy: Positive
415	Marxist Analysis: Positive
416	Anti-Growth Economy: Positive

Domain 5: Welfare and Quality of Life
501	Environmental Protection: Positive
502	Culture: Positive
503	Social Justice: Positive
504	Welfare State Expansion: Positive
505	Welfare State Limitation: Positive
506	Education Expansion: Positive
507	Education Limitation: Positive

Domain 6: Fabric of Society
601	National Way of Life: Positive
602	National Way of Life: Negative

Table II.1. (*Continued*)

603	Traditional Morality: Positive
604	Traditional Morality: Negative
605	Law and Order: Positive
606	Social Harmony: Positive
607	Multiculturalism: Positive
608	Multiculturalism: Negative
Domain 7: Social Groups	
701	Labour Groups: Positive
702	Labour Groups: Negative
703	Farmers: Positive
704	Middle Class and Professional Groups: Positive
705	Underprivileged Minority Groups: Positive
706	Non-Economic Demographic Groups: Positive

105	- ban chemical weapons;
105	- refuse to deploy cruise missiles;
105	- begin discussions for the removal of nuclear bases;
107	- increase aid to developing countries;
201	- take action to protect the status of refugees.

Step No. 2: Classifying the Quasi-Sentences

Read the whole of the first paragraph before you start coding the first quasi-sentence because the context may give you hints how to code an otherwise ambiguous argument. Look to see whether one of the fifty-six categories definitely captures the sense of the first identified quasi-sentence and note down the respective number of the category at the margin of the page. Repeat this procedure for all the quasi-sentences of the first paragraph. Then proceed with the next paragraph by repeating Step No. 1.

4.2.1. Categories with Country-Specific Meanings

In most of the cases, the categories have clear meanings which are applicable to all countries. But some categories have country-specific contents or require country-specific definitions. The categories (101) 'Foreign Special Relations: Positive' and (102) 'Foreign Special Relations: Negative' have country-specific meanings. Here, the coder has to decide in advance with which other country or countries the manifesto country (i.e. the country he or she is coding) has a 'special foreign relationship'; for example, in the British case: former colonies, in the Swedish case: the rest of Scandinavia. Equally, the category (705) 'Minorities' requires a definition of what groups are considered as underprivileged in the manifesto country. The specific content of these categories must be spelled out as notes in a coding protocol.

Step No. 3: Coding Protocol for All Country-Specific Categories and Coding

Note down definitions for all country-specific categories in a coding protocol. The coding has to be done in as uniform a way as possible. For comparative reasons, the greatest possible standardization has to be achieved. Therefore, the coder must note down every coding decision he or she made if the procedure is not specifically mentioned in these guidelines.

4.2.2. *Coding Problems and Difficulties*

Not all of the arguments are as clear as the examples given above. Three difficulties may appear in the process of applying Step No. 2:

a.   No category seems to apply.

b.   More than one category seem to apply.

c.   The statement seems unclear.

a. No category seems to apply

The coding frame was created to capture the total platform content. Nonetheless, it may be that no category is available for a particular problem in a particular country. These quasi-sentences are treated as uncodable (000). It is important to realize that 'uncoded' does not necessarily mean that a sentence is devoid of meaning (although of course it may be), only that it cannot be fitted into the present coding frame. However, the *general rule* is that sentences should be coded if at all possible. To follow this general rule there are a number of specific decision rules on how to tackle with difficult coding decisions.

In many countries some of the categories are not used much (for instance (405) 'Corporatism' and (409) 'Keynesian Demand Management'), but are vital for comparative reasons. Therefore, some categories may be left empty at the end of the coding procedure. On the other hand seldom used categories are the most difficult to handle.

Decision Rule No. 1: Checking Definitions of All Categories in Policy Domains

Whenever tempted to treat a quasi-sentence as uncodable, read the definitions of categories in the relevant policy domains again because it might well be that the quasi-sentence contains a policy position that is taken only rarely. Therefore, the specific definition of the respective category may just have been forgotten.

A quasi-sentence may be without intrinsic meaning but may nevertheless be part of the discussion of a problem and have a stylistic or a linking function, for example:

'The next government will do everything in its power to defend the interests of the farmers. To this end, we envisage several measures. Firstly, we will increase payments of all kinds to farmers. ... '

These are three quasi-sentences. The middle sentence itself is devoid of any policy content but is a part of the same argument. Therefore, category (703) 'Agriculture' is coded three times.

Decision Rule No. 2: Identifying Connecting Sentences

Some sentences, which may otherwise be uncodable, may just be connecting sentences between two arguments (for instance: Therefore, we are going to do three things). These connecting sentences themselves do not constitute meaningful arguments but are part of an ongoing argument. Therefore, connecting sentences should be coded in the same category as surrounding sentences or as the bulk of the paragraph they appear in.

Because of the *general rule* to classify quasi-sentences if at all possible, all quasi-sentences treated as uncodable must be checked again after coding the total programme. Uncoded quasi-sentences may be biased in meaning, that is, they may have a common thrust. Some quasi-sentences may contain country-specific issues which are not mentioned specifically in the definition of the category but nonetheless be subsumable under one of the fifty-six standard categories. Should this be the case, it must be noted down in the coding protocol according to Step No. 3. Other quasi-sentences may have a country-specific bias too strong to be subsumed under one of the fifty-six standard categories. For these quasi-sentences a new subcategory may be developed to capture the content of these otherwise uncodable sentences. Examples of subcategories, used for coding the programmes of parties in transitional democracies, are given in Section 9. Subcategories must *always* be nested into the fifty-six standard categories so that they can be aggregated up to one of the fifty-six standard categories. For instance 1011 is nested into 101, 2011 is nested into 201.

Decision Rule No. 3: Creating Subcategories

Look at all uncoded sentences a second time and try to figure out whether some of these statements have an equivalent meaning. Make sure that there really is no related standard category that captures the sense of these quasi-sentences. Should many quasi-sentences contain the same arguments which are not subsumable under one of the fifty-six standard categories, note down a temporary 4-digit code and a temporary definition for a new subcategory and contact the supervisor. **Do not** *create subcategories for each and every single issue because this is useless even when comparing parties from the same party system.* **Never** *create new categories without checking with the supervisor because you may destroy the comparability of the data.*

The subcategories set out in Table II.2 are used for CEE countries.

Note that even trained coders tend to create too many subcategories, that is, subcategories containing one or two quasi-sentences, only. From more than eighty subcategories that had been created for transitional countries, thirty were re-aggregated into the main standard categories because they were almost empty. The remaining fifty-four subcategories, listed in Section 8, must be coded for all programmes from parties in CEE countries.

b. More than one category seem to apply

The opposite difficulty of uncodable sentences is that more than one category seems to apply. This difficulty can be dealt with applying the following decision rules:

Decision Rule No. 4: Section Headings as Guidelines

Look at the section heading of the quasi-sentence in question. Then, take the category which covers the topic of the section or the heading. Thus, section headings are taken as guidelines for coding, although section headings themselves are not to be coded.

If headings are not given or do not apply to the argument in question, a couple of decision rules are to be followed for the most common cases. The problem of choosing between two categories often occurs with respect to group politics, for instance: 'We want more social security for workers'. In this case, category (701) 'Labour Groups' or category (504) 'Welfare State Expansion' may apply.

Decision Rule No. 5: Specific Policy Positions 'Beat' Group Politics except Group (703) 'Agriculture'

Whenever there is a choice between a specific policy position given in Policy Domains 1, 2, 3, 4, 5, or 6 on the one hand and a social group from Domain 7 on the other hand, take the specific policy position. **This rule does not apply to category (703) 'Agriculture'.** *All quasi-sentences devoted to agriculture are to be coded into category 703, even if a specific policy position such as (402) 'Incentives' or (410) 'Economic Growth' is taken to further the interests of farmers.*

Table II.2. Subcategories

1011	Russsia/USSR/CIS: Positive
1012	Western States: Positive
1013	Eastern European Countries: Positive
1014	Baltic States: Positive
1015	Nordic Council: Positive
1016	SFR Yugoslavia: Positive
1021	Russia/USSR/CIS: Negative
1022	Western States: Negative
1023	East European Countries: Negative
1024	Baltic States: Negative
1025	Nordic Council: Negative
1026	SFR Yugoslavia: Negative
1031	Russian Army: Negative
1032	Independence: Positive
1033	Rights of Nations: Positive
2021	Transition to Democracy
2022	Restrictive Citizenship: Positive
2023	Lax Citizenship: Positive
2031	Presidential Regime: Positive
2032	Republic: Positive
2033	Checks and Balances: Positive
2041	Monarchy: Positive
3011	Republican Powers: Positive
3051	Public Situation: Negative
3052	Communist: Positive
3053	Communist: Negative
3054	Rehabilitation and Compensation: Positive
3055	Political Coalitions: Positive
4011	Privatization: Positive
4012	Control of Economy: Negative
4013	Property-Restitution: Positive
4014	Privatization Vouchers: Positive
4121	Social Ownership: Positive
4122	Mixed Economy: Positive
4123	Publicly Owned Industry: Positive
4124	Socialist Property: Positive
4131	Property-Restitution: Negative
4132	Privatization: Negative
5021	Private–Public Mix in Culture: Positive
5031	Private–Public Mix in Social Justice: Positive
5041	Private–Public Mix in Welfare: Positive
5061	Private–Public Mix in Education: Positive
6011	The Karabakh Issue: Positive
6012	Rebuilding the USSR: Positive
6013	National Security: Positive
6061	General Crisis
6071	Cultural Autonomy: Positive
6072	Multiculturalism pro Roma: Positive
6081	Multiculturalism pro Roma: Negative
7051	Minorities Inland: Positive
7052	Minorities Abroad: Positive
7061	War Participants: Positive
7062	Refugees: Positive

Decision Rule No. 6: Specific Policy Positions 'Beat' (305) 'Political Authority'

*Whenever there is a choice between category (305) 'Political Authority', defined as the party's **general** competence to govern or the **general** critique of opponent parties' competence, on the one hand and another category from Policy Domains 1 to 7, the specific policy position is to be chosen.*

Decision Rule No. 7: Specific Policy Positions 'Beat' (408) 'General Economic Goals'

Whenever there is a choice between a more specific policy position given in Policy Domains 1 to 7 and category (408) 'General Economic Goals', the specific policy positions (for instance (410) 'Economic Growth') is to be chosen instead of 408.

For all other cases in which more than one category seem to apply, the coder has to decide what the most important concern of the argument is since one, and only one, category has to be chosen for each argument. There is only one exception to the 'one-and-only-one' rule:

Decision Rule No 8: European Level and National/Regional Level

Policies at the European level may be discussed with respect to their impact at the national or regional level. In these cases, (108) 'European Community: positive' or (110) 'European Community: negative' as well as the specific national position in Policy Domains 2 to 7 have to be coded.

c. The statement seems unclear

Even after applying decision rules 1 to 8, one may still not be sure where an argument is leading. Many of these problems may be solved by taking the context of the ambiguous quasi-sentence into account. Coders should first of all take into account the following sentences because the first (quasi-)sentence may be part of an argument which is explicated in the next sentences. Therefore, it is always useful to start the coding procedure by reading the whole paragraph.

In some cases, crucial decisions have to be made with respect to the manifest or latent content of statements. No inferences should be made with respect to the meaning of statements. The coder has to code what the statement says, not what he or she thinks it may lead to in the end. As with uncodable sentences, all unclear statements should be marked and reread at the end of coding.

Some of the coding problems will be solved with growing experience. However, whenever the coder is unsure about which category is to be taken, the supervisor (volkens@wz-berlin.de) should be contacted. The sentences in question can be translated into English and the coding decision is then taken and explained by the supervisor.

4.3. Coding Sheet

After finishing the coding of a platform, a tally is kept on a coding sheet given in this section. The coding sheet shows the respective country, party, and election year and gives the number of quasi-sentences coded into each standard category of the Standard Coding Frame as well as the total number of quasi-sentences. However, before even starting with Step No. 1, first of all take the following step:

Step No. 0: Do not start with Step No. 1 before having done the reliability test given in this handbook because the reliability test is used for identifying coding mistakes. Thus, wait for the reply of the supervisor or you might have to do it all over again!

Coding Sheet

COUNTRY:		PARTY:	YEAR:
000:	410:	1011:	4011:
101:	411:	1012:	4012:
102:	412:	1013:	4013:
103:	413:	1014:	4014:
104:	414:	1015:	4121:
105:	415:	1016:	4122:
106:	416:	1021:	4123:
107:	501:	1022:	4124:
108:	502:	1023:	4131:
109:	503:	1024:	4132:
110:	504:	1025:	5021:
201:	505:	1026:	5031:
202:	506:	1031:	5041:
203:	507:	1032:	5061:
204:	601:	1033:	6011:
301:	602:	2021:	6012:
302:	603:	2022:	6013:
303:	604:	2023:	6061:
304:	605:	2031:	6071:
305:	606:	2032:	6072:
401:	607:	2033:	6081:
402:	608:	2041:	7051:
403:	701:	3011:	7052:
404:	702:	3051:	7061:
405:	703:	3052:	7062:
406:	704:	3053:	
407:	705:	3054:	
408:	706:	3055:	
409:			Total N:

5. Coding Exercise

The following sample texts with solutions for the identification of quasi-sentences and categories serve as exercises for coding.

GREAT BRITAIN, The Liberal/SDP Alliance 1983

'Working together for Britain'

(Extracts)

The General Election on 9th June 1983 will be seen as a watershed in British politics. /   **000**

It may be recalled as the fateful day when depression became hopelessness and the   **000**
slide of the post-war years accelerated into the depths of decline. ▮Alternatively it   **000**
may be remembered as the turning point when the people of this country, at the
eleventh hour, decided to turn their backs on dogma and bitterness and chose a
new road of partnership and progress. ▮

It is to offer real hope of a fresh start for Britain that the Alliance between our two   **305**
parties has been created. ▮What we have done is unique in the history of British   **305**
parliamentary democracy. ▮Two parties, one with a proud history, and one born   **606**
only two years ago out of a frustration with the old systems of politics, have come
together to offer an alternative government pledged to bring the country together
again. ▮

The Conservative and Labour parties between them have made an industrial   **305**
wasteland out of a country which was once the workshop of the world. ▮
Manufacturing output from Britain is back to the level of nearly twenty years   **410**
ago. ▮Unemployment is still rising and there are now generations of   **408**
school-leavers who no longer even hope for work. ▮Mrs Thatcher's government   **305**
stands idly by, hoping that the blind forces of the marketplace will restore the jobs
and factories that its indifference has destroyed. ▮The Labour Party's response is   **305**
massive further nationalization, a centralized state socialist economy and rigid
controls over enterprise. ▮The choice which Tories and Socialists offer at this   **305**
election is one between neglect and interference. ▮Neither of them understands   **606**
that it is only by working together in the companies and communities of Britain
that we can overcome the economic problems which beset us. ▮Meanwhile the   **606**
very fabric of our common life together deteriorates. ▮The record wave of   **605**
violence and crime and increased personal stress are all signs of a society at war
with itself. ▮Rundown cities and declining rural services alike tell a story of a   **606**
warped sense of priorities by successive governments. ▮Mrs Thatcher promised   **606**
'to bring harmony where there is discord'. ▮Instead her own example of   **606**
confrontation has inflamed the bitterness so many people feel at what has
happened to their own lives and local communities. ▮

Our Alliance wants to call a halt to confrontation politics. ▮We believe we have   **606**
set an example by working together as two separate parties within an alliance of   **606**
principle. ▮Our whole approach is based on cooperation: not just between our   **606**
parties but between management and workers, between people of different races   **202**
and above all between government and people. ▮Because we are not prisoners of
ideology we shall listen to the people we represent and ensure that the good sense
of the voters is allowed to illuminate the corridors of Westminster and
Whitehall. ▮

THE IMMEDIATE CRISIS: JOBS AND PRICES

Our economic crisis demands tough immediate action. ▮It also requires a   **305**
government with the courage to implement those strategic and structural reforms   **305**
which alone can end the civil war between the two sides of industry. ▮

The immediate priority is to reduce unemployment. Why? ▮To the Alliance   **408**
unemployment is a scandal; ▮   **408**

robbing men and women of their careers; ▌blighting the prospects for a quarter   701
of all our young people, ▌wasting our national resources, ▌aborting our chances   706
of industrial recovery, ▌dividing our nation ▌and fuelling hopelessness and   410
crime. ▌   408
    606
    605

Much of the present unemployment is a direct result of the civil war in British   408
industry, of restrictive practices and low investment. ▌But in addition,   408
Conservative government policies have caused unemployment to rise. ▌An   408
Alliance government would cause unemployment to fall. How? ▌Can it be done   414
without releasing a fresh wave of inflation? ▌

We believe it can. ▌We propose a carefully devised and costed jobs programme   414
aimed at reducing unemployment by 1 million over two years. ▌This programme   504
will be supported by immediate measures to help those hardest hit by the   503
slump—the disadvantaged, the pensioners, the poor. ▌

Ours is a programme of mind, heart, and will. ▌It is a programme that will work!   404
The programme has three points: ▌Fiscal and Financial Policies for Growth;   404
▌Direct Action to provide jobs; ▌An Incomes Strategy that will stick. ▌   410
    504
    701

STRATEGY FOR INDUSTRIAL SUCCESS

The Alliance is alone in recognizing that Britain's industrial crisis cannot be solved   606
by short-term measures such as import controls or money supply targets. ▌Our   606
crisis goes deep. ▌Its roots lie in the class divisions of our society, ▌in the vested   606
interests of the Tory and Labour parties, ▌in the refusal of management and   606
unions to wide democracy in industry, ▌in the way profits and risks are   202
shared. ▌   606

The policies offered by the two class-based parties will further divide the nation   606
North versus South, Management versus Labour. ▌Our greatest need is to build a   606
sense of belonging to one community. ▌We are all in it together. ▌It is   606
impossible for one side or the other in Britain to 'win'. ▌Conflict in industrial   606
relations means that we all lose. ▌   606

The Alliance is committed to policies which will invest resources in the
high-technology industries of the future. ▌We are committed to a major new   411
effort in education and training. ▌We are pledged to trade union reform to tough   506
anti-monopoly measures. ▌   403

PARTNERSHIP IN INDUSTRY

Britain has made little progress towards industrial democracy, yet several of our
European partners have long traditions of participation and cooperation backed by
legislation. ▌They do not face the obstacles to progress with which our divisive   202
industrial relations present us. ▌To be fully effective, proposals for participation   606
in industry need to be buttressed by action on two fronts: ▌a major extension of   202
profit sharing and worker share-ownership to give people a real stake where they   701
work as well as the ability to participate in decision-taking, ▌and reform of the   202
trade unions to make them genuinely representative institutions. ▌

PARTICIPATION AT WORK

We propose enabling legislation that will offer a flexible and sensible approach: ∎ 202

An Industrial Democracy Act to provide for the introduction of employee
participation at all levels, ∎ incentives for employee share-ownership, ∎ employee 202
rights to information, ∎ and an Industrial Democracy Agency (IDA) to advise on 701
and monitor the introduction of these measures: ∎ 201
202

Employee Councils covering each place of work (subject to exemption for small
units) for all companies employing over 1,000 people. ∎ Smaller companies would 202
also be encouraged to introduce Employee Councils. ∎ 202

GOVERNMENT AND INDUSTRY

Priority for Industry

The role of an Alliance government in relation to private industry will be to
provide selective assistance taking a number of forms: ∎ 402

an industrial credit scheme to provide low-interest, long-term finance for projects
directed at modernizing industry; ∎ 402

A national innovation policy, to provide selective assistance for high-risk projects,
∎∎ particularly involving the development of new technologies ∎ and for 402
research and development in potential growth industries; ∎ 411
410

public purchasing policies to stimulate innovation, ∎ encourage the introduction 411
of crucial technologies ∎ and aid small businesses; ∎ 411
402

we will establish a cabinet committee chaired by the prime minster at the centre of
decision-taking on all policies with a bearing on the performance of industry. ∎ 303

The Alliance will strengthen the Monopolies' and Mergers' Commission to ensure
its ability to prevent monopoly and unhealthy concentrations of industrial and 403
commercial power. ∎ The aim is to guarantee fair competition and to protect the 403
interests of employers, consumers, and shareholders. ∎

New and Small Business

To encourage the growth of new and small businesses, we will attack red tape and
provide further financial and management assistance by: ∎ 402

extending the Loan Guarantee Scheme, in the first instance raising the maximum
permitted loan to £150,000; ∎ and the Business Start-Up Scheme, raising the 402
upper limit for investment to £75,000; ∎ and introducing Small Firm Investment 402
Companies to provide financial and management help; ∎ 402

zero-rating building repairs and maintenance for VAT purposes ∎ and reducing 402
commercial rates by 10 per cent; ∎ 402

making sure the Department of Industry coordinates and publicises schemes for
small businesses ∎ and that government aid ceases to discriminate against small 402
businesses; ∎ 402

tailoring national legislation such as the Health and Safety Regulations to the needs
of small businesses ▌and amending the statutory sick pay scheme to exclude small   402
businesses. ▌   402

Agriculture and Fisheries

Agriculture is an important industry and employer. ▌To encourage its further   703
development we will: ▌   703

increase government support for effective agricultural marketing at home and   703
abroad▌and continue support for 'Food from Britain'; ▌   703

ensure that agriculture has access like other industries to the industrial credit
scheme we propose; ▌   703
encourage greater access to farming, especially by young entrants. ▌   703

The Alliance is determined to safeguard the future of our fishing industry which
needs help to re-build after years of uncertainty and the drastic consequences for   703
the deep-sea fleet of 200-mile limits in the waters they used to fish. ▌

Education and training

The third basic condition for industrial success is a people with the skills and
self-confidence that will be needed for the challenges of new technology. ▌The   411
education and training systems are not providing enough people with the skills   411
necessary to make them employable and the country successful in competition   411
with its rivals. ▌We are falling further behind. ▌Japan on present plans will be   506
educating all its young people to the age of 18 by 1990. ▌More than 90 per cent of   411
the 16–19 age group in Germany gain recognized technical qualifications. ▌And it   506
is not just a matter of school-leavers. ▌Our managers are less professionally   411
qualified than our main competitors. ▌From the bottom to top we are   411
underskilled, and this has to be put right if we are to prosper in future. ▌To do   411
this, to raise standards in education and training and to improve their effectiveness
is the object of proposals set out in the next section. ▌

NEW ZEALAND, National Party 1972

'A Guide to what the next National Government will do for New Zealand'
(Extracts)

THE ECONOMY

In 1972 New Zealand had, for the first time, more overseas reserves than total
overseas debt. ▌Labour has dissipated these reserves, borrowed about $200   414
million overseas and incurred annual interest charges mortgaging almost our total   414
export earnings from butter and cheese. ▌

Inflation in 1972 was about 5 per cent, the second lowest of the OECD nations.
▌Today it is about 15 per cent, well above the OECD average, ▌and New Zealand   414
has an external deficit per head of population second only to Iceland. ▌   414
                                                                                                  414

The first three years of the coming National Government will be very largely
devoted to restoring New Zealand's shattered economy. ▌   408

Continuous attention to economic trends and problems will replace stop-go and panic measures. ∎And the taxation system will be used to give incentives for desirable economic activity. ∎	408 402

We will take steps to stimulate savings. ∎Saving accounts, limited as to amount, will be established. ∎The deposits of individuals will earn an interest rate at least equal to the annual rate of inflation thus preserving the purchasing power of savings. ∎	414 414 414

We believe that continued double-figure inflation will destroy the basis of the New Zealand economy and cause untold misery. ∎The fight against increases in the cost of living is the most important single issue in economic management. ∎	414 414

People without jobs represent waste of productive effort: ∎National supports a policy of full employment ∎and the dignity of labour. ∎We do not accept unemployment as a balancing factor in economic management. ∎	410 408 701 701

Finally, the National Development Council will be restored and consultation resumed between government departments, academic specialists, and private industry, including farming and organized labour. ∎The vital role of every section of productive industry will be recognized. ∎	405 405

It is these moves which will put New Zealand on the way to economic recovery. ∎And reduce the spiralling rate of inflation. ∎	408 414

SUPERANNUATION

Seldom has any policy released by an opposition party had the impact that the National Superannuation scheme has had. ∎It is designed to give every New Zealander dignity and a decent income in retirement. ∎Here is how it will operate: ∎	504 504 504

Anyone who is 60 years old, or more, and who has lived in New Zealand for at least ten years will receive National Superannuation, starting next year. ∎And with three big annual jumps in the rate of benefit it will be fully operating by 1978. ∎	504 504

To guarantee our elderly retired folk a decent minimum income, the full rate of National Superannuation, for a married couple, will be 80 per cent of the average weekly ordinary time wage. ∎It will be recalculated every six months. ∎	504 504

In 1976, to start the scheme, the rate will be 65 per cent of the average wage; ∎in 1977 it will be raised to 70 per cent ∎and in 1978 to the full 80 per cent. ∎The rate for single persons, at all times, will be 60% of the married rate. ∎	504 504 504 504

The present average weekly wage is $99 and so, if there is no increase at all in wage rates in the next three years, the rates of National Superannuation will be shown in the box* below (*box not shown). ∎	504

Next year, under National, the age and universal superannuation benefits will merge to form National Superannuation. ∎	504

At present both these benefits pay $51.26 to a married couple and $30.75 to a single person, so even in the first year of National Superannuation, a married couple over 60 who have no other income will have $6.18 a week more to spend than they do now and a single beneficiary will receive, after tax, $3.15 a week more than he now gets by way of age benefits, or universal superannuation. ▍   **504**

Of course those with other income will receive the benefit too, but they will pay more tax on their bigger incomes. ▍   **503**

By 1978 a married couple will receive a net $18.06 a week more than the present age benefit or universal annuation and a single person will be receiving a net $10.17 a week more. ▍ For the single person, that is a pay rise of more than 33 per cent. ▍   **504** **504**

The big and comforting thing about National Superannuation is that everyone gets it, just so long as they have lived in New Zealand for ten years or more and are aged 60 or over. ▍   **504**

They will not, nor will anyone, be expected to make special contributions over a period of years, in order to qualify. ▍ The scheme is financed out of ordinary taxation, so there is nothing to be deducted from wages; no special payments of any kind. ▍   **504** **504**

This means that the present age beneficiary will receive National Superannuation next year. ▍ So will the retired government servant (in addition to the pension from the government superannuation fund which he had paid for). ▍ And so will all the people who are drawing pensions from company and other private superannuation schemes. ▍   **504** **504** **504**

In recent weeks, the government has been making moves to compensate for the weaknesses revealed in their own scheme, when compared with National's. ▍ But the fact remains that National's is the only superannuation scheme that offers a fair deal to everyone in their years of retirement. ▍   **503** **503**

WOMEN'S RIGHTS

Since 1975 is International Women's Year, it can be expected that all political parties will talk a great deal about their 'women's policies'. ▍ Unfortunately, most will be little more than window dressing. ▍ National's plans go far beyond this. ▍   **706** **706** **706**

We will begin by introducing legislation to remove existing legal discrimination relating to women, ▍ and to prohibit discrimination against any person by reason of sex. ▍   **503** **503**

We will also establish a Human Rights Commission which will ensure that equal rights legislation is enforced and that women have an effective and inexpensive means of redress. ▍ The Commission will investigate cases of discrimination presented to it and recommend civil action to the Attorney General. ▍   **503** **503**

Full consideration will be given to the recommendations of the Select Committee on Women's Rights. ▍ We will set priorities for implementation, in consultation with women's organizations. ▍   **706** **706**

We will legislate to ensure that all areas of discrimination in employment are removed ▉ and that merit is the sole criterion in respect of job applications, selection, and promotion. ▉	503 503
To encourage women who wish to enter, return to or remain in employment, National will encourage employers to establish flexible working patterns, such as glide time, part-time, job sharing, and multi-shift work. ▉ Thus assisting women who undertake the dual role of worker and mother. ▉	706 706
We will give special attention to the problems associated with re-entry to the workforce and ensure that greater job retraining opportunities are available. ▉	706
Maternity leave without pay will be available to women for a period of up to twelve weeks, without loss of job security, promotion, or superannuation rights, providing this does not cause undue disruption to a business enterprise. ▉	706
The new National Government will appoint women to boards, commissions, and tribunals and will give consideration to the appointment of women as industrial mediators. ▉	706
We will also support increased participation of women in the judicial system and recognize no sex barriers in the exercise of any judicial office. ▉ Suitably qualified women will be given exactly the same consideration as men. ▉	503 503
National will ensure that early childhood education is generally available (where feasible) as an integral part of the education system. ▉ Priority will be given to such areas as new housing suburbs and regenerated inner city areas. ▉	506 411
Financial assistance will be provided through approved voluntary agencies to establish centres for those children who need day care but whose parents cannot afford to pay the full cost. ▉	504
National will also promote and encourage job training and retraining, 'second chance' education ▉ and promote a policy of life-long education for women. ▉	411 706
We will tackle the problems women face with housing. ▉ Under National the Housing Corporation will not differentiate between men and women borrowers on grounds of sex. ▉	706 503
We will introduce a flexible principal repayment plan to meet those cases where the wife works, leaves the workforce to raise a family and then returns to work. ▉	706
The National party believes all women must have the opportunity to participate on the basis of full equality in the social, cultural, economic, and political spheres of New Zealand society. ▉	503

6. Reliability Test

The following pages have to be coded for a reliability test. A copy of this text with the marked quasi-sentences and the number of identified categories in the margin of the pages has to be checked by the supervisor before the actual coding is started to check whether the correspondence in coding is sufficiently high.

AUSTRALIA, National Country Party 1966:

'WE WILL GROW, PROSPER'

The Deputy Prime Minister (Mr McEwen) said last night all the government's policies were aimed at building an Australia respected and trusted throughout the world. Mr McEwen, delivering the Country party policy speech at Sheparton, said: The Country party, the government, has one constant and continuing policy objective—to make Australia strong, safe, prosperous; to build a modern Australia, with equal opportunity for all:

where the aged, and the infirm, are looked after;

where the young are well educated, properly trained, to play their part in making the greater Australia of the future;

where every man, woman, and child—native-born Australians and migrants alike—can live in freedom, enjoying the rewards of their own efforts, obtaining their just share of the wealth of the community.

Under our coalition government's policies, Australia's advance has been remarkable. Here are the results of the seventeen years of our responsibility in government:

3.5 million more people since we came to office—half of them migrants;

1.25 million new jobs (1.6 million new homes built);

tremendous increases in wool production; wheat, meat, sugar, dairy products, fruit, and so on—with fewer workers.

The volume of exports more than doubled.

More than 20,000 new factories; factory production increased two and a half times.

Mineral production more than doubled.

2.5 million more vehicles on the road—a car for every four people;

unprecedented developments in community services; roads, dams, power houses, hospitals, and schools.

Industries everywhere are creating new wealth, ultimately distributed for all the people in better wages, social services, and health, in education and defence.

In seventeen years the total production of Australia, including all primary and secondary industries and the service industries which go with them, has doubled.

If in 1949, in a policy speech I had said: 'Put the Country party and the Liberal party in power and our policies will double the size of the Australian economy in 17 years', this would have been treated with derision. But we have done it!

This is a story of growth; of increasing national strength, greater safety, higher prosperity, and sharing the prosperity.

Three years ago, we said our policies would produce 25 per cent growth over 5 years. Despite the disastrous drought, this objective is well in sight. I now say the next five years will see this rate continued.

We are determined that successive generations of Australians will enjoy in even greater measure than we do, an Australian way of life of which we can be proud, and the rest of the world envy.

ALLIANCES

In today's world, no country can stand alone. Safety and security demand that our own growing strength be allied with that of others who share our beliefs in the right of free people to remain free. This is the basis of our foreign policy. We must be sure that if our freedom is threatened we will not be left to stand alone. So, we are concerned with the integrity of other small, free countries. The respect for Australia as a staunch and reliable ally has never been higher. Our great association with Britain and the Commonwealth has been strengthened. We have stood with Britain in preserving the security of Malaysia. Under the ANZUS Treaty we, with New England, have established a great alliance with the USA. Under SEATO we are linked with Britain, the USA, and France, and with Asian countries from Pakistan to the Philippines.

PRUDENCE

We help the less-developed countries with aid, and we were the first in the world to give tariff preference to them. We strive constantly for peace, through the United Nations, and will do so unceasingly. But prudence and security demand that we work also for strong and lasting alliances. The most powerful country in the world—the USA—will be with us to protect our freedom if we are threatened with aggression, just as the USA today is protecting the freedom of the people of South Vietnam from Communist aggression. The USA seeks no material gain, fighting this distant war. Australia seeks only to prove that aggression will not succeed. And as Australia herself would expect help if in need, we now demonstrate that we are willing to extend our help to a small, free people under attack. We want to so conduct ourselves that the USA will not hesitate to stand between Australia and an aggressor. America is the one country that can do this. Our troops in South Vietnam earn for us the right to the protection of the USA and our other treaty allies, should Australia be threatened. Voluntary recruiting has not produced the numbers of men required for the Army. The Government did try, long and hard, to enlist sufficient men as volunteers. Despite all its efforts not enough men came forward to enable us to play our present part with the British in Malaysia and the Americans in South Vietnam. So, we have added to the ranks of our volunteer regular army the necessary numbers of national servicemen to meet the nation's requirements. To say that we would honour our obligations with the USA and our other allies only if enough volunteers came forward would show Australia as a very uncertain ally. American conscripts have helped to save us once. No Australian would suggest that we were not grateful that they defended us in our day of peril. Surely no responsible Australian would suggest that, in the absence of sufficient volunteers we should wait until war reaches Australia itself before we called conscripts to the protection of our homeland. We in the government are sure that we have acted properly in bringing in National Service so that we may join with America in her stand to prevent the outward expansion of aggressive Communism.

Of course, safety is not secured only by modern defence forces and alliances. There must be great economic strength—an industrial base capable of servicing and maintaining today's complex military operations, food and mineral production for our own needs, and to earn foreign exchange, good roads and railways, efficient ports.

Defence security and economic strength go hand in hand. Our policies promote these. Look at the primary industries.

By 1964, before the calamitous drought total farm output was 67 per cent higher than when we came to office.

Wool, still the great foreign country earner, has nearly doubled in production since the war. Wool has been helped by the Japanese Trade Treaty, taxation incentives, huge expenditure on research and technology, and government-supported promotion activity.

CROP RECORD

Wheat growers are about to harvest what could be an all-time record crop; double the average crop of the early 'fifties'. The guaranteed price covers more than 200 million bushels each harvest. This has given the industry the confidence necessary for expansion.

Total bounty payments provided by our government to the dairy industry, to offset high costs and difficult markets, have amounted to just on 3,500 million. A quarter of a million people depend on the dairy industry.

The great sugar industry has a fair price in the home market; a good price for sales under the agreement with Britain; negotiated access for profitable sales to America. The Japanese Trade Treaty has made Japan our biggest sugar customer.

In my policy speech, three years ago, I said: 'If problems arise, we will be ready to help.' We have helped.

The sugar industry, through no fault of its own, is in serious temporary difficulty. It asked for, and our government has given a loan of $19 million to augment pool payments from this year's crop.

For Australian beef producers, negotiated access to the USA market, and now to Japan, has been worth millions.

We have legislated to give effect to marketing or stabilization plans for canned and dried fruits, for eggs, and also for tobacco, which has been lifted from a peasant industry to one of high-average incomes.

Cotton is taking dramatic strides forward under the stimulus of our policies.

There are problems—in the apple and pear industry; in dairying; the British move towards the European Common Market; the never-ending job of gaining access to markets. Much has been achieved in meeting these problems. We will never let up in our efforts.

EXPANSION

Our policies for secondary industry are policies for growth, sound expansion, jobs, jobs for a growing, well-paid workforce, more than 100,000 new jobs a year.

Tariff machinery is continually improved to give prompt and adequate tariff protection; to prevent damage by dumping and disruptive imports.

We give efficient secondary industry a secure grip on the home market. From this base we encourage it to develop exports with the help of a variety of export incentives.

Investment in manufacturing has risen from $120 million a year to $1,000 million a year.

Great new industries are providing well-paid employment for more and more Australians. Average earnings in real 'spending-power terms' are up 50 per cent.

Help is provided for the aged, the infirm, the sick, health and social-service payments lifted from $162 million to $1,020 million a year.

Australia can and must look after the needs of the aged and the infirm. They must be given a full share of benefit from the nation's growth.

FREIGHTS

We have initiated moves to stem overseas freight rises by rationalization of overseas shipping services; for containerization and other modern cargo-handling methods, and by establishment of modern port facilities.

Industry stabilization plans form part of the compensation to export industries for the burden of costs arising from fast national growth.

So does the $28 million-a-year subsidy on superphosphate, and our new subsidy on nitrogenous fertilisers of $30 per ton nitrogen content.

Petrol prices have been reduced to no higher than fourpence a gallon over city prices. Many inland people have been saved more than a shilling a gallon. For years the Country party policy urged this plan.

Special taxation allowance has been granted to primary producers, huge sums provided for agricultural research and extension, massive help for wool promotion.

Suitable long-term credit at lower interest rates has been made available for rural and other development needs.

The Commonwealth Development Bank, the trading banks, term loan fund of $246 million, adds a new dimension to the array of credit facilities available to farmers.

Decentralization requires practical policies which make country areas profitable locations for industry and attractive places for people to live. Housing must be available, so must phones and TV, air services—including freight.

For Commonwealth Aid Roads grants we are providing $750 million in the current five-year period; $150 million this year, rising to $170 million the year after next and $126 million is being found for nearly 2,000 miles of rail standardization and reconstruction.

Our government acted through state government to help those affected by the drought. So far $57 million has been provided. Ways must be found to mitigate the effects of drought; to reduce and alleviate the personal heartbreak and national losses which go with them.

BEEF ROADS

We have given special attention to developing the North and 4,000 miles of beef roads have been approved. More are under study and $57 million is being provided for beef roads in Queensland, Western Australia and the Northern Territory.

We have found millions of dollars for port facilities in Western Australia and Queensland: at Weipa in Queensland, and help at Gladstone; in Western Australia more than $6 million for port improvements at Derby, Wyndham, and Broome.

We have found $12 million for stage one of the Ord irrigation project.

In Queensland vast areas—11 million acres—are being turned into high-productive pastures. We are finding $23 million for this and $1 million is being provided this year for research into tropical pastures.

Freight on superphosphate to Darwin will be subsidized and tax concessions allowed for mining with $42 million for oil search subsidies.

INDUSTRIES

Nothing contributes more to northern development than the sound and profitable expansion of the industries already located in the north.

What has been done for sugar, tobacco, beef, and for mineral development is conscious major policy for northern development.

These are parts of the whole pattern of policies for the development of the north and the balanced development of the whole of Australia.

I said at the beginning that we had a constant objective, to make Australia strong and safe, prosperous at home, respected and trusted throughout the world. I have spoken of some of the things we have done, of what we are doing.

These are not disjointed actions, independent of one another; thought up to get some votes, or some credit, or to appease some group.

They are all parts of a total, policies all designed for the one overriding purpose, to make Australia strong, safe, and prosperous.

We can be proud of what has been achieved; of Australia's great and growing economic strength, of high and rising living standards, of the continuous improvements in education, housing, and social services.

Because we have honoured our obligations and are playing our part in resisting aggression today we can be confident of our own future safety and security, of the strength of our alliances, of the assured protection of the USA should we ever be threatened.

The Australia of today is a base on which an even stronger, safer, more prosperous Australia will be built over the next decade.

Notes:

The particular countries with which Australia has a special relationship are defined as the Commonwealth countries.

ANZUS is a regional security treaty.

7. Definition of Categories

DOMAIN 1: External Relations

101 Foreign Special Relationships: Positive

Favourable mention of particular countries with which the manifesto country has a special relationship. For example, in the British case: former colonies; in the Swedish case: the rest of Scandinavia; the need for cooperation with and/or aid to such countries.

102 Foreign Special Relationships: Negative

Negative mention of particular countries with which the manifesto country has a special relationship; otherwise as 101, but negative.

103 Anti-Imperialism: Positive

Negative reference to exerting strong influence (political, military, or commercial) over other states; negative reference to controlling other countries as if they were part of an empire; favourable mention of decolonization; favourable reference to greater self-government and independence for colonies; negative reference to the imperial behaviour of the manifesto and/or other countries.

104 Military: Positive

Need to maintain or increase military expenditure, modernizing armed forces and improvement in military strength, rearmament and self-defence, need to keep military treaty obligations, need to secure adequate manpower in the military.

105 Military: Negative

Favourable mention of decreasing military expenditures; disarmament; 'evils of war'; promises to reduce conscription, otherwise as 104, but negative.

106 Peace: Positive

Peace as a general goal, declarations of belief in peace and peaceful means of solving crises, desirability of countries joining in negotiations with hostile countries.

107 Internationalism: Positive

Need for international cooperation, cooperation with specific countries other than those coded in 101, need for aid to developing countries, need for world planning of resources, need for international courts, support for any international goal or world state, support for UN.

108 European Integration: Positive
Favourable mention of European integration in general, desirability of expanding the EU and/or of increasing its competence, desirability of the manifesto country joining (or remaining a member).

109 Internationalism: Negative
Favourable mention of national independence and sovereignty as opposed to internationalism; otherwise as 107, but negative.

110 European Integration: Negative
Hostile mention of the EU, opposition to specific European policies which are preferred by European authorities, otherwise as 108, but negative.

DOMAIN 2: Freedom and Democracy
201 Freedom and Human Rights: Positive
Favourable mention of importance of personal freedom and civil rights, freedom from bureaucratic control, freedom of speech, freedom from coercion in the political and economic spheres, individualism in the manifesto country and in other countries.

202 Democracy: Positive
Favourable mention of democracy as a method or goal in national and other organizations; involvement of all citizens in decision-making as well as generalized support for the manifesto country's democracy.

203 Constitutionalism: Positive
Support for specific aspects of the constitution; use of constitutionalism as an argument for policy as well as general approval of the constitutional way of doing things.

204 Constitutionalism: Negative
Opposition to the constitution in general or to specific aspects; otherwise as 203, but negative.

DOMAIN 3: Political System
301 Decentralization: Positive
Support for federalism or devolution; more regional autonomy for policy or economy; support for keeping up local and regional customs and symbols; favourable mention of special consideration for local areas; deference to local expertise.

302 Centralization: Positive
Opposition to political decision-making at lower political levels; support for more centralization in political and administrative procedures; otherwise as 301, but negative.

303 Governmental and Administrative Efficiency: Positive
Need for efficiency and economy in government and administration; cutting down civil service; improving governmental procedures; general appeal to make the process of government and administration cheaper and more effective.

304 Political Corruption: Negative
Need to eliminate corruption, and associated abuse, in political and public life.

305 Political Authority: Positive
Favourable mention of strong government, including government stability; manifesto party's competence to govern and/or other party's lack of such competence.

DOMAIN 4: Economy
401 Free Enterprise: Positive

Favourable mention of free enterprise capitalism; superiority of individual enterprise over state and control systems; favourable mention of private property rights, personal enterprise and initiative; need for unhampered individual enterprises.

402 Incentives: Positive
Need for wage and tax policies to induce enterprise; encouragement to start enterprises; need for financial and other incentives.

403 Market Regulation: Positive
Need for regulations designed to make private enterprises work better; actions against monopolies and trusts, and in defence of consumer and small business; encouraging economic competition; social market economy.

404 Economic Planning: Positive
Favourable mention of long-standing economic planning of a consultative or indicative nature, need for government to create such a plan.

405 Corporatism: Positive
Favourable mention of the need for collaboration of employers and trade union organizations in overall economic planning and direction through the medium of tripartite bodies of government, employers, and trade unions.

406 Protectionism: Positive
Favourable mention of extension or maintenance of tariffs to protect internal markets; other domestic economic protectionism such as quota restrictions.

407 Protectionism: Negative
Support for the concept of free trade; otherwise as 406, but negative.

408 Economic Goals
Statements of intent to pursue any economic goals not covered by other categories in domain 4. This category is created to catch an overall interest of parties in economics and, therefore, covers a variety of economic goals.

409 Keynesian Demand Management: Positive
Demand-oriented economic policy; economic policy devoted to avoiding depression, mitigating effects of depression and/ or to increasing private demand through boosting public demand and/or through increasing social expenditure.

410 Productivity: Positive
Need to encourage or facilitate greater production; need to take measures to aid this; appeal for greater production and importance of productivity to the economy; the paradigm of growth.

411 Technology and Infrastructure: Positive
Importance of modernization of industry and methods of transport and communication; importance of science and technological developments in industry; need for training and research. This does not imply education in general (see category 506).

412 Controlled Economy: Positive
General need for direct government control of economy, control over prices, wages, rents, etc.

413 Nationalization: Positive
Favourable mention of government ownership, partial or complete, including government ownership of land.

414 Economic Orthodoxy: Positive
Need for traditional economic orthodoxy, for example, reduction of budget deficits, retrenchment in crisis, thrift and savings; support for traditional economic institutions such as stock market and banking system; support for strong currency.

415 Marxist Analysis: Positive
Positive reference (typically but not necessarily by communist parties) to the specific use of Marxist-Leninist terminology and analysis of situations which are otherwise uncodable.

416 Anti-Growth Economy: Positive
Favourable mention of anti-growth politics and steady state economy; ecologism/ 'Green politics' especially as applied to economic policy; sustainable development.

501 Environmental Protection: Positive
Preservation of countryside, forests, etc.; general preservation of natural resources against selfish interests; proper use of national parks; soil banks, etc.; environmental improvement. 'Ecologism' /'Green' politics as applied to environmental policy.

502 Culture: Positive
Need to provide cultural and leisure facilities including arts and sport; need to spend money on museums, art galleries, etc.; need to encourage worthwhile leisure activities and cultural mass media.

503 Social Justice: Positive
Concept of equality; need for fair treatment of all people; special protection for underprivileged; need for fair distribution of resources; removal of class barriers; end to discrimination on the grounds of race, sex, gender, disability, age, sexual orientation, etc.

504 Welfare State Expansion: Positive
Favourable mention of need to introduce, maintain, or expand any social service or social security scheme; support for social services such as health service or social housing.
Note: This category excludes education.

505 Welfare State Limitation: Positive
Limiting expenditure on social services or social security; otherwise as 504, but negative.

506 Education Expansion: Positive
Need to expand and/or improve educational provision at all levels. This excludes technical training which is coded under 411.

507 Education Limitation: Positive
Limiting expenditure on education; otherwise as 506, but negative.

DOMAIN 6: Fabric of Society
601 National Way of Life: Positive
Appeals to patriotism and/or nationalism; suspension of some freedoms in order to protect the state against subversion; support for established national ideas.

602 National Way of Life: Negative
Opposition to patriotism and/or nationalism; opposition to the existing national state; otherwise as 601, but negative.

603 Traditional Morality: Positive
Favourable mention of traditional moral values; prohibition, censorship and suppression of immorality and unseemly behaviour; maintenance and stability of family; religion.
604 Traditional Morality: Negative

Opposition to traditional moral values; support for divorce, abortion etc.; otherwise as 603, but negative.

605 Law and Order: Positive
Enforcement of all laws; actions against crime; support for resources for police, etc.; tougher attitudes in courts.

606 Social Harmony: Positive
Appeal for national effort and solidarity; need for society to see itself as united; appeal for public spiritedness; decrying anti-social attitudes in times of crisis; support for the public interest.

607 Multiculturalism: Positive
Favourable mention of cultural diversity, communalism, cultural plurality, and pillariza-tion; preservation of autonomy of religious, linguistic heritages within the country includ-ing special educational provisions.

608 Multiculturalism: Negative
Enforcement or encouragement of cultural integration; otherwise as 607, but negative.

DOMAIN 7 Social Groups
701 Labour Groups: Positive
Favourable reference to labour groups, working class, unemployed; support for trade unions; good treatment of employees.

702 Labour Groups: Negative
Abuse of power by trade unions; otherwise as 701, but negative.

703 Farmers: Positive
Support for agriculture and farmers; any policy aimed specifically at benefiting these.

704 Middle Class and Professional Groups: Positive
Favourable reference to middle class, professional groups, such as physicians or lawyers; old and new middle class.

705 Underprivileged Minority Groups: Positive
Favourable reference to underprivileged minorities who are defined neither in economic nor in demographic terms, for example, the handicapped, homosexuals, immigrants, etc.

706 Non-economic Demographic Groups: Positive
Favourable mention of, or need for, assistance to women, the elderly, young people, lin-guistic groups, etc.; special interest groups of all kinds.

8. Subcategories Used for CEE Countries

1011 Russia/USSR/CIS: Positive
Favourable mention of Russia, the USSR, the CMEA bloc, or the Community of Indepen-dent States.

1012 Western States: Positive
Favourable mention of Western states, including the USA and Germany.

1013 Eastern European Countries: positive
Favourable mention of Eastern European countries in general.

1014 Baltic States: Positive
Favourable mention of the Baltic states, including other states bordering the Baltic Sea.

1015 Nordic Council: Positive
Favourable mention of the Nordic Council.

1016 SFR Yugoslavia: Positive
Favourable mention of countries formerly belonging to SFR Yugoslavia including special relationships with Montenegro, Macedonia, Slovenia, Croatia and Bosnia-Herzegovina.

1021 Russia/USSR/CIS: Negative
Negative mention of Russia, the USSR, or the Community of Independent States.

1022 Western States: Negative
Negative mention of Western states, including the USA and Germany.

1023 East European Countries: Negative
Negative mention of Eastern European countries in general.

1024 Baltic States: Negative
Negative reference to the Baltic states.

1025 Nordic Council: Negative
Negative reference to the Nordic Council.

1026 SFR Yugoslavia: Negative
Negative mention of countries formerly belonging to SFR Yugoslavia including negative reference to Montenegro, Macedonia, Slovenia, Croatia, and Bosnia-Herzegovina.

1031 Russian Army: Negative
Need to withdraw the Russian army from the territory of the manifesto country; need to receive reparations for damage caused by the Russian army or other Soviet institutions.

1032 Independence: Positive
Favourable mention of the independence and sovereignty of the manifesto country.

1033 Rights of Nations: Positive
Favourable mention of freedom, rights, and interests of nations.

2021 Transition to Democracy
General reference to the transition process of one-party states to pluralist democracy.

2022 Restrictive Citizenship: Positive
Favourable mention of restrictions in citizenship; restrictions in enfranchisement with respect to (ethnic) groups.

2023 Lax Citizenship: Positive
Favourable mention of lax citizenship and election laws; no or few restrictions in enfranchisement.

2031 Presidential Regime: Positive
Support for current presidential regime; statements in favour of a powerful presidency.

2032 Republic: Positive
Support for republican forms of government.

2033 Checks and Balances: Positive
Support for checks and balances and separation of powers, and specifically for limiting the powers of the presidency by increasing legislative/judicial powers, or transferring some executive powers to the legislature or judiciary.

2041 Monarchy: Positive
Support for a monarchy, including conceptions of constitutional monarchy.

3011 Republican Powers: Positive
Favourable mention of stronger republican powers.

3051 Public Situation: Negative
Negative reference to the situation in public life after the founding elections.

3052 Communist: Positive
Cooperation with former authorities/communists in the transition period; pro-communist involvement in the transition process; and 'let sleeping dogs lie' in dealing with the nomenclature.

3053 Communist: Negative
Against communist involvement in democratic government; weeding out the collaborators from governmental service; need for political coalition except communist parties.

3054 Rehabilitation and Compensation: Positive
Favourable reference to civic rehabilitation of politically persecuted people in the communist era; reference to juridical compensation concerning communist expropriations; moral compensation.

3055 Political Coalitions: Positive
Reference to the need of broader political coalition; need for cooperation at the political level; necessity of collaboration among all political forces.

4011 Privatization: Positive
Favourable reference to privatization.

4012 Control of Economy: Negative
Negative reference to the general need for direct governmental control of the economy.

4013 Property Restitution: Positive
Favourable reference to the physical restitution of property to previous owners.

4014 Privatization Vouchers: Positive
Favourable reference to privatization vouchers.

4121 Social Ownership: Positive
Favourable reference to the creation or preservation of cooperative or non-state social ownership within a market economy.

4122 Mixed Economy: Positive
Favourable reference to mixed ownership within a market economy.

4123 Publicly Owned Industry: Positive
Positive reference to the concept of publicly owned industries.

4124 Socialist Property: Positive
Positive reference to socialist property, including public and cooperative property; negative reference to privatization.

4131 Property Restitution: Negative
Negative reference to the physical restitution of property to previous owners.

4132 Privatization: Negative
Negative reference to the privatization system; need to change the privatization system.

5021 Private–Public Mix in Culture: Positive
Necessity of private provisions due to economic constraints; support for private funding in addition to public activity.

5031 Private–Public Mix in Social Justice: Positive
Necessity for private initiatives due to economic constraints.

5041 Private–Public Mix in Welfare: Positive
Necessity for private welfare provisions due to economic constraints; desirability of competition in welfare service provisions; private funding in addition to public activity.

5061 Private–Public Mix in Education: Positive
Necessity for private education due to economic constraints; desirability of competition in education.

6011 The Karabakh Issue: Positive
Positive reference to the unity of Karabakh and Armenia or the recognition for an independent Republic of Karabakh; rendering assistance to Karabakh.

6012 Rebuilding the USSR: Positive
Favourable mention of the reunification of all republics and nations living on the former territory of the USSR into a new common (democratic) state or into a common economic space; negative reference to the dissolution of the USSR and the respective treaties.

6013 National Security: Positive
Support for or need to maintain national security in all spheres of social life; policies devoted to this goal.

6061 General Crisis
Identification of a general crisis in the country.

6071 Cultural Autonomy: Positive
Favourable mention of cultural autonomy.

6072 Multiculturalism pro Roma: Positive
Favourable mention of cultural autonomy of Roma.

6081 Multiculturalism pro Roma: Negative
Negative mention of cultural autonomy of Roma.

7051 Minorities Inland: Positive
Favourable reference to manifesto country minorities in foreign countries; positive reference to manifesto country minorities.

7052 Minorities Abroad: Positive
Favourable reference to ethnic minorities living in the manifesto country such as Latvians living in Estonia.

7061 War Participants: Positive
Favourable mention of, or need for, assistance to people taking part in the war on the territory of former Yugoslavia.

7062 Refugees: Positive
Favourable mention of, or need for, assistance to people who left their homes because of the war (e.g. on the territory of former Yugoslavia) or were forcibly displaced.

References

Berelson, Bernard (1952), *Content Analysis in Communication Research*. New York: Hafner Publishing Company.
Budge, Ian, Klingemann, Hans-Dieter, Volkens, Andrea, Bara, Judith, Tanenbaum, Eric with Fording, Richard C., Hearl, Derek J., Kim, Hee Min, McDonald, Michael, and Mendés,

Silvia (2001), *Mapping Policy Preference. Estimates for Parties, Electors, and Governments 1945–1998*. Oxford: Oxford University Press.

Budge, Ian, Robertson, David, and Hearl, Derek (eds.) (1987), *Ideology, Strategy and Party Change. Spatial Analysis of Post-War Election Programmes in 19 Democracies*. Cambridge: Cambridge University Press.

Klingemann, Hans-Dieter, Hofferbert, Richard I., Budge, Ian with Keman, Hans, Pétry, Francois, Bergman, Torbjörn, and Strøm, Kaare (1994), *Parties, Policies, and Democracy*. Boulder, CO: Westview Press.

Laver, Michael, and Budge Ian (eds.) (1992), *Party Policy and Coalition Government*. New York: St. Martin's Press.

Robertson, David (1976), *A Theory of Party Competition*. London: Wiley & Sons.

Sartori, Giovanni (1976), *Parties and Party Systems. A Framework for Analysis*. Cambridge: Cambridge University Press.

Further Reading

Krippendorf, Klaus (2003), *Content Analysis: An Introduction to its Methodology*. Beverley Hills, CA: Sage.

Neuendorf, Kimberley A. (2002), *The Content Analysis Guidebook*. Thousand Oaks, CA; New Delhi, London: Sage.

Riffe, Daniel, Stephen Lacy and Frederick G. Fico (1998), *Analyzing Media Messages: Using Quantitative Content Analysis in Research*. Mahwah, NJ; Lawrence Erlbaum.

Roberts, Carl W. (ed.) (1997), *Text Analysis for the Social Sciences*. Mahwah, NJ: Lawrence Erlbaum.

Political Parties Included in the Data-Set

Appendix III lists all parties in the Manifesto data-set by country in alphabetical order including (I.) 24 OECD countries, (II.) 24 CEE countries, and (III) 1 other country (Israel). For each party in the 49 countries, the following information is provided:

1. Parties	1.1	Acronyms as usually used in original language, except Japan: acronyms of English names.
	1.2	Names of parties in original language mostly as given in Arthur S. Banks (ed.): *Political Handbook of the World*, Binghamton: CSA Publications/New York: McGraw-Hill (various editions).
	1.3	Name of party in English (if original is not English).
	1.4	Changes in names of parties. In all appended documentation, the latest name of a party is used.
2. Elections	2.1	First and last election of time period covered.
	2.2	Number of elections in time period covered. This number equals the number of cases for each party, including its coded platforms, joint platforms, and estimated cases.
3. MDS-ID		Identification number in Manifesto data-set MDS-ID 11110 to ID 98951. The party identification code consists of five digits. The first two digits repeat the country code. The third, fourth, and fifth digits are running numbers.

I. OECD Countries
1.1 Australian Parties Covered

	Parties	Elections		MDS-ID
		first–last	no	
ALP	Australian Labor Party	1990–2001	5	63320
AD	Australian Democrats	1990–2001	4	63321
LPA	Liberal Party of Australia	1990–2001	5	63620
CP	Country Party	1990–2001	5	63810
NCP	renamed: National Country Party	in 1975		
NPA	renamed: National Party of Australia	in 1982		

Total number of cases	19

1.2 Austrian Parties Covered

	Parties	Elections		MDS-ID
		first–last	no	
GA	Die Grüne Alternative (Green Alternative)	1990–2002	5	42110
	renamed: Die Grünen (Green Party)	in 1993		
KPÖ	Kommunistische Partei Österreichs (Communist Party)	2002	1	42220
SPÖ	Sozialdemokratische Partei Österreichs (Austrian Social Democratic Party)	1990–2002	5	42320
VdU	Verband der Unabhängigen (League of Independents)	1990–2002	5	42420
FPÖ	renamed: Freiheitliche Partei Österreichs (Austrian Freedom Party)	in 1956		
	renamed: Die Freiheitlichen (Freedom Movement)	in 1995		
LF	Liberales Forum (Liberal Forum)	1994 + 1995	2	42421
ÖVP	Österreichische Volkspartei (Austrian People's Party)	1990–2002	5	42520

Total number of cases   23

1.3 Belgian Parties Covered

	Parties	Elections		MDS-ID
		first–last	no	
ECOLO	Écologistes Confédérés pour l'Organisation de Luttes Originales (Francophone Ecologists)	1991–2003	4	21111
AGA LEV	Anders Gaan Leven (Live Differently—Flemish-speaking Ecologists, also called Groen!)	1991–1999	3	21112
BSP	Belgische Socialistische Partij (Flemish Socialist Party)	1991–1999	3	21321
SP	renamed: Socialistische Partij (Flemish Socialist Party)	in 1980		
PS	Parti Socialiste (Francophone Socialist Party)	1991–2003	4	21322
PVV	Partij voor Vrijheid en Vooruitgang (Party of Liberty and Progress)	1991–2003	4	21421
VLD	renamed: Vlaamse Liberalen en Demokraten (Flemish Liberals and Democrats)	in 1992		
PLP	Parti de la Liberté et du Progrès (Party of Liberty and Progress)	1991	1	21422
PRLW	renamed: Parti des Réformes et de la Liberté de Wallonie (Francophone Liberals)	in 1976		
PRL	renamed: Parti Réformateur Libéral (Francophone Liberals)	in 1979		

PRL-FDF	Parti Réformateur Libéral—Front Démocratique des Francophones (Liberal Reformation Party—Francophone Democratic Front)	1995	1	21423
PRL-FDF-MCC	Parti réformateur libéral—Front démocratique francophone—Mouvement des Citoyens pour la Changement (Liberal Reformation Party—Francophone Democratic Front—Citizens' Movement for Change)	1999	1	21425
CVP	Christelijke Volkspartij (Christian People's Party)	1991–2003	4	21521
PSC	Parti Social Chrétien (Christian Social Party)	1991–2003	4	21522
FDF	Front Démocratique des Bruxellois Francophones (Francophone Democratic Front)	1991	1	21912
	Frontpartij (Front Party)	1991 + 1995	2	21913
VNV	renamed: Vlaamsch Nationaal Verbond (Flemish National League)	in 1936		
	renamed: Vlaamsch Concentratie (Flemish Concentration)	in 1949		
	renamed: Christelijke Vlaamse Volksunie (Flemish Christian Peoples' Union)	in 1954		
VU	renamed: De Volksunie (Peoples' Union)	in 1987		
VB	Vlaams Blok (Flemish Bloc)	1991–2003	4	21914
VU-ID21	De Volksunie—Ideen voor de 21ste eeuw (People's Union—Ideas for the 21st century)	1999	1	21915

Total number of cases   37

1.4 Canadian Parties Covered

	Parties	Elections		MDS-ID
		first–last	no	
CCF	Cooperative Commonwealth Federation	1993–2000	3	62320
NDP	renamed: New Democratic Party	in 1961		
LP	Liberal Party of Canada	1993–2000	3	62420
PCP	Progressive Conservative Party	1993–2000	3	62620
RPC	Reform Party of Canada	1993 + 1997	2	62621
CA	Canadian Reform Conservative Alliance including RPC	2000	1	62622
BQ	Bloc Québécois	1993–2000	3	62901

Total number of cases   15

1.5 Danish Parties Covered

	Parties	Elections		MDS-ID
		first–last	no	
EL	Enhedslisten—De Rød-Grønne (Red-Green Unity List) composed of: Valforbund Enhedslisten: De Grønne, Solidarisk Alternativ, Invendrerlisten, Christianialisten, Arbeidsløshedsparteit, Kærlighedspartiet, Miljøparti	1994–2001	3	13229
SF	Socialistisk Folkeparti (Socialist People's Party)	1990–2001	4	13230
SD	Socialdemokratiet (Social Democratic Party)	1990–2001	4	13320
CD	Centrum-Demokraterne (Centre Democrats)	1990–1998	3	13330
RV	Det Radikale Venstre (Radical Party)	1990–2001	4	13410
V	Venstre (Liberals)	1990–2001	4	13420
KrF	Kristeligt Folkeparti (Christian People's Party)	1990–2001	4	13520
KF	Konservative Folkeparti (Conservative People's Party)	1990–2001	4	13620
DF	Danske Folkeparti (Danish People's Party)	1998–2001	2	13720
FP	Fremkridtspartiet (Progress Party)	1990–1998	3	13951

Total number of cases   35

1.6 Finnish Parties Covered

	Parties	Elections		MDS-ID
		first–last	no	
VL	Vihreä Liitto (Green Union)	1991–2003	4	14110
VL	Vasemmistoliitto (Left Wing Alliance)	1991–2003	4	14223
SSDP	Suomen Sosialidemokraattinen Puolue (Finnish Social Democrats)	1991–2003	4	14320
	Kansallinen Edistyspuolue (National Progressive Party)	1991	1	14420
	renamed: Suomen Kansanpuolue (Finnish People's Party)	in 1951		
LKP	renamed: Liberaalinen Kansanpuolue (Liberal People's Party)	in 1966		
NSP	Nuorsuomalainen Puolue (Progressive Finnish Party, also known as Young Finns)	1995	1	14430
SKL	Suomen Kristillinen Liitto (Finnish Christian Union)	1991–2003	4	14520
KK	Kansallinen Kokoomus (National Coalition)	1991–2003	4	14620
	Maalaisliitto (Agrarian Union)	1991–2003	4	14810
	renamed: Keskustapuolue (Centre Party)	in 1965		
SK	renamed: Suomen Keskusta (Finnish Centre)	in 1988		
	Suomen Pientalonpoiken Puolue (Finnish Smallholder's Party)	1991–2003	4	14820
SMP	renamed: Soumen Maaseudun Puolue (Finnish Rural Party)	in 1966		

| PS | renamed: Perussuomalaiset (True Finns) | in 1998 | | |
| RKP/SFP | Ruotsalainen Kansanpuolue/Svenska Folkpartiet (Swedish People's Party) | 1991–2003 | 4 | 14901 |

Total number of cases   34

1.7 French Parties Covered

	Parties	Elections first–last	no	MDS-ID
	Écologistes (Greens) in 1997: Les Verts	1993–2002	3	31110
GE	Generation Écologie (Ecology Generation)	1997	1	31111
PCF	Parti Communiste Français (French Communist Party)	1993–2002	3	31220
SFIO	Section Française de l'Internationale Ouvriére (Socialist Party)	1993–2002	3	31320
PS	renamed: Parti Socialiste (Socialist Party)	in 1969		
UDF	Union pour la Démocratie Française (Union for French Democracy)	1993–2002	3	31624
RPR	Rassemblement pour la République (Rally for the Republic)	1993 + 1997	2	31625
UMP	Union pour la majorité presidentielle (Union for the Presidential Majority) composed of: RPR Rassemblement pour la République (Rally for the Republic) and DL Démocratie Libérale (Liberal Democracy); after the election part of UDF joined the Union	2002	1	31626
FN	Front National (National Front)	1993–2002	3	31720

Total number of cases   19

1.8 German Parties Covered

	Parties	Elections first–last	no	MDS-ID
Greens/90	Grüne/Bündnis'90 (Greens/Alliance'90)	1990	1	41112
90/Greens	Bündnis'90/Die Grünen (Alliance'90/Greens)	1994–2002	3	41113
PDS	Partei des Demokratischen Sozialismus (Party of Democratic Socialism)	1990–2002	4	41221
SPD	Sozialdemokratische Partei Deutschlands (Social Democratic Party of Germany)	1990–2002	4	41320
FDP	Freie Demokratische Partei (Free Democratic Party)	1990–2002	4	41420
CDU/CSU	Christlich-Demokratische Union/Christlich-Soziale Union (Christian Democratic Union/Christian Social Union)	1990–2002	4	41521

Total number of cases   20

1.9 Greek Parties Covered

Parties		Elections		MDS-ID
		first–last	no	
KKE	Kommounistiko Komma Elladas (Communist Party of Greece)	1993–2000	3	34210
SAP	Synaspismos tis Aristeras kai tis Proodou (Progressive Left Coalition)	1990–2000	3	34211
PASOK	Panhellinio Socialistiko Kinema (Panhellenic Socialist Movement)	1990–2000	4	34313
DIKKI	Dimokratiki Kinoniki Kinema (Democratic Social Movement)	1996	1	34314
ND	Nea Dimokratia (New Democracy)	1990–2000	4	34511
Pola	Politiki Anixi (Political Spring)	1993 + 1996	2	34512

Total number of cases 17

1.10 Icelandic Parties Covered

Parties		Elections		MDS-ID
		first–last	no	
VGF	Vinstrihreyfing—Grænt Frambod (Left Green Movement)	1999 + 2003	2	15111
	Sósiálistaflokkurinn (United Socialist Party)	1991 + 1995	2	15220
Ab	renamed: Alþhýðubandalagid (People's Alliance)	in 1956		
A	Alþhýðuflokkurinn (Social Democratic Party)	1991 + 1995	2	15320
	Þjóðvaki (Awakening of the Nation)	1995	1	15323
S	Samfylkingin (Alliance of Ab, A, and Kv)	1999 + 2003	2	15328
FF	Frjálslyndi Flokkurinn (Liberal Party)	1999 + 2003	2	15420
Sj	Sjálfstaedisflokkurinn (Independence Party)	1991–2003	4	15620
F	Framsóknarflokkurinn (Progressive Party)	1991–2003	4	15810
Kv	Samtök um Kvennalista (Women's Alliance)	1991 + 1995	2	15951

Total number of cases 21

1.11 Irish Parties Covered

Parties		Elections		MDS-ID
		first–last	no	
Greens	Ecology Party/Green Party/Comhaontas Glas	1992–2002	3	53110
DLP	Democratic Left Party	1992 + 1997	2	53221
LP	Páirti Lucht Oibre (Labour Party)	1992–2002	3	53320
PD	Progressive Democrats	1992–2002	3	53420
FG	Fine Gael (Family of the Irish)	1992–2002	3	53520

FF	Fianna Fáil (Soldiers of Destiny)	1992–2002	3	53620
Sinn Fein	Ourselves III	1997 + 2002	2	53951

Total number of cases　　　　　　　　　　　　　　　　19

1.12 Italian Parties Covered

	Parties	Elections		MDS-ID
		first–last	no	
FdV	Federazione dei Liste Verdi (Green Federation)	1992–1996	3	32110
	Il Girasole (Greens and Social Democrats)	2001	1	31111
RC	Rifondazione Comunista (Newly Founded Communists)	1992–2001	4	32212
PDCI	Partito dei Comunisti Italiano (Italian Communists)	2001	1	32213
PCI	Partito Comunista Italiano (Communist Party)	1992–2001	4	32220
PDS	renamed: Partito Democratico della Sinistra (Democratic Party of the Left)	in 1990		
DS	renamed: Democratici di Sinistra (Democrats of the Left)	in 1998		
PR	Partito Radicale (Radical Party)	1992–1996	3	32310
	renamed: Lista Panella	in 1992		
	renamed: Lista Panella—Riformatori	in 1994		
	renamed: Lista Sgarbi-Panella	in 1996		
PSI	Partito Socialista Italiano (Socialist Party)	1992 + 1994	2	32320
RI	Rinnovamento Italiano (Italian Renewal)	1996	1	32321
	Ulivo (Olive Tree) composed of: Il Girasole, PDCI, PDS, and La Margherita	2001	1	32329
PSLI	Partito Socialista dei Lavoratori Italiani (Socialist Party of Italian Workers)	1992	1	32330
PSDI	renamed: Partito Socialista Democratico Italiano (Italian Democratic Socialist Party)	in 1972		
PRI	Partito Repubblicano Italiano (Republican Party)	1992	1	32410
PLI	Partito Liberale Italiano (Liberal Party)	1992	1	32420
	La Margherita (Daisy)	2001	1	32421
DC	Democrazia Cristiana (Christian Democrats)	1992–1996	3	32520
PPI	renamed: Partito Populare Italiano (Italian Popular Party)	in 1994		
CCD	Centro Cristiano Democratico (Christian Democratic Centre)	1996	1	32521
	Biancofiore (White Flower)	2001	1	32522
PI	Patto per l'Italia (Pact for Italy)	1994	1	32528
AD	Alleanza Democratica (Democratic Alliance)	1994 + 1996	2	32529
FI	Forza Italia (Go Italy)	1994–2001	3	32610
NPSI	Nuovo Partito Socialista Italiano (New Socialist Party)	2001	1	32611
	Casa della Libertá (House of Freedom) composed of: Biancofiore, FI, NDSI, AN, LN	2001	1	32629
MSI	Movimento Sociale Italiano (Italian Social Movement)	1992–2001	4	32710

MSI-DN	renamed: Movimento Sociale Italiano-Destra Nazionale (Italian Social Movement-National Right)	in 1972		
AN	renamed: Alleanza Nazionale (National Alliance)	in 1994		
LN	La Lega Nord (Northern League)	1992–2001	4	32720
DE	Democrazia Europea (European Democracy)	2001	1	32901
	Lista di Pietro Italia del Valori (List Di Pietro Italy of Values)	2001	1	32902
LR	La Rete/Movimento per la Democrazia (The Network/Movement for Democracy)	1992 + 1994	2	32951

Total number of cases   49

1.13 Japanese Parties Covered

	Parties	Elections first–last	no	MDS-ID
JCP	Nihon Kyosan-to (Japan Communist Party)	1990–2003	5	71220
JSP	Nihon Shakai-to (Japan Socialist Party)	1990–2003	5	71320
DSP	Minshu-Shakai-to (Democratic Socialist Party)	1990 + 1993	2	71321
SDF	Shaminren (Social Democratic Federation)	1990	1	71322
CGP	Komei-to (Clean Government Party)	1990–2003	4	71530
LDP	Jiyu-Minshu-to (Liberal Democratic Party)	1990–2003	5	71620
JRP	Shinsei-to (Japan Renewal Party)	1993	1	71622
NFP	Sinshin (New Frontier Party)	1996	1	71623
DPJ	Minshu (Democratic Party of Japan)	1996–2003	3	71624
LP	Jiyo-to (Liberal Party)	2000	1	71625
NCP	Hoshu-to (New Conservative Party)	2000	1	71626
NP	Sakigake (New Party)	1993 + 1996	2	71951
JNP	Nihon Shin-to (Japan New Party)	1993	1	71952

Total number of cases   32

1.14 Luxembourgian Parties Covered

	Parties	Elections first–last	no	MDS-ID
GLEI-GAP	Greng Lëscht Ekologesch Initiativ-Di Grëng Alternativ (Green Left Ecological Initiative-Green Alternative)	1994 + 1999	2	23113
POSL/LSAP	Parti Ouvrier Socialiste Luxembourgeois/Letzeburger Sozialistesch Arbeiterpartei (Socialist Workers' Party)	1994 + 1999	2	23320
	Groupement Patriotique et Démocratique (Patriotic and Democratic Group)	1994 + 1999	2	23420
	renamed: Groupement Démocratique (Democratic Group)	in 1954		

PD/DP	renamed: Parti Démocratique/Demokratesch Partei (Democratic Party)	in 1959		
PCS/CSV	Parti Chrétien Social/Chrëschtlech Sozial Vollekspartei (Christian Social People's Party)	1994 + 1999	2	23520
ADR	Aktiounskomitee fir Demokratie a Rentegerechtegkeet (Action Committee for Democracy and Pension Justice)	1994 + 1999	2	23951

Total number of cases   10

1.15 Dutch Parties Covered

	Parties	Elections		MDS-ID
		first–last	no	
GL	Groen Links (Green Left)	1994–2003	4	22110
SP	Socialistische Partij (Socialist Party)	1994–2003	4	22220
PvdA	Partij van de Arbeid (Labour Party)	1994–2003	4	22320
D'66	Democraten'66 (Democrats'66)	1994–2003	4	22330
VVD	Volkspartij voor Vrijheid en Democratie (People's Party for Freedom and Democracy)	1994–2003	4	22420
LN	Leefbaar Nederland (Livable Netherlands)	2002 + 2003	2	22430
CDA	Christen-Democratisch Appel (Christian Democratic Appeal)	1994–2003	4	22521
CU	Christen Unie (Christian Union)	2002 + 2003	2	22526
LPF	Lijst Pim Fortuyn (List Pim Fortuyn)	2002 + 2003	2	22720

Total number of cases   30

1.16 New Zealand Parties Covered

	Parties	Elections		MDS-ID
		first–last	no	
	Green Party of Aotearoa	1999 + 2002	2	64110
LP	Labour Party	1990–2002	5	64320
	Alliance	1993–1999	3	64321
	ACT	1996–2002	3	64420
	United Future	2002	1	64421
	Jim Anderton's Progressive Coalition	2002	1	64422
NP	National Party	1990–2002	5	64620
NZFP	New Zealand First Party	1993–2002	4	64621
	Social Credit/Democratic Party	1990	1	64951

Total number of cases   25

1.17 Norwegian Parties Covered

	Parties	Elections		MDS-ID
		first–last	no	
	Sosialistisk Folkeparti (Socialist People's Party)	1993–2001	3	12221
SV	renamed: Sosialistisk Venstreparti (Socialist Left Party)	in 1975		
DNA	Det Norske Arbeiderparti (Norwegian Labour Party)	1993–2001	3	12320
V	Venstre (Liberal Party)	1993–2001	3	12420
KrF	Kristelig Folkeparti (Christian People's Party)	1993–2001	3	12520
H	Høyre (Conservative Party)	1993–2001	3	12620
	Bondepartiet (Farmers' Party)	1993–2001	3	12810
SP	renamed: Senterpartiet (Centre Party)	in 1959		
	Anders Langes Parti (Anders Lange's Party)	1993–2001	3	12951
FrP	renamed: Fremskrittspartiet (Progress Party)	in 1977		

Total number of cases 21

1.18 Portuguese Parties Covered

	Parties	Elections		MDS-ID
		first–last	no	
BE	Bloco De Esquerda (Left Bloc)	1999 + 2002	2	35211
PCP	Partido Comunista Português (Portuguese Communist Party)	1991–1999	3	35220
CDU	Coligação Democrática Unitária (Unified Democratic Coalition)	1991–2002	4	35229
PSP	Partido Socialista Português (Portuguese Socialist Party)	1991–2002	4	35311
PPD	Partido Popular Democrático (Popular Democratic Party)	1991–2002	4	35313
PSD	renamed: Partido Social Democrata (Social Democratic Party)	in 1977		
CDS	Partido do Centro Democrático Social (Centre Social Democrats)	1991–2002	4	35314
PP	renamed: Partido Popular (Popular Party)	in 1995		
PSN	Partido de Solidariedade Nacional (National Solidarity Party)	1991	1	35951

Total number of cases 22

1.19 Spanish Parties Covered

	Parties	Elections		MDS-ID
		first–last	no	
PCE/PSUC	Partido Communista de España (Communist Party)	1993–2000	3	33220

IU	renamed: Izquierda Unida (United Left)	in 1989		
PSOE	Partido Socialista Obrero Español (Spanish Socialist Workers' Party)	1993–2000	3	33320
CDS	Centró Democrático y Social (Centre Democrats)	1993	1	33512
AP	Alianza Popular (Popular Alliance)	1993–2000	3	33610
PP	renamed: Partido Popular (Popular Party)	in 1989		
CiU	Convergència i Unió (Convergence and Union)	1993–2000	3	33611
PNV/EAJ	Partido Nacionalista Vasco/Euskadi Alberti Jetzale (Basque Nationalist Party)	1993–2000	3	33902
EA	Eusko Alkartasuna (Basque Solidarity)	1993–2000	3	33903
PAR	Partido Argonés Regionalista (Aragonese Regionalist Party)	1993 + 2000	2	33904
ERC	Esquerra Republicana de Catalunya (Catalan Republican Left)	1993–2000	3	33905
PA	Partidu Andalucista (Andalusian Party)	1993 + 2000	2	33906
CC	Coalicion Canaria (Canarian Coalition)	1993–2000	3	33907
BNG	Bloque Nacionalista Galego (Galician Nationalist Bloc)	1996 + 2000	2	33908

Total number of cases   31

1.20 Swedish Parties Covered

	Parties	Elections first–last	no	MDS-ID
	Miljöpartiet de Gröna (Green Ecology Party)	1991–2002	4	11110
	Sveriges Kommunistiska Parti (Communist Party of Sweden)	1991–2002	4	11220
Vk	renamed: Vänsterpartiet Kommunisterna (Left Communists Party)	in 1967		
Vp	renamed: Vänsterpartiet (Left Party)	in 1990		
SdaP	Socialdemokratistiska Arbetarepartiet (Social Democratic Labour Party)	1991–2002	4	11320
FP	Folkpartiet (People's Party)	1991–2002	4	11420
FP	renamed: Folkpartiet Liberalerna (Liberal People's Party)	in 1990		
KdS	Kristdemokratiska Samhällspartiet (Christian Democratic Community Party)	1991–2002	4	11520
	Hogerpartiet (Right Party)	1991–2002	4	11620
MSP	renamed: Moderata Samlingspartiet (Moderate Coalition Party)	in 1969		
	Bondeforbundet (Agrarian Party);	1991–2002	4	11810
CP	renamed: Centerpartiet (Centre Party)	in 1957		
NyD	Ny Demokrati (New Democracy)	1991	1	11951

Total number of cases   29

1.21 Swiss Parties Covered

	Parties	Elections first–last	no	MDS-ID
	Grüne (Greens)	1991–2003	4	43110
	renamed: Föderation der Grünen Parteien der Schweiz/Fédération Suisse des Partis Écologistes (Federation of Green Parties)	in 1983		
GPS/PES	renamed: Grüne Partei der Schweiz/Parti Écologiste Suisse (Green Party of Switzerland)	in 1987		
PdA	Partei der Arbeit der Schweiz/Parti suisse du travail (Swiss Labour Party)	1991–2003	4	43220
SPS/PSS	Sozialdemokratische Partei der Schweiz/Parti Socialiste Suisse (Social Democratic Party)	1991–2003	4	43320
LdU/ADI	Landesring der Unabhängigen/Alliance des Indépendants (Independents' Alliance)	1991–1999	3	43321
FDP/PRD	Freisinnig-Demokratische Partei der Schweiz/Parti Radical-Démocratique Suisse (Radical Democratic Party)	1991–2003	4	43420
	Schweizerische Konservative Volkspartei/Parti Populaire Conservateur Suisse (Conservative People's Party)	1991–2003	4	43520
	renamed: Konservativ-Christlich Soziale Partei/Parti Conservateur Chretien Social (Conservative Christian Social Party)	in 1957		
CVP/PDC	renamed: Christlich Demokratische Volkspartei der Schweiz/Parti Démocrate-Chrétien Suisse (Christian Democratic People's Party)	in 1971		
EVP/PEP	Evangelische Volkspartei der Schweiz/Parti Populaire Evangelique Suisse (Protestant People's Party)	1991–2003	4	43530
LPS/PLS	Liberale Partei der Schweiz/Parti libéral suisse (Liberal Party of Switzerland)	1991–2003	4	43531
	Nationale Aktion gegen die Überfremdung von Volk und Heimat/Action Nationale contre l'Emprise et la Surpopulation Etrangère (National Action against Foreign Domination)	1991–2003	4	43710
NA/AN	renamed: Nationale Aktion für Volk und Heimat/Action Nationale pour le Peuple et la Patrie (National Action for People and Fatherland)	in 1979		
SD	renamed: Schweizer Demokraten/Démocrates Suisses (Swiss Democrats)	in 1991		
EDU	Eidgenössisch-Demokratische Union (Federal Democratic Union)	1991–2003	4	43711
BGB	Schweizerische Bauern-, Gewerbe- und Bürgerpartei/Parti Suisse des Paysans, Artisans et Bourgeois (Farmers', Traders' and Citizens' Party)	1991–2003	4	43810
SVP/UDC	renamed: Schweizerische Volkspartei/Union Démocratique du Centre (Swiss People's Party)	in 1971		
	Schweizer Auto Partei/Parti Automobiliste Suisse (Swiss Motorists' Party)	1991 + 1995	2	43951

FPS	renamed: Freiheitspartei der Schweiz (Freedom Party of Switzerland)	in 1994

Total number of cases	45

1.22 Turkish Parties Covered

	Parties	Elections		MDS-ID
		first–last	no	
CHP	Cumhuriyet Halk Partisi (Republican People's Party)	1995–2002	3	74321
SHP	Sosyal Demokrat Halçi Parti (Social Democratic Populist Party)	1991	1	74323
DSP	Demokratik Sol Parti (Democratic Left Party)	1991–2002	4	74324
ANAP	Anavatan Partisi (Motherland Party)	1991–2002	4	74623
DYP	Doğru Yol Partisi (True Path Party)	1991–1999	3	74624
BBP	Büyük Birlik Partisi (Grand Unity Party)	1999	1	74626
DTP	Demokrat Türkiye Partisi (Democratic Turkey Party)	1999	1	74627
MHP	Milliyetçi Hareket Partisi (National Action Party)	1999	1	74712
RP	Refah Partisi (Welfare Party)	1991 + 1995	2	74715
FP	Falizet Partisi (Virtue Party)	1999	1	74716

Total number of cases	21

1.23 British Parties Covered

	Parties	Elections		MDS-ID
		first–last	no	
	Sinn Fein	1997 + 2001	2	51210
	Labour Party	1992–2005	4	51320
LDP	Liberal Democratic Party	1992–2005	4	51421
	Conservative Party	1992–2005	4	51620
UUP	Ulster Unionist Party	1992–2001	3	51621
SNP	Scottish National Party	1992–2001	3	51902
DUP	Democratic Unionist Party	1992–2001	3	51903
UKIP	United Kingdom Independence Party	2001	1	51951

Total number of cases	24

1.24 US-American Parties Covered

	Parties	Elections		MDS-ID
		first–last	no	
	Democratic Party	1992–2004	4	61320
	Republican Party	1992–2004	4	61620

Total number of cases	8

II. CEE Countries

2.1 Albanian Parties Covered

	Parties	Elections first–last	no	ID
PPSH	Partia ë Punës ë Shqipërisë (Albanian Party of Labour)	1991–2001	5	75220
PSS	renamed: Partia Socialiste Shqipërisë (Albanian Socialist Party)	in 1991		
PSDS	Partia Socialdemokratike ë Shqipërisë (Social Democratic Party of Albania)	1991–2001	5	75320
PADS	Partia Aliancë Demokratica e Shqipërisë (Democratic Alliance Party of Albania)	1992–2001	4	75421
PP	Partia Popullore (People's Party) formerly: APLP Albanian People's League Party	1991	1	75621
PUK	Partia e Unitetit Kombëtare (Party of National Unity)	1992	1	75622
PLL	Partia Lëvizja e Legalitetit (Legality Movement Party)	1991–1997	3	75623
PDSH	Partia Demokratike ë Shqipërisë (Democratic Party of Albania)	1991–1997	4	75624
PBK	Partia Balli Kombetar (Party of National Front)	1996 + 1997	2	75721
PRSH	Partia Republikana Shqipërisë (Albanian Republican Party)	1991–1997	4	75722
PASH	Partia Agrare Shqiptare (Agrarian Party of Albania)	1991–2001	4	75810
OMONIA	Bashkimia Demokratik i Minoritet Grek (Democratic Union of the Greek Minority)	1991–2001	5	75951
PDNJ	reorganized: Partia Bashkimi per te Drejtat e Njeriut (Union for Human Rights Party)	in 1992		

Total number of cases   38

2.2 Armenian Parties Covered

	Parties	Elections first–last	no	ID
HKK	Hayastani Komunistakan Kusakstyun (Communist Party of Armenia)	1995 + 1999	2	76222
HHD	Hai Heghapokhakan Dashnaktsutyun (Armenian Revolutionary Federation)	1999 + 2003	2	76321
MAC	Miavorvac Ashkhatanquin Cusaqcutsun (United Labour Party)	2003	1	76322
OR	Orinats Erkir (Counry of Law)	1999 + 2003	2	76420
A	Adartyun (Justice Alliance)	2003	1	76421
AIM	Azgayin Inknoroshum Miavorum (National Self-Determination Union)	1995	1	76521
HHK	Hayastani Hanrepetakan Kusakstutyun (Republican Party of Armenia)	2003	1	76610
HA	Hanrabedutyun Alliance (Bloc Republic)	1995	1	76711

AGzM	Azgayin Gzoghovrdakan Miutyen (National Democratic Union)	1995 + 1999	2	76712
	Shamiram (Women's Organization)	1995	1	76901
IM	Iravunk ev Miabanutiun (Right and Unity) composed of: National Unity, Constitutional Law, Artsakj Haiastan, and Gardmak	1999	1	76902
M	Miasnutiun (Unity) composed of: HZhK People's Party and HHK Republican Party	1999	1	76903
AM	Azgain Miagnutsum (National Unity Party)	2003	1	76904

Total number of cases   17

2.3 Azerbaijani Parties Covered

	Parties	Elections		ID
		first–last	no	
YAP	Yeni Azerbaycan Partiyasi (New Azerbaijan Party)	1995 + 2000	2	77220
AKP	Azerbaycan Kommunist Partiyasi (Azerbaijan Communist Party)	2000	1	77221
AXC	Azerbaycan Xalq Cebhesi (Popular Front Party of Azerbaijan)	1995 + 2000	2	77420
AMDP	Azerbaycan Müstequil Democrat Partiyasi (Democratic Party of Owners)	1995	1	77430
AMIP	Azerbaycan Milli Istiqlal (National Independence Party of Azerbaijan)	1995 + 2000	2	77710
VHP	Vätändas Hämrä'yliyi Partiyasi (Citizens Solidarity Party)	2000	1	77951

Total number of cases   9

2.4 Belarusian Parties Covered

	Parties	Elections		ID
		first–last	no	
KPB	Kommunisticeskaja Partija Belarusi (Party of Communists of Belarus)	1995	1	78211
APB	Agrarnaja Partija Belarusi (Agrarian Party)	1995	1	78212
BKhP	Belaruskaya Krest'yanskaya Partyia (Peasant's Party)	1995	1	78213
BPR	Belaruski Patryatychny Rukh (Patriotic Movement of Belarus)	1995	1	78214
PNZ	Partija Narodnaj Zgody (Party of People's Consent)	1995	1	78410
ADPB	Ab'jadnanaja Demakratycnaja Partija Belarusi (United Democratic Party of Belarus)	1995	1	78430
BSDG	Belaruskaja Sacyjal-Deakratycnaja Partija 'Gramada' (Belarusian Social-Democratic Party 'Gramada')	1995	1	78710
PWN	Party of Women 'Nadzeja'	1995	1	78901

Total number of cases   8

2.5 Parties in Bosnia-Herzegovina Covered

Parties		Elections		ID
		first–last	no	
SK BiH-SDP	Savez Komunista Bosne i Hercegovine-Stranka Demokraskih Promjena (League of Communists of Bosnia and Herzegovina-Party of Democratic Changes)	1990	1	79221
SRS	Savez Reformskih Snaga (Alliance of Reform Forces)	1990	1	79222
SPRS	Socijalisticka Partija Republike Srpske (Socialist Party of the Republic Serbia)	1996	1	79223
SDP BiH	Socijal-Demokratska Partija Bosne i Hercegovine (Social Democratic Party of Bosnia and Herzegovina)	1998–2002	3	79321
KzCD BiH	Koalicija za Cjelovitu I Demokratsku Bosne i Hercegovine (Coalition for a United and Democratic Bosnia and Herzegovina)	1998	1	79421
PDP RS	Partija Demokratskog Progresa Republike Srpske (Democratic Progress Party of the Republic Serbia)	2000 + 2002	2	79422
NHI	Nova Hrvatska Inicijativa (New Croatian Initiative)	2000	1	79423
SRS RS	Srpska Radikalna Stranka Republike Srpske (Serbian Radical Party of the Republic Serbia)	1998	1	79721
RS RS	Radikalna Stranka Republike Srpske (Radical Party of the Republic Serbia)	1998	1	79722
S BiH	Stranka za Bosne i Hercegovine (Party of Bosnia and Herzegovina)	1996–2002	3	79723
DNZ BiH	Demokratska Narodna Zajednica Bosne i Hercegovine (Democratic Peoples' Community of Bosnia and Herzegovina)	2000	1	79901
SDA	Stranka Demokratske Akcije (Party of Democratic Action)	1990–2002	4	79951
SDS BiH	Srpska Demokratska Stranka Bosne i Hercegovine (Serbian Democratic Party of Bosnia and Herzegovina)	1990	1	79952
HDZ BiH	Hrvatska Demokratska Zajednica Bosne i Hercegovine (Croatian Democratic Community of Bosnia and Herzegovina)	1990–2002	5	79953
MBO	Muslimanska-Bosnjacka Organizacija (Bosnian Muslim Organization)	1990	1	79954
SDS	Srpska Demokratska Stranka (Serbian Democratic Party)	1996–2002	4	79955

Total number of cases 31

2.6 Bulgarian Parties Covered

	Parties	Elections first–last	no	ID
DE	Dvisenie Ekoglasnost (Ekoglasnost Movement, also called the Green Party)	1994 + 1997	2	80110
BSP	Bulgarska Socialisticheska Partiya (Bulgarian Socialist Party)	1990–1997	4	80220
BSP K	BSP Koalitisija (BSP Coalition) composed of: BSP Bulgarska Socialisticheska Partiya (Bulgarian Socialist Party) and eight minor parties	1991 + 1994	2	80228
	BSP Koalitisija (BSP Coalition) composed of: BSP Bulgarska Socialisticheska Partiya (Bulgarian Socialist Party) BZNS-AS Bulgarski Zemedelski Naroden Sajuz - Aleksander Stanboliynski (Bulgarian Agrarian People's Union - Alexander Stamboliysky) DE Dvisenie Ekoglasnost (Movement Ekoglasnost)	1997	1	80229
DL	renamed: Demokratiènata Levica (Democratic Left)	in 1997		
KzB	Koalizija za Balgarija (Coalition for Bulgaria, leading member: BSP)	2001	1	80221
KE	Koalicija Evrolevica (Coalition Euro-Left)	1997	1	80320
SDS	Soyuz na Demokratichnite Sili (Union of Democratic Forces) founding members: BSDP Bulgarska Sotsial-demokraticheska Partiya (Bulgarian Social Democratic Party), BZNS-NP Bulgarki Zemedelski Naroden Sayuz (Bulgarian Agrarian National Union - Nikolai Petkov), Komitet za Zashtita na Relioznite Prava, Svobodata na Savestta i Duhovnite Tsenosti (Committee for Religious Rights, Freedom of Conscience, and Spiritual Values); Klub na Represiranite sled 1945 Godina (Club for the Victims of Repression after 1945), GI Grazhdanska Initsiativa (Citizens' Initiative), Federattsiya na Nezavisimi Studentki Druzhestva (Federation of Independents' Students Societies), Nezavisimo Druzhestvo za Zashtita na Choveshkite Prava v Bulgariya (Independent Association for the Defence of Human Rights in Bulgaria), Nezavisima Federatsiya na Truda Podkrepa (Independent Labour Federation Pokrepa); additional members in 1989 and 1990: RDP Radikalna Demokraticheska Partiya (Radical Democratic Party), ZP Zelena Partiya (Green Party), HDF Hristiyan-Demokraticheska Fronta (Christian Democratic Front), ASP Alternativna Sotsialierlna Partiya (Alternative Socialist Party)	1990–1994	3	80410
ODS	Obedineni Demokraticni Sili (United Democratic Forces, leading member: SDS)	1997 + 2001	2	80411
ODS-NS-Alliance	Obedineni Demokraticni Sili–Naroden Sajuz (United Democratic Forces–People's Union Alliance)	2001	1	80418

BZNS	Bulgarski Zemedelski Naroden Soyuz (Bulgarian Agrarian National Union)	1990	1	80810
NS	Naroden Sajuz BZNS/DP (People's Union) composed of: BZNS Bulgarski Zemedelski Naroden Soyuz (Bulgarian Agrarian National Union) DP Demokraticheska Partiya (Democratic Party)	1994	1	80811
BZNS AS	Bulgarski Zemedelski Naroden Sayuz Alexander Stamboliysky (Bulgarian Agrarian National Union Alexander Stamboliysky)	1994	1	80812
BBB	Bulgarski Business Bloc (Bulgarian Business Bloc)	1994 + 1997	2	80901
NDST	Nacionalno Dvizenie Simeon Tvori (National Movement Simeon the Second)	2001	1	80902
DPS	Dvizhenie za Prava i Svobodi (Movement for Rights and Freedom)	1990–2001	5	80951
ONS	Obedinenie za Nacionalno (Union of National Salvation)	1997	1	80952

Total number of cases   29

2.7 Croatian Parties Covered

	Parties	Elections		ID
		first–last	no	
SZH	Savez Zelenih Hrvatske (Green Union of Croatia)	1990	1	81111
SKH-SDP	Savez Komunista Hrvatske–Stranka Demokratskih Promjena (League of Communists of Croatia–Party of Democratic Change)	1990–1995	3	81220
SDPH	renamed: Socijaldemokratska Stranka Hrvatske–Stranka Demokratskih Promjena (Socialdemokratic Party of Croatia–Party of Democratic Change)	in 1992		
Left Bloc	composed of: SKH-SDP Savez Komunista Hrvatske–Stranka Demokratskih Promjena (League of Communists of Croatia–Party of Democratic Change)	1990	1	81229
SSH	Socijalisticka Stranka Hrvatske (Socialist Party of Croatia) and joint candidates with:	1990	1	81221
SSOH	Savez Socijalisticke Omladine Hrvatske (Union of Socialist Youth of Croatia)	1990	1	81222
ZAS	Zelena Akcija–Split (Green Action of Split)	1990	1	81112
SPD	Socijademokratska Partija Hrvatska (Social Democratic Party of Croatia)	1995	1	81223
HSLS	Hrvatska Socijalno-Liberalna Stranka (Croatian Social-Liberal Party)	1992 + 1995	2	81410
KNS	Koalicija Narodnog Sporazuma (Coalition of People's Agreement) composed of: HSLS Hrvatska Socijalno-Liberalna Stranka (Croatian Social-Liberal Party), HKDS Hrvatska Krscanska Demokratska	1990	1	81420

	Stranka (Croatian Christian Democratic Party) SDSH Socijaldemokratska Stranka Hrvatske (Social-Democratic Party of Croatia)			
HND	Hrvatska Narodna Stranka (Croatian Independent Democrats)	1995	1	81430
HDZ	Hrvatska Demokratska Zajednica (Croatian Democratic Union)	1990–2003	5	81711
HNS	Hrvatska Narodna Stranka (Croatian People's Party)	1992 + 1995	2	81712
HSP	Hrvatska Stranka Prava (Croatian Party of Rights)	1992 + 1995	2	81713
HSS	Hrvatska Seljacka Stranka (Croatian Peasant Party)	1992–2003	3	81810
SNS	Srpska Narodna Stranka (Serbian People's Party)	1992	1	81951
CRP	(Coalititon of Regional Parties) composed of:	1992	1	81959
IDS	Istarski Demokratski Sabor (Istrian Democratic Assembly)	1992	1	81953
DA	Dalmatinska Akcija (Dalmatian Action)	1992	1	81954
RDS	Rijecki Demokratski Savez (Democratic Alliance of Rijeka)	1992	1	81955
ZL	Zajednica Lista (Joint List Bloc) composed of:	1995 + 2000	2	81899
	SBSH Slavonsko-Baranjska Hrvatska Stranka (Croatian Party of Slavonia and Baranja) HSS Hrvatska Seljacka Stranka (Croatian Peasant Party) IDS Istarski Demokratski Sabor (Istrian Democratic Assembly) HNS Hrvatska Narodna Stranka (Croatian People's Party) HKDU Hrvatska Krscanska Demokratska Unija (Croatian Christian Democratic Union)	1995	1	81956

Total number of cases   33

2.8 Czech Parties Covered

	Parties	Elections		ID
		first–last	no	
KSC	Kommunistická Strana Ceskoslovenska (Communist Party of Czechoslovakia)	1990–2002	4	82220
KSBM	renamed: Komunisticka strana Bohemia a Moravy (Communist Party of Bohemia and Moravia)	in 1992		
LB	Levy Bloc (Left Bloc) composed of: KSCM Komunisticka strana Bohemia a Moravy (Communist Party of Bohemia and Moravia) DL Demokratická Levice (Democratic Left of the CSFR)	1992	1	82221
CSSD	Ceskoslovenska socialni demokracie (Czechoslovak Social Democratic Party)	1992–2002	4	82320

CSSD	renamed: Ceská Strana Sociálně Demokratická (Czech Social Democratic Party)	in 1993		
OF	Obcanské fórum (Civic Forum) composed of: ASD Asociace socialnich demokratu (Association of Social Democrats) ODA Obcanska demokraticka alliance (Civic Democratic Alliance) KAN Klub Neangažovanych Nestaniku (Policitally Involved Non-Party Members Club) HOS Hnuté Za Občanskou Svobodu (Movement for Civic Freedom), LDS Liberalne demokraticka strana (Liberal Democratic Party) RS Republikánská strana (Republican Party)	1990	1	82410
ODA	Obcanska demokraticka alliance (Civic Democratic Alliance)	1992 + 1996	2	82412
ODS	Obcanska demokraticka strana (Civic Democratic Party)	1992–2002	4	82413
ODS-KDS	Alliance composed of: ODS Obcanska demokraticka strana (Civic Democratic Party) KDS Krestanskodemokraticka strana (Christian Democratic Party)	1992	1	82419
LSU	Liberalne socialni unie (Liberal Social Union) composed of: CSS Ceskoslovenska strana socialisticka (Czechoslovak Socialist Party), ZS Zemédélská strana (Farmers' Party), SZ Strana zelenych (Green Party)	1992	1	82420
US	Unie Svobody (Freedom Union)	1998	1	82421
CSL	Ceskoslovenska strana lidova (Czechoslovak People's Party)	1990	1	82520
KDS	Krestanskodemokraticka strana (Christian Democratic Party)	1992	1	82521
KDU-CSL-Alliance	Alliance composed of: KDU Krestanská a Demokratická Unie (Christian and Democratic Union) CSL Ceskoslovenska strana lidova (Czechoslovak People's Party) organized as a party	1992–1998 in 1992	3	82523
Koalice	(Coalition) composed of: KDU Krestanská a Demokratická Unie (Christian and Democratic Union) CSL Ceskoslovenska strana lidova (Czechoslovak People's Party) US Unie Svobody–Democraticke Unie (Freedom Union–Democratic Union) DEU Demokratická Unie (Democratic Union) US and DEU combined into one party	2002 in 2001	1	82524

KDU	Krestanská a Demokratická Unie (Christian and Democratic Union) composed of: KDS Krestanskodemokraticka strana (Christian Democratic Party) KDH Křest'anskodemokratické Hnuti (Christian and Democratic Movement) PA Podnikatelské Asociace (Association of Entrepreneurs) ZS Zemédélská Strana (Farmers' Party)	1990	1	82529
SPR-RSC	Sduzeni pro republiku–Republikanska strana Ceskoslovenska (Coalition for the Republic–Republican Party of Czechoslovakia)	1992–1998	3	82710
DZJ	Duchodei za Zivotni Jistoty (Movement of Pensioners for Life Securities)	1996 + 1998	2	82901
HSD-SMS	Hnutí za Samosprávnou Demokracii–Spolecnost pro Moravu a Slezko (Movement for an Autonomous Democracy–Society for Moravia-Silesia)	1990 + 1992	2	82951

Total number of cases   33

2.9 Estonian Parties Covered

	Parties	Elections		ID
		first–last	no	
KK	Kindel Kodu (Secure Home) composed of: K Eesti Koonderakond (Coalition Party) EM Eesti Maalit (Estonian Rural Union) EDO Eesti Demokraatlik Öiglusliit (Estonian Democratic Justice) EPL Eesti Pensionärde Liit-EPL (Estonian Pensioner's Union)	1992	1	83220
Moodukad	Rahvaerakond Moodukad (People's Party Moderates) composed of:	1992–2003	4	83410
	ESDP Eesti Sotsiaaldemokraatlik Partei (Social Democratic Party) EMK Eesti Maa-Keskerakond (Rural Centre Party)	1992	1	83320
Kesk	Eesti Keskerakond (Estonian Center Party, successor to Rahvarinne)	1995–2003	3	83411
Rahvarinne	(Estonian Popular Front Coalition) composed of: ERPT Eestima Rahvarinne Perestroika Toetuseks (Popular Front) ERKE Eesti Rahva-Keskerakond (Centre People's Party) EN Eesti Naisliit (Womens' Union)	1992	1	83421
ER	Eesti Reformierakond (Estonian Reform Party)	1995–2003	3	83430

Paremoolsed	Vabriiklate ja Konservatiivide Rahvaerakond (Rightists) composed of: EV Eesti Vabriiklaste (Estonian Republican Coalition Party) EKR Eesti Konservativne Rahvaerakond (Estonian Conservative People's Party)	1995	1	83610
VKRE	combined into: Vabriiklate ja Konservatiivide Rahvaerakond (Republican and Conservative People's Party)	in 1995		
ResP	Ühendus Vabariigi Eest–Res Publica (Union for the Republic–Res Publica)	2003	1	83611
Rahvaliit	Eestimaa Rahvaliit (Estonians People's Union)	2003	1	83612
IERSP	Electoral Union composed of: Isamaa (Fatherland) ERSP Eesti Rahvusliku Soltumatuse Partei (Estonian National Independence Party)	1995	1	83709
	combined into: Isamaaliit (Pro Patria Union)	in 1995		
Isamaa	Erakond Isamaaliit (Pro Patria Union) composed of: EKR Eesti Konservativne Rahvaerakond (Estonian Conservative Party) EKDE Eesti Kristlik-Demokraatlik Erakond (Estonian Christian Democratic Party) EKDL Eesti Kristlik-Demokraatlik Liit (Estonian Christian Democratic Union) ELP Eesti Liberaaldemokraatlik Partei (Estonian Liberal Democratic Party) ELL Eesti Liberaldemokraatlik Liit (Estonian Liberal Democratic Union)	1992–2003	3	83710
ERSP	Eesti Rahvusliku Soltumatuse Partei (Estonian National Independence Party)	1992	1	83711
EK	Eesti Kodanik (Estonian Citizen Coalition) composed of: EVP Eesti Vabariigi Partei (Estonian Republic Party) Noarootsi (Living Health Association)	1992	1	83712
KMÜ	Koonderakond ja Maarahva Ühendus (Coalition Party and Rural Union) composed of:	1995	1	83719
	EKK Eesti Koonderakond (Coalition Party)	1995 + 1999	2	83713
	EM Eesti Maalit (Estonian Rural Union)			
EME	Eesti Maarahva Erakond (Estonian Country People's Party)	1999	1	83810
IR	Independent Royalists composed of: RP Royalist Party VT Vaba Toome (Royalist Union)	1992	1	83901
NDE	Nash Dom–Estonia! (Our Home–Estonia!)	1995	1	83951
EÜRP	Eesti Ühendatud Rahvapartei (Estonian United People's Party)	1999	1	83952

Total number of cases	29

2.10 Georgian Parties Covered

	Parties	Elections		ID
		first–last	no	
Greens	Sakartvelos Mtsvaneta Partia (Green Party)	1992	1	84110
Mshvidoba	Bloki 'Mshvidoba' (Peace Bloc) composed of: DU Democratic Union JPG Justice Party of Georgia LESRG League of Economic and Social Revival of Georgia AU Agrarian Union MCP Monarchist-Conservative Party LEM Association URA Union for the Revival of Ajaria	1992	1	84221
SMSP	Sakartvelos Mshromelta Sotsialisturi Partia (Socialist Workers' Party)	1992	1	84222
SSP	Sakartvelos Sotsialisturi Partia (Socialist Party of Georgia)	1995 + 1999	2	84223
SSDP	Sakartvelos Sotsial-Demokratiuli Partia (Social Democratic Party)	1992	1	84321
SSSK	Sakartvelos Sotsialuri Samartlianobis Kavshiri (Social Justice Union)	1992	1	84322
SMK	Sakartvelos Mokalaketa Kavshiri (Citizens' Union of Georgia)	1995 + 1999	2	84323
	Kartia–91 (Charter 91)	1992	1	84411
	Tertmeti Oktomberi (Oktober 11) composed of: GPF Georgian Popular Front DCG Democratic Choice for Georgia CDU Christian-Democratic Union RP Republican Party	1992	1	84421
	Ertoba (Unity Bloc) composed of: LDNP Liberal-Democratic National Party PPF Party of Peace and Freedom	1992	1	84422
DP	Demokratiuli Partia (Democratic Party)	1992	1	84423
SSAK	Sruliad Sakartvelos Aghordzinebis Kavshiri (All-Georgian Revival Union)	1995 + 1999	2	84424
DAP	renamed: Demokratiuli Aghordzinebis Pavshiri (Democratic Union of Revival)	in 2003		
BP	Bloki 'Progressi' (Bloc 'Progress')	1995	1	84425
PKT	Politikuri Kavshiri 'Tanadgoma' ('Stand-by' Political Alliance)	1995	1	84426
SRKET	Sakartvelos Reformatorta Kavshiri–Erovnuli Tankhmoba (Reformators' Union–National Concord)	1995	1	84427
MGS	Mretsvelopba Gadaarchens Sakartvelos (Industry will save Georgia)	1999	1	84428
SGK	Sakartvelos Ghvtisshvilta Kavshiri (Union of God's Children)	1992	1	84521

KTK	Kartvel Traditsionalista Kavshiri (Union of Georgian Traditionalists)	1992 + 1995	2	84710
EDP	Erovnul Demokratiuli Partia (National Democratic Party)	1992 + 1995	2	84711
ICS	Ilia Chavchavadzis Sazogadoeba (Ilia Chavchavadze Society)	1992	1	84712
SSMKS	Sruliad Sakartvelos Merab Kostavas Sazogadoeba (Merab Kostava Society)	1992	1	84713
SETAK	Sakartvelos Erovnuli Tankhmobis da Aghorzinebis Kavshiri (Union of National Agreement and Revival)	1992	1	84714
SEDP	Sakartvelos Erovnuli Damoukideblobis Partia (National Independent Party)	1992	1	84715
SSFK	Sruliad Sakartvelos Fermerta Kavshiri (All-Georgian Farmers' Union)	1992	1	84810
KMSP	Khalkhta Megobrobis da Samartlianobis Partia (People's Friendship and Justice)	1992	1	84951

Total number of cases   30

2.11 German Democratic Republic Parties Covered

| | Parties | Elections | | ID |
		first–last	no	
Grüne-UFV	Grüne–UFV (Greens–IWM) composed of: GP Grüne Partei (Green Party) UFV Unabhängiger Frauenverband (Independent Women's League)	1990	1	85111
B 90	Bündnis 90 (Alliance 90) composed of: Neues Forum (New Forum) Demokratie Jetzt (Democracy Now) IFM Initiative für Frieden und Menschenrechte (Initiative for Peace and Human Rights)	1990	1	85112
AVL	Aktionsbündnis Vereinigte Linke (United Left Action Alliance)	1990	1	85210
PDS	Partei des Demokratischen Sozialismus (Party for Democratic Socialism)	1990	1	85221
SPD	Sozialdemokratische Partei Deutschlands (Social Democratic Party of Germany)	1990	1	85320
BFD	Bündnis der Freien Demokraten (Alliance of Free Democrats) composed of:	1990	1	85429
	FDP Freie Demokratische Partei (Free Democratic Party)	1990	1	85421
	LDP Liberal Demokratische Partei (Liberal Democratic Party)	1990	1	85422
	DFP Deutsche Forumpartei (German Forum Party)	1990	1	85423

NDPD	National-Demokratische Partei Deutschlands (National Democratic Party of Germany)	1990	1	85424
CDU	Christlich Demokratische Union (Christian Democratic Union)	1990	1	85521
DSU	Deutsche Soziale Union (German Social Union)	1990	1	85522
DA	Demokratischer Aufbruch–'sozial und ökologisch' (Democratic Opening)	1990	1	85523
DBD	Demokratische Bauernpartei Deutschlands (Democratic Peasants' Party of Germany)	1990	1	85524
DFD	Demokratischer Frauenbund Deutschlands (Democratic Women's League)	1990	1	85901

Total number of cases		15

2.12 Hungarian Parties Covered

	Parties	Elections		ID
		first–last	no	
MSzP	Magyar Szocialista Párt (Hungarian Socialist Party)	1990–2002	4	86220
MSzDP	Magyarországi Szociáldemokrata Párt (Hungarian Social Democratic Party)	1990	1	86320
FiDeSz	Fiatal Demokraták Szövetsége (Federation of Young Democrats) in 1998 in some electoral districts and in	1990–2002	4	86421
FiDeSz-	2002 in alliance with:			
MPP-MDF Alliance	Magyar Polgari Párt (Hungarian Civic Party) and Magyar Demokrata Fórum (Hungarian Democratic Forum)	1998 + 2002	2	86429
SzDSz	Szabad Demokraták Szövetsége (Alliance of Free Democrats)	1990–2002	4	86422
MDF	Magyar Demokrata Fórum (Hungarian Democratic Forum) in 1998 in some electoral districts in alliance with:	1990–1998	3	86521
MDF- FiDeSz-MPP-Alliance	Fiatal Demokraták Szövetsége (Federation of Young Democrats) and Magyar Polgari Párt (Hungarian Civic Party)	1998	1	86529
KDNP	Kereszténydemokrata Néppárt (Christian Democratic People's Party)	1990 + 1994	2	86522
MIEP	Magyar Igazság és Elet Pártja (Hungarian Justice and Life Party)	1998	1	86620
FKgP	Független Kisgazda Párt (Independent Smallholders' Party)	1990–1998	3	86810
FKFPP	renamed: Független Kisgazda-Földmunkás és Polgári Párt (Independent Smallhoders' and Civic Party)	in 2003		

ASz	Agrárszövetség (Agrarian Alliance) composed of: ARS Agrár Reformkörör Szövetsége (Agrarian Reform Circle Movement) ARM Agrár Reformkörör Mozgalom (Association of Agrarian Reform Circles) one joint candidate with: SFV Szövetség a Faluért, Vidékért (Alliance for the Village and the Countryside)	1990	1	86811

Total number of cases 26

2.13 Latvian Parties Covered

	Parties	Elections first–last	no	ID
ZZS	Zalo un Zemnieku savieniba (Green and Farmers' Union)	2002	1	87110
SLAT	Saskana Latvijai–atdzimsana tautsaimniecibai (Concord for Latvia–Rebirth of the Economy)	1993	1	87220
LSP	Latvijas Socialistika Partija (Latvian Socialist Party)	1995	1	87310
LSDA	Latvijas Socialdemokratu Apvieniba (Latvian Social-Democratic Alliance)	1998	1	87311
LVP	Latvijas Vienibas Partija (Latvian Unity Party)	1995	1	87320
LC	Latvijas celš (Latvia's Way)	1993–2002	4	87410
DPS	Demokratiska Partija 'Saimnieks' (Democratic Party 'Saimnieks')	1995	1	87411
LLP	Latvijas Liberāla Partija (Latvian Liberal Party)	1993	1	87420
TSP	Tautas Saskanas Partija (National Harmony Party)	1995 + 1998	2	87421
PCTVL	Par cilvēka tiesībām vienotā Latvijā (For Human Rights in a United Latvia)	2002	1	87422
JL	Jaunais laiks (New Era)	2002	1	87423
DCP	Demokratiska centra partija (Democratic Centre Party)	1993	1	87430
JP	Jauna Partija (New Party)	1998	1	87431
LKDS	Latvijas Kristigo demokratu savieniba (Latvia's Christian Democratic Union)	1993	1	87520
LPP	Latvijas Pirmā Partija (Latvia's First Party) including: Latvijas Kristigo demokratu savieniba (Christian Democratic Union)	2002	1	87521
TP	Tautas Partija (People's Party)	1998 + 2002	2	87610
LNKP-LZP-Alliance	Latvijas Nacionala Konservativa Partija–Latvijas Zala Partija (Latvian National Conservative Party–Green Party of Latvia)	1995	1	87611

LNNK	Latvijas Nacionalas neatkaribas kustiba (National Independence Movement of Latvia)	1993	1	87710
TUB	Tevzemei un brivibai (For the Fatherland and Freedom)	1993 + 1995	2	87721
TKL	Tautas Kustiba Latvija (Zigerista Partija) (Popular Movement for Latvia (Siegerist))	1995	1	87722
TB-LNNK-Alliance	Apvieniba 'Tevzemei un brivibai'– Latvijas Nacionalas neatkaribas kustiba (For Fatherland and Freedom–National Independence Movement of Latvia)	1998 + 2002	2	87723
LZS	Latvijas Zemnieku savieniba (Latvia's Farmers' Union)	1993	1	87810
ZS-LKDS-LDP-Alliance	Electoral Union composed of: ZS Latvijas Zemnieku Savieniba (Farmer's Union of Latvia) LKDS Latvijas Kristigo demokratu savieniba (Latvia's Christian Democratic Union) LDP Latvijas Demokratiska Partija (Latvia's Democratic Party)	1995	1	87811
L	Lidztiesiba (Equal Rights)	1993	1	87951

Total number of cases   31

2.14 Lithuanian Parties Covered

	Parties	Elections		ID
		first–last	no	
LDDP	Lietuvos demokratiné darbo partija (Lithuanian Democratic Labour Party)	1992 + 1996	2	88220
LSDP	Lietuvos socialdemokratu partija (Lithuanian Social Democratic Party)	1992 + 1996	2	88320
BSDK	Brazausko socialdemokratiné koalicija (Brazauskas Social Democratic Coalition) composed of: LSDP Lietuvos socialdemokratu partija (Lithuanian Social Democratic Party) LDDP Lietuvos demokratiné darbo partija (Lithuanian Democratic Labour Party) NDP Naujosios demokratijos partija (New Democratic Party) LRS Lietuvos rusu sajunga (Lithuanian Russian Union)	2000	1	88321
NS	Naujoji sajunga (New Union)	2000	1	88410
LCJ	Lietuvos centro judejimas (Centre Movement of Lithuania)	1992–2000	3	88420
LCS	renamed: Lietuvos centro sajunga (Lithuanian Centre Union)	in 1996		

SK	Sajudzio koalicija (Sajudis Coalition) composed of: Sajudis LZP Lietuvos zaliloji partija (Lithuanian Green Party) PC Pilieciu chartija (Citizens' Charter) LPKP Lietuvos politiniu kaliniu partija (Union of Political Prisoners)	1992	1	88421
LLS	Lietuvos liberalu sajunga (Lithuanian Liberal Union)	2000	1	88422
LKDPK	Lietuvos krikscioniu demokratu partijos koalicija (Lithuanian Christian Democratic Party Coalition) composed of:	1992	1	88529
LKDP	Lietuvos krikščioniu demokratu partija (Lithuanian Christian Democratic Party)	1992–2000	3	88521
LDP	Lietuvos demokratu partijos jungtinis sajungos (Lithuanian Democratic Party)	1992 + 1996	2	88522
LPKTS	Lietuvos politiniu kaliniu ir tremtiniu sajungos (Union of Lithuanian Political Prisoners and Deportees)	1992	1	88523
TS	Tevynes Sájunga (Homeland Union)	1996 + 2000	2	88620
LTSS	Lietuviu tautininku sajungos sarasas (Lithuanian National Union List) composed of: LLS Lietuviu tautininku sajunga (Lithuanian National Union) NP Nepriklausomybes partija (Independence Party)	1992	1	88710
LVP	Lietuvos valstiecu partija (Lithuanian Agrarian Party)	2000	1	88810
LLS	Lietuvos lenkų sajunga (Union of Poles of Lithuania)	1992 + 2000	2	88951
LLRA	renamed: Lietuvos lenku rinkimu akcija (Election Action of Lithuania's Poles)	in 2000		

Total number of cases   24

2.15 Macedonian Parties Covered

	Parties	Elections		ID
		first–last	no	
KM-PDP	Sojuz na Komunistite na Makedonija–Partija za Demokratska Preobrazba (League of Communists of Macedonia–Party of Democratic Change)	1990–1998	3	89221
SDSM	renamed: Socijaldemokratski Sojuz na Makedonija (Social-Democratic League of Macedonia)	in 1991		
RSM	Reformiskite Sili na Makedonija (Reform Forces of Macedonia)	1990 + 1994	2	89222
LP	renamed: Liberalna Partija (Liberal Party)	in 1998		

MDPSM	Mlada Demokratsko-Progresivna Stranka na Makedonija (Young Democratic Progressive Party of Macedonia)	1990	1	89223
LDP	Liberalno Demokratska Partija (Liberal Democratic Party)	1998	1	89224
SLB	Social-Liberal Bloc composed of: SDSM Socijaldemokratski Sojuz na Makedonija (Socialdemocratic League of Macedonia) LP Liberalna Partia (Liberal Party) SPM Socijalisticki Partija na Makedonija (Socialist Party of Macedonia)	1994	1	89227
Joint Candidates RSM/LP, MDPSM, and SPM		1990	1	89228
Joint Candidates RSM/LP, MDPSM, SPM, and PCER		1990	1	89229
SPM	Socijalisticki Partija na Makedonija (Socialist Party of Macedonia)	1990–1998	3	89320
DA	Demokratska Alternativa (Democratic Alternative)	1998	1	89321
SJM	Stranka na Jugoslovenite vo Makedonija (Party of Yugoslavs in Macedonia)	1990	1	89420
VMRO-DPMNE	Vnatresna Makedonska Revolucionerna Organizacija–Demokratska Partija za Makedonsko Nacionalno Edinstvo (Internal Macedonian Revolutionary Organization–Democratic Party for Macedonian National Unity), formerly: MAAK Pan-Macedonian Action	1990 + 1998	2	89710
PDPM	Partija za Demokratski Prosperitet vo Makedonija (Party for Democratic Prosperity in Macedonia)	1990–2002	4	89951
PDP	Partis Demokratis Populore (People's Democratic Party)	1990	1	89952
PCER	Partija za Celosna Emancipacija na Romite (Party for the Complete Emancipation of Romany Gypsies)	1990	1	89953
NDP	Narodna Demokratska Partija (People's Democratic Party)	1994 + 1998	2	89954
Joint Candidates PDPM and PDP		1990	1	89959

Total number of cases	26

2.16 Moldovan Parties Covered

	Parties	Elections		ID
		first–last	no	
PSMUE	Blocul electoral Partidul Socialist si Miscarea 'Unitat-Edinstvo' (Electoral Bloc) composed of: PS Partidul Socialist (Socialist Party) Yedinstvo	1994	1	90220
AFPCD	Blocul electoral Alianta Frontului Popular Crestin Democrat (Alliance of the Popular Christian Democratic Front)	1994	1	90520

PDAM	Partidul Democrat Agrar din Moldova (Agrarian Democratic Party)	1994	1	90810
BTI	Blocul Taranilior si Intelectualilor (Peasant and Intellectual Bloc) including: PPM Peasant's Party of Moldova and CI Congress of Intelligensia	1994	1	90951

Total number of cases   4

2.17 Montenegrin Parties Covered

	Parties	Elections		ID
		first–last	no	
SKCG	Savez Komunista Crne Gore (League of Communists of Montenegro)	1990–1996	3	91220
DPS	renamed: Demokratska Partija Socijalista (Democratic Party of Socialists)	in 1992		
SRSCG	Savez Reformskih Snaga za Crnu Goru (Alliance of Reform Forces for Montenegro) composed of: LZCG Liberalna Savez Crne Gore (Liberal Alliance of Montenegro)	1990	1	91229
PSCG	Partija Socijalista Crne Gore (Socialist Party of Montenegro)	1990	1	91222
SP	Socijalisticka Partija (Socialist Party)	1990	1	91223
SNPCG	Socijalisticka Narodna Partija Crne Gore (Socialist People's Party of Montenegro)	1998	1	91224
SDPR	Socijal-Demokratska Partija Reformista (Social-Democratic Party of Reformists)	1992	1	91320
SDPCG	Socijaldemokratska Partija Crne Gore (Social-Democratic Party of Montenegro)	1996	1	91321
DPSCG	Demokratska Partija Socijalista Crne Gore (Democratic Party of Socialists of Montenegro) main member of:	1998	1	91322
DZB	Da zivimo bolje (For a Better Living)	1998	1	91323
LSCG	Liberalna Savez Crne Gore (Liberal Alliance of Montenegro)	1990–2002	5	91420
NS	Narodna Stranka (People's Party)	1990–1996	3	91710
SRS	Srpska Radikalna Stranka (Serbian Radical Party)	1992	1	91711
DK	Democratic Coalition, composed of:	1990	1	91959
SNR	Stranka Nacionalne Ravnopravnosti (Party of National Equality)	1990	1	91951
DSCG	Demokratski Savez U Crnoj Gori (Democratic League in Montenegro)	1990	1	91952
SDACG	Stranka Demokratske Akcije Crne Gore (Democratic Action Party of Montenegro)	1996	1	91953

Total number of cases   24

2.18 Polish Parties Covered

	Parties	Elections first–last	no	ID
SLD	Sojusz Lewicy Demokratycznej (Democratic Left Alliance)	1991–1997	3	92210
SD	Stronnictwo Demokratyczne (Democratic Party)	1991	1	92211
SLD-UP	Coalition	2001	1	92212
NSZZ	Niezalezny Samorzadny Zwiazek Zawodowych 'Solidarnosc' (Self-governed Trade Union 'Solidarity')	1991	1	92320
SP	Solidarnosc Pracy (Solidarity of Labour)	1991	1	92321
UP	Unia Pracy (Union of Labour)	1993 + 1997	2	92322
UD	Unia Demokratyczna (Democratic Union) merger between: UD Unia Demokratyczna (Democratic Union) ROAD Ruch Obywatelski-Akcja Demokratyczna (Democratic Action Civic Movement) FPD Forum Prawicy Demokratycznej (Forum of the Democratic Right)	1991 + 1993	2	92410
KLD	Kongres Liberalno-Demokratyczny (Liberal-Democratic Congress)	1991	1	92420
PPPP	Polska Partia Przyjaciol Piwa (Polish Beer-Lovers Party)	1991	1	92431
UPR	Unia Polityki Realnej (Union of Real Politics)	1991	1	92432
PPG	Polish Economic Program merger of: KLD and PPPP	1991	1	92433
UW	Unia Wolnosci (Freedom Union)	1997	1	92434
PO	Platforma Obywatelska (Citizens' Platform)	2001	1	92435
PiS	Prawo i Sprawieliwość (Law and Justice)	2001	1	92436
ChD	Chrzescijansko-Demokratycznego Stronnictwo Pracy (Christian Democratic Party)	1991	1	92520
POC	Porozumienie Obywatelskie Centrum (Centre Citizens' Alliance)	1991	1	92521
PChD	Partia Chrzescijanskich Demokratów (Party of Christian Democrats)	1991	1	92522
RDR	Movement for Res Publica	1991	1	92523
WAK	Wyborcza Akcja Katolickia (Catholic Elector Action), composed of: ZChN Zjednoczenie Chrzescijansko-Narodowe (Christian National Union) KP Konwencja Polska (Polish Convention) SChL Stronnictwo Chrzecijansko-Ludowe (Christian Farmers' Alliance)	1991	1	92530
AWS	Akcja Wyborcza Solidarność (Electoral Action Solidarity)	1997	1	92620

ROP	Ruch Odbudowy Polski (Movement for the Reconstruction of Poland)	1997	1	92621
SRP	Samoobrona Rzeczypospolitej Polskiej (Self defence of the Polish Republic)	2001	1	92622
KPN	Konfederacja Polski Niepodleglej (Confederation for Independent Poland)	1991 + 1993	2	92710
PZZ	Polski Zwiazek Zachodni (Polish Western Union)	1991	1	92711
PX	Partia X (Party X)	1991	1	92712
LPR	Liga Polskich Rodzin (League of Polish Families)	2001	1	92713
PL	Porozumienie Ludowe (Peasant Accord)	1991	1	92810
PSL	Polskie Stronnictwo Ludowe (Polish Peasant Party), merger between: PSLO Polski Stronnictwo Ludowe–Odrodzenie (Reborn Polish Peasant Party) PSLW Polski Stronnictwo Ludowe–Wilanowskie (Peasant Party–Wilanow)	1991–2001	4	92811
BBWR	Bezpartyjny Blok Wspierania Reform (Non-Party Bloc in Support of Reforms, Walesa Support Party)	1993	1	92901
RAS	Ruch Automomii Slaska (Movement for the Autonomy of Silasia)	1991	1	92952
MN	Mniejszosc Niemiecka (German Minority) composed of: Opole ZSMNW Zwiazku Stowarzyszen Mniejszosci Niemieckiej Wojewodztwa (German Social-Cultural Society)	1991–2001	4	92953

Total number of cases 42

2.19 Political Parties in Romania

	Parties	Elections first–last	no	ID
MER	Miscarea Ecologista din Romania (Ecological Movement of Romania)	1990	1	93111
PER	Partidul Ecologist Român (Romanian Ecological Party)	1990	1	93112
FSN	Frontul Salvarii Nationale (National Salvation Front)	1990–2000	3	93221
PD	renamed: Partidul Democrat (Democratic Party)	in 1993		
PSR	Partidul Socialist Democratic Român (Romanian Socialist Democrat Party)	1990	1	93222
FDSN	Frontul Democrat al Salvarii nazionale (Democratic National Salvation Front)	1992–2000	3	93223

PDSR	renamed: Partidul Democratiei Sosiale din Romania (Party of Social Democracy of Romania)	in 1993		
	leading member of: PDSR Polul Democrat-Social din Romania (Democratic Social Pole of Romania)	in 2000		
PSDR	Partidul Social-Democrat Român (Romanian Social Democrat Party)	1990	1	93320
USD	Uniunea Social Democrat (Social Democratic Union)	1996	1	93322
CDR	ConvenÞia Democratā Românā (Democratic Convention of Romania)	1992 + 1996	2	93411
	composed of: 17 parties PNT-cd, PER, PSDR, FER, PAC, AFDPdR, SU, AR21Dec89, MRV, UMRL, UU, UNS, PL1993, PUD, PUDC, SPFMTR, PNL-CD	in 1992		
	composed of: 13 parties PNT-cd, PNL, PNL-CD, PER, PAR, FER, AC, AFDPR, SU, AR21Dec89, MRV, UMRL, UNS	in 1996		
PNL	Partidul National Liberal (National Liberal Party)	1990 + 2000	2	93430
PNTCD	Partidul National Taranesc-Crestin si Democrat (National Christian Democratic Peasants' Party)	1990	1	93521
GDC	Grupul Democrat de Centru (Democratic Group of the Centre)	1990	1	93529
PND	composed of: Partidul National Democrat (National Democratic Party)	1990	1	93523
FDRT	Frontul Democrat Roman din Timisoara (Romanian Democratic Front from Timisoara) plus 6 parties without seats in parliament: PDS Partidul Dreptatii Sociale din Romania (Social Justice Party of Romania) PNP Partidul National Progresist (National Progressist Party) PDC Partidul Democrat din Cluj (Democratic Party from Cluj) MDM Miscarea Democratia Moderna (Modern Democratic Movement) MDI Miscarea Democratia din Iasi (Modern Democracy from Iasi) PE Partidul Ecologist (Ecologist Party)	1990	1	93524
PUNR	Partidul UnitāÞii NaÞionale Române (Party of Romanian National Unity)	1990–1996	3	93711
PRM	Partidul Romania Mare (Greater Romania Party)	1992–2000	3	93712
PSM	Partidul Socialist al Muncii (Socialist Labour Party)	1992	1	93713
AUR	Alainta pentru Unitatea Romanilor (Romanian Unity Alliance), composed of: PUNR Partidul UnitāÞii NaÞionale Române (Party of Romanian National Unity)	1990	1	93719

228

Mapping Policy Preferences II

PR	Partidul Republican (Republican Party)	1990	1	93714
PDAR	Partidul Democrat Agrar din Romania (Democratic Agrarian Party of Romania)	1990 + 1992	2	93810
PCDMR	Partidul Crestin Democrat Maghiar din Romania (Hungarian Democratic Federation of Romania), reorganized as:	1990–2000	4	93951
UDMR	Uniunea Democrată Maghiară România/Romániai Magyar Demokrata Szövetseg (Hungarian Democratic Alliance of Romania)	in 1990		

Total number of cases   34

2.20 Russian Parties Covered

	Parties	Elections		ID
		first–last	no	
KPRF	Kommunisticheskaya Partiya Rossiiskoi Federatsii (Communist Party of the Russian Federation)	1993–2003	4	94221
APR	Agrarnaya Partiya Rossii (Agrarian Party)	1993–2003	3	94222
ZhR	Politicheskoe Dvizhenie Zhenshchiny Rossii (Women of Russia)	1993 + 1995	2	94223
DIM	Dostoinstvoi I Miloserdie (Dignity and Charity)	1993	1	94224
VN	Viast narodu! (Power to the People!)	1995	1	94225
Rodina	Rodina–Narodno Patrioticheskij Souz Rossii (Motherland–Popular Patriotic Union of Russia)	2003	1	94310
RDDR	Rosiiskoe Dvizhenie Demokraticheskikh Reform (Russian Movement for Democratic Reform)	1993	1	94320
IBIR	Blok Ivana Rybkina (Ivana Rybkin's Bloc)	1995	1	94321
DVR	Demokraticheskii Vybor Rossii (Russia's Democratic Choice)	1993 + 1995	2	94421
Yabloko	Yavlinsky-Boldryev-Lukin Bloc (Yabloko-Bloc)	1993–2003	4	94422
PRES	Partiya Rossiskoyo Edinstva I Soglasiy (Party of Russian Unity and Accord)	1993	1	94423
NDR	Nash Dom Rossiya (Our Home is Russia)	1995 + 1999	2	94424
VR	Vpered, Rossiya! (Russia, Go Forward!)	1995	1	94425
PGL	Pamfilova–Gurov–V. Lysenko, Respublikanskaja Partija Rossi (Republican Party of the Russian Federation)	1995	1	94426
DVR-OD	Demokraticheskii Vybor Rossii–Ob'edinenny Demokraty (Russia's Democratic Choice–United Democrats) composed of: DVR Demokraticheskiy Vibor Rossi (Russia's Democratic Choice) RPSD Russian Party for Social-Democracy RPP Russia's Peasant Party WS Woman for Solidarity SfD Soldiers for Democracy CNAR Congress of National Associations of Russia	1995	1	94427

MEDVED	Mezhregional'noye Dvizhenie Yedinstvo (Inter-Regional Movement Unity)	1999	1	94620
SPS	Soyuz Pravikh Sil (Union of Right Forces)	1999 + 2003	2	94621
OVR	Otechestvo Vsya Rossija (Fatherland All Russia)	1999	1	94622
BZ	Bloc Zhirinovskogo (Zhirinovsky Bloc)	1999	1	94710
LDPR	Liberal'no Demokraticheskaya Partija Rossii (Liberal Democratic Party of Russia)	1993–2003	3	94711
DPR	Demokraticheskaya Partija Rossii (Democratic Party of Russia)	1993	1	94712
KRO	Kongres Russkikh Obshchin (Congress of Russian Communities)	1995	1	94713
ER	Edinaja Rossja (United Russia)	2003	1	94951

Total number of cases 37

2.21 Serbian Parties Covered

	Parties	Elections		ID
		first–last	no	
SPS	Socijalisticka Partija Srbije (Socialist Party of Serbia)	1990–2000	5	95221
SRSV	Savez Reformskih Snaga Vojvodine (Alliance of Reform Forces of Vojvodina)	1990 + 1992	2	95222
LC	Leftist Coalition, composed of: SPS Socijalisticka Partija Srbije (Socialist Party of Serbia)	1997	1	95229
	JL Jugoslovenska Unianska Levika (Yugoslav Left) ND Nova Demokratija (New Democracy)	1997	1	95223
DEPOS	DEPOS Coalition, formerly: USDO Udruzena Srpska Demokratska Opozicija (Associated Serbian Democratic Opposition), composed of: ND Nova Demokratija (New Democracy) SPO Srpski Pokret Obnove (Serbian Movement for Renewal) DSS Demokratska Stranka Srbije (Democratic Party of Serbia)	1992 + 1993	2	95420
GSS	Gradjanski Savez Srbije (Civic Alliance of Serbia)	1993	1	95421
ND	Nova Demokratija (New Democracy)	1992–1997	3	95422
DOS	Demokratska Opozicija Srbije (Democratic Opposition of Serbia)	2000	1	95423
DS	Demokratska Stranka (Democratic Party)	1990–1993	3	95430
SPO	Srpski Pokret Obnove (Serbian Movement for Renewal)	1990–1997	3	95710
SRS	Srpska Radikalna Stranka (Serbian Radical Party)	1992–2000	4	95711

DPS	Demokratska Partija Srbije (Democratic Party of Serbia–Vojislav Kostunica)	1993	1	95712
StSSljS	Stranka Saveza Seljaka Srbije (Party of the Alliance of Peasants of Serbia)	1990 + 1992	2	95810
DZVM	Demokratska Zajednica Vojvodjanskih Madjara (Democratic Community of Magyars of Vojvodina)	1990–1997	4	95951
KV	renamed: Koalicija Vojvodina (Coalition Vojvodina)	in 1997		
SDA	Stranka Demokratske Akcije (Party of Democratic Action of Muslims)	1990	1	95952
KAP	Koalicija Albanskih Partija (Coalition of Albanian Parties), composed of:	1993	1	95954
PDD	Partija za Demokratsko Delovanje (Party for Democratic Activity) and DPA Demokratska Partija Albanaca (Democratic Party of Albanians)	1993	1	95955

Total number of cases   36

2.22 Slovak Parties Covered

	Parties	Elections		ID
		first–last	no	
SZ	Strana Zelenych (Green Party)	1990	1	96111
ZRS	Zdruzenie robotníkov Slovenska (Workers' Association of Slovakia)	1994	1	96210
KSC	Komunistická strana Ceskoslovenka (Communist Party of Czechoslovakia)	1990–2002	4	96220
SDL	renamed: Strana demokratickej ľavice (Party of the Democratic Left)	in 1990		
SV	Spolocna Vol'ba (Common Choice) composed of: SDA Strana demokratickej ľavice (Party of the Democratic Left) SDSS Socialno-demokratická strana Slovenska (Social Democratic Party) SZS Strana zelenýnch na Slovenska (Green Party) HP Hnutie polnohospodárov (Peasant Movement)	1994	1	96221
KSS	Komunistická strana Slovenská (Communist Party of Slovakia)	2002	1	96222
DS	Demokratická Strana (Democratic Party)	1990	1	96420
DU	Demokratická Unia (Democratic Union) including candidates of:	1994	1	96421
	NDS Národnodemokraticka strana (National Democratic Party, NDP participated in government 03.94–09.94)	1994	1	96712

SOP	Strana obéianskeho porozumenia (Party of Civic Understanding)	1998	1	96422
	Smer (Direction)	2002	1	96423
ANO	Aliancia nového obcana (Alliance of a New Citizen)	2002	1	96424
VPN	Verejnost prosti násiliu (Public Against Violence)	1990	1	96430
ADSR	Aliancia Demokratov Slovenskej Republiky (Alliance of Democrats, in March 1993 8 deputies left HZDS to form ADSR; these participated in govenment 03.94–09.94)	1992	1	96431
KDH	Krestanskodemokratické hnutie (Christian Democratic Movement)	1990–2002	4	96521
SDK	Slovenská demokratická koalicia (Slovak Democratic Coalition) composed of: KDH, DU, SDSS, and SZS	1998	1	96522
SDKU	Slovenská demokratická a krest'anská únia (Slovak Democratic and Christian Union)	2002	1	96523
SNS	Slovenská národná strana (Slovak National Party)	1990–1998	4	96710
HZDS	Hnutie za demokraticke Slovensko (Movement for a Democratic Slovakia)	1992–2002	4	96711
	with tiny coalition partner: RRS Peasants' Party of Slovakia and including candidates of SGA	in 1994		
ESWS-MKDH	Koalicia Mad'arské krestánsko-demokratické hnutie, Együttéles-Spoluzitie-Coexistensia (Coalition Political Movement Coexistence and the Hungarian Christian-Democratic Movement), composed of	1990–2002	5	96952
	Együttélés (Coexistence) MKDH Madarské krestansko-demokratické hnutie (Hungarian Christian Democratic Movement), reorganized as:	1992 + 1994	2	96951
MK	Madárská koalícia (Hungarian Coalition) composed of: Együttélés (Coexistence)	in 1994		
MKDH	Madarské krestansko-demokratické hnutie (Hungarian Christian Democratic Movement)	1994	1	96953
MOS	Mad'arská Obcianka Strana (Hungarian Civic Party), renamed:	1994	1	96954
SMK-MKP	Strana mad'arskej koalície–Magyar Koalícía Pártja (Party of the Hungarian Coalition)	in 1998		

Total number of cases   39

2.23 Slovenian Parties Covered

	Parties	Elections		ID
		first–last	no	
ZS	Zeleni Slovenije (Greens of Slovenia)	1990 + 1992	2	97110
ZL	Zdruzena Lista (Unity, Asssociated List) alliance of centre-left groups headed by:	1992	1	97223
ZKS	Zveza Komunista Slovenije (League of Communists of Slovenia)	1990	1	97220
SDSS	Socialdemokraticna Stranka Slovenije (Social-Democratic Party of Slovenia)	1990–2000	4	97320
ZLSD	Zdruzena Lista Socialninh Demokratov (Associated List of Social Democrats)	1996 + 2000	2	97321
LDS	Liberalna Democraticna Stranka (Liberal Democratic Party), formerly: ZSMS Liberalna Stranka (Liberal Party)	1990–2000	4	97421
LDS	reorganized as: Liberalna Democracija Slovenije (Liberal Democracy of Slovenia)	in 1994		
DSS	Demokratska Stranka Slovenje (Democratic Party of Slovenia)	1990 + 1992	2	97430
SKD	Slovenska Krscanski Demokrati (Slovene Christian Democrats)	1990–1996	3	97520
SLS	Slovenska Ljudska Stranka (Slovenian People's Party)	1990–1996	3	97521
Nsi	Nova Slovenija Krščanski Ljudska Stranka (New Slovene Christian People's Party)	2000	1	97522
SLS-SKD	Slovenska Ljudska Stranka (Slovenian People's Party)	2000	1	97620
SNS	Slovenska Nacionalna Stranka (Slovene National Party)	1992–2000	3	97710
SKZ	Slovenska Kmecka Zveza (Slovene Peasant League)	1990	1	97810
Desus	Demokraticna Stranka Upokojencev Slovenije (Democratic Party of Pensioners of Slovenia)	1996 + 2000	2	97951
SMS	Stranka Mladih Slovenije (Party of Slovenian Youth)	2000	1	97952

Total number of cases	31

2.24 Ukrainian Parties Covered

	Parties	Elections		ID
		first–last	no	
PZU	Partiyia Zelenykh Ukrainy (Green Party)	1998	1	98111
KPU	Komunistychna Partiyia Ukrainy (Communist Party of Ukraine)	1994–2002	3	98221
SPU	Socialistychna Partiyia Ukrainy (Socialist Party of the Ukraine)	1994 + 2002	2	98321
PSPU	Prohresyvna Sotsialstychna Partiyia Ukrainy (Progressive Socialist Party of the Ukraine)	1998	1	98322
BSP-SP	Blok Sotsiallistychna Partiyia I Selyans'ka Partiyia (Socialist Party of Ukraine–Peasant Party of Ukraine)	1998	1	98323
	Hromada (Community)	1998	1	98324
SDPU	Sotsial-Demokratychna Partiyia Ukrainy (Social Democracy Party)	1994	1	98325
	Kuchma (International Bloc for Reforms)	1994	1	98421
PVDU	Partiyia Demokratychnsho Vidrodzhennya Ukrainy (Party of the Democratic Rebirth of Ukraine)	1994	1	98422
PPU	Partiyia Pratsi Ukrainy (Labour Party)	1994	1	98423
HKU	Hrodmadyans'kyi Konhres Ukrainy (Civic Congress)	1994	1	98424
NDPU	Narodno-demokratychna Partiyia Ukrainy (People's Democratic Party)	1998	1	98426
SDPU-o	Sotsial Demokratychna Partiyia Ukrainy–obyednana (Social Democratic Party of Ukraine–associated)	1998 + 2002	2	98427
	Vpered, Ukraina (Go Ahead, Ukraine)	1998	1	98428
ZYU	Za Yedinu Ukrainu (For United Ukraine)	2002	1	98429
KhDPU	Khrystyyans'ko-demokratychna Partiyia Ukrainy (Christian-Democratic Party)	1994 + 1998	2	98521
Rukh	Narodnyi Rukh Ukrainy (Popular Movement of Ukraine)	1994 + 1998	2	98611
URP	Ukrains'ka Respublikans'ka Partiyia (Ukrainian Republican Party)	1994	1	98612
DemPU	Demokratychna Partiyia Ukrainy (Democratic Party of the Ukraine)	1994	1	98613
NF	Natsional'nyi Front (National Front)	1998	1	98614
NU	Bloc Viktora Iushchenka Nasha Ucraina (Viktor Yushchenko Bloc Our Ukraine)	2002	1	98615
JT	Vibortsyj Bloc Julii Tymoshenko (Juliya Tymoshenko Election Bloc)	2002	1	98616
KUN	Konhres Ukrains'kykh Natsionalistiv (Congress of Ukrainian Nationalists)	1994	1	98711
UKRP	Ukrains'ka Konservatyva Respublikans'ka Partiyia (Ukrainian Conservative Republican Party)	1994	1	98712

UNA	Ukrainska Natsionalna Assembleia (Ukrainian National Assembly)	1994	1	98713
SelPU	Selyans'ka Partiyia Ukrainy (Peasant Party of Ukraine)	1994	1	98810
APU	Ahrarna Partiyia Ukrainy (Agrarian Party of Ukraine)	1998	1	98811
RC	Party of Economic Rebirth (Renaissance of Crimea)	1994	1	98951

Total number of cases   34

III. OTHER COUNTRIES
3.1 Israeli Parties Covered

Parties		Elections		ID
		first–last	no	
HADASH	Hazit Democratit le Shalom ve-Shivayon (Democratic Front for Peace and Equality)	1992–1999	3	72225
	Hadash-Balad (Democratic National Party)	in 1996		
RATZ	Hatenva Lezhiot Ha'ezrach (Citizens Rights Movement)	1973–1988		
MAPAM	Mifleget Ha'Poalim Hameuchad (United Workers Party)	1949–1965		
		1988		
MERETZ	Merger between RATZ and MAPAM	1992–1999	3	72326
ILP	Mifleget Ha'avodah Ha'Israelit (Israel Labour Party)	1992–1996	2	72323
	Israel Echad (One Israel—Electoral alignment between Israel Labour and two small lists)	1999	1	72327
	Centre Party	1999	1	72415
	Haderech Ha'shlishit (The Third Way)	1996	1	72427
	Yisrael Ba'aliya (Israel for Immigration)	1996 + 1999	2	72428
MAFDAL	Miflaga Datit Leumit (National Religious Party)	1992–1999	3	72530
SHAS	Shomrei Torah Sephardim (Sephardi Torah Guardians)	1992–1999	3	72533
	Yahadut Ha Torah (United Torah Judaism) (Merger between Agudat Israel and Degel haTorah)	1992–1999	3	72535
Tehiya	Tenuat Hatehiya (Renaissance Movement)	1992	1	72612
Tsomet	HaTenua LeHithadashot Zionit Vevilti (Crossroads-non-aligned movement for Zionist renewal)	1992	1	72613
Moledet	Moledet (Homeland)	1992–1996	2	72614
	Likud	1992–1999	3	72622
	National Union	1999	1	72624
	Yisrael Beiteinu (Israel Our Home)	1999	1	72625
	HaReshima HaAravit HaMeuchedet	1992–1996	2	72901

Total   number of cases   33

3.2 Cypriot Parties Covered

	Parties	Elections		ID
		first–last	no	
AKEL	Anorthotikon Komma Ergazemenou Laou (Progressive Party of the Working People)	1996 + 2001	2	55321
EDEK	Socialtistiki Komma Kyprou EDEK (Socialist Party of Cyprus EDEK)	1996	1	55322
KISOS	Kinima Sosialdimokratikon (Social Democrat Movement)	2001	1	55322
KF	Komma Fileleftheron (Liberal Party)	1996	1	55421
DIKO	Dimokratikon Komma (Democratic Party)	1996 + 2001	2	55422
KED	Kinima ton Eleftheron Dimokratikon (Movement of Free Democrats)	1996	1	55423
DISY	Dimokratikos Sinagermos (Democratic Coalition)	1996 + 2001	2	55711
Total	number of cases		10	

3.3 Maltese Parties Covered

	Parties	Elections		ID
		first–last	no	
PL	Partit Laburista (Labour Party)	1996 + 1998	2	54320
PN	Partit Nazzjonalista (Nationalist Party)	1996 + 1998	2	54322
Total	number of cases		4	

APPENDIX IV

Missing Party Documents

The following list of missing election programmes relates to all parties represented in the twenty-four parliaments of OECD countries between 1990 and 2003 and all parties with at least two seats in the parliaments of the twenty-four CEE countries (except parties subsumed under 'other parties' in election statistics) for which no programmatic data are available. It shows that our manifesto data-set includes all parties that are judged to be relevant in national contexts because, as a rule, missing parties occupy very few seats. If you have any platform from the following list, we would be very glad if you could send a copy to one of the authors.

I. OECD Countries

Countries	Parties	Election years	Number of seats
Australia	Country-Liberal Party	1996	1
Belgium	Banana	1991	3
	National Front	1991, 1995, 1999	1,2,1
Denmark	Danish People's Party	1998	13
Finland	Ecological Party	1995	1
	REM Reformgroup	1999	1
France	PR Republican Pole	2002	1
Greece	Independent Muslim List	1990	2
	Democratic Renewal	1990	1
	Ecological Alternatives	1990	1
	Left Coalition	1990	4
Ireland	Socialist Party	1997, 2002	1,1
Italy	South Tyrol People's Party	1992, 1994, 2001	3,3,3
	List Aosta Valley	1992, 1994	1,1
	Venetian League	1992	1
	Pensioners	1992	1
	Southern Action League	1994	1
	Valdostian League	2001	1
Japan	United Democratic Socialists	1993	4
	Democratic Reform Union	1996	1
	Independents Party	2000	5
	Liberal League	2000	1
Luxembourg	DL The Left	1999	1
Netherlands	Political Reformed Party	1994, 1998, 2002, 2003	2,3,2,2
	Reformed Political Union	1994, 1998	2,2
	Reformed Political Federation	1994, 1998	3,3
	Centre Democrats	1994	3

	AOV Elderly People	1994	6
	Union 55 +	1994	1
New Zealand	NLP New Labour Party	1990	1
	United New Zealand	1996, 1999	1,1
Norway	Red Electoral Alliance	1993	1
	Coastal Party	1997	1
Spain	HB United People	1993, 1996	2,2
	UV Valencian Union	1993, 1996	1,1
	BNPG Galician National Popular Bloc	1996, 2000	2,3
	AV-MEC Catalan Green Alternative	2000	1
Sweden	Red Electoral Alliance 93	1993	1
Switzerland	United Socialist Party	1991	1
	Feminist Green Alternative	1991, 1995	1,2
	League of the Tessins	1991, 1995, 1999, 2003	2,1,2,1
	Christian Social Party	1991, 1995, 2003	1,1,1
	Solidarity	2003	1
	Socialist Green Alternative	2003	1
Great Britain	Social Democratic and Labour Party	1992, 1997, 2001, 2005	4,3,3
	Ulster Popular Unionist Party	1992	1
	Party of Wales	1992, 1997, 2001, 2005	4,4,4

II. CEE Countries

Bosnia	ZL United List	1996	2
	NSSM-SMP Peoples Union for Peace–Union for Peace	1996	2
	Sloga Unity	1998	4
	Social-Democrats of Bosnia-Hercegovina	1998	2
Bulgaria	Fatherland Front	1990	2
Montenegro	Democratic Alliance of Montenegro	1996	2
	Democratic Union of Albanians	1996	2
Poland	Germans of Opole Silesia	1997	
Russia	OPD All-Russian Political Movement in Support of the Army	1999	2
	ROS Russian All People's Union	1999	2
Serbia	RDSV Reform Democratic Party of Voijvodina	1992	2
	GC Group of Citizens–Arkan	1992	5
	SVM Alliance of Voijvodina Hungarians	1997	4
	Coalition 'List for Sandzhak'	1997	3
	PSU Serbian Unity Party	2000	14
Slovenia	SSS Socialist Party of Slovenia	1990	5
	SOPS Craftsmen and Entrepreneurial Party–Center Party	1990	3
Ukraine	PRP Party of Reforms and Order	1998	3
	PRVU Party of Regional Revival	1998	2

III. Other Countries

Israel	All parties	2003	120

General Bibliography

Adams, James (1998), 'A Theory of Spatial Competition With Biased Voters', Paper, Department of Political Science, University of California, Santa Barbara.

——— (2001), 'A Theory of Spatial Competition with Biased Voters', *British Journal of Political Science*, 31: 210–23.

——— (2005), Comment, 199–202 of McDonald, Michael and Budge, Ian, Elections, Parties, Democracy.

——— and Merrill, Samuel (1998), 'Spatial Competition with Biased Voters', Paper, Department of Political Science, University of California at Santa Barbara.

——— Clark, Michael, Ezrow, Lawrence and Glasgow, Garrett (2004), 'Understanding Change and Stability in Party Ideologies: Do Parties Respond to Public Opinion or to Past Election Results?', *British Journal of Political Science*, 34(4): 589–610.

Anderson, Christopher and Guillory, C. (1997), 'Political Institutions and Satisfaction with Democracy', *American Political Science Review*, 91: 66–81.

Bara, Judith (2001*a*), 'Tracking Estimates of Public Opinion and Party Policy Intentions in Britain and the USA' in Laver, Michael (ed.) *Estimating the Policy Positions of Political Actors*. London: Routledge.

——— (2001*b*), 'Using Manifesto Estimates to Validate Computerized Analysis' in Budge et al. (eds.) *Mapping Policy Preferences: Estimates for Parties, Governments and Electors 1945–1998*. Oxford: Oxford University Press.

——— (2006), 'Do Parties Reflect Public Concerns?' in Bara, Judith and Weale, Albert (eds.) *Democratic Politics and Party Competition*. London: Routledge

——— and Budge, Ian (2001), 'Party Policy and Ideology: Still New Labour?' in Norris, Pippa (ed.) *Britain Votes 2001*. Oxford, UK: Oxford University Press.

Bartolini, S. and Mair, Peter (1990), *Identity, Competition and Electoral Availability: The Stabilisation of European Electorates 1885–1985*. Cambridge: Cambridge University Press.

Benoit, Kenneth and Laver, Michael (2006), *Party Policy in Modern Democracies*. London: Routledge.

Berelson, Bernard (1952), *Content Analysis in Communications Research*. Glencoe, IL: Free Press.

——— (1954), 'Content Analysis' in Lindzey, Gordon (ed.) *Handbook of Social Psychology, Volume I*. Reading, MA: Addison-Wesley.

——— (1971), *Content Analysis in Communications Research*. New York: Hafner.

Birch, Sarah (1998), 'In the Shadow of Moscow: Ukraine, Moldova and the Baltic Republics' in White, Stephen, Batt, Judy and Lewis, Paul G. (eds.) *Developments in Soviet and East European Politics 2*. Basingstoke, UK: Macmillan.

——— (2001), 'Electoral Systems and Party Systems', *Perspectives on European Politics and Society*, 2(3): 355–77.

——— Millard, Frances, Popescu, Marina and Williams, Kieran (2002), *Embodying Democracy: Electoral System Design in Post-Communist Europe*. Basingstoke, UK: Palgrave.

Blais, Andre, Blake, Donald and Dion, Stephane (1993), 'Do Parties Make a Difference: Parties and the Size of Government in Liberal Democracies', *American Journal of Political Science*, 37: 40–62.

Browne, Eric and Franklin, M. (1973), 'Coalition Payoffs in European Parliamentary Democracies', *American Political Science Review*, 67: 453–64.

Budge, Ian (1994), 'A New Spatial Theory of Party Competition: Uncertainty, Ideology and Party Equilibria', *British Journal of Political Science*, 14: 443–67.

—— (1999), 'Party Policy and Ideology: Reversing the 1950s' in Evans, Geoffrey and Norris, Pippa (eds.) *Critical Elections*. London: Routledge.

—— (2000), 'Expert Judgements of Party Policy Positions: Uses and Limitations in Political Research', *European Journal of Political Research*, 37: 103–13.

—— (2001), 'Validating Party Policy Placements', *British Journal of Political Science*, 31: 210–23.

—— and Farlie, Dennis J. (1977), *Voting and Party Competition*. London and New York: John Wiley & Sons.

—— —— (1978), 'The Potentiality of Dimensional Analyses for Explaining Voting and Party Competition', *European Journal of Political Research*, 6: 203–31.

—— and Hofferbert, Richard I. (1990), 'Mandates and Policy Outcomes: US Party Platforms and Federal Expenditure', *American Political Science Review*, 84: 111–31.

—— —— (1992*a*), 'The Party Mandate and the Westminster Model: Party Programmes and Government Spending in Britain, 1948–1985', *British Journal of Political Science*, 22.

—— —— (1992*b*), 'Party Platforms, Mandates and Government Spending', *American Political Science Review*, 87: 744–50.

—— and Laver, Michael (1986), 'Policy, Ideology and Party Distance: Analysis of Election Programmes in 19 Democracies', *Legislative Studies Quarterly*, 11: 607–15.

—— —— (1993), 'The Policy Basis of Government Coalitions: A Comparative Investigation', *British Journal of Political Sciences*, 23: 499–519.

—— and Pennings, P. J. M. (2007*a*) 'Do They work? Validating Computerized Word-Frequency Estimates Against Policy Series', in Special edition of Marks, Gary (ed.) *Electoral Studies*.

—— —— (2007*b*) 'Missing the Message and Shooting the Messenger: Benoit and Laver's "Response"', in Special edition of Marks, Gary (ed.) *Electoral Studies*.

—— and Robertson, David (1987), 'Do Parties Differ and How? Comparative Discriminant and Factor Analyses' in Budge, Ian, Robertson, David and Hearl, Derek J. (eds.) *Ideology, Strategy and Party Change: Spatial Analyses of Post-War Election Programmes in 19 Democracies*. Cambridge: Cambridge University Press.

—— Robertson, David and Hearl, Derek J. (eds.) (1987), *Ideology, Strategy and Party Change: Spatial Analyses of Post-War Election Programmes in 19 Democracies*. Cambridge: Cambridge University Press.

—— Crewe, Ivor, McKay, David and Newton, Kenneth (1998, 2000), *The New British Politics*. London: Pearson.

—— Tanenbaum, Eric and Bara, Judith (1999), *Monitoring Democratic Five-Year Plans: Multiple Coding of British Manifestos and US Platforms*. Swindon: ESRC Report R00022289.

—— Klingemann, Hans-Dieter, Volkens, Andrea, Bara, Judith and Tanenbaum, Eric (2001), *Mapping Policy Preferences: Estimates for Parties, Governments and Electors 1945–1998*. Oxford: Oxford University Press.

—— et al. (1997), *The Politics of the New Europe: Atlantic to Urals*. London: Longman.

Burke, Edmund (1790/1955), *Reflections on the Revolution in France*. New York: The Library of Liberal Arts Press.

Burt, Gordon (1997), 'Party Policy: Decision Rule or Chance? A Note on Budge's New Spatial Theory of Party Competition', *British Journal of Political Science*, 27: 647–58.

Cameron, David R. (1978), 'The Expansion of the Political Economy', *American Political Science Review*, 78: 1243–61.

Castles, F. (ed.) (1982), *The Impact of Parties*. Beverley Hills, CA: Sage.

_____ and Mair, P. (1984), 'Left-Right Political Scales: Some Expert Judgements', *European Journal of Political Research*, 12: 73–88.

Converse, Philip E. (1964), 'The Nature of Belief Systems in Mass Publics' in Apter, David (ed.) *Ideology and Discontent*. New York, NY: Free Press.

_____ (1970), 'Attitudes and Non-Attitudes: Continuation of a Dialogue' in Tufte, Edward R. (ed.) *The Quantitative Analysis of Social Problems*. Reading, MA: Addison-Wesley.

_____ (2000). 'Assessing the Capacity of Mass Publics', *Annual Review of Political Science*, 3: 331–53.

Dahrendorf, Ralf (1990), *Reflections on the Revolution in Europe*. New York: Random House.

Downs, Anthony (1957), *An Economic Theory of Democracy*. New York: Harper.

Duvold, Kjetil and Mindaugas, Jurkynas (2004), 'Lithuania' in Berglund, Sten, Ekman, Joakim and Aarebrot, Frank H. (eds.) *The Handbook of Political Change in Eastern Europe*. Cheltenham, UK and Northampton, MA, USA: Edward Elgar.

Erikson, Robert S., MacKuen, Michael B. and Stimson, James A. (2001), *The Macro Polity*. New York: Cambridge University Press.

Evans, Geoffrey and Norris, Pippa (eds.) (1999), *Critical Elections: British Parties and Voters in Long-Term Perspective*. London: Sage.

_____ Heath, Anthony and Payne, Clive (1999), 'Class: Labour as a Catch-All Party' in Evans, Geoffrey and Norris, Pippa (eds.) *Critical Elections: British Parties and Voters in Long-Term Perspective*. London: Sage.

Farrell, David M. and Webb, Paul (2000), 'Political Parties as Campaign Organizations' in Dalton, Russell J. and Wattenberg, Martin P. (eds.) *Parties Without Partisans: Political Change in Advanced Industrial Democracies*. Oxford, UK: Oxford University Press.

Fuchs, Dieter and Klingemann, Hans-Dieter (1990), 'The Left-Right Schema' in Jennings, M. Kent et al. (eds.) *Continuities in Political Action*. Berlin: Walter de Gruyter.

Gabel, Mathew and Huber, John (2000), 'Putting Parties in Their Place', *American Journal of Political Sciences*, 44: 94–103.

Gibbons, Matthew (2000), *Election Programmes in New Zealand Politics*. Ph.D. Thesis, University of Waikato, New Zealand.

Grzybowski, Marian and Mikuli, Piotr (2004), 'Poland' in Berglund, Sten, Ekman, Joakim and Aarebrot, Frank H. (eds.) *The Handbook of Political Change in Eastern Europe*. Cheltenham, UK and Northampton, MA, USA: Edward Elgar.

Harmel, Robert, Janda, Kenneth and Tan, A. (1995), 'Substance vs Packaging: An Empirical Analysis of Parties' Issue Profiles', Paper presented to Annual Meeting of American Political Science Association, Chicago.

Hearl, Derek J. (1988), 'Ambivalence Revisited: An Analysis of Liberal Party Manifestos Since 1945' in Kirchner, Emil (ed.) *Liberal Parties in Western Democracies*. Cambridge: Cambridge University Press.

_____ (1990), *Political Manifestos of the World*. Munich: Microfiche Bowker-Sauer.

_____ (2001), 'Checking the Party Policy Estimates: Reliability' in Budge, Ian et al. (eds.) *Mapping Policy Preferences: Estimates for Parties, Electors, and Governments 1945–1998*. Oxford, UK: Oxford University Press.

Heise, David R. (1969), 'Separating Reliability and Stability in Test-Retest Correlation', *American Sociological Review*, 33: 93–101.

Hofferbert, Richard I. and Budge, Ian (1992), 'The Party Mandate and the Westminster Model: Election Programmes and Government Spending in Britain 1948–1985', *British Journal of Political Sciences*, 22: 151–82.

_____ _____ and McDonald, Michael D. (1993), 'Party Platforms, Mandates and Government Spending', *American Political Science Review*, 87: 747–50.

_____ and Klingemann, Hans-Dieter (1990), 'The Policy Impact of Party Programmes and Government Declarations in the Federal Republic of Germany', *European Journal of Political Research*, 18: 277–304.

Huber, John and Inglehart, Ronald (1995), 'Expert Interpretations of Party Space and Party Locations in 42 Societies', *Party Politics*, 1: 73–111.

Inglehart, Ronald and Klingemann, Hans-Dieter (1976), 'Party Identification, Ideological Preference and the Left-Right Dimension among Western Mass Publics' in Budge, Ian, Crewe, Ivor and Farlie, Dennis (eds.) *Party Identification and Beyond: Representations of Voting and Party Competition*. London: John Wiley & Sons.

Janda, Kenneth (1980), *Political Parties: A Cross-National Survey*. New York: Free Press.

_____ Harmel, Robert, Edens, Christine and Goff, Patricia (1995), 'Changes in Party Identity: Evidence From Party Manifestos', *Party Politics*, 1: 171–96.

Jasiewicz, Krysztof (2003), 'Elections and Voting Behaviour' in White, Stephen, Batt, Judy and Lewis, Paul G. (eds.) *Developments in Central and East European Politics 3*. Basingstoke, UK: Palgrave.

Karasimeonov, Georgi (2004), 'Bulgaria' in Berglund, Sten, Ekman, Joakim and Aarebrot, Frank H. (eds.) *The Handbook of Political Change in Eastern Europe*. Cheltenham, UK and Northampton, MA, USA: Edward Elgar.

Keman, Hans (ed.) (1997), *The Politics of Problem-Solving in Post-War Democracies*. Basingstoke, UK: Macmillan.

Kim, Hee-Min and Fording, Richard C. (1998), 'Voter Ideology in Western Democracies 1946–1989', *European Journal of Political Research*, 33: 73–97.

_____ _____ (2000), 'Government Partisanship in Western Democracies, 1945–1989', Unpublished manuscript, Florida State University and the University of Kentucky.

_____ _____ (2001*a*), Extending Party Estimates to Governments and Electors' in Budge, Ian et al. (eds.) *Mapping Policy Preferences*. Oxford: Oxford University Press, pp. 157–78.

_____ _____ (2001*b*), 'Does Tactical Voting Matter? The Political Impact of Tactical Voting in Recent British Elections', *Comparative Political Studies*, 34(3): 294–311.

King, Gary and Laver, Michael (1993), 'Party Platforms, Mandates and Government Spending', *American Political Science Review*, 87: 744–58.

_____ _____ (1999), 'Many Publications But Still No Evidence', *Electoral Studies*, 18: 597–8.

Kitschelt, Herbert (1994), *The Transformation of European Social Democracy*. Cambridge: Cambridge University Press.

Kleinnijenhuis, Jan and Pennings, Paul (1999), 'Measurement of Party Positions on the Basis of Party Programs, Media Coverage and Voter Perceptions', Paper presented to European Consortium for Political Research Joint Sessions of Workshops, Mannheim.

_____ _____ (2001), 'Measurement of Party Positions on the Basis of Party Programmes' in Laver, Michael (ed.) *Estimating the Policy Position of Political Actors*. London: Routledge, pp. 162–8.

Klingemann, Hans-Dieter (1995), 'Party Positions and Voter Orientations' in Klingemann, Hans-Dieter and Fuchs, Dieter (eds.) *Citizens and the State*. Oxford: Oxford University Press.

_____ and Fuchs, Dieter (eds.) (1995), *Citizens and the State*. Oxford: Oxford University Press.

——— Hofferbert, Richard I., Budge, Ian et al. (1994), *Parties, Policies and Democracy.* Boulder, CO: Westview.

——— Fuchs, Dieter and Zielonka, J. (2006), *Democracy and Political Culture in Eastern Europe.* London: Routledge.

Kollman, Ken, Miller, John H. and Page, Scott E. (1992), 'Adaptive Parties in Spatial Elections', *American Political Science Review*, 86(4): 929–37.

——— ——— ——— (1998), 'Political Parties and Electoral Landscapes', *British Journal of Political Science*, 28: 129–58.

Krippendorf, Klaus (2003), *Content Analysis: An Introduction to Its Methodology.* Beverley Hills, CA: Sage.

Laver, Michael (ed.) (2001), *Estimating the Policy Positions of Political Actors.* London: Routledge.

——— and Budge, Ian (eds.) (1992), *Party Policy and Government Coalitions.* London: Macmillan/New York: St. Martins.

——— and Garry, John (1998), 'Estimating Policy Positions From Party Manifestos', Paper presented at European Consortium for Political Research Joint Sessions of Workshops, Warwick.

——— ——— (1999), 'Estimating Policy Positions From Party Manifestos', Paper presented at European Consortium for Political Research Joint Sessions of Workshops, Mannheim.

——— ——— (2000), 'Estimating Policy Positions From Political Texts', *American Journal of Political Science*, 44: 619–34.

——— and Hunt, W. Ben (1992), *Policy and Party Competition.* New York and London: Routledge.

——— and Schofield, Norman (1990), *Multiparty Government: The Politics of Coalition in Europe.* Oxford and New York: Oxford University Press.

——— Benoit, Kenneth and Garry, John (2003), 'Extracting Policy Positions From Political Texts Using Words as Data', *American Political Science Review*, 97(2): 311–31.

Levitan, Teresa E. and Miller, Warren (1979), 'Ideological Interpretations of Presidential Elections', *American Political Science Review*, 73: 751–71.

Lewis, Paul G. (2003), 'Political Parties' in White, Stephen, Batt, Judy and Lewis, Paul G. (eds.) *Developments in Central and East European Politics 3.* Basingstoke, UK: Palgrave.

Lewis-Beck, Michael (1988), *Economics and Elections.* Ann Arbor, MI: University of Michigan Press.

Lijphart, Arend (1984), *Democracies: Patterns of Majoritarian and Consensus Government in 21 Countries.* New Haven, CT: Yale University Press.

——— (1999), *Patterns of Democracy: Government Forms and Performance in Thirty-Six Countries.* New Haven, CT: Yale University Press.

Lipset S. M. and Stein, Rokkan (1967), *Party Systems and Voter Alignments.* New York, NY: Doubleday.

McDonald, Michael (2006), 'Parties in Democracy, Democracy in Parties: Lessons From Ian Budge and the CMP Data' in Bara, Judith and Weale, Albert (eds.) *Democratic Politics and Party Competition.* London: Routledge.

——— and Budge, Ian (2005), *Elections, Parties, Democracy: Conferring the Median Mandate.* Oxford: Oxford University Press.

——— and Mendés, Silvia M. (1999), 'The Policy Space of Party Manifestos', Paper presented at European Consortium for Political Research Joint Sessions of Workshops, Mannheim.

——— ——— (2001), 'Checking the Party Policy Estimates: Convergent Validity' in Budge et al. (eds.) *Mapping Policy Preferences: Estimates for Parties, Governments and Electors 1945–1998.* Oxford: Oxford University Press.

McDonald, Budge, Ian and Hofferbert, Richard (1999), 'Party Mandate Theory and Time Series Analysis', *Electoral Studies*, 18: 587–96.

—— —— and Pennings, Paul (2004), 'Choice Versus Sensitivity: Party Reactions to Public Concerns', *European Journal of Political Research*, 43(6): 845–68.

—— Mendés, Silvia M. and Kim, Myunghee (2007), 'Cross-Temporal and Cross-National Comparisons of Party Left-Right Positions', Special edition of *Electoral Studies* (forthcoming).

Mair, Peter (1986), 'Locating Irish Political Parties on a Left-Right Dimension: An Empirical Enquiry', *Political Studies*, 44: 456–65.

—— (1987), *The Changing Irish Party System: Organization, Ideology and Electoral Competition*. London: Pinter.

—— (2001), 'Searching for the Positions of Political Actors: A Review of Approaches and a Critical Evaluation of Expert Surveys' in Laver, Michael (ed.) *Estimating the Policy Position of Political Actors*. London: Routledge.

—— and Castles, Francis G. (1997), 'Revisiting Expert Judgements', European Journal of Political Science, 31: 150–7.

Marks, Gary (ed.) (2007), 'Comparing Data Sets on the Positioning of Political Parties', Special edition of *Electoral Studies* (forthcoming).

May, J. D. (1978) 'The Definition of Democracy: A plea for Clarity', *Political Studies*, 36: 138–52.

Michels, Roberto (1949), *Political Parties: A Sociological Study of Ideological Tendencies of Modern Democracy* [translated by Eden Paul and Cedar Paul]. New York: Dover.

Millard, Frances (2004), *Elections, Representation and Parties in Post-Communist Europe*. Basingstoke, UK: Palgrave.

Miller, S. (1977), 'News Coverage of Congress: The Search for the Ultimate Spokesman', *Journalism Quarterly*, 54: 459–65.

Müller, Wolfgang C. (2000), 'Austria: Tight Coalitions and Stable Government' in Müller, Wolfgang C. and Strøm, Kaare (eds.) *Coalition Governments in Western Europe*. Oxford: Oxford University Press.

—— and Strøm, Kaare (eds.) (2000a), *Coalition Governments in Western Europe*. Oxford: Oxford University Press.

—— (2000b), 'Coalition Governance in Western Europe' in Müller, Wolfgang C. and Strøm, Kaare (eds.) *Coalition Governments in Western Europe*. Oxford: Oxford University Press.

Narud, Hanne-Marthe and Strøm, Kaare (2000), 'Norway: A Fragile Coalitional Order' in Müller, Wolfgang C. and Strøm, Kaare (eds.) *Coalition Governments in Western Europe*. Oxford: Oxford University Press.

Norris, Pippa (2005), *Radical Right: Voters & Parties in the Regulated Market*. New York: Cambridge University Press.

Neuendorf, Kimberley (2002), *The Content Analysis Guidebook*. Thousand Oaks, CA, New Delhi and London: Sage.

Pelizzo, Riccardo (2003), 'Party Positions or Party Direction?: An Analysis of Party Manifesto Data', *West European Politics*, 26(2): 67–89.

Pennings, Paul (1998), 'Party Responsiveness and Socio-Economic Problem-Solving in Western Democracies', *Party Politics*, 4: 393–404.

—— and Lane, J. E. (eds.) (1998), *Comparing Party System Change*. London: Routledge.

Pierce, Roy (1999), 'Mass-Elite Linkages and the responsible Party Model of Representation' in Miller, Warren E., Pierce, Roy, Thomassen, Jacques, Herrera, Richard, Holmberg,

Sören, Esaiasson, Peter and Wessels, Bernhard, (eds.) *Policy Representation in Western Democracies*. Oxford: Oxford University Press.

Powell, G. Bingham (2000), *Elections as Instruments of Democracy Majoritarian and Proportional Visions*. New Haven, CT: Yale University Press.

Price, Simon and Sanders, David (1993), 'Modelling Government Popularity in Postwar Britain: A Methodological Example', *American Journal of Political Science*, 37: 317–34.

Rallings, Colin (1987), 'The Influence of Election Programmes: Britain and Canada 1945–1979' in Budge, Ian, Robertson, David and Hearl, Derek J. (eds.) *Ideology, Strategy and Party Change: Spatial Analyses of Post-War Election Programmes in 19 Democracies.* Cambridge: Cambridge University Press.

Ranney, Austin (ed.) (1962), *Essays in the Behavioural Study of Politics*. Urbana, IL: University of Illinois Press.

Riffe, Daniel, Lacy, Stephen and Fico, Frederick G. (1998), *Analyzing Media Messages: Using Quantitative Content Analysis in Research*. Mahwah, NJ: Lawrence Earlbaum.

Riker, William (1962), *The Theory of Political Coalitions*. New Haven, CT: Yale University Press.

——— (ed.) (1993), *Agenda Formation*. Ann Arbor, MI: University of Michigan Press.

Roberts, Carl W. (ed.) (1997), *Text Analysis for the Social Sciences*. Mahwah, NJ: Lawrence Earlbaum.

Robertson, David (1976), *A Theory of Party Competition*. London and New York: John Wiley & Sons.

——— (1987), 'Britain, Australia, New Zealand and the United States 1946–1981: An Initial Comparative Analysis' in Budge, Ian, Robertson, David and Hearl, Derek J. (eds.) *Ideology, Strategy and Party Change: Spatial Analyses of Post-War Election Programmes in 19 Democracies*. Cambridge: Cambridge University Press.

Rose, Richard (1964), 'Parties, Factions and Tendencies in Britain', *Political Studies*, 12: 33–46.

——— (1969), 'The Variability of Party Government', *Political Studies*, 17: 413–45.

——— (1974), *The Problem of Party Government*. London: Macmillan.

Rueda, David and Pontusson, Jonas (2000), 'Wage Inequalities and Varieties of Capitalism', *World Politics*, 52: 350–83.

Sartori, Giovanni (1976), *Parties and Party Systems: A Framework for Analysis*. Cambridge: Cambridge University Press.

Sanders, David and Price, Simon (1991), *Economic Competence, Rational Expectations and Government Popularity in Post-War Britain*. Colchester: ESRC Research Centre in Micro-Social Change.

Saward, Michael (1998), *The Terms of Democracy*. Cambridge, Polity.

Schofield, Norman (1993), 'Political Competition and Multiparty Coalition Governments', *European Journal of Political Research*, 23: 1–33.

——— and Laver, Michael (1985), 'Bargaining Theory and Portfolio Payoffs in European Coalition Governments, 1945–1983', *British Journal of Political Science*, 15: 143–64.

Schumpeter, Joseph (1962), *Capitalism, Socialism and Democracy*. New York: Harper & Row.

Smith-Sivertsen, Hermann (2004), in Berglund, Sten, Ekman, Joakim and Aarebrot, Frank H. (eds.) *The Handbook of Political Change in Eastern Europe*. Cheltenham, UK and Northampton, MA, USA: Edward Elgar.

Spafford, Duff (1971), 'A Note on the Equilibrium Division of the Vote', *American Political Science Review*, 65: 180–3.

Stimson, James A. (n.d.). 'Party Proximity to the Median Voter in U.S. Presidential Elections', Unpublished manuscript, University of North Carolina at Chapel Hill.

_____ McKuen, Michael S. and Erikson, Robert S. (1995), 'Dynamic Representation', *American Political Science Review*, 89: 543–65.

Stokes, Donald E. (1966), 'Spatial Models of Party Competition' in Campbell, Angus, Converse, Philip E., Miller, Warren E. and Stokes, Donald E. (eds.) *Elections and the Political Order*. New York: John Wiley & Sons.

_____ and Iversen, Gudmund R. (1962), 'On the Existence of Forces Restoring Party Competition', *Public Opinion Quarterly*, 26: 159–71.

Stone, P. J., Dunphy, D. C., Smith, M. S. and Ogilvie, D. M. (eds.) (1966), *The General Inquirer: A Computer Approach to Content Analysis*. Cambridge, MA: MIT Press.

Strøm, Kaare and Liepart, Jorn (1989), 'Ideology, Strategy and Party Competition in Post-War Norway', *European Journal of Political Research*, 17: 263–88.

Thomassen, Jacques (ed.) (2005), *The European Voter*. Oxford: Oxford University Press.

Thome, Helmut (1999), 'Party Mandate Theory and Time-Series Analysis: A Methodological Comment', *Electoral Studies*, 18: 569–85.

Thomson, Robert (1999), *The Party Mandate: Election Pledges and Government Actions in the Netherlands*. Amsterdam: CT Press.

Tóka, Gabor (2004), in Berglund, Sten, Ekman, Joakim and Aarebrot, Frank H. (eds.) *The Handbook of Political Change in Eastern Europe*. Cheltenham, UK and Northampton, MA, USA: Edward Elgar.

Volkens, Andrea (1992), *Content Analysis of Party Programmes in Comparative Perspective: Handbook and Coding Instructions*. Berlin: Wissenschaftszentrum.

_____ (1994), *Comparative Manifestos Project: Data-Set CMP94*. Berlin: Wissenschaftszentrum.

_____ (2000), *Die PDS im Parteiensystem*. Berlin: Bundesstiftung Rosa Luxemburg and Dietz Verlag.

_____ (2001), 'Manifesto Research Since 1979: From Reliability to Validity' in Laver, Michael (ed.) *Estimating the Policy Positions of Political Actors*. London: Routledge.

_____ (2006), 'Policy Changes of Parties in European Parliament Party Groups' in Bara, Judith and Weale, Albert (eds.) *Democratic Politics and Party Competition*. London: Routledge.

Von Beyme, Klaus (1985), *Political Parties in Western Democracies*. Aldershot, UK: Gower.

_____ (2001), 'Parties in the Process of Consolidation in East-central Europe' in Pridham, Geoffrey and Agh, Attila (eds.) *Prospects for Democratic Consolidation in East-Central Europe*. Manchester, UK and New York: Manchester University Press.

Ware, Alan (1996), *Political Parties and Party Systems*. Oxford: Oxford University Press.

Warwick, Paul V. (1992), 'Ideological Diversity and Government Survival in Western European Parliamentary Democracies', *Comparative Political Studies*, 25: 332–61.

_____ (2000), 'Policy Horizons in West European Parliamentary Systems', *European Journal of Political Research*, 38: 37–61.

Webb, Paul (2000), *The Modern British Party System*. London: Sage.

Weber, Robert P. (1990), *Basic Content Analysis*, 2nd edn. Newbury Park, CA: Sage.

Wiley, David E. and Wiley, James A. (1970), 'The Estimation of Measurement Error in Panel Data', *American Sociological Review*, 35: 112–17.

Williams, Kieran (2003), 'The Czech Republic and Slovakia' in White, Stephen, Batt, Judy and Lewis, Paul G. (eds.) *Developments in Central and East European Politics 3*. Basingstoke, UK: Palgrave.

Woldendorp, Jaap, Keman, Hans and Budge, Ian (1993), 'Party Government in 20 Democracies', *European Journal of Political Research*, 24: 1107 (Special edition: *Political Data 1945–1990*).

———— ———— ———— (1998), 'Party Government in 48 Democracies: An Update, 1993–1995', *European Journal of Political Research*, 33: 125–64.

———— ———— ———— (2000), *Party Government in 48 Democracies, 1945–1998*. Dordrecht, the Netherlands, Boston, MA and London: Kluwer.

Zajc, Drago and Boh, Tomaž (2004), 'Slovenia' in Berglund, Sten, Ekman, Joakim and Aarebrot, Frank H. (eds.) *The Handbook of Political Change in Eastern Europe*. Cheltenham, UK and Northampton, MA, USA: Edward Elgar.

Select Bibliography of Manifesto-Related Research

Adams, James (2001), 'A Theory of Spatial Competition with Biased Voters', *British Journal of Political Science*, 31: 210–23.

—— (2005), Comment, 199–202 of McDonald, Michael and Budge, Ian, *Elections, Parties, Democracy*.

—— Clark, Michael, Ezrow, Lawrence and Glasgow, Garrett (2004), 'Understanding Change and Stability in Party Ideologies: Do Parties Respond to Public Opinion or to Past Election Results?', *British Journal of Political Science*, 34(4): 589–610.

—— and Merrill, Samuel (1998), 'Spatial Competition with Biased Voters', Department of Political Science, University of California at Santa Barbara.

Agasøster, Bodil (2001), 'A Framework for Analysing Local Party Policy Emphases in Scotland' in Laver, Michael (ed.) *Estimating the Policy Positions of Political Actors*. London: Sage, pp. 76–89.

—— (2001), *Party Cohesion and Local Agendas: A Study of Variations in Local Campaign Strategies in Scotland*. PhD Thesis, University of Aberdeen.

Bara, Judith (2005), 'With a Little Help From Our Friends: An Analysis of the Transfer of Policy Expressions Between British and American parties', Annual meeting of the American Political Science Association, Washington, DC, September 2005.

—— (2001), 'Tracking Estimates of Public Opinion and Party Policy Intentions in Britain and the USA' in Laver, Michael (ed.) *Estimating the Policy Positions of Political Actors*. London: Routledge.

—— (2006), 'Do Parties Reflect Public Concerns?' in Bara, Judith and Weale, Albert (eds.) *Democratic Politics and Party Competition*. London: Routledge.

—— and Budge, Ian (2001), 'Party Policy and Ideology: Still New Labour?' in Norris, Pippa (ed.) *Britain Votes 2001*. Oxford, UK: Oxford University Press.

Baron, David (1991), 'A Strategic Bargaining Theory of Government Formation in Parliamentary Systems', *American Political Science Review*, 85: 137–64.

Bartolini, S. and Mair, Peter (1990), *Identity, Competition and Electoral Availability: The Stabilisation of European Electorates 1885–1985*. Cambridge: Cambridge University Press.

Budge, Ian (1994), 'A New Spatial Theory of Party Competition: Uncertainty, Ideology and Party Equilibria', *British Journal of Political Science*, 14: 443–67.

—— (1999), 'Party Policy and Ideology: Reversing the 1950s' in Evans, Geoffrey and Norris, Pippa (eds.) *Critical Elections*. London: Routledge.

—— (2000), 'Expert Judgements of Party Policy Positions: Uses and Limitations in Political Research', *European Journal of Political Research*, 37: 103–13.

—— (2001), 'Validating Party Policy Placements', *British Journal of Political Science*, 31: 210–23.

—— and Farlie, Dennis J. (1977), *Voting and Party Competition*. London and New York: John Wiley & Sons.

—— —— (1978), 'The Potentiality of Dimensional Analyses for Explaining Voting and Party Competition', *European Journal of Political Research*, 6: 203–31.

—— and Hofferbert, Richard I. (1990), 'Mandates and Policy Outcomes: US Party Platforms and Federal Expenditure', *American Political Science Review*, 84: 111–31.

Budge, Ian and Hofferbert, Richard I. (1990) Mandates and 'Policy Outcomes', *American Political Science Review*, 84: 111–31.

_____ and Laver, Michael (1986), 'Policy, Ideology and Party Distance: Analysis of Election Programmes in 19 Democracies', *Legislative Studies Quarterly*, 11: 607–15.

_____ _____ (1993), 'The Policy Basis of Government Coalitions: A Comparative Investigation', *British Journal of Political Science*, 23: 499–519.

_____ and Pennings P. J. M. (2007*a*) 'Do They Work? Validating Computerized Word-Frequency Estimates against Policy Series' in Special edition of Marks, Gary (ed.) *Electoral Studies*.

_____ _____ (2007*b*) 'Missing the Message and Shooting the Messenger: Benoit and Laver's "Response" ' in Special edition of Marks, Gary (ed.) *Electoral Studies*.

_____ and Robertson, David (1987), 'Do Parties Differ and How?' Comparative Discriminant and Factor Analyses' in Budge, Ian, Robertson, David and Hearl, Derek J. (eds.) *Ideology, Strategy and Party Change: Spatial Analyses of Post-War Election Programmes in 19 Democracies*. Cambridge: Cambridge University Press.

_____ _____ and Hearl, Derek J. (eds.) (1987), *Ideology, Strategy and Party Change: Spatial Analyses of Post-War Election Programmes in 19 Democracies*. Cambridge: Cambridge University Press.

_____ Tanenbaum, Eric and Bara, Judith (1999), *Monitoring Democratic Five-Year Plans: Multiple Coding of British Manifestos and US Platforms*. Swindon: ESRC Report R00022289.

_____ Klingemann, Hans-Dieter, Volkens, Andrea, Bara, Judith and Tanenbaum, Eric (2001), *Mapping Policy Preferences: Estimates for Parties, Governments and Electors 1945–1998*. Oxford: Oxford University Press.

Carkoglu, Ali (1995), 'Election Manifestos and Policy-Oriented Economic Voting. A Pooled Cross-National Analysis', *European Journal of Political Research*, 27: 293–317.

Caul, Miki and Gray, Mark M. (2000), 'From Platform Declarations to Policy Outcomes: Changing Party Profiles and Partisan Influence Over Policy', in Dalton, Russell J. and Wattenberg, Martin P. (eds.) *Parties Without Partisans: Political Change in Advanced Industrial Democracies*. Oxford: Oxford University Press.

Dalton, Russell J. and Wattenberg, Martin P. (eds.) (2000), *Parties without Partisans: Political Change in Advanced Industrial Democracies*. Oxford: Oxford University Press.

Erikson, Robert S., MacKuen, Michael B. and Stimson, James A. (2001), *The Macro Polity*. New York: Cambridge University Press.

Evans, Geoffrey, Heath, Anthony and Payne, Clive (1999), 'Class: Labour as a Catch-All Party?' in Evans, Geoffrey and Norris, Pippa (eds.) *Critical Elections. British Parties and Voters in Long-Term Perspective*. London: Sage, pp. 97–102.

Gabel, Mathew and Huber, John (2000), 'Putting Parties in Their Place', *American Journal of Political Sciences*, 44: 94–103.

Gibbons, Matthew (2000), *Election Programmes in New Zealand Politics*. Ph.D. Thesis, University of Waikato, New Zealand.

_____ (2004), 'Review: Parties, Policies, and Democracy', *ECPR European Political Science (EPS)*, 3(3): 23–38.

Hearl, Derek J. (1988*a*), 'Ambivalence Revisited: An Analysis of Liberal Party Manifestos Since 1945' in Kirchner, Emil (ed.) *Liberal Parties in Western Democracies*. Cambridge: Cambridge University Press.

_____ (1988*b*), 'The Luxemburg Liberal Party' in Kirchner, Emil (ed.) *Liberal Parties in Western Democracies*. Cambridge: Cambridge University Press.

Hearl, Derek J. (2001), 'Checking the Party Policy Estimates: Reliability' in Budge, Ian et al. (eds.) *Mapping Policy Preferences: Estimates for Parties, Electors, and Governments 1945– 1998.* Oxford, UK: Oxford University Press.

Hofferbert, Richard I. and Budge, Ian (1992), 'The Party Mandate and the Westminster Model: Election Programmes and Government Spending in Britain 1948–1985', *British Journal of Political Science*, 22: 151–82.

——— and Klingemann, Hans-Dieter (1990), 'The Policy Impact of Party Programmes and Government Declarations in the Federal Republic of Germany', *European Journal of Political Research*, 18: 277–304.

——— ——— Budge, Ian and McDonald, Michael D. (1993), 'Party Platforms, Mandates and Government Spending', *American Political Science Review*, 87: 747–50.

Imbeau, Louis M. and McKinley, Robert (eds.) (1996), *Comparing Government Activity.* London: Macmillan.

Janda, Kenneth, Harmel, Robert, Edens, Christine and Goff, Patricia (1995), 'Changes in Party Identity: Evidence From Party Manifestos', *Party Politics*, 1: 171–96.

Keman, Hans (ed.) (1997), *The Politics of Problem-Solving in Post-War Democracies.* Basingstoke, UK: Macmillan.

Kim, Hee Min and Fording, Richard C. (1998), 'Voter Ideology in Western Democracies 1946–1989', *European Journal of Political Research*, 33: 73–97.

——— ——— (2000), 'Government Partisanship in Western Democracies, 1945–1989', Unpublished manuscript, Florida State University and the University of Kentucky.

——— ——— (2001*a*), 'Extending Party Estimates to Governments and Electors', in Budge et al. (eds.) *Mapping Policy Preferences.* Oxford: Oxford University Press, pp. 157– 78.

——— ——— (2001*b*), 'Does Tactical Voting Matter? The Political Impact of Tactical Voting in Recent British Elections', *Comparative Political Studies.*

King, Gary, and Laver, Michael (1993), 'Party Platforms, Mandates and Government Spending', *American Political Science Review*, 87: 744–7.

——— ——— (1999), 'Many Publications But Still No Evidence', *Electoral Studies*, 18: 597–8.

Kleinnijenhuis, Jan and Pennings, Paul (1999), 'Measurement of Party Positions on the Basis of Party Programs, Media Coverage and Voter Perceptions', Paper presented to European Consortium for Political Research Joint Sessions of Workshops, Mannheim.

Klingemann, Hans-Dieter (1995), 'Party Positions and Voter Orientations' in Klingemann, H. D. and Fuchs, Dieter (eds.) *Citizens and the State.* Oxford: Oxford University Press.

——— and Fuchs, Dieter (eds.) (1995), *Citizens and the State.* Oxford: Oxford University Press.

——— Hofferbert, Richard I., Budge, Ian et al. (1994), *Parties, Policies and Democracy.* Boulder, CO: Westview.

——— Fuchs, Dieter and Zielonka, J. (2006), *Democracy and Political Culture in Eastern Europe.* London: Routledge.

König, Thomas, Volkens, Andrea and Bräuninger, Thomas (1999), 'Regierungserklärungen von 1949 bis 1998. Eine vergleichende Untersuchung ihrer regierungsinternen und— externen Bestimmungsfaktoren', *Zeitschrift für Parlamentsfragen*, 29: 641–59.

Krouwel, Andre (1998), *The Catch-All Party in Western Europe: A Study in Arrested Development.* Amsterdam: CT Press.

Laver, Michael (ed.) (2001), *Estimating the Policy Positions of Political Actors.* London: Routledge.

———— and Budge, Ian (eds.) (1992), *Party Policy and Government Coalitions*. London: Macmillan and New York: St. Martins.

———— and Garry, John (1998), 'Estimating Policy Positions From Party Manifestos', Paper presented at European Consortium for Political Research Joint Sessions of Workshops, Warwick.

Laver, Michael and Garry, John (1999), 'Estimating Policy Positions From Party Manifestos', Paper presented at European Consortium for Political Research Joint Sessions of Workshops, Mannheim.

———— (2000), 'Estimating Policy Positions From Political Texts', *American Journal of Political Science*, 44: 619–34.

———— Benoit, Kenneth and Garry, John (2003), 'Extracting Policy Positions from Political Texts Using Words as Data', *American Political Science Review*, 97(2): 311–31.

McDonald, Michael and Budge, Ian (2005), *Elections, Parties, Democracy: Conferring the Median Mandate*. Oxford: Oxford University Press.

———— and Mendés, Silvia M. (1999), 'The Policy Space of Party Manifestos', Paper presented at European Consortium for Political Research Joint Sessions of Workshops, Mannheim.

———— Budge, Ian and Hofferbert, Richard (1999), 'Party Mandate Theory and Time Series Analysis', *Electoral Studies*, 18: 587–96.

———— ———— and Pennings, Paul (2004), 'Choice Versus Sensitivity: Party Reactions to Public Concerns', *European Journal of Political Research*, 43(6): 845–68.

———— ———— and Kim, Myunghee (2007), 'Cross-temporal and Cross-national Comparisons of Party Left-Right Positions', Special Issue of *Electoral Studies*, (forthcoming).

Mair, Peter (1986), 'Locating Irish Political Parties on a Left-Right Dimension: An Empirical Enquiry', *Political Studies*, 44: 456–65.

———— (1987), *The Changing Irish Party System: Organization, Ideology and Electoral Competition*. London: Pinter.

Marcinkowski, Frank (1998), *Massenmedien und Politikinhalte. Empirische Fallstudie auf einem unterbelichteten Forschungsfeld. Duisburger Materialen zur Politik- und Verwaltungswissenschaft*. Duisburg: Gerhard-Mercator-Universität Duisburg.

Marks, Gary (ed.) (2007), 'Comparing Data Sets on the Positioning of Political Parties', Special edition of *Electoral Studies* (forthcoming).

Michels, Ank M. B. (1993), *Nederlandse politieke partijen en hun kiezers (1970–1989)*. Ph.D. Thesis, Universiteit Twente.

Neidhardt, Friedhelm, Eilders, Christiane and Pfetsch, Barbara (1998), *Die Stimme der Medien im politischen Prozeß: Themen und Meinungen in Pressekommentaren*. Discussionpaper FS III 98-106, Berlin: Wissenschaftszentrum Berlin für Sozialforschung.

Pelizzo, Riccardo (2003), 'Party Positions or Party Direction?: An Analysis of Party Manifesto Data', *West European Politics*, 26(2): 67–89.

Pennings, Paul (1998), 'Party Responsiveness and Socio-Economic Problem-Solving in Western Democracies', *Party Politics*, 4: 393–404.

Pétry, François (1988), 'The Policy Impact of Canadian Party Programs', *Canadian Public Policy*, 14: 376–89.

———— (1991), 'Fragile Mandate: Party Programmes and Public Expenditures in the French Fifth Republic', *European Journal of Political Research*, 20: 149–71.

———— (1995), 'The Party Agenda Model: Election Programmes and Government Spending in Canada', *Canadian Journal of Political Sciences*, 28: 51–84.

Pétry, François (2002), *Les Parti québécois. bilan des engagements électoraux, 1994–2000*. Québec: Presses de l'Université Laval.

——and Landry, Réjean (2001), 'Estimating Interparty Policy Distances from Election Programmes in Quebec, 1970–1989', in Laver, Michael (ed.) *Estimating the Policy Positions of Political Actors*. London: Sage, pp. 131–46.

Rallings, Colin (1987), 'The Influence of Election Programmes: Britain and Canada 1945–1979' in Budge, Ian, Robertson, David and Hearl, Derek J. (eds.) *Ideology, Strategy and Party Change: Spatial Analyses of Post-War Election Programmes in 19 Democracies*. Cambridge: Cambridge University Press.

Ray, Leonard (2001), 'A Natural Sentence Approach to the Computer Coding of Party Manifestos' in Laver, Michael (ed.) *Estimating the Policy Positions of Political Actors*. London: Sage, pp. 149–61.

Riker, William (ed.) (1993), *Agenda Formation*. Ann Arbor, MI: University of Michigan Press.

Robertson, David (1976), *A Theory of Party Competition*. London and New York: John Wiley & Sons.

——(1987), 'Britain, Australia, New Zealand and the United States 1946–1981: An Initial Comparative Analysis' in Budge, Ian, Robertson, David and Hearl, Derek J. (eds.) *Ideology, Strategy and Party Change: Spatial Analyses of Post-War Election Programmes in 19 Democracies*. Cambridge: Cambridge University Press.

Rölle, Daniel (2000), 'Wahlprogramme als Richtschnur parlamentarischen Handelns', *Zeitschrift für Parlamentsfragen*: 821–33.

Römmele, Andrea (1999), 'Direkte Kommunikation zwischen Parteien und Wählern: Direct-Mailing bei SPD und CDU', *Zeitschrift für Parlamentsfragen*, (2): 305–15.

——(1997), 'Communicating with Their Voters: The Use of Direct Mailing by the SPD and the CDU', *German Politics*, 16: 120–31.

Rucht, Dieter and Volkens, Andrea (1998), 'Der Einfluß von politischem Protest auf Wahlprogramme in der Bundesrepublik Deutschland. Eine quantitative Analyse' in Albach, Horst, Dierkes, Meinolf, Berthoin Antal, Ariane and Vaillant, Kristina (eds.) *Organisationslernen–institutionelle und kulturelle Dimensionen, WZB Jahrbuch 1998*. Berlin: Edition Sigma, pp. 311–31.

Saglie, Jo (1998), 'A Struggle for the Agenda? Norwegian parties and the European Issues 1989–1995', *Party Politics*, 4: 262–84.

Schofield, Norman (1993), 'Political Competition and Multiparty Coalition Governments', *European Journal of Political Research*, 23: 1–33.

——and Laver, Michael (1985), 'Bargaining Theory and Portfolio Payoffs in European Coalition Governments, 1945–1983', *British Journal of Political Science*, 15: 143–62.

Stimson, James A. (n.d.). 'Party Proximity to the Median Voter in U.S. Presidential Elections', Unpublished manuscript, University of North Carolina at Chapel Hill.

——McKuen, Michael S. and Erikson, Robert S. (1995), 'Dynamic Representation', *American Political Science Review*, 89: 543–65.

Stokes, Donald E. (1966), 'Spatial Models of Party Competition' in Campbell, Angus, Converse, Philip, Miller, Warren E. and Stokes, Donald E., *Elections and the Public Order*. New York, Wiley.

Strøm, Kaare and Liepart, Jorn (1989), 'Ideology, Strategy and Party Competition in Post-War Norway', *European Journal of Political Research*, 17: 263–88.

Thome, Helmut (1999), 'Party Mandate Theory and Time-Series Analysis: A Methodological Comment', *Electoral Studies*, 18: 569–85.

Thomson, Robert (1999), *The Party Mandate: Election Pledges and Government Actions in the Netherlands*. Amsterdam: CT Press.

Volkens, Andrea (1992), *Content Analysis of Party Programmes in Comparative Perspective: Handbook and Coding Instructions*. Berlin: Wissenschaftszentrum.

——— (1994), *Comparative Manifestos Project: Data-Set CMP94*. Berlin: Wissenschaftszentrum.

——— (2000), *Die PDS im Parteiensystem*. Berlin: Bundesstiftung Rosa Luxemburg/Dietz Verlag.

——— (2001), 'Manifesto Research Since 1979: From Reliability to Validity' in Laver, Michael (ed.) *Estimating the Policy Positions of Political Actors*. London: Routledge.

Volkens, Andrea (2006), 'Policy Changes of Parties in European Parliament Party Groups' in Bara, Judith and Weale, Albert (eds.) *Democratic Politics and Party Competition*. London: Routledge.

Warwick, Paul V. (1992), 'Ideological Diversity and Government Survival in Western European Parliamentary Democracies', *Comparative Political Studies*, 25: 332–61.

——— (2000), 'Policy Horizons in West European Parliamentary Systems', *European Journal of Political Research*, 38: 37–61.

Webb, Paul (2000), *The Modern British Party System*. London: Sage.

Bibliography of Electoral Data Sources

I. OECD Countries
General:

Banks, Arthur S. (ed.) (diverse), *Political Handbook of the World*. Binghamton: CSA Publications and New York: McGraw-Hill.

Keesing's *Record of World Events* (diverse).

Mackie, Thomas T. (1992), 'General Elections in Western Nations during 1990', *European Journal of Political Research*, 21: 317–32.

_____ and Rose, Richard (1991), *The International Almanac of Electoral History*, 3rd edn. Houndmills, Basingstoke, Hampshire, London: Macmillan.

1.1 Australian Election Statistics

Mackerras, Malcolm (2002), 'Australia', *European Journal of Political Research*, 41: 897–905.

_____ and Mcallister, Ian (1999), 'Australia', *European Journal of Political Research*, 36: 317–25.

1.2 Austrian Election Statistics

Fallend, Franz (1999), 'Austria', *European Journal of Political Research*, 36: 327–37.

_____ (2002), 'Austria', *European Journal of Political Research*, 41: 906–14.

Müller, Wolfgang C. (1995), 'Austria', *European Journal of Political Research*, 28: 277–89.

_____ (1996), 'Austria', *European Journal of Political Research*, 30: 275–85.

1.3 Belgian Election Statistics

Belgian Federal Electoral Commission, http://polling2003.belgium.be/electionshome/uk/result/chamber/table_top.html (20/07/04).

Deruette, Serge (1996), 'Belgium', *European Journal of Political Research*, 30: 287–98.

_____ and Loeb-Mayer, Nicole (1992), 'Belgium', *European Journal of Political Research*, 22: 363–72.

Rihoux, Benoît (2000), 'Belgium', *European Journal of Political Research*, 38: 338–47.

1.4 Canadian Election Statistics

Carty, Roland Kenneth (1994), 'Canada', *European Journal of Political Research*, 26: 255–68.

_____ (1998), 'Canada', *European Journal of Political Research*, 34: 363–71.

_____ (2001), 'Canada', *European Journal of Political Research*, 40: 263–70.

1.5 Danish Election Statistics

Bille, Lars (1995), 'Denmark', *European Journal of Political Research*, 28: 313–21.

_____ (2002), 'Denmark', *European Journal of Political Research*, 41: 941–6.

Parline database, http://www.ipu.org/parline-e/reports/2087_E.htm (07/03/05).

1.6 Finnish Election Statistics

Ministry of Justice, http://192.49.229.35/e/aanaktiivisuus/aanestys1.htm and http://192.49.229.35/e/tulos/lasktila.html (26/03/03).

Sundberg, Jan (1992), 'Finland', *European Journal of Political Research*, 22: 391–9.
—— (1996), 'Finland', *European Journal of Political Research*, 30: 321–30.
—— (2000), 'Finland', *European Journal of Political Research*, 38: 374–81.

1.7 French Election Statistics

Ysmal, Colette (2003), 'France', *European Journal of Political Research*, 42: 943–56.

1.8 German Election Statistics

Bundeswahlleiter (2002), Endgültiges Wahlergebnis der Bundestagswahl 2002, http://www.bundeswahlleiter.de/bundestagswahl2002/deutsch/ergebnis2002/bund_land/wahlkreis/kr99999.htm (04/11/02).
Poguntke, Thomas (1995), 'Germany', *European Journal of Political Research*, 28: 341–52.

1.9 Greek Election Statistics

Mavrogordatos, Gorge Th. (1994), 'Greece', *European Journal of Political Research*, 26: 313–18.
—— (1997), 'Greece', *European Journal of Political Research*, 32: 375–81.
—— (2001), 'Greece', *European Journal of Political Research*, 40: 313–19.

1.10 Icelandic Election Statistics

Hardarson, Ólafur Th. (1992), 'Iceland', *European Journal of Political Research*, 22: 429–35.
—— (1996), 'Iceland', *European Journal of Political Research*, 30: 367–76.
—— and Kristinsson, Gunnar Helgi (2000), 'Iceland', *European Journal of Political Research*, 38: 408–19.
Parline database, http://www.ipu.org/parline-e/reports/2143_E.htm (03/07/03).

1.11 Irish Election Statistics

Marsh, Michael (1993), 'Ireland', *European Journal of Political Research*, 24: 455–66.
—— and O'Malley, Eoin (2003), 'Ireland', *European Journal of Political Research*, 42: 979–85.

1.12 Italian Election Statistics

Ignazi, Piero (1993), 'Italy', *European Journal of Political Research*, 24: 175–83.
—— (1995), 'Italy', *European Journal of Political Research*, 28: 393–405.
—— (2002), 'Italy', *European Journal of Political Research*, 41: 992–1000.
'National Elections. The Cycle of Elections—Italy' (1996), *Electoral Studies*, 15: 595.

1.13 Japanese Election Statistics

Kato, Junko (2001), 'Japan', *European Journal of Political Research*, 40: 348–60.
—— (2004), 'Japan', *European Journal of Political Research*, 43: 1047–53.
Shiratori, Rei (1994), 'Japan', *European Journal of Political Research*, 26: 355-60.
—— (1997), 'Japan', *European Journal of Political Research*, 32: 425–33.

1.14 Luxembourgian Election Statistics

Hirsch, Mario (1995), 'Luxembourg', *European Journal of Political Research*, 28: 415–20.
—— (2000), 'Luxembourg', *European Journal of Political Research*, 38: 453–7.
Parline database, http://www.ipu.org/parline%2De/reports/2191%5Fe.htm (25/03/02).

1.15 Dutch Election Statistics

Lucardie, Paul (2003), 'The Netherlands', *European Journal of Political Research*, 42: 1029–36.

—— and Voerman, Gerrit (1995), 'The Netherlands', *European Journal of Political Research*, 28: 427–36.

—— —— (2004), 'The Netherlands', *European Journal of Political Research*, 43: 1084–92.

1.16 New Zealand Election Statistics

Vowles, Jack (1994), 'New Zealand', *European Journal of Political Research*, 26: 375–87.

—— (2000), 'New Zealand', *European Journal of Political Research*, 38: 470–80.

—— (2003), 'New Zealand', *European Journal of Political Research*, 42: 1037–47.

1.17 Norwegian Election Statistics

Aalberg, Torii (2002), 'Norway', *European Journal of Political Research*, 41: 1047–56.

Heidar, Knut (1994), 'Norway', *European Journal of Political Research*, 26: 389–95.

Narud, Hanne Marthe (1998), 'Norway', *European Journal of Political Research*, 34: 485–92.

1.18 Portuguese Election Statistics

Stock, Maria (1992), 'Portugal', *European Journal of Political Research*, 22: 505–11.

Stock, Maria José and Magone, José Maria (1996), 'Portugal', *European Journal of Political Research*, 30: 445–52.

Magone, José Maria (2000), 'Portugal', *European Journal of Political Research*, 38: 499–510.

—— (2003), 'Portugal', *European Journal of Political Research*, 42: 1058–66.

1.19 Spanish Election Statistics

Del Castillo, Pilar and López Nieto, Lourdes (1994), 'Spain', *European Journal of Political Research*, 26: 423–9.

Delgado, Irene and López Nieto, Lourdes (2001), 'Spain', *European Journal of Political Research*, 40: 413–20.

1.20 Swedish Election Statistics

Widfeldt, Anders (2003), 'Sweden', *European Journal of Political Research*, 42: 1091–101.

—— and Pierre, Jon (1992), 'Sweden', *European Journal of Political Research*, 22: 519–26.

—— —— (1995), 'Sweden', *European Journal of Political Research*, 28: 477–85.

1.21 Swiss Election Statistics

Hardmeier, Sibylle (2000), 'Switzerland', *European Journal of Political Research*, 38: 529–41.

—— (2004), 'Switzerland', *European Journal of Political Research*, 43: 1151–9.

Ladner, Andreas (1992), 'Switzerland', *European Journal of Political Research*, 22: 527–36.

—— (1996), 'Switzerland', *European Journal of Political Research*, 30: 469–78.

Parline database, http://www.ipu.org/parline-e/reports/2305_E.htm (04/07/04).

1.22 Turkish Election Statistics

Parline database, http://www.ipu.org/parline%2De/reports/2323%5Fe.htm (09.01.03).

State Institute of Statistics (1992): *Results of General Election*.

1.23 British Election Statistics

Fisher, Justin (2002), 'United Kingdom', *European Journal of Political Research*, 41: 1101–10.

Mackie, Thomas T. (1993), 'United Kingdom', *European Journal of Political Research*, 24: 555–62.

Webb, Paul (1998), 'United Kingdom', *European Journal of Political Research*, 34: 539-49.

Rallings, Colin and Thrasher, Michael (2005), 'The 2005 General Election: Analysis of Results' (London: Electoral Commission).

1.24 US-American Election Statistics

Katz, Richard S. (1993), 'United States of America', *European Journal of Political Research*, 24: 563–72.

_____ (1997), 'United States of America', *European Journal of Political Research*, 32: 517–28.

_____ (2002), 'United States of America', *European Journal of Political Research*, 41: 1111–18.

Federal Election Commission (2005), 'Federal Elections, 2004: Election Results for the US President, the US Senate and the US House of Representatives' (Washington DC: Federal Election Commission).

II. CEE Countries
General

Banks, Arthur S. (ed.) (diverse), *Political Handbook of the World*. Binghamton, CSA Publications and New York: McGraw-Hill.

Keesing's *Record of World Events* (diverse).

Mackie, Thomas T. (1992), 'General Elections in Western Nations during 1990', *European Journal of Political Research*, 21: 317–32.

2.1 Albanian Election Statistics

Hoppe, Hans-Joachim (1992), 'Demokratischer Machtwechsel in Albanien', *Osteuropa. Zeitschrift für Gegenwartsfragen des Ostens*, 42: 609–20.

Parline database, http://www.ipu.org/parline-e/reports/2001_E.htm (05/06/03).

Parline database, http://www.ipu.org/parline-e/reports/2001_E.htm (09/12/05).

Statistical Yearbook of Albania, 1991.

Szajkowski, Bogdan (1992), 'The Albanian Election of 1991', *Electoral Studies*, 11: 157–61.

Zanaj, Fatmir (2004), 'The First Two Pluralist Elections and the Cleavage Structure in Postcommunist Albania' in Barjaba, Kosta (ed.) *Albania's Democratic Elections, 1991–1997. Analyses, Documents and Data*. Berlin: Edition sigma.

2.2 Armenian Election Statistics

Data for 1995 provided by Liz Fuller, source: *Golos Armenii*, 13 July 1995; *Noyan Tapan*, 13 July 1995, 17 July 1995, and 3 August 1995.

Figures for 1999 elections provided by Ronald Shaiko, USAID, Center for Democracy and Governance, Washington, DC.

IFES database, http://209.50.195.230/eguide/resultsum/armenia_par03.htm (01/04/04).

2.3 Azerbaijani Election Statistics

'Aserbaidschan: Wahlen nach örtlichen Traditionen' (1996), *Wostok*, 1: 16–18.

Data for 1995 provided by Teimuraz Chubinishivli, Techinform Institute Tblisi, Georgia.

Nohlen, Dieter, Grotz, Florian and Hartmann, Christof (eds.) (2001), *Elections in Asia and the Pacific. A Data Handbook, Volume I.* Oxford: Oxford University Press.

2.4 Belarusian Election Statistics

Data for 1995 provided by David Rotman, Belarus Sociological Service 'Public Opinion', Minsk, Belarus.
Inter-parliamentary Union (diverse), *Chronicle of Parliamentary Elections and Developments*, 6/1994–6/1995.

2.5 Bosnian Election Statistics

Data for 1990 and 1996 provided by Prof. Dr. Vladimir Goati, Institute of Social Sciences, Center of Political and Public Opinion Research, Narodnog fronta 45, Beograd.
Election Update, Report on Eastern Europe, 49/1990: 27.
Electionworld database, http://www.electionworld.org/election/bosnia.htm (16/01/02).
Parline database, http://www.ipu.org/parline-e/reports 2039_E.htm (06/08/03).

2.6 Bulgarian Election Statistics

Essex database, http://www2.essex.ac.uk/elect/electer/bg_er_nl.htm (07/02/01).

2.7 Croatian Election Statistics

Kasapović, Mirjana, Grdešić, Ivan and Zakošek, Nenad (1995), Die parlamentarischen Wahlen im Oktober 1995. Paper of the Faculty of Political Science, University of Zagreb, Croatia.
Parline database, http://www.ipu.org/parline-e/reports/2077_E.htm (06/08/03).
Šiber, Ivan (ed.) (1997), *The 1990 and 1992/93 Sabor Elections in Croatia. Analyses, Documents and Data.* Berlin: Edition Sigma.

2.8 Czech Election Statistics

Brokl, Lubomir and Mansfeldová, Zdenka (1999), 'Czech Republic', *European Journal of Political Research*, 36: 349–69.
Essex database, http://www2.essex.ac.uk/elect/electer/czech_er_nl.htm (17/04/01).
Essex database, http://www2.essex.ac.uk/elect/electer/czech_er_nl.htm (03/02/03).

2.9 Estonian Election Statistics

Essex database, http://www2.essex.ac.uk/elect/electer/est_er_nl.htm (17/04/01).
Pettai, Velo (2004), 'Estonia', *European Journal of Political Research*, 43: 993–9.

2.10 Georgian Election Statistics

Allison, Lincoln (1996), 'The Georgian Elections of November 1995', *Electoral Studies*, 2: 275–80.
Central Electoral Commisson of Georgia, Final Record of Results of Georgian Parliament Elections 1995, http://www.parliament.ge/ELECTIONS/parties.html.
Fuller, Elizabeth (1992), 'The Georgian Parliamentary Elections', *Radio Free Europe, RFE/RL Research Reports*, 47: 1–4.
IFES database, http://www.ifes.org/eguide/resultsum/georgiares.htm (03/06/03).
Inter-parliamentary Union (diverse), *Chronicle of Parliamentary Elections and Developments*, 6/1992–6/1993.
Slider, Darrell (1992), 'The October 1992 Elections in Georgia', Paper presented at the National Convention of the AAASS, Phoenix, 19 November 1992.

2.11 German Democratic Republic's Election Statistics

Mackie, Thomas T. (1992), 'General Elections in Western Nations During 1990', *European Journal of Political Research*, 21: 323.

2.12 Hungarian Election Statistics

Essex database, http://www2.essex.ac.uk/elect/electer/hu_er_nl.htm (10/06/02).
Ilonzki, Gabriella and Kurtán, Sándor (2003), 'Hungary', *European Journal of Political Research*, 42: 967–74.

2.13 Latvian Election Statistics

Electionworld database, http://www.electionworld.org/election/latvia.htm (13/08/03).
Essex database, http://www2.essex.ac.uk/elect/electer/latvia_er_nl.htm (17/04/01).
Essex database, http://www2.essex.ac.uk/elect/database/indexElections.asp?country=LATVIA&election=lv2002 (23/06/02).

2.14 Lithuanian Election Statistics

Essex database, http://www2.essex.ac.uk/elect/electer/lt_er_nl.htm (17.04.01).

2.15 Macedonian Election Statistics

Adrejevich, Milan (1990), 'The Election Scorecard for Serbia, Montenegro, and Macedonia', *Radio Free Europe, Reports on Eastern Europe*, 51: 37–9.
IFES database, http://209.50.195.230/eguide/resultsum/macedonia_par_res02.htm (21/05/03).
Inter-parliamentary Union (diverse), *Chronicle of Parliamentary Elections and Developments*, 6/1994–6/1995.
Republic Election Committee (diverse), *Reports on the Elections of 1990 and 1994*.

2.16 Moldovan Election Statistics

Essex database, http://www2.essex.ac.uk/elect/database/indexElections.asp?opt=leg&country=MOLDOVA&election=md94.
Essex database, http://www2.essex.ac.uk/elect/database/indexElections.asp?country=MOLDOVA&election=md98.
Essex database, http://www2.essex.ac.uk/elect/database/indexElections.asp?country=MOLDOVA&election =md2001.

2.17 Montenegrin Election Statistics

Data for 1990 to 1998 provided by Prof. Dr. Vladimir Goati, Institute of Social Sciences, Center of Political and Public Opinion Research, Belgrade, Serbia and Montenegro.
Goati, Vladimir (ed.) (1998), *Elections to the Federal and Republican Parliaments of Yugoslavia (Serbia and Montenegro) 1990–1996. Analyses, Documents and Data.* Berlin: Edition Sigma, pp. 192–9.
IFES database, http://www.ifes.org/eguide/resultsum/montenegro_par02.htm (02/06/03).

2.18 Polish Election Statistics

Essex database, http://www2.essex.ac.uk/elect/electer/pl_er_nl.htm (14/02/01).
Essex database, http://www2.essex.ac.uk/elect/database/indexElections.asp?country=POLAND&election=pl2001 (23/06/03).
Jasiewicz, Krzysztof (1992), 'Poland', *European Journal of Political Research*, 22: 489–504.

Jasiewicz, Krzysztof and Gebethner, Stanislaw (1999), 'Poland', *European Journal of Political Research*, 36: 489–95.

2.19 Romanian Election Statistics

Essex database, http://www2.essex.ac.uk/elect/electer/ro_er_nl.htm (27/03/01).

2.20 Russian Election Statistics

Essex database, http://www2.essex.ac.uk/elect/electer/rus_prelr.htm (17/04/01). IFES database, http://ifes.org/eguide/resultsum/russia_par03.htm (04/07/04). Schneider, Eberhard (1996), 'Duma-Wahlen 1995 (III). Ergebnisse, Informationen, Analysen', *Osteuropa*, 5: 430–48.

Sejnis, Viktor (2000), 'Wie Rußland gewählt hat. Zum Fazit der Parlaments- und Präsidentenwahlen Dezember 1999/März 2000', *Osteuropa*, 7: 758–78.

2.21 Serbian Election Statistics

Allock, John B. (1991), 'Yugoslavia' in Szajkowski, Bogdan (ed.) *New Political Parties of Eastern Europe and the Soviet Union*. Essex: Longman.

Andrejevich, Milan (1993), 'The Radicalization of Serbian Politics' in *Radio Free Europe, RFE/RL Research Reports*, 13: 14–24.

OSCE/ODIHR Election Observation Mission (2001), Final Report on the Parliamentary Elections in the Republic of Serbia, p. 16.

Vukomanovic, Dijana (1995), 'Documentary Appendix' in Goati, Vladimir (ed.) *Challenges of Parliamentarism. The Case of Serbia in the Early Nineties*. Belgrade: National Library of Serbia, p. 268.

2.22 Slovak Election Statistics

Essex database, http://www2.essex.ac.uk/elect/electer/slovakia_er_nl.htm (28/05/01).

Slovakian Electoral Commission, http://www.slovakia.eu.net/slovakia/elections.html (05/11/00).

Essex database, http://www2.essex.ac.uk/elect/database/indexElections.asp?country=SLOVAKIA&election=sk2002 (23/06/03).

2.23 Slovenian Election Statistics

IFES database, http://www.ifes.org/eguide/resultsum/sloveniares.htm (22/06/04).

Slovenian Electoral Commission, www.sigov.si/elections (19/07/01).

2.24 Ukrainian Election Statistics

Electionworld database, http://www.electionworld.org/election/ukraine.htm (12/08/03).

Essex database, http://www2.essex.ac.uk/elect/electer/ukr_er_nl.htm (17/04/01).

Essex database, http://www2.essex.ac.uk/elect/database/indexElections.asp?country=UKRAINE&election=ukr2002 (23/06/03).

III. Other Countries
3.1 Israeli Election Statistics

Diskin, Abraham (1993), 'Israel', *European Journal of Political Research*, 24: 467–74.

Jerusalem Post, 31 May 1996, pages 1–5 on breakdown of results for Elections to 14th Knesset, 1996.

Sorene, James (1999), *Elections in Israel: Background Information*, 3rd edn. Embassy of Israel, UK.

State of Israel, (1990), *Statistical Abstract of Israel, 41, 1990, 550ff.* Jerusalem, Central Bureau of Statistics.

3.2 Cyprus Election Statistics

Political Handbook of the World 2000–02. Binghamton, NY: CSA Publications, 2003.

3.3 Malta Election Statistics

Parties' National Vote: Totals and Percentages. Government of Malta. http://www.maltadata.com/np-total.htm (04/06/06).

Index

Appendices, figures, tables, and notes are indexed as **ap**, **f**, **n**, and **t**. More than one item appearing on the same page are indexed as **a** and **b**.